ultimate success of Corwin's book: the ability to realistically demonstrate the challenges and triumphs of top detectives seeking both answers and justice." —Amazon.com official site review

"While not recounting every homicide case he observed, the author vividly renders a handful that exemplify the range of entrenched social fissures and seedy criminality that have long defined Los Angeles. . . . With a touch of Chandleresque panache, Corwin's true crime reads like vintage noir, delivering taut dialogue sprinkled with off-color wisecracks and lyrical passages." —*Publishers Weekly*

"Combining a deft, elegant prose style with the acute eye of a veteran crime reporter, Miles Corwin has created a compelling portrait of seasoned homicide cops at work. This is L.A.'s darkest side."

—Jonathan Kellerman

The Killing Season

"Gripping drama and pathos . . . Rarely has the genre been worked to better effect." —*The New York Times Book Review*

"A grab-you-by-the-throat page-turner." —*Los Angeles Times*

"A fascinating, gripping, and at times heart-wrenching story."

—Michael Connelly

"Haunting and thrilling, this is a beautifully told story of violence and courage, and an unforgettable look behind the yellow crime-scene tape."

—*Kirkus Reviews*

And Still We Rise

"An impressive, important work of narrative journalism . . . A more gifted reporter can barely be imagined." —*San Francisco Chronicle*

"A book that both lifts the heart and afflicts the soul."

—Samuel Freedman, author of *Small Victories*

"Splendid." —*Los Angeles Times Book Review*

MILES

CORWIN

HOMICIDE

A Year with the LAPD's Elite Detective Unit

SPECIAL

A HOLT PAPERBACK

HENRY HOLT AND COMPANY

NEW YORK

Holt Paperbacks
Henry Holt and Company, LLC
Publishers since 1866
175 Fifth Avenue
New York, New York 10010
www.henryholt.com

A Holt Paperback® and ® are registered trademarks of
Henry Holt and Company, LLC.

Library of Congress Cataloging-in-Publication Data

Corwin, Miles.
    Homicide Special : a year with the LAPD's elite detective unit / Miles Corwin.—1st ed.
      p.   cm.
    ISBN-13: 978-0-8050-7694-3
    ISBN-10: 0-8050-7694-8
    1. Los Angeles (Calif.) Police Dept. 2. Detectives—California—Los Angeles.
3. Homicide investigation—California—Los Angeles. I. Title.
HV8148.L55C67   2003
363.25'9523'0979494—dc21   2003047883

Henry Holt books are available for special promotions and
premiums. For details contact: Director, Special Markets.

Originally published in hardcover in 2004
by Henry Holt and Company

First Holt Paperbacks Edition 2004

Designed by Fritz Metsch

Printed in the United States of America
5 7 9 10 8 6

For Diane

Homicide

Special

Prologue

On a scorching, smoggy Friday afternoon in August, a Homicide Special lieutenant in downtown Los Angeles answers a call from a detective supervisor in North Hollywood.

"I might have one for you," he says. "We had a call-out last night in Studio City. A Russian lady shot in the chest. Lots of condoms around. Probably a call girl. Very attractive. But here's the kicker: the FBI has a tap on her phone."

"Why?" the lieutenant asks.

"Don't know. That's why we're calling you. You want it?"

"I'll send some guys over this afternoon."

The lieutenant crosses the squad room and briefs Detectives Chuck Knolls and Rich Haro. This is their last day as partners. They had hoped to make it through the night without a corpse, but Knolls is first on the weekend on-call list, which officially began at noon today. He has to take the case. His new partner, currently on vacation, won't show until tomorrow. So Knolls and Haro will track a homicide together one last time.

Haro, who is fifty-five, has tired eyes, a thick black mustache, and a sun-lined face. The oldest detective in the unit, he is on the verge of retirement. A case he picked up two years ago—the murder of a 468-pound Hell's Angel known as Large Larry and his girlfriend—is scheduled for trial Monday. He will be tied up in court for months. After the trial, Haro wants to stay at Homicide Special just long enough to solve a Guatemalan triple murder he has been investigating for the past year and a half. Then he will pull the plug.

Haro knows this might be his last homicide, and he is already feeling nostalgic about leaving the unit. During his sixteen years at Homicide Special and, before that, as a divisional detective, he has investigated hundreds of murders and has solved many of them. It has been a good run, but he is getting too old to stand on his feet all night at murder scenes, to jump out of bed at three A.M. after call-outs, to work twenty-four hours straight, grab a nap, and then work another shift. He thinks back to his first interview at the unit, when a grizzled homicide detective known as Jigsaw John leaned over, Canadian whiskey on his breath, and asked, "You speak any language besides Spanish?"

"Yeah," replied Haro curtly, aware that there was only one other Latino in Homicide Special. "English."

Everyone in the room laughed, and he was accepted into the unit.

Haro has never been the diplomatic sort. When he arrived at Homicide Special, he addressed any colleague who annoyed him as "Butt Licker." Butt Licker, or B.L., became his nickname, and he derived a perverse pleasure in the sobriquet; in the pre-politically correct days of police work, he handed out business cards with the initials "B.L." beneath his name.

Haro feels like a dinosaur and worries that his style of investigation is outmoded. When he first joined the unit, detectives slowly, methodically sifted through leads and clues and hints of evidence. Because his caseload was lighter then, he worked at his own deliberate pace. The wave of intense detectives who have recently joined the unit are so harried and impatient that Haro believes the quality of their investigations suffers.

Knolls, who just spent a grueling five years investigating murders in South-Central Los Angeles and has been at Homicide Special only nine months, is one of these new, driven detectives. He is forty-four, with pale green, hard-to-read poker eyes, thinning sandy brown hair, and a solid build from daily weight-lifting sessions. Blunt, stubborn, and accustomed to taking charge, Knolls has clashed in the past with Haro, his only partner at Homicide Special. Neither detective regrets splitting up.

As the lieutenant finishes up his briefing, Haro wonders whether the case will keep him out all night. He has lost track of the number of mornings he has arrived at home as his family was waking up. This is one element of the job he is not going to miss.

Haro and Knolls grab their suit jackets and roll out in separate cars.

The detectives cruise through downtown, heat waves shimmering in the distance, the horizon veiled by a tawny band of smog. Less than an hour after the call-out, they speed on the freeway toward North Hollywood.

On another day, in another century, in a city that even then was famous for its dark and disturbing crimes, private detective Philip Marlowe climbed the redwood steps to his small house in the Hollywood Hills, fixed himself a stiff drink, and listened to the cars rumble through a canyon pass. "I . . . looked at the glare of the big angry city hanging over the shoulder of the hills. . . . Far off the banshee wail of police or fire sirens rose and fell, never for very long completely silent. . . . Twenty-four hours a day somebody is running, somebody else is trying to catch him."

Today, half a century after Raymond Chandler wrote *The Long Goodbye,* twenty-four hours a day somebody is still running in Los Angeles. But while there are many more killers in this sprawling city now, and many more detectives trying to catch them, one thing has remained unchanged: a select downtown unit with citywide jurisdiction is still assigned to investigate the most brutal, most complex, most high-profile murders in Los Angeles. This unit is called Homicide Special.

Murders that involve celebrities are transferred from the local police divisions to Homicide Special. Organized-crime killings, serial murders, cases that require great expertise or sophisticated technology are investigated by Homicide Special. Any murder that is considered a priority by the chief of police is sent to Homicide Special.

A unit that tracks such singular murders is perfectly suited to Los Angeles. Teetering on the edge of the continent, the city has always been an urban outpost, conceived in violence, nurtured by deception, enriched by graft, riven by racial enmity, and plagued throughout its history by heinous homicides.

In the mid–nineteenth century, Los Angeles was known as the most murderous town in the entire West, a way station for the most vicious desperadoes, gamblers, grifters, and drifters. The only police chief in the city's history to die in the line of duty was murdered in 1870. East Coast reporters suggested that Los Angeles should change its name to Los Diablos. By 1900, L.A. was a cow town of about 100,000 people, unable to grow because of its limited water supply. The event that precipitated the city's population explosion and transformed it into a major metropolis was itself a crime: civic leaders hornswoggled farmers in the Owens Valley, 233 miles away, and siphoned off their water, enriching a handful of prominent men who had devised a real estate scam.

Once the water was flowing, millions poured into the city, lured by the promise of sunny days, balmy nights, ocean breezes, and the fragrance of orange blossoms. But beneath the palm trees and the pastel bungalows with their velvety lawns simmered the rage and resentment of rootless people whose troubles did not dissolve in the hazy sunshine. The burgeoning crime rate served as a sinister counterpoint to the utopia promised by civic boosters and real estate hucksters. The seemingly benign, subtropical landscape also proved violent, beset by earthquakes, wildfires, flash floods, and deadly mud slides.

In the 1930s and '40s, the city's dark side inspired the noir genre, spawning such writers as Chandler and James M. Cain and a spate of nihilistic movies. During this era, Los Angeles suffered an increasing number of complex, sadistic murders. Soon, the LAPD began assigning these cases to a specialized downtown unit composed of the most skilled, most experienced homicide detectives in the department. In 1947, this unit—which eventually evolved into Homicide Special—investigated the most infamous unsolved murder in the history of the city, a murder that forever shattered the myth that Los Angeles was a placid paradise. The nude corpse of Elizabeth Short, a twenty-two-year-old aspiring actress, was found in a weed-choked lot, neatly sliced in half at the waist. Her organs had been removed, her body drained of blood. A ghastly ear-to-ear grin was carved on her face. Short was christened the Black Dahlia because of her tight-fitting black dress and dyed-black hair, which she wore in a swirling bouffant.

During the next half century, detectives from the unit tracked countless other notorious cases, from Marilyn Monroe's overdose, to the Manson Family murders, to the assassination of Robert Kennedy. During the 1970s and '80s, the detectives caught a number of serial killers who terrorized the populace, such as the Skid Row Stabber, who killed ten transients; the Koreatown Slasher, who killed six people and wounded seven; and the Sunset Slayer, who shot six young women and had sex with the corpses. They handled other serial murder cases as well, with varying degrees of success. But their failures were rarely scrutinized, and Homicide Special retained its reputation as the department's premier investigative unit, with the best detectives in the city.

Astute LAPD detectives in other divisions, however, predicted problems ahead. Homicide Special, they said, was becoming a good-old-boys' club, a complacent fraternity of middle-aged detectives. Their techniques were outmoded, their best investigative days behind them. Because the workload was so light, some aging detectives spent more time on the golf course than at homicide scenes. Detectives picked up so few "fresh blood" cases that their crime scene expertise and investigative skills were rusty. There was little turnover in the unit, so the best young detectives often were excluded.

These criticisms proved particularly prescient when, on a June morning in 1994, the bodies of Nicole Brown Simpson and her friend Ronald Goldman, both of whom had been stabbed and slashed more than thirty times, were found at her Brentwood condominium. Police officials transferred the case to Homicide Special, expecting exemplary detective work. But during the trial of O. J. Simpson, Nicole Brown Simpson's husband, people throughout the country watched defense attorneys eviscerate Homicide Special detectives and their maladroit investigation.

Homicide Special's reputation was at rock bottom. But in the wake of the Simpson acquittal, the unit underwent an extensive overhaul. Most of the detectives and both lieutenants retired or were transferred. Today, only a handful of investigators remain from the days of the Simpson case.

Captain Jim Tatreau, the new head of Robbery-Homicide Division—which includes Homicide Special, Rape Special, Robbery Special, and the Officer Involved Shooting team—has brought in almost twenty new homicide detectives. Most are much younger than the previous crew, and their workload has increased considerably.

During the past few years, Homicide Special's status has risen as detectives have solved a number of nationally publicized cases: The granddaughter of Bernard Parks, the Los Angeles chief of police, was shot and killed by a gangbanger who was aiming for her companion. An Academy Award–winning actor, Haing S. Ngor, who had survived the horrors of the Cambodian killing fields, was shot outside his apartment, and initial reports indicated that he was killed by Khmer Rouge hit men. The first female Secret Service agent to die in the line of duty was blasted by a shotgun while on a stakeout. Bill Cosby's son Ennis was murdered during a robbery attempt.

When a jury convicted a Ukrainian immigrant named Mikail Markhasev in the Cosby case after only a few hours of deliberation, the *Los*

Angeles Times—which had blasted the LAPD during the Simpson trial—published a laudatory editorial: "Important differences . . . between the Markhasev and Simpson cases explain the different trials and verdicts. Most important . . . was the solid professional work in the Ennis Cosby . . . investigation as opposed to unbelievably sloppy police work in the Nicole Brown Simpson and Ronald Goldman double-murder investigation."

The unit, however, has endured recent failures as well. But Homicide Special detectives have learned that they cannot exult after their successes or dwell on their failures for too long. They simply do not have that luxury.

Because, in Los Angeles, *twenty-four hours a day somebody is running.*

And when a killer has committed a murder deemed sufficiently bizarre, or intractable, or newsworthy, the detectives assigned the task of trying to catch him are still from Homicide Special.

Part I

THE VALLEY

1

Chuck Knolls and Rich Haro arrive at the North Hollywood Division station in midafternoon. Although they are visitors, they stride through the room with authority.

A female detective in Sex Crimes nods at Knolls, whom she has worked with before.

"This one's more interesting than the usual," she says.

"How so?" Knolls asks.

"I'll let the homicide guys fill you in."

The station, with its bureaucratic brown carpeting and honeycomb of cubicles, has the subdued ambiance of a suburban sheriff's outpost. Despite its name, the San Fernando Valley community of North Hollywood has little in common with its glitzy neighbor, Hollywood, twelve miles south.

Knolls and Haro sit on the edge of a desk as two North Hollywood detectives and their supervisor update them.

"I see the condoms and the neighbor says she hears a lot of bed squeaking," says Detective Martin Pinner. "I figure she's a prostitute. So at ten this morning I try to put a tap on the phone to find out who her customers are. The phone company says, 'You can't have a tap. Someone else already has one.' "

Pinner adds that the phone company refused to reveal who ordered the tap, even after he threatened to subpoena the records. They told him the subscriber would contact him.

"A few minutes later," he says, rapping his knuckles on the phone for effect, "the FBI calls me."

Knolls sighs. FBI involvement means the case is beyond a dead hooker. Russian organized crime could be involved. The cast of characters and suspects could be scattered across the country—even the world.

"Was she clothed?" Knolls asks.

"Just panties—not torn," says Mike Coffey, the detective supervisor. "And a babydoll robe. Open."

"How many shots?" Haro asks.

"Single gunshot two inches above left nipple," Coffey says. "Pierced her lung. Blew apart her heart." He lifts his thumb, aims his index finger, and adds, "Almost a straight shot. More than two feet away. She was beaten savagely around the face. Multiple blunt force."

"He just *kicked* her ass," Pinner says.

"There were some unusual marks on her," Coffey says, "three long, thin, parallel marks." He slashes the air with three fingers. "I thought she was pistol-whipped, but those marks don't really match up with a pistol."

"You get the bullet?" Knolls asks.

"At the autopsy," Coffey says. "Lodged in the spine. A monster .45 round. Full metal copper jacket. Mushroomed in front a bit. Otherwise, it's in beautiful shape."

"Casing?" Knolls asks.

"Ejected fifteen feet to the side of the bed," Coffey says. "We picked up three condoms from the trash can and a black pubic hair—not hers—in her IUD. So we'll have good DNA. We got eight messages off her answering machine—all in Russian."

The victim's name is Lyudmyla Petushenko, Coffey says. Her friends call her Luda, but since she has not been identified by a family member and her documents have not been authenticated she is officially known as Jane Doe No. 45.

Coffey adds that they have caught a break: a video camera outside the apartment's front door. Patrol officers at the scene on Thursday— the day of the murder—collected the tape.

Knolls nods appreciatively. "Was she raped?"

"No trauma to the vagina," Coffey says.

"Who found the body?" Knolls asks.

"Leyla—a friend. She calls a guy named Mher, who also goes by Mike. He rents the apartment for the victim. We hear he's pimping for her. Anyway, he freaks out, calls 911, and then shows up. The paramedics are already there. We interviewed him at the station. And here's something interesting. A Russian girl, an ex-hooker, was found cut up in a sewer in Marina Del Rey a few months ago. You know who her pimp is? Mher."

Haro and Knolls exchange uneasy glances: they might be tracking a serial murderer, which would significantly compound the variables. Another detective interrupts to inform Coffey that the FBI agent is in the lobby.

Minutes later, Knolls, Haro, and the North Hollywood detectives join the FBI agent and a few other investigators from organized crime and rape units in a conference room. The territorial undercurrents are strong. Since investigations by the FBI and the LAPD have intersected, the two agencies must establish jurisdictional guidelines. Meetings between local law enforcement and the FBI are always dicey, poker games between detectives and federal agents battling for turf. Agents will bluff and pretend to know more—or less—about a case than they really do, whatever stance will elicit more information from their counterpart. Detectives sometimes stonewall, reluctant to share any scrap unless they are certain they will receive equal value in return.

The FBI agent bears little resemblance to the stuffy, dark-suited stiff portrayed in the stock cop shows. Jennifer Amo, who works in the FBI's Russian organized crime squad, is in her late twenties, slight, a few inches over five feet, with blond shoulder-length hair. She is soft-spoken and, surrounded by stone-faced LAPD detectives, clearly ill at ease, like a graduate student defending her thesis before a faculty committee.

Coffey brusquely gives Agent Amo a quick synopsis, informing her that since the Russian mafia might complicate the case and the FBI's involved, detectives from the LAPD's Robbery-Homicide Division will take over from North Hollywood.

"The victim is a pretty blond prostitute brought here from the Ukraine by Mher and his wife," Amo begins, marking her territory. "The victim's phone is in his name. Mher and his wife set up girls in apartments and they run ads in some of the weekly papers. Johns call a central number and they send the guys to the call girls."

"Any indication our victim was doing some business on the sly and pissed off Mher?" Knolls asks.

"No," Amo says. "The girls are afraid. They know these people can get to their families in Kiev."

"Any dope involved?" Knolls asks.

"Well, they *are* prostitutes—but nothing big," says Amo. She pulls out two photos of Mher and his wife, enlarged California driver's license pictures. Mher is swarthy, with a heavy beard and sleepy black eyes; his wife is fair and fleshy, with a vacant stare.

"What can you tell us about the phone tap that will help us?" Haro asks impatiently.

Amo is courteous but reserved. She explains that because of "legal issues and confidentiality," she is prohibited from discussing the telephone conversations. She will only reveal that monitoring of the victim's phone began six days before her death.

Haro presses Amo, who reiterates her position. Coffey, attempting to ease the tension, gives Amo more background on the murder, including the fact that Luda was shot with a .45-caliber handgun. Haro abruptly rises and storms out of the room, motioning for the North Hollywood detectives to follow him. This may be his last day on the case, but he is furious. He did not want the caliber of the bullet released to the FBI.

"This is bullshit," he says through clenched teeth, in the hallway. "They want everything we have without giving anything in return. I've been through this before with them."

"Yeah," Coffey says, "I've been though it, too."

"I don't want *her* getting all of our information," Haro says. "They're interested in solving their smuggling and white slavery case. They could care less about our murder."

Haro tells the detectives about an old Armenian-Russian organized crime murder he once handled that is still unsolved. "The FBI had an informant feeding them information," Haro says. "In the beginning, we gave them what we had. They wouldn't give us anything. Eventually, I wouldn't even talk to the FBI. If they wanted to reach us, they had to call my partner. I still don't trust 'em."

Coffey, another LAPD veteran, nods in agreement.

Knolls joins the group in the hallway and angrily addresses Haro. "Let's just conclude this meeting. I don't want to keep that FBI agent just sitting in the conference room, twiddling her thumbs. We can't afford to piss her off right now." Haro can settle past scores; he will be off the case tomorrow. But Knolls will need Amo later on. He quickly ushers Haro and the others back into the conference room.

"I've been doing this a long time, and I've had problems with the FBI in the past," Coffey announces. "They haven't shared information with us on cases. They'd come in, ask if they could look at our murder books and crime scene photos. Then they'd leave, say thanks, and not give us anything."

"I've heard that before," Amo says warily.

Knolls fumes as he calculates how he and his new partner will have to slink over to the FBI building and make amends with Amo. After an uncomfortable silence, an LAPD detective from the rape unit says she does not think Luda was sexually assaulted. "She had real long fingernails. None were broken. She was beaten badly on the face and the head. I don't think it was a trick. It was personal. Sex wasn't the motive. Robbery wasn't the motive. Anger was the motive. *She* was the motive."

Ten minutes later, after the detectives and Amo realize they are at an impasse, the meeting breaks up. Amo leaves and the LAPD investigators linger in the room. A female detective in the organized crime unit tells Knolls and Haro that she has worked with Amo before. "She withholds some stuff, but she *has* given us things. She's better than the previous agents I've worked with."

"The thing is, it's *our* case, not theirs," Haro says.

"What else did you find in the apartment?" Knolls asks Coffey, eager to change the subject.

"About twenty-two hundred in cash hidden in purses and envelopes around the bedroom," Coffey says. "But her leather organizer was missing. People we've talked to said it was there and now it's gone."

He adds that North Hollywood detectives have already interviewed about half a dozen people. Mher and his wife claim they rented the Studio City apartment because they were going to lease their house to a group of musicians. The deal fell apart and they were stuck, but then they met Luda at a coffee shop and arranged a sublet.

"Total bullshit," Coffey tells Haro and Knolls.

Mher admitted he visited Luda the night before the murder, which Coffey does believe. The next day, after calling 911, Mher arrived at the apartment with two other men. At the station, the detectives examined their hands for gunshot residue. The tests were negative.

The detectives also interviewed a Russian named Serge, whose telephone number they found at Luda's apartment. He claims to be in the car auction business, but detectives in the organized crime unit suspect he is involved with the Russian mafia. Serge also says he met Luda at a coffee shop. She should be in the hookers' hall of fame, he told the detectives. She was a nympho who loved her job, and the sex was so great, he says, she even stopped charging him.

Next, Coffey mentions an eighteen-year-old Russian community college student who called Luda's apartment repeatedly on Thursday afternoon after the body was discovered. At the station, the student, who claimed not to have known that Luda was dead, said he planned to take her to an amusement park that day. He explained that he met her at the shoe store where he worked part-time. The previous Saturday he had attended her birthday party at a Russian nightclub in Studio City.

"He's an odd duck," Coffey says. "He claims he did not know she was a prostitute. Says they were just friends."

"You believe him?" Knolls asks.

"I don't know," Coffey says. "He called a lot."

"Sounds obsessed," Haro interrupts.

"We also talked to her sugar daddy," Coffey says. "A guy named Mischa. He didn't have a lot to say."

"Any idea what those slash marks are?" Knolls asks.

"They're a real mystery," Coffey says.

"Any leather or B-and-D equipment around?"

Coffey shakes his head.

"She have any family here?" Haro asks.

"No," Coffey says. "Another witness said she had a little girl in Russia. Said she wanted to save money, go to computer school, and bring her daughter to the U.S."

"Since she was trying to get her daughter out here, maybe she was skimming and that pissed off the pimp," Coffey says.

"Yeah," Knolls says. "She *did* have twenty-two hundred stashed in the apartment."

At about five o'clock, Knolls thanks the North Hollywood team for their help. The detectives drive back downtown in their own cars. As Knolls inches south on the Hollywood Freeway, he contemplates the case. He knows he could spend months investigating the murder—maybe years, if Russian organized crime is involved. He speculates about how the killer exited the apartment, and wonders whether the crime scene was chaotic, with kicked-in doors and broken mirrors, or if the victim was quickly bludgeoned and shot—brutal questions he never would have faced had he stayed in the grocery business.

Fourteen years ago, Knolls was promoted to manager at a chain super-market. The money was excellent, with lucrative bonuses. He had a wife, two kids, and a house in the Valley. His life was set, he figured.

In August, he prepared for Christmas. After New Year's, he ordered supplies for Valentine's Day. On Valentine's Day, he ordered Easter merchandise. After Easter, he stocked pallets of charcoal and picnic supplies for the summer. Then in August he did it all over again, year after year.

But one morning, shortly after he turned thirty, he decided he simply could not put in the next thirty years at the supermarket. His father had worked at Sears for forty years, running a warehouse and later selling tires, but Knolls wanted a different kind of life. He always had an interest in law enforcement because the job seemed stimulating and adventurous. For ten years he had considered quitting and apply-ing to the LAPD or Sheriff's Department. Knolls finally realized that if he was going to sign up, he could not put if off any longer. He quit his job, took a $20,000 pay cut, and entered the LAPD academy as a thirty-year-old "boot."

Knolls, about a decade older than most of the young recruits, could not afford to languish in a patrol car. Because of his maturity, drive, and aptitude, he advanced quickly: in less than seven years, he was promoted to detective, quickly developing a reputation as a dogged investigator and skilled interviewer. He was a natural candidate for Homicide Special. He transferred to the unit in 1999, during the post–O. J. Simpson housecleaning.

Knolls has an intimate knowledge of how fragile life is, how impor-tant it is not to put off goals indefinitely. At the age of five, he was diagnosed with cancer of the parotid gland. He had extensive radiation treatment beneath his left ear, where a surgeon removed a section of his jawbone, leaving thick scar tissue and a deep cavity. Knolls has a ruggedly handsome right profile. The remnants of the cancer surgery are visible only from the left side.

If he could survive cancer, Knolls believed, he could accomplish anything. As a result, he has never suffered from a lack of confidence.

Knolls and his new partner, Brian McCartin, meet the next day at the North Hollywood station. They worked in the same squad room in South-Central and, more recently, at Homicide Special, but they greet each other without the bonhomie that many detectives in the unit share. Because of their disparate backgrounds and bearing, they have been merely acquaintances, not friends. Knolls has lived his entire life in the suburban San Fernando Valley. Despite the occasional cantankerous outburst, he has a casual, low-key demeanor. McCartin, slender with a ruddy complexion, is a blunt New Yorker with an abundance of restless energy who moved to Los Angeles and joined the LAPD after working as a fireman in Harlem for a year. Although Knolls is a veteran detective, he is a relative newcomer to the unit. McCartin, who is forty, has been assigned to Homicide Special for four and a half years, and is more integrated into RHD—Robbery-Homicide Division—more comfortable with its rituals.

Although it is the weekend, both detectives wear conservative dark suits and ties. Knolls briefs McCartin on the murder, the phone tap, the possible suspects, and how Haro and Coffey probably alienated Agent Amo.

"And she's got an informant," Knolls says.

"Oh, man," McCartin says. "We're going to have to nurture her. These old guys still think Hoover's in charge of the FBI. But it's changing." During the mid-1990s, McCartin was selected to join a new LAPD-FBI task force investigating unsolved murders in South-Central L.A. As a result, he has had more exposure to the FBI than most police detectives, and enjoys a better relationship with the agents.

In the North Hollywood conference room, McCartin and Knolls examine stacks of the victim's documents, paperwork, and photographs. A striking woman with platinum hair and green eyes, Luda defies the hard-looking, dissipated hooker stereotype. In one of the photos found at her apartment she is at a nightclub with a pudgy, gray-haired man who the detectives believe may be Mischa, the sugar daddy. Other pictures show her posing with an unidentified man in Las Vegas and basking beside a hotel swimming pool in a green bikini.

The crime scene photos offer a stark contrast. Luda is bloody and battered, lying on her back, her white silk robe open, the sash still loosely tied around her waist. A pair of high heels flank her head. Blood streams from her mouth. Purplish bruises cover her face. Her lips are pursed, turned down in a slight grimace, as if she is cringing or anticipating another blow. A ghastly collage of red, purple, and pink bruises mottles her face, and both eyes are deeply blackened.

On her neck and cheek and the side of her face are the distinctive slash marks—three horizontal lines—that Coffey described. Drops of blood snake from her left nipple to the top of her shoulder. The left side of her face, from her mouth to her ear, is smudged with blood. A side-view photograph reveals an ornate green and red butterfly tattoo on the small of her back.

"Someone sure wanted her dead," McCartin says. "He beat the shit out of her, then coup-de-grâced her. What do you think of Mher?"

"He cops to being there the night before with his cousin. But get this: another of his girls was found dismembered in a storm drain."

McCartin looks up from the picture. "Do we have a serial killer?" Knolls gazes at the crime scene photos without responding.

"Did they print the shit out of the place?" McCartin asks.

"I hope so."

"Did the manager seal the apartment off?"

"I don't know," Knolls says. "That's why I want to get my ass out there."

Luda lived in a four-story luxury apartment, a white stucco building, perched on a narrow, winding street. Palm trees and banana plants shade the lushly landscaped complex, which is bordered by pink geraniums, purple and crimson snapdragons, puffy white azaleas, and spiky orange and blue birds-of-paradise. The building is in the San Fernando Valley, separated from Hollywood by a strip of the Hollywood Hills, in a community whose name, Studio City, reflects the area's early role in the movie industry. During the mid-1920s, not far from Luda's apartment, a lettuce ranch was converted into a movie studio for Mack Sennett, who made the Keystone Kops comedies during the silent film era.

The building's residents must punch in a code to enter; the manager buzzes the detectives in. On their way to the elevator they pass the entrance to the pool, where several young women sunbathe in lounge chairs. A group of men chat in the Jacuzzi. It is a typical sweltering summer afternoon in the Valley—temperature in the mid-nineties, with a few tattered clouds above a dusky, polluted horizon. But for a woman probably fleeing poverty and despair in the Ukraine, Knolls figures, a summer day by the pool must have seemed idyllic.

The manager looks queasy as she lingers by the door to Luda's second-floor apartment. "Do I have to go inside?" she asks.

When Knolls shakes his head, she pulls out a ring of keys, opens the door, and flees down the stairs. The apartment is as sterile as a motel room, with no photographs on the walls, no personal or idiosyncratic decorating touches. The generic furnishings look as if they were all quickly purchased from the same Ikea store display. The white kitchen and bathroom counters, and the white furniture in the living room and bedroom are streaked with sooty fingerprint dust. The sole personal item in the apartment is displayed on a bedroom end table; it is a small silver-framed photo of Luda's little girl. She wears a blue-and-white striped sundress and smiles broadly at the camera.

Initially, the victim was just a faceless Russian hooker to Knolls. But now that he knows she has a young daughter whom she struggled to bring to America, Luda Petushenko has been transformed into a corporeal, fully formed woman, and Knolls feels more motivated to find her killer.

The detectives study an archipelago of blood spots a few feet from the bed, red smudges that glare like neon in Luda's all-white world. They then examine the waist-high blood-splatter pattern on a wall. McCartin traces the path of the bullet casing, walking to the side of the bed because casings usually eject to the right.

"This guy must have been very pissed off to whale on her like that," McCartin says, more to himself than to Knolls. "What could piss someone off like that?"

Knolls studies a vent on the bedroom ceiling. "Just checking on the off chance she was videotaping in the bedroom for blackmail." But he finds no trace of a camera.

The detectives, who have tossed hundreds of homes, move systematically from room to room. Without speaking, they divide up the duties: Knolls examines closets and the bathroom, while McCartin probes the drawers and cabinets in the kitchen and bedroom. Knolls soon stacks up several piles of identification cards, keys, scraps of paper with phone numbers and addresses, receipts—many for children's clothing—and matchbooks from a number of Beverly Hills hotels. Knolls dumps out the trash can in the bathroom and spots several used condoms that the North Hollywood detectives apparently missed.

"Those *blessed* guys," he barks.

McCartin picks up a Russian-English dictionary with an inscription: "Thank you for a good time in L.A.—Francis."

"Here's your first English lesson, baby," he says, playing the part of a customer, jerking his thumb toward the bed. Moving to the kitchen, he opens the refrigerator with a pair of pliers to avoid leaving fingerprints and finds a few bottles of pickles, mayonnaise and horseradish, a jar of borscht, a package of carrots, a container of yogurt, and a half-filled bottle of Merlot. A dozen desiccated red roses hang, drying, upside down from a nearby towel rack.

Knolls fills several plastic garbage bags and joins McCartin on the balcony, which overlooks a courtyard framed by ficus trees and yucca plants coated with dust. Although it is a sunny summer afternoon, the windows and drapes are closed in all the adjacent apartments. The courtyard is silent except for the hum of air conditioners. The detectives now realize why no neighbors heard the shot.

"How did he get out of here?" Knolls asks.

McCartin peers below. "It's about a ten-foot drop. But he could have climbed down to the first floor."

"This ain't no smoking-gun case," Knolls says.

"It doesn't make it any easier with the FBI pissed at us," McCartin says. "Let's hope we can repair the damage. I'll call them first thing Monday morning."

"Good idea," Knolls says. "We need all the help we can get."

2

Shortly before eight o'clock Monday morning, McCartin crosses the squad room on the way to his desk. Haro stops him.

"How's your case look?" Haro asks.

"We locked up the suspect yesterday," McCartin says, attempting to suppress a smile.

"Yesterday?" Haro asks incredulously.

"You got it. That's what happens when you put a *real* detective on the case," McCartin says, chuckling as he hurries to his desk.

"Butt licker," Haro mutters.

Back in their own squad room, at their own desks, which are side by side, McCartin and Knolls sift through the growing mound of paperwork on Luda's murder. Robbery-Homicide Division is on the third floor of Parker Center, nicknamed the Glass House by the prisoners transported to its holding cells. The eight-story structure stands in the heart of downtown Los Angeles, a block from city hall, the city's best-known architectural landmark. While city hall is a classic Art Deco skyscraper with distinctive serrated, sloping walls, Parker Center is a bland glass and steel building that it looks like an enormous refrigerator. Built in 1955, the LAPD headquarters—renamed, in 1966, to honor former chief William H. Parker—was shoddily constructed and is now decrepit and cramped. The floors sag. The plumbing leaks. Paint peels in the hallways. Some of the offices have furniture and décor right out of Jack Webb's *Dragnet*.

RHD also has changed little in decades. Robbery Special and Rape Special have their own small squad rooms. Homicide Special, adjacent to the two units, consists of one large room with two rows of twelve battered metal desks flanking a narrow passageway. One lieutenant supervises the detectives on the west side of the room and another is responsible for those on the east side. The large white "on-call" board, which looms on the front wall of the squad room, lists detective teams that are available to be dispatched to fresh homicides. Detectives from the two sides of the room—known as Homicide I and Homicide II— alternate by the week. Although they are separated only by an aisle, there is a subtle rivalry between the two squads; detectives develop a strong loyalty to their side of the room. They are sometimes reluctant to share information and have, on occasion, accused their counterparts of leaking news to the press. The unit handles about twelve to fifteen complex murder cases a year, with the workload split between the two groups.

A speckled black-and-white linoleum hallway leads to the splintered squad-room door. With its ancient wooden filing cabinets, dusty venetian blinds, harsh overhead fluorescent lights, and black-and-white wanted posters taped to the walls, Homicide Special has the feel of a 1940s film noir precinct. Only the computers appear anachronistic. The detectives still do not have voice mail and there is no receptionist. They are frequently interrupted by the ringing phone and impatiently scribble messages for one another.

The Homicide Special detectives do not seem out of place in this relic of a room. All twenty-four are men. (The two female detectives are both working on task forces in other buildings.) Most are white. Almost everyone wears a dark suit, pressed white shirt, conservative tie, and shoes buffed to a gleam. Decades ago, supervisors in the unit decided that because Homicide Special detectives were supposed to be the city's best detectives, they should look like its best detectives. The tradition continues. McCartin is dressed today in a formal dark blue suit, white shirt, and blue-and-red print tie; Knolls wears a gray suit, white shirt, and green print tie.

Their lieutenant, Don Hartwell, who is in charge of Homicide II, was once a chef in one of the city's best French restaurants. This morning he is regaling a detective with a detailed account of a meal he enjoyed Saturday night at the renowned Westside restaurant Vincenti. The mullet, he says with a look of wonder, was flown in from Italy. He cuts his gastronomic reverie short, however, when he spots McCartin and Knolls. He wants to hear about their visit to Luda's apartment.

At the division stations, supervisors often micromanage detectives' cases, but at Homicide Special the two lieutenants and the captain of the unit give investigators a great deal of latitude. They believe that if a detective is promoted to RHD, he has earned the perquisite of independence. Many, having handled more than a hundred murders before they transferred to the unit, have their own, idiosyncratic ways of working. All the Homicide Special investigators are detectives second or third grade—the top rank for an investigator. If they were at division stations they would supervise other detectives.

The competition for positions at Homicide Special is intense, with more than a dozen applicants, all of whom have extensive homicide experience, for each opening. The two lieutenants interview the candidates, question their supervisors, assess their investigative background, and then rank them. They are seeking poised, articulate detectives. Many of the victims in the cases Homicide Special investigates are prominent people, and the investigators must be able to establish a rapport with witnesses from all strata of society. The lieutenants eventually present their assessments to the head of RHD, Captain Tatreau, who makes the final decision.

Homicide Special was once a more cohesive unit. Because the detectives had lighter caseloads, they had more time for the socializing that engendered an esprit de corps. They spent many nights after work drinking in the downtown bars, and they often golfed or hunted together on weekends. Today, the Homicide Special detectives are younger and many have small children; they have less time for drinking and golfing. The two-man teams often work independently, without help from other detectives. As a result, the unit feels fragmented, with a dozen pairs of partners orbiting around the squad room, only occasionally revolving in unison.

After the detectives brief Hartwell, they scrupulously log every scrap of paper, notebook, photograph, greeting card, note, document, bill, receipt, and matchbook recovered from the apartment. The rest of the morning is spent compiling the murder book, the three-ring, royal blue plastic binder that summarizes a homicide case. It contains all the data gathered during an investigation, including evidence lists, crime scene photographs and diagrams, statements from patrol officers, suspects, and witnesses, and a day-to-day—sometimes hour-to-hour—chronology of the investigation.

When the detectives finish organizing the murder book, McCartin calls the homicide detective who investigated the murder of the dismembered Russian hooker found in the storm drain near the ocean. The detective confirms that her pimp was Mher, but says she had been out of the business awhile. He does not believe that Mher killed her. Still, Knolls and McCartin are concerned that the two murders might be connected.

The detectives have no witnesses to Luda's murder, not even a neighbor who heard a shot. They do, however, have two potentially devastating pieces of evidence: the videotape and the shell casing. Every weapon engraves distinctive groove patterns on the bullet it releases. For decades, ballistics technicians have used these patterns to match recovered bullets with suspects' guns. With semiautomatic pistols, however, detectives can use a still more advanced and reliable method of identification. A new computer process makes it possible to create digital images of the unique markings of spent cartridges (or shell casings). An FBI database can compare and match these markings with ammunition found at crime scenes nationwide. If the same gun was used, detectives can now quickly connect shootings from different jurisdictions.

Later in the afternoon, the detectives drop off the casing at the LAPD ballistics lab. They also plan to obtain the bullet, removed at the autopsy, so ballistics technicians can analyze it. When they return to the office, McCartin calls Jennifer Amo and sets up an appointment for the next day.

The FBI's office in West Los Angeles is located on the seventeenth floor of the Federal Building, a boxy, unadorned white tower on Wilshire Boulevard. Amo and her female supervisor greet the detectives in the FBI lobby and escort them to a conference room. The women seem stiff and reserved.

"I really have to apologize for the way some of the LAPD guys acted the other day," Knolls says when everyone is seated. "That's just old-school thinking. But we want to start fresh."

McCartin mentions his work with FBI agents on the unsolved-murder task force. "I know the FBI has changed," he says. "I'm very open and more than willing to work with you. If we can work together, I'll give you what we have."

"When we find the shooter, we'll be out of your hair," Knolls adds.

Amo and her supervisor appear to relax. The supervisor says she will do what she can to help them.

Amo tells the detectives they are investigating Russian white slavery.

She and her supervisor then briefly explain how crime rings with contacts in the former Soviet Union and Los Angeles obtain Mexican tourist visas for young Russian and Ukrainian girls. The girls, some of whom are naïve aspiring models, are smuggled into the United States from Mexico and "purchased" by madams. The girls are forced to pay off their passage by working as prostitutes.

Spreading several dozen enlarged driver's license photos of pimps, madams, prostitutes, and smugglers on the table, the agents point to a few of the players and give the detectives thumbnail background sketches.

Luda, Amo says, was smuggled into the country in May. She worked for Mher and his wife, as well as for Lana, another Russian madam. Mher is Armenian, but he grew up in Los Angeles. An FBI informant claims that since the murder, no one has seen him.

The meeting is short but productive. The agents and the detectives agree to share information during the course of their respective investigations.

The detectives always work an eight A.M.-to-four P.M. shift, and although it is "end of watch" by the time they leave the FBI building they agree to drive to Hollywood and interview a few Russian hookers whom Amo had identified during the meeting. During the first few weeks of a fresh case, Homicide Special lieutenants do not complain about overtime.

They decide to approach the case's dramatis personae in concentric circles, interviewing peripheral players—the prostitutes—first, then gradually moving inward, to madams, pimps, smugglers, and, finally, potential suspects, such as Mher. To interview him now would be useless; they have no witnesses, no concrete evidence, and no leverage.

McCartin drives his unmarked blue Chevrolet Malibu east on Santa Monica Boulevard, through Beverly Hills, north on La Cienega, moving slowly through rush-hour traffic. He then heads east on Sunset to Hollywood. Although the gentrification of Hollywood is under way, the section of east Hollywood they pass is a shabby neighborhood of strip malls and fast-food restaurants. The detectives decide to eat before the interviews, and McCartin suggests the Boston Market he has spotted on a corner.

"Since we're just starting out as partners, one thing you should know about me: I don't like chains," Knolls says. He points to another corner and says, "Let's eat at that hole-in-the-wall Mexican place. That looks good."

Over soda and excellent tacos laced with cilantro, they examine the photos and jot down the addresses of the women identified by Amo as prostitutes. They decide to "door-knock" the women without calling first. McCartin drives west toward a spectacular sunset, the fiery, sinking sun irradiating the smog on the horizon with splashes of burnt orange. They pass the Château Marmont, where John Belushi overdosed on a cocaine-and-heroin speedball, and then south to West Hollywood, past hip, trendy Melrose Avenue.

The first woman they hope to interview lives just south of a stretch of Melrose lined with art galleries and antique shops. Homes in the Hollywood Hills glimmer in the distance. A warm breeze carries the fruity, tropical smell of night-blooming jasmine.

The woman who answers the door is in her mid-twenties and blonde, in a low-cut pink velour top and skintight jeans. She has long lavender fingernails and wears a wooden cross around her neck. A flicker of anxiety clouds her eyes when the detectives identify themselves, but she invites them in and sits cross-legged on a sofa. Until recently, she says, in heavily accented English, she lived here with her boyfriend, a professional boxer. This piques Knolls's and McCartin's interest because Luda's face was so badly beaten. But the name the woman mentions isn't familiar to either detective.

The woman says she works as a hairdresser and denies knowing Luda. McCartin shows her the driver's license photographs that Amo provided them. She says she cannot identify anyone.

Knolls knows she is lying, so he asks, sounding exasperated, "Do you know *anyone* who is a criminal?"

"No," she says. "I wish I could help you. But I can't."

The interview lasts less than ten minutes. The detectives learn absolutely nothing. As they walk back to the car, Knolls says, "I don't believe a fucking word she says."

"When I shook her hand, it was really sweating," McCartin says. "We need to get her to the station and poly"—polygraph—"the shit out of her."

The next apartment they visit is located in a down-at-the-heels section of east Hollywood, a Russian immigrant neighborhood of crumbling duplexes and apartment buildings. When an elderly, stout woman opens the door, the scent of overcooked cabbage and onions spills into the hallway. She speaks no English, so she finds a neighbor, who explains that the young woman the detectives are looking for moved some time ago. But the neighbor knows her phone number and calls her. She agrees to meet them in front of her old apartment. When she arrives, they drive her to the Hollywood Division station, a two-story redbrick building across the street from a rickety bail-bonds office.

Perched on a metal chair, in the corner of a small, spare interview room, the woman attempts to appear nonchalant. But a twitching jaw muscle reveals her apprehension. She is petite and wears no makeup; her blond hair, which looks natural, is cut in a short pageboy. She is dressed in a conservative white sleeveless blouse and black slacks. The woman says she is twenty-four, but she could pass for a UCLA sophomore.

She tells the detectives in passable English that she emigrated from the Ukraine four and a half years earlier. After Knolls asks a few preliminary questions, McCartin points at her.

"Are you a prostitute?"

"No," she says without conviction.

"I don't believe you," he says, glowering.

She takes sip of water and stares at a wall.

While her gaze is averted, Knolls scowls at McCartin, irritated that he has confronted the woman so quickly. Knolls had planned a number of softball questions to draw her out.

McCartin and Knolls have worked together for only three days and can't yet read each other, can't discern when to let the other detective take the lead and when to interject a question.

Sometimes, Homicide Special partners take longer to meld into a team than detectives in the local divisions do. They are experienced, skilled investigators, accustomed to following their instincts and solving murders their own way. Homicide Special detectives were promoted downtown because they had been successful employing their own sometimes idiosyncratic methods. As a result, many are unwilling to compromise or change their approach.

Knolls shows the woman a picture of Luda and several driver's license photographs. She does not identify anyone.

McCartin taps a pen beside the picture. "What happened to her could happen to *you* if we don't find these people."

"I don't care about drugs," Knolls says, counting on his fingers; "I don't care about prostitution. I don't care about illegal immigration. I don't care about tax evasion. I'm a homicide detective. All I care about is who killed this girl."

"I don't *know* nothing," she says, sullenly.

"Are you afraid that if you talk to us, someone will hurt your family back in the Ukraine?" Knolls asks.

Her eyes widen for a moment and she appears as if she is about to nod. Instead, she shakes her head. "I don't know her. I don't know nothing."

After a few more questions, the detectives realize the interview is pointless. They watch the woman walk out of the station, undulating like a Hollywood Boulevard hooker.

"That's no welfare walk," Knolls says. "She *swings* it."

McCartin watches with disgust. "We've got too many barriers here: language, culture, attitude. We've got to get a Russian speaker on board, working with us every day. It's like we're going to bat blindfolded. I worked in the ghetto too long. I can't read these Russian white people."

Knolls riffles through the stack of photographs. "We need to find the weak link."

"It could be a crazy ex-boyfriend who beat her to teach her a lesson," McCartin says.

"But why kill her?" Knolls asks.

"Could go a lot of ways. Our guy may be Russian mafia. It's quite open now."

Although the interviews tonight produced no useful information, they have at least "tickled the wire," McCartin says. The two girls will probably call others being monitored by the FBI, to discuss the detectives' questions and, Knolls and McCartin hope, Luda's murder.

As they drive back downtown to Parker Center, Knolls confronts McCartin. "You're like a bull in a china shop."

"What do you mean?" McCartin asks.

Knolls says angrily, "I'm trying to get her to relax. But you go after her almost as soon as she sits down." He imitates McCartin's New York accent and barks, " 'Hey, you a hookah?' "

"I felt we needed a different approach," McCartin says, sounding defensive. "I'm sick of these bitches lying to us. You weren't going to get shit with her anyway."

"It's worth a try. Why blast her right away?"

"I thought that was the best way to go."

"You're a bull, all right," Knolls says. "A New York bull."

They ride the rest of the way in silence.

McCartin's background is typical for the NYPD, but unusual for the LAPD. The son of a New York City fireman, he grew up in the Bronx, and moved to Westchester County in grammar school. His father and his four grandparents were born in Ireland. His father's father, who was wanted by the British because of his IRA activities, slipped out of Ireland in 1919, boarding a steamer in Wales, and made his way to New York, where he worked as a sandhog on the Lincoln Tunnel. Unlike some Southern Californians, who have tenuous attachments to their roots and their jobs, McCartin has a strong identity. He's an Irish cop.

After high school, McCartin attended Norwich University, a private military college in Vermont. At the end of his sophomore year, he enlisted, eventually joining the elite 82nd Airborne Division and making thirty-seven jumps. His next goal was flight school, but his father, who now owned a hardware store in the Bronx, had suffered a heart attack and McCartin was needed at home. For the next few years, he managed the store during the day and attended college at night. After graduation, he joined the New York City Fire Department and was assigned to a station in Harlem at 139th Street and Amsterdam Avenue.

But after a year he craved something different, a break from his father's routine. In college he had taken a police science class. One of the other students, a small-town cop, had mentioned that the LAPD was "a sharp department" with a beautiful academy, and Los Angeles was a city where it was sunny almost every day. McCartin decided to apply.

On a vacation in February 1983, McCartin flew to Los Angeles and took the LAPD entrance exam. During his two weeks in Southern California, it rained for twelve straight days, but when the LAPD accepted him, he moved immediately.

During the next decade, he walked a beat in a South-Central housing project, cruised Venice in a patrol car, and served as a training officer. In the early 1990s he was promoted to detective and soon made it to homicide, where he was overwhelmed with more than twenty murders a year.

Several of the gang murders McCartin investigated were as complex, brutal, and rife with witness intimidation as the organized crime cases he used to read about in the New York tabloids. McCartin was assigned to a task force that investigated Cleamon "Big Evil" Johnson, the leader of the notorious 89 Family Bloods; Johnson had killed more than twenty people, detectives suspected, but had evaded arrest because witnesses were too terrified to talk. The task force eventually brought Big Evil down, sending him to death row. McCartin's work on the case and his assignment to an FBI-LAPD unsolved-murder team helped facilitate his promotion to RHD.

McCartin's life now is a world away from the Bronx. He lives more than sixty miles east of downtown, in rural Riverside County, on two and a half acres. His wife and children love horses, so he plans to build a barn and tack room. The commute, however, is hellish. He usually rises at four A.M. to avoid the morning traffic, arrives at Parker Center at 5:30, and works out in the basement gym before starting his shift. On occasion, McCartin takes the train to the downtown station. Because of his dark business suits, fellow commuters probably assume he is a corporate lawyer or a sales executive. His cop eyes, however, give him away; they exude suspicion and a certainty that almost everyone he encounters during his workday will lie to him.

On Wednesday morning McCartin calls Amo for background on the two women he and Knolls interviewed Tuesday night. She confirms that the first, the one whose ex-boyfriend is a boxer, is a call girl. The demure-looking woman, Amo says, "is a prostitute and up-and-coming madam who is big time in the organization."

Later in the morning, an Armenian-American detective who has heard about the murder stops by RHD to share information on a Russian stolen-car ring he is investigating. Knolls says he has an Armenian suspect—Mher—who grew up in Los Angeles. Could Mher be involved with the Russian mafia? Knolls asks. The other detective explains that the Russian mob hires members of Armenian Power—an Armenian-American street gang based in Hollywood—as enforcers.

"Great," Knolls says sarcastically. "If we can't get through to the dollies, how are we going to get through to *these* gangsters?"

Homicide Special detectives often pick up cases late, after the divisional detectives realize the complexity of the investigation. Fortunately, the Luda Petushenko case was assigned only a day after the murder, but Knolls and McCartin still missed the fresh crime scene, the initial interviews, and the autopsy.

On Wednesday afternoon, they decide to stop by the coroner's office to talk to the pathologist and examine the body. Usually, they would rely on the autopsy notes compiled by the original detectives. But the slash marks on Luda's face and neck pique their interest.

The pathologist removes Luda's body from a metal rack in the "cooler," sets it on a gurney, and wheels it to a corridor outside the autopsy room where he meets the detectives. Luda's corpse is in a clear plastic body bag, tied with twine at the ankles, thighs, and waist. The body is stiff, slightly decomposed, and the skin is waxy. The partly opened body bag leaves her upper torso exposed. Thick, crude stitches run down the center of her chest where her internal organs were removed during the autopsy. Slightly above the left nipple, there is a dime-sized, red-rimmed circle: the entry point of the .45-caliber slug.

As doctors and technicians scurry down the hallway, the pathologist studies the deep, plum-colored bruises that streak and speckle Luda's face and neck. "There's a lot of contusions on the jawbone and side of the face," he says. "There's a large hemorrhage on the back of the neck. But I don't think she was strangled. I've done a lot of cases with women who were strangled and their nails were usually damaged from the struggle." He points to Luda's ice-blue acrylic fingernails. "No damage at all. In all my time here, I've never seen one that went down so quickly. Boom, boom. It happened like that," he says, snapping his fingers. He shadowboxes, throwing a few crisp punches. "There was bruising on the brain. It was like a shot from a boxer."

McCartin and Knolls nod simultaneously.

The pathologist waves a palm above Luda's arm and says, "They're clean. No bruising at all. That's unusual regarding trauma and women." He adds, "she was taken down first. Punched or struck with an object. She was alive when she was shot. There was a lot of blood in the cavity on her left side."

Knolls crouches beside the gurney and points to the slashes on her neck, the side of her face, and cheek. "What do you think made those marks?"

"One of our criminologists suggested it was the butt end of a forty-five," the pathologist says.

"Could he have stomped on her?" McCartin asks. "Maybe those are boot marks."

"Don't think so," the pathologist says.

"Could he have braced her against something?" Knolls asks. "Maybe the object he jammed her against made those marks."

"I was thinking the same thing," the pathologist says. "Maybe an end table."

"Or a bed," McCartin says.

The pathologist scrutinizes Luda's neck. "There's a real linear pattern to it."

"Maybe someone was torturing her," Knolls says. "Or maybe someone coldcocked her with a three- or four-knuckle ring."

McCartin asks the pathologist if he can determine the time of death.

Luda's body was discovered early Thursday morning. The pathologist estimates that she was killed Wednesday morning at about six o'clock. "Most people peak at full rigor mortis in eighteen hours in ambient temperature," he says.

"But we believe she was on the phone at nine o'clock the morning she was killed," Knolls says. "Is that possible?"

"Heat will accelerate it," the pathologist says. "Cold will delay it."

"The North Hollywood guys said the air-conditioning was on full blast," McCartin says. "Somebody didn't want that body stinking and discovered. It was cold as a meat locker in there."

The pathologist nods. "Then she could have been alive at nine o'clock."

When they return to the squad room, McCartin studies the videotape shot outside the front door of Luda's apartment building, attempting to compare the images with the driver's license photos from the FBI. The video runs so fast he cannot clearly see the faces. He plans to ask the LAPD electronics lab for help.

Knolls tracks down Leyla, the Russian woman who found Luda's body. Because her English is so limited, he arranges for a Russian-speaking detective from another LAPD division to translate. The detective has a busy caseload and is only free for the day.

Almost six feet tall, Leyla is a zaftig young woman in tight black pants, a gold anklet, and a diaphanous blouse. Her lacy black bra is clearly visible. She has an Eastern European cast to her features, with high cheekbones, an oval face, and cupid's-bow lips.

McCartin hands her a cup of coffee. Knolls flashes his business card and points to the word "Homicide." "That's *all* I'm interested in," he says, as the Russian-American detective translates. Knolls then delivers his mantra: "I don't care about dope, immigration, prostitution, green cards. All I want to know is who killed this girl. We want the *truth*."

Leyla nods nervously. She tells them she met Luda at Troyka, a

Russian market in Hollywood. Both were buying telephone cards to call home. They exchanged phone numbers and a week later Luda called.

"How many times were you at her Studio City apartment?" Knolls asks.

"Four or five times," she says.

"Was Luda working?" Knolls asks.

"No. She didn't have a work permit."

"How'd she get money?" Knolls asks.

"I don't know. That doesn't interest me."

Knolls sighs with exasperation.

"So if I tell you she was a prostitute, you'd be shocked?" McCartin says sarcastically.

Leyla spots a straw on the table, drops it into her coffee, and takes a delicate sip. "If I knew she was a prostitute, I'd never go to her house."

McCartin fixes Leyla with a suspicious look. "Are *you* a prostitute?"

She does not wait for the translator. "*Nyet.*"

"Then how do you pay your rent?"

She sips her coffee through the straw. "My parents send me money."

"What do *they* do?" McCartin asks.

She says her father is a police chief in the Ukraine, adding that she knows nothing about smuggling rings, prostitution, escort services, or Russian criminals.

Frustrated, the detectives leave the room to confer. They know she is lying, but agree that they do not want to push too hard at this initial stage. They do not want to alienate her. If Leyla asks for a lawyer, the interview is over.

They return to the room and ask her to recount the day of the murder. She begins by saying that Luda asked her for a 9:30 wake-up call. They planned to buy hair-care products at a nearby mall that afternoon. Leyla called at 9:30, but nobody answered and she figured that Luda was sunbathing by the pool. At 1:45 she drove to the apartment and waited by the underground garage. When someone opened the garage security gate, she sprinted inside and rode the elevator to Luda's apartment, which was usually unlocked.

The detectives are disappointed to hear how Leyla slipped into the apartment building. The videotape may be less helpful than they had hoped.

"It was very quiet inside," Leyla continues. "I thought she was by the pool. I went to use the restroom, then, out of the corner of my eye, I saw something on the floor, lying next to the bed. I realized it was Luda. I thought she was drunk or asleep. But then I saw her face. It was very swollen and blood was on her neck."

Leyla takes another sip of coffee and says, "I bent over and saw a little hole in her chest. Blood was coming out of her ears. I checked the pulse on her arm, but it was already very cold."

She then called Mher on her cell phone. She tells the detectives she did not call the police because she is not comfortable speaking English.

McCartin shows her a picture of Mher and asks, "Can you identify him?"

"That's Mher, the man I called."

"How'd you end up with his phone number?" Knolls asks.

"Because Luda was a guest at his house for a time and she told me if I ever needed to get hold of her to call him."

"How did Luda meet Mher?" McCartin asks.

"At a restaurant, I think."

"You think he could have killed her?" McCartin asks.

"No. He went to the police several times on his own because he wanted to know what happened."

"You don't seem too upset about stumbling onto a murder scene," McCartin says.

"That's just my character," she says, smiling cryptically. "I don't show my emotions in front of other people."

"You involved in anything illegal?" McCartin asks.

"No."

"You willing to take a polygraph?" McCartin asks.

"Sure," she says uncertainly.

"You realize we have a lot of interviews left," McCartin says. "If we find out you're lying to us, you could be deported or tossed in jail."

"I said what I said," she says flatly.

"When you were in the apartment and saw her body, was a television on?" Knolls wonders if the sound could have muffled the gunshot.

"She didn't have a television," Leyla says. "Even though she had a lot of cash, she didn't want to spend the money. She was saving all her money so she could bring her daughter over."

"Did she talk about her daughter a lot?"

"All the time. She told me: 'I want to see my daughter. I'm dying. I can't live without her.' She had a picture of her daughter in her wallet. Whenever she pulled it out, she kissed it."

If Luda did not work, McCartin asks, how did she plan to pay for her daughter's passage to the U.S.?

She tells him that Luda had a boyfriend—Mischa, a wealthy Russian man. The Saturday night before the murder, Mischa hosted a birthday party for Luda, which Leyla attended, at a Russian nightclub in Hollywood. A teenage boy, a friend of Luda's, was also at the party.

"She was separated and her husband's still in Kiev," Leyla says. "She talked about marrying again—this time to a rich guy. Maybe Mischa. She said if she could not find a rich guy to marry her this year, she would go back home."

At the end of the interview, Knolls asks if she has Mischa's telephone number. He is surprised when she nods and opens her telephone book.

McCartin and Knolls head back downtown, frustrated with the interview and each other. McCartin feels that often, when he asks a question, Knolls interrupts too quickly, breaking his line of inquiry. Knolls believes that McCartin is too abrupt and confrontational. To avoid another argument, they segue to a strained chat about Leyla.

As McCartin pulls onto the freeway, he says, "These broads are tough as nails. They're emotionless."

"Can't get a straight answer out of them," Knolls says.

"They'd deny the earth is round," McCartin says. "But at least Leyla put us onto Mischa. I'm going to call him when we get back. I'll try to get him to come by tomorrow."

The next afternoon, while the detectives wait for Mischa, they tell Lieutenant Hartwell about the fruitless interview with Leyla.

"You've got all these Russian girls who've only been here a few years, with no apparent jobs, yet they're all well dressed, driving nice cars, looking prosperous, living in beautiful apartments," Hartwell says, laughing. "Isn't America a great country?"

McCartin could not find an LAPD Russian speaker on such short notice, but he has managed to procure the services of a Los Angeles County Sheriff's Department translator. Mischa shows up in mid-afternoon and follows the translator and the detectives to a small interview cubicle in the back of the squad room. Short and pudgy with gray hair and gold-rimmed bifocals, he looks more like a grandfather from the old country than a sugar daddy. His clothes, however, are flashy: he wears black suede shoes with shiny silver buckles, a long-sleeved black silk shirt, and lime green linen pants.

Mischa, who immigrated to the United States in 1977, insists he does not need a translator. Knolls starts with some brief biographical questions. Mischa says he is in his mid-fifties and works as a salesman for a Russian vodka company. Three months ago he met Luda at the Troyka, the same Russian market where Leyla said she met her. He was never inside Luda's apartment; he always picked her up outside, and they spent nights at his house. The last time he saw Luda was at her birthday party. On the day she was murdered, they were supposed to stop by a pawnshop, where he planned to buy her a television. But when Mischa called the apartment, a detective answered and instructed him to drive to the North Hollywood station, where he was inter-viewed the first time.

When McCartin asks him how Luda supported herself, Mischa responds earnestly that she sold clothing in the Ukraine, and he assumed she continued to operate the business while in Los Angeles. He feigns surprise when McCartin tells him that Luda was a prostitute. They dated about once a week and, he insists, he never paid her.

McCartin and Knolls look disgusted, tired of the hookers and crooks snowing them.

The translator suddenly jabs a forefinger at Mischa. "You're a *vor v zakonye*" (a fraternal order of professional criminals in Russia that dates back hundreds of years). He points to Mischa's hands. On one is a faded tattoo of a heart pierced by a sword, on the other, a sunflower.

"Those are gulag tattoos," the translator says.

"That's bullshit!" Mischa shouts. "I got those when I was nineteen and I was in the Russian army."

So far McCartin has restrained himself, but now that the translator has challenged Mischa, he feels free to go after him.

"If you keep lying, we'll throw you in an INS holding tank right now," McCartin bluffs.

"I don't know who killed her, I swear to God," Mischa sputters. "I have a daughter. If something like this would happen to her, I don't know what I'd do. I come to the police station on my own. What more can I do?"

Mischa is flushed now, breathing heavily through his nose and wheezing.

Knolls raises a palm. "Okay, okay. Let's all calm down."

The detectives and the translator confer outside in the squad room. They need some leverage, McCartin says, or Mischa will continue to lie.

"That's right," the translator says. "A guy like him isn't afraid of the American police. You're Boy Scouts compared to those Russian cops. The prisons here are country clubs compared to the gulags."

McCartin tells the translator they found a picture at the apartment of Luda and Mischa posing together at her birthday party. If they threatened to run the photograph in Los Angeles's Russian newspaper, he asks, would that encourage Mischa to talk?

"Maybe," the translator says. "His associates might think he's attracting too much attention."

When they return to the interview room, Knolls tosses the picture on the table. "We need some way to officially confirm her identity. We're going to run this picture in the Russian paper if we don't get any information by next week."

"No problem," Mischa says, attempting to appear unconcerned. Then he asks, "Why do you need to run that picture?"

"We need information," McCartin says.

"Can the information be anonymous?" Mischa asks.

"That'll work," McCartin says.

"She used to send clothes to her daughter in the Ukraine," Mischa says, suddenly helpful. He names the shipping service she used. "They must have some records that could help you officially identify her."

Mischa tells the detectives he'll ask around about Luda. "One thing I can tell you, though. It's not an old-school type who did this murder. It's a newcomer. It's that *new* breed." He shakes his head in disgust, like a father who cannot understand why his son wears an earring.

Before the interview ends, McCartin again asks Mischa if he ever visited Luda's apartment. Mischa denies even entering the building. If he is caught on the videotape, however, or if his DNA matches the semen in one of the condoms, McCartin knows they might have enough to arrest him for the murder.

After Mischa and the translator leave, McCartin and Knolls slump in their chairs and put their feet up on their desks. The squad room is empty on this late Friday afternoon and they sit in silence for several minutes. Glaring through the venetian blinds, the harsh summer sun casts striped shadows on the desks and walls. The detectives look dispirited and enervated.

Exactly one week ago they picked up the case, and their progress has been negligible. Everybody they interview lies to them. The cultural chasm frustrates them. They have heard other detectives mutter that their case is a loser, consigned to unsolved purgatory. Haro never solved his Russian-Armenian organized crime murder. McCartin and Knolls worry that their case is headed in the same direction.

But Homicide Special detectives have one singular advantage: time. Divisional detectives might spend a week or two investigating a murder before they are assigned the next case. They might be forced to juggle half a dozen investigations simultaneously. Homicide Special detectives have the luxury of focusing on a single case for an extended period of time.

While the investigation seems stalled, the afternoon has yielded one positive development: their request for a full-time Russian translator has been granted. He begins next week.

3

The translator, David Krumer, arrives early Monday morning. A young LAPD officer born in the Ukraine, he immigrated to the United States when he was three, and grew up speaking Russian at home. One of only four Russian speakers in the department, he has spent the past year patrolling the Valley in a squad car. He is clearly excited about his new assignment.

After McCartin and Knolls deliver a synopsis of the case, they provide Krumer with the phone numbers for Luda's mother and husband in Kiev. Start with the husband, Knolls tells Krumer, even though they were separated.

McCartin calls the manager of Luda's apartment building. When he hangs up, he is chuckling. "You know the first thing the manager says?" he asks Knolls. "He asked me what the victim's 'backstory' was."

"Everyone's gone Hollywood," Knolls says.

McCartin carries the videotapes from the apartment building upstairs to the LAPD electronics lab. He wants freeze-frame images of everyone who entered the apartment the day of the murder.

Krumer talks to the husband, Igor, for about fifteen minutes. "He already knew she was dead," Krumer tells Knolls. "He got an anonymous call last week. He sounded very calm. Not upset at all. He told me that Luda studied to be a hairdresser, but ended up working in an open-air market in Kiev, selling food products. He said the economy there sucks."

Next, Krumer calls Luda's mother. "Hello, this is David Krumer from the Los Angeles Police Department. Have you spoken to Igor, regarding your daughter? . . . Well, I have very bad news. It turns out your daughter has passed away. . . ."

Krumer hangs up, looking unnerved. Responding to hot shot calls from a squad car has not prepared him for informing a woman that her daughter has been murdered. "The mother didn't know she was killed," Krumer tells Knolls. "She was really crying and wailing. The first question she asked was odd. She asked: 'Did it happen outside or inside her apartment?' "

Knolls deposits several boxes of Luda's documents, photographs, travel receipts, letters, and notebooks in an interview room. Krumer will begin translating the papers, while McCartin studies the videotapes and Knolls works the phones and organizes the murder book.

In the afternoon, the detectives stop by the Troyka market. Krumer, whose father owns a San Fernando Valley bakery, is familiar with the market: as a teenager he delivered crates of his father's bread here. At the edge of a Russian neighborhood in Hollywood, the Troyka is tucked into a Sunset Boulevard strip mall that also houses an Indian tandoori restaurant, a Chinese noodle shop, and a Russian bakery; across the street are a taco stand and a Thai restaurant.

From a distance, Krumer could pass for a Homicide Special detective. But a closer look reveals a patrol officer fresh off the streets. He is twenty-eight—most detectives in the unit are in their forties and fifties—and his bristling, street cop buzz cut makes him look younger. He is not accustomed to dressing up for work. He owns one suit and one sports coat, and instead of a dress belt, he wears the thick black service belt that usually straps around his uniform.

The owner of the Troyka is a middle-aged, brittle-haired blonde in a leopard-pattern blouse and gray apron. When Krumer asks the woman, who speaks no English, her name, she furiously waves a hand and whispers, "Nyet!"

Krumer talks with her for a few minutes and then translates. "The lady says she's afraid word will get around that she spoke to us. That's why she doesn't want her name used. But she'll answer our questions."

She leads the detectives to a corner of the market, behind a glass cooler filled with mushrooms, pickles, meatballs, and cooked cabbage. Garlicky sausages hang from the ceiling. The shelves are filled with jars of beets, mustard, onions, and horseradish. Russian newspapers and magazines line a periodical rack by the entrance.

Krumer interviews the owner over the din of the electric slicer as the butcher carves sausages for a customer. He shows her photographs of Luda, Mischa, Leyla, and Mher.

"She says Mischa *did* meet Luda here," Krumer tells the detectives. "He's a regular customer and one day she came in. She was a long way from her apartment and he offered to give her a ride."

"At least he told us the truth about *one* thing," McCartin says.

"Luda used to stop by the market once a week to buy phone cards," Krumer says. "The owner and Luda struck up a conversation because they're both from Kiev. The last time she saw Luda was in early June, the day she met Mischa. She recognizes Leyla because she used to come in and buy phone cards, too, but she cannot identify Mher. By the way Luda dressed, she suspected she was a prostitute. In fact, the girls who work at the store had a running bet on whether she was one or not."

Knolls tells him to ask the woman if she knew about the murder. "She *did* know about the murder," Krumer says. "The guy who sells phone cards told her."

"Did she hear any details?" McCartin asks.

"Nyet! Nyet! Nyet!" the woman says.

"Does she think Armenians were involved in her murder?" McCartin asks.

"She says, 'I don't know. I don't want to know,' " Krumer tells the detectives.

McCartin hands the woman his business card and says to Krumer, "Tell her if any of Luda's friends come in, have them call me."

As they walk out the door, Krumer points out a loaf of his father's black bread on the shelf. The label reads, "Soldier's Bread," and the package features a drawing of Krumer's father in a Russian army uniform. The bread is sold by the half loaf, Krumer explains, because that is the ration a Russian soldier carries.

The next morning, the detectives in the squad room angrily dissect a *Los Angeles Times* article about a federal judge who has ruled that the LAPD could be sued under an antiracketeering law. The ruling stems from one of the worst scandals in the department's history: more than a hundred convictions have been overturned and five officers so far have been arrested and criminally charged.

The scandal centers on the LAPD's Rampart Division, headquartered in a gritty neighborhood west of downtown with a large Central American population. Officers have been charged with beating and threatening suspects—and in one case shooting an unarmed man—as well as with planting weapons and drugs on them and with lying in court.

The Homicide Special detectives are proud to work in the division, proud they have been selected to work in a unit with such a storied reputation. Many have immaculate records. Yet they fear those reputations have been tarnished along with the dirty cops'. During the past year, it seems to them, all news about the LAPD has been bad. They support the arrest of crooked cops, but to label an entire police department of more than nine thousand officers a criminal enterprise is an outrage, the detectives complain.

Otis Marlow, one of the few veterans remaining in the unit, strides through the squad room door shortly before eight o'clock, salutes the detectives sharply, and announces cheerily: "Good morning, fellow racketeers."

In a homicide squad room, black humor usually trumps melancholy. Now, the morning's ugly mood quickly dissipates. The detectives chuckle and return to their homicide chronologies, or witness statements, or murder books, or crime scene photographs.

After several days holed up in the interview room, Krumer walks the detectives through his translations. First, he points to a document that appears to be Luda's trick sheet. Neatly drawn columns list the names of johns, the times of the appointments, the fees—about $200 to $300 per customer—and the split with the madam, which was usually fifty-fifty. Beneath the name of every john, Luda wrote brief descriptions: "producer," "lawyer," "shy," or "rabid." From May 24 to June 9, she netted $3,300.

Krumer also translated Luda's route to the United States. She traveled from the Ukraine by train, arriving in Moscow on April 9. Two days later, she arrived in Frankfurt, and then flew to Mexico. She spent about three weeks in Mexico City, Tecate, and Tijuana. On May 5, she was smuggled into the United States. After five nights in San Diego, she arrived in Los Angeles. Three and a half months later she was murdered.

The detectives praise Krumer's thorough work and then crowd around a photo found at Luda's apartment, a shot of several scantily clad, provocatively posed young women. Knolls speculates about whether Luda was smuggled into the United States with these girls, or whether she earned extra money procuring customers for them.

Krumer shows them other paperwork that indicates Luda owed Mher $5,000.

"Interesting," Knolls says. "Maybe Mher was tired of waiting for his money and wanted to teach the other girls a lesson."

"Or if she was running her own business, that could have pissed off the competition," McCartin says.

Krumer points out several diary entries and an unmailed letter from Luda to her mother, sister, and daughter: "I love you a lot. I am lonely here without you. It's very frightening. I only wish to make money faster and bring you to me. It's all possible. All it takes is time. Here it's very beautiful. Freedom is everything. A lot of our own are here. I relax every day, sunbathe in the pools. . . . When I see small children in the pool, I see my own Anastasia and imagine how I will relax with her. . . . Everything is great. The only thing missing is you. Kissing you. Hard hugs. Protect Anastasia and hope she does not forget me. Bye. I love you all."

When McCartin first gazes upward at Ivan, the eighteen-year-old who called Luda's apartment repeatedly on the day of the murder, he immediately recalls the pathologist who described a punch so powerful that it bruised Luda's brain. Ivan, who is six foot seven, is big enough to have delivered that blow. And clearly, he is terrified. Nervously, he strokes the stubble on his chin while responding to the detectives' preliminary questions. He immigrated several years ago and attended two years of high school in Los Angeles, so his English is excellent.

Luda had been in the United States for just two weeks when she visited the shoe store where Ivan works part-time. They chatted and exchanged phone numbers. Ivan insists that their relationship was never sexual; he merely showed her the sights of Los Angeles. He kept calling her the day of the murder because they had planned to spend the afternoon at the Magic Mountain amusement park.

McCartin taps his pen on the metal table. Leyla had told them that she and Luda planned to buy hair-care products that afternoon at a nearby mall. Mischa claimed that he and Luda had planned to buy a television at a pawnshop. Now Ivan says they had planned to visit an amusement park. McCartin wonders who is lying.

Luda did not have a job, Ivan says, so Mischa probably paid some bills. He was also under the impression that someone in the Ukraine sent her money.

"I don't believe a *friggin'* word you've said." McCartin throws the pen down.

Ivan nervously pinches his calf.

"She was a prostitute, and you know it. You better start leveling with us, or *you* will be in trouble."

Ivan stares at his shoes for several minutes, looks up and says, "I'm afraid of these people. When I was in Russia, I saw how these people worked. I saw people killed."

"It's not my job to investigate one murder and end up with a second one," McCartin says.

Ivan scratches his chin and jiggles his foot.

"Who do you think killed her?" Knolls asks.

"She was always saying: 'This guy doesn't want to give me back my money.' But I don't know who she was talking about." Ivan then says that at Luda's birthday party a girl named Olena told him about being threatened by a Russian mafia thug.

"She told me at the nightclub that this guy warned her that if she didn't work for him, he'd send some black guys to rape her and he'd kill all her family in Kiev. But she didn't tell me any more about it, or any details."

McCartin spreads out on the table the photographs found at Luda's apartment. Ivan identifies the prettiest, youngest, and most voluptuous of the girls as Olena. She is topless—her crossed arms partly cover her breasts—and she wears white lace panties and thigh-high white stockings. Ivan does not know her last name.

The detectives speculate that the thug who threatened her was Mher. They show Mher's enlarged driver's license photograph to Ivan, but he cannot identify him.

"Could this guy who threatened her have been after Luda too?" McCartin asks.

"Maybe."

"Why?"

"I don't know."

At the end of the interview, Krumer speaks up. "Let me ask you something, just for myself. Did your mother tell you not to say anything to the police?" This is a question, Krumer later points out, that perhaps only a Jewish cop would ask a Jewish witness.

Ivan pauses, looks as if he is about to nod, but instead quickly shakes his head.

After Ivan leaves, McCartin and Knolls decide that the Russian thug belongs on their rapidly expanding list of suspects. Now they have to identify him. And the quickest way to do so is to interview Olena. But first they have to find her.

On the Tuesday after Labor Day, Krumer calls a couple in Denver who were friends with Luda and her husband in the Ukraine. He found their phone number in Luda's papers. "Luda confided in them in the past," Krumer tells McCartin and Knolls. "She told them about a run-in she had with some Russian-Armenian guy. He threatened to kill her over a business deal."

In the afternoon, one of the FBI agents investigating Russian prostitution calls and tells McCartin that he has a Russian informant who knew Luda's business associates. The informant told the agent that he heard Mher was there when Luda was killed, although he did not know how, exactly, Mher was involved. He also heard that a boxer had something to do with the murder.

The detectives picked up the case two and a half weeks ago and still have more questions than answers. Is the Armenian gangster who threatened Olena the same one who threatened Luda? Is Mher the Armenian gangster? Is Ivan an obsessed, spurned suitor? Did Mischa the sugar daddy have a reason to kill Luda? And, finally, is this a run-of-the-mill hooker murder, or a complex investigation inextricably entwined with the Russian mafia?

Russian organized crime, the detectives realize, is a misnomer. The criminals are neither Russian nor organized. Many are immigrants from Armenia, the Ukraine, Georgia, and other former Soviet republics. Unlike the Italian Mafia, with its large criminal families and hierarchy, the Russian mob has no centralized organization and consists of many small syndicates, known as brigades. All pursue their own illegal schemes, but collectively, they are known as the Russian mafia.

During the 1970s, when Soviet authorities allowed hundreds of thousands of Jews to immigrate to the United States, a number of criminals—including some with marginal Jewish status or who simply passed as Jews—set up their operations in the Brighton Beach section of Brooklyn. Because they had lived in a totalitarian state and had extensive experience evading Soviet regulations, the Russian mobsters soon became adept at defrauding the U.S. government and corporations. These immigrant criminals specialized in crimes such as medical and insurance fraud, tax scams, credit card forgery, and check kiting.

The next wave of Soviet criminals entered the United States in the early 1990s during the economic turmoil and political upheaval accompanying the Soviet Union's dissolution. Many pursued white-collar crime, like their predecessors. But they also branched out into more traditional criminal enterprises, including drug smuggling, auto theft, prostitution, counterfeiting, and extortion, and some were infamous for their brutal methods.

Brooklyn is still the hub, but Los Angeles, which has the nation's second-largest Russian population, is another major hot spot.

The detectives, disheartened by the sluggish pace of the investigation, decide to leapfrog over the peripheral players and interview someone closer to the epicenter—Serge, the man who boasted that Luda waived her usual fee because they had had such passionate sex. He told the North Hollywood detectives, who found his telephone number at Luda's apartment, that he met her at a coffee shop; McCartin and Knolls are convinced he is lying. They know that Serge is a target of a joint investigation involving LAPD auto theft detectives, the FBI, and the U.S. Customs Service, focused on a crime ring that ships stolen cars to Russia and smuggles Russians into the United States.

McCartin tells Knolls that unless they have some leverage over Serge, the interview will be fruitless. He suggests the "cold poly" approach. When he worked in South-Central, he polygraphed a number of gang murder suspects first and questioned them afterward. If a suspect failed the polygraph, McCartin believed he gained added clout and authority during the subsequent interrogation. He suggests employing this method with Serge. Knolls is skeptical, but McCartin insists.

Polygraphs cannot determine guilt or innocence; they are merely indicators of a subject's veracity and are not admissible in court. Investigators often use them, however, to assess the truthfulness of witnesses, verify data, and develop leads.

Knolls and McCartin are edgy all day as they prepare for Serge's arrival. He could be the key to their investigation. If he "lies and denies," McCartin tells Knolls and Krumer, they might be chasing leads on this murder until they retire.

In the late afternoon, Serge breezes into the squad room, looking blasé, checking out the detectives with an expression of curiosity, rather than concern. He is in his mid-thirties, tall, tan, and broad-shouldered, with close-cropped light brown hair. He wears jeans, a tight T-shirt, and black boots. He might be considered handsome, except that a constant smirk and his eyes, which glitter with calculation, give his sharp features a reptilian cast. Serge grew up in Russia, but his family was allowed to leave the country during the wave of Jewish emigration in the 1970s, he tells the detectives, in lightly accented English. He is a car dealer, he says, but is between jobs.

"This is going to be a tough one for you," he says in a slightly condescending tone. "All the Russian prostitutes in L.A. are so scared they went underground."

His cocky manner irritates McCartin, but he contains himself, casually asking Serge whether he minds taking a polygraph before the interview. McCartin assures him that this is a standard procedure. After a split-second hesitation, Serge agrees. They walk down a back corridor and wait for a service elevator. Several garbage cans overflow with trash, and the floor is strewn with newspapers and candy wrappers.

Serge surveys the clutter and sniffs, "*This* isn't what I expected."

On the fourth floor, the polygraph examiner escorts Serge to a small chamber and leads him to a seat. The examiner then hooks a blood-pressure cuff around Serge's arm, attaches small metal plates to the ring and index fingers of his right hand, and wraps rubber tubes around his chest and stomach. The instruments are attached to a computer, which will analyze Serge's heart rate, blood pressure, breathing patterns, and perspiration levels. The detectives watch the exam on a video monitor in a room down the hall.

"How much sleep did you get last night?" the examiner asks.

"Ten hours," Serge says.

McCartin grumbles, "Lucky bastard. I had to get up at four o'clock this morning to make it to work in time."

While the examiner asks Serge several preliminary questions, McCartin tells Knolls and Krumer about one of the dimmest criminals he ever interviewed. The suspect, who continually called the test a "polycure," wanted the examiner to ask him whether he loved his girlfriend—so he would finally know definitively how he felt about her.

Prior to the polygraph, the detectives had outlined several basic questions for the examiner: Did you inflict any of Luda's injuries? Were you present when Luda was shot? Do you know for sure who shot Luda?

After the first round of questions, the examiner leaves the polygraph chamber to go over the results with the detectives. "Oh, man!" he says, falling into a chair. "I don't like these results. The charts are going in both directions at once. They aren't consistent. The new terminology for this kind of result is 'no opinion.' We used to call it 'inconclusive.' "

"Could this mean he was there, but he didn't do it?" Knolls asks.

The examiner nods. He says that although there are a number of possible explanations, he is certain that Serge knows more than he has revealed.

The examiner returns to his subject. "You didn't pass the test. You're not telling me the complete truth. . . ." He pauses, then bluffs. "Everything points to you."

Serge, slouching in his chair, legs crossed, immediately sits upright, as if jolted by an electric shock. His nonchalant façade dissolves in an instant. "That freaks me out. It's just so absurd," he sputters. He points to the polygraph and says, "That's an absolutely useless pile of junk. And you should know."

They return to the RHD interview room and Krumer brings Serge, who is flushed, a cup of coffee. Knolls attempts to calm him down, gradually working up to a few introductory questions. McCartin fingers the FBI's photos, which he is about to spring on Serge, but Knolls motions for him to wait. McCartin soon grows impatient with Knolls's leisurely pace. Finally, he barks, "How many girls you bring over?"

Knolls is miffed. He believes McCartin is pushing too hard, too fast.

"We want the truth, not bullshit," McCartin says. "Tell me what you know."

"If I talk about illegal things, how do I know you cops won't get me into trouble?" Serge sips his coffee nervously.

"We're not here to nail you," McCartin says. "All we care about is the murder."

Serge puts his elbows on the table, cradling his chin with his palms. After a few minutes, he says, "Let me try to explain. I had a scam going. . . ."

Serge begins to tick off the details of his business operation. A group of his associates who own a travel agency in Kiev obtain Mexican visas for Ukrainians. Some pay a fee up front. The young women work off their passage as prostitutes when they arrive in the United States. Serge owns a boat on which he and a female partner smuggle the Ukrainians—as many as twenty-five at a time—into the United States, from Tijuana to San Diego.

"Where'd you get the boat?" McCartin asks.

Serge smiles sheepishly and says, "It was a trawler. I bought it from the Boy Scouts."

Knolls chuckles. Even McCartin manages a faint smile. Krumer shakes his head and says, "A Boy Scout boat running hookers. I can't believe it."

"Is this going to get me into trouble?" Serge asks.

"I could give a rat's ass about all this," Knolls says. "All I care about is the murder."

Serge explains that he first met Luda in Mexico, shortly after she arrived, but he did not bring her to L.A. A group of Armenian smugglers arranged her trip. Luda was a quick study, Serge says. And she was desperate for money because she wanted to bring her daughter to the United States.

"So Luda became my new partner."

"*Your* partner," Knolls says, catching McCartin's eye. McCartin looks equally surprised.

"Yeah. She had connections in Kiev. I had the boat. She needed me. I needed her."

Luda, Serge explains, arranged for six Ukrainian women to obtain visas and fly to Mexico. Serge's trawler transported them to the United States. In San Diego, Luda picked up the girls and drove them to Los Angeles. She "sold" four of them to a madam named Lana, whom she worked for. Two slipped away because they did not want to turn tricks. Serge, who claims he felt sorry for them, found them a place to live. Lana was angry with him and Luda. A few weeks before the murder, Lana called and accused him of stealing her hookers.

McCartin asks him whether he was afraid.

"Not of her. But she was working with an Armenian guy named Mike. He's some kind of strong-arm type, an enforcer guy. He calls and tells me: 'You stole my hookers. Do you know who you're talking to?' " Serge pauses. "He's trying to take over. I heard they did the same thing in New York. Ex-KGB people were hitting on all the hookers and madams, trying to take over their business. Everyone's afraid of this guy. After Luda was murdered, I heard that Michael told Lana, 'If things don't go my way, something will happen again.' "

"Why go after Luda and not you?" McCartin asks.

"Maybe because they couldn't find me. I live in a pretty remote area of the Hollywood Hills. No one knows where it is."

"You think Luda had any contact with him?" Knolls asks.

"Yes, but I'm not sure. A few days before the murder she said four Armenians came to her house and asked her who she worked for."

The detectives know that Mher is also known as Mike. They wonder if the Armenian enforcer is Mher.

"So why kill her?" McCartin asks.

Serge shrugs.

"My opinion is they were pissed off at you and they were sending you a message," Knolls says.

"Did they know you were screwing her?" McCartin asks.

"It was no secret."

"Anyone knows what Michael looks like?" Knolls asks.

"One of the girls does. He tracked her down. He went to her apartment and raped her."

McCartin shows him the picture of Olena.

"That's the one."

"Did Mike threaten her family in Russia?" Knolls asks.

"That's what she said."

The detectives leave Serge and confer in the squad room.

"You're being a New York bull again," Knolls says to McCartin.

"I asked him some questions and he opened up right away," McCartin says defensively.

"You wanted to show him the pictures right away. Let's slow down."

"Why wait? I gotta tell you, there were times when I was trying to establish a line of questioning in there, but you kept interrupting me."

Worn out, the detectives pause, like fighters staggering back to their corners at the end of a round. Although Knolls and McCartin sometimes seem to work at cross-purposes, Serge is proof that their inadvertent good cop–bad cop routine is becoming quite effective.

Back in the interview room, McCartin produces the pictures of the six women, and Serge confirms that he and Luda smuggled them into the United States.

McCartin then shows Serge a series of the driver's license photos supplied by the FBI. Serge immediately identifies one unshaven, rough-looking character with a buzz cut: "That's Boxer." Boxer, he adds, is now dating one of the six Ukrainian girls transported from Mexico. He is in the naval reserves.

The detectives are intrigued. "Is he helping you out with the boat operation?" asks McCartin.

Serge laughs. "He doesn't know shit about boats."

"And he's in the *navy*?" Knolls says incredulously.

"That's right."

McCartin asks him to contact Olena and help set up an interview with her. Serge insists that Olena would be too frightened to talk to the detectives, but says she might feel more comfortable alone with Krumer, since he is from the Ukraine. The detectives agree, and Serge says he will contact her and propose the interview.

Serge meekly asks the detectives whether they can forget about his smuggling operation because he has assisted them with their homicide case.

"Why would we jeopardize our murder investigation to burn you?" Knolls says.

The detectives do not intend to burn Serge. Yet. To ensure the FBI agents' continued cooperation, McCartin and Knolls plan to offer them any new information about prostitution and smuggling if they will delay arrests until the Luda case is completed.

Knolls and McCartin know Serge will claim he was framed when he discovers that his statements incriminated him. But detectives may legally deceive suspects in order to determine the truth about a crime. Police can use deception, the courts have ruled, as long as their tactics are not so egregious that they force an innocent person to confess.

At the end of the interview Serge declares in a self-righteous tone, "I do this with a clear conscience. I bring people here who are starving at home and have nothing to lose. They have a better life here." Before he leaves, he says, "Now tell me, did I really fail the polygraph?"

"You were deceptive," Knolls says. "You were holding something back."

Serge shakes the detectives' hands and says he will contact them about Olena. McCartin watches with satisfaction as he shuffles out the door a lot less confident than when he entered hours earlier.

The detectives return to the empty squad room. Outside, it is dark and the neon lights of downtown glow in the distance. Knolls pours himself a cup of coffee. Krumer finishes off a candy bar. McCartin loosens his tie. The detectives are tired and hungry, but they are buoyed by the interview. After all of the half-truths, self-serving statements, evasive answers, and brazen lies of the past few weeks, they have finally uncovered a semblance of the truth. This is the break they had hoped for. They now have some insight into Luda's past, her journey to the United States, her life in Los Angeles, and, possibly, her death. She is not the typical hapless-hooker victim. Prostitution was not her only illegal enterprise. The detectives have a possible motive, a potential suspect. And, most important, they have a witness who can identify the suspect.

"All in all, a pretty productive day," Krumer says.

"This Armenian Mike might be a totally different guy from Mher," McCartin says.

"I agree," Knolls says. "But that FBI informant said Mher might have been there. So if this Armenian Mike isn't Mher, I think Mher might have driven him there and been there during the murder. We got to get Mher in here and poly him."

"This guy might have come out from New York to take over," McCartin says. "I don't think we have his picture."

"Serge is trying to put us onto Armenian Mike," Knolls says. "Maybe he's a threat to him."

"Could be," McCartin says. "But I think he was being truthful."

As the detectives lock their desks, grab their briefcases, and head for the door, McCartin smiles. "Guys," he says, "we're getting close."

4

The next morning, Knolls and McCartin decide to celebrate with a late breakfast at Howard's Café, which is a few miles west of downtown in the corner of a Pico Union strip mall lined with Salvadoran businesses. Howard's, which has a sign in front advertising CHINESE & AMERICAN FOOD, is jammed with cops, bus drivers, and city workers who dine on eggs and fried rice and other unorthodox combinations. The detectives and Krumer order the Howard's Special No. 8, a heaping plate of barbecued pork and fried rice for $5.95.

"I never met Jews like Serge and Mischa before," McCartin tells Knolls and Krumer, between mouthfuls. "I never met Jews who were crooks and thugs like this. Growing up in New York, all the Jews I ever met were doctors and lawyers."

Krumer attended law school but grew disillusioned and joined the police force instead of studying for the bar. The parents of his academy classmates were proud to have a son who worked as a cop, but in a Jewish family, he grumbles, a cop is a disappointment.

"Not in an Irish family," McCartin says, laughing.

After breakfast, they pile into McCartin's Malibu and he heads west on the Santa Monica Freeway, negotiating the side streets of Westwood and pulling up in front of a luxurious Wilshire Boulevard highrise. According to the FBI, a madam named Svetlana lives here, but the detectives decide to start with the manager. Knolls warns McCartin not to intimidate her by broaching the subject of prostitution right away. He plans to introduce the subject later in the interview, delicately.

After the manager ferries them into her office, Knolls says, "We'd like to ask you a few questions about some Russian tenants."

"Well," the manager says, "we had a group of Russian hookers here a little while back."

McCartin flashes Knolls a barely perceptible smile.

"We had to throw them out at the end of last year," the manager says. "They had a big argument on the fifteenth floor and a neighbor complained. Some Russian guy threatened the neighbor with a gun."

Knolls shows her a picture of Mher.

"That's *him*," she says immediately. "It's totally him. I had several face-to-face conversations with him."

Svetlana moved months ago, the manager says, and she does not have her forwarding address. Knolls shows her pictures of the Ukrainian girls, but she cannot identify them. The hookers used to spend their days by the pool, she says, so after the interview Knolls declares with mock gravity that he must be meticulous and visit the pool to check for Ukrainian "dollies" lounging in their bikinis. The detectives, however, are disappointed to find the pool deserted. In their dark suits, white shirts, and polished black shoes, they look anomalous and awkward standing beside the water in the bright sunshine.

This morning, outside Howard's Café, the air was still and oppressive and the smog so thick the sky was an adobe-colored vault. But in Westwood the ocean breezes blow away the smog and temper the harsh summer sun. Thinned of pollutants, the light is radiant here, the sky neon blue, the shadows razor sharp. The flaming bougainvillea and pink oleander blossoms that frame the pool are strikingly vivid. After being holed up in the squad room the past few weeks, the detectives are in no hurry to return. So instead of driving back to RHD, they meander east along Wilshire Boulevard.

McCartin, who worked in West Los Angeles when he was a young patrolman, knows the area well and decides to show Knolls and Krumer the small mortuary where Marilyn Monroe's body is interred. He drives through a narrow passageway off Wilshire, behind a soaring Westwood office tower, and parks beside a satiny strip of grass dotted with headstones. Walking to a marble wall across from the graveyard, he points: "There she is, boys." On one of the crypts is a simple brass plaque: MARILYN MONROE 1926–1962." A brass vase affixed to the vault is filled with fresh yellow and white daisies. Until the 1980s, her ex-husband Joe DiMaggio paid for fresh flowers to be delivered to the vase. Now only visitors uphold the tradition.

McCartin tells them that Marilyn Monroe's first husband was a "copper" who worked on the LAPD shooting range. After the detectives spend a few minutes walking about the small cemetery, McCartin drives them east on Wilshire and then north through Beverly Hills, past some of the most expensive mansions in the country. He pulls up in front of an incongruously bucolic home, known as the Witches' Cottage, which would be more appropriate in a Brothers Grimm fairy tale than in an exclusive Beverly Hills neighborhood. It features two steeply peaked gables, an undulating cedar-shake roof, leaded glass windows, rough-cut wooden shutters, and a lawn split by a moat. The cottage, built in 1921, was originally designed as a movie set and office for a production company and was later moved to this neighborhood.

As McCartin threads the Malibu through traffic he says, "Mher's the key to this case. Either he was there, he did it, or he knows who did it. Let's stop by his house."

Last year, Mher and his wife claimed on their tax returns that they earned $148,000 operating a flower shop. But the address listed for the shop is in a residential neighborhood near Hollywood. Knolls and McCartin have no intention of contacting Mher yet; they simply want to verify that he lives here. McCartin drives down a shady street and parks near the house, which is bright yellow and looks as if it has recently been remodeled and landscaped. A new Mercedes without license plates is parked in the driveway.

When McCartin and Knolls walk to the front porch, trying to determine whether someone actually operates a flower business at the house, Mher suddenly opens the door. He wears a sleeveless undershirt and blue sweat pants and has a large gold cross around his neck. Knolls quickly introduces himself and McCartin and tells him they are investigating Luda's murder.

"We'd like to have you come down to the station and look at some pictures," he says casually.

"Sure," Mher says. "When?"

"We'll let you know," Knolls says. "What's the best number to reach you?"

Mher gives Knolls his cell phone number. He tells the detectives he rented Luda's apartment and later sublet the unit to her. "When can I get my stuff?" he asks.

"You're getting evicted," McCartin says coldly.

Knolls suggests that Mher call the manager.

When they return to the car, Knolls tells McCartin, "You're pretty damn blunt." He imitates McCartin's New York accent: "Ya gettin' evicted, ya fuckin' asshole."

"Why pussyfoot around?" McCartin retorts, shrugging. "Anyway, my personality doesn't matter. We'll be booking his ass soon."

The next Monday morning, Knolls and McCartin are in the middle of a debate: are Mher and Armenian Mike the same person?

"I think so," Knolls says.

"I'm not convinced yet," McCartin says.

"I think Serge knows it," Knolls says. "He just won't ID him because he doesn't want to go to court."

Krumer calls the Ukraine, interviews Luda's mother again, and gleans another interesting detail about Serge: he owed Luda $15,000. McCartin suggests that the debt could have colored his interpretation of events. Later, the detectives drive to a bank near Luda's apartment and meet with a representative from the county office that administers the estates of foreign nationals. Luda's safety deposit box contains her passport and an envelope with twenty crisp $100 bills. Her savings account total is about $7,000, and $2,200 in cash was found in her apartment.

"In about four months, since she arrived in the U.S., she's got $11,500 in cash," Knolls tells McCartin. "That's not counting the money Serge owes her and all the cash she sent back to the Ukraine. She was raking it in."

The one constant in Luda's uncertain life, the detectives know from Krumer's interviews, was her love for her daughter, Anastasia. Knolls and McCartin want to make sure that the money is sent to Anastasia, not to Luda's estranged husband. Anastasia lives with Luda's mother and the husband sees her only occasionally.

The detectives ask the county worker how they can ensure that the cash will be sent to the daughter. She says the county is required to secure the money first and determine later how it is disbursed.

Knolls says, "I'm thinking of taking the cash into evidence." This would circumvent the county worker.

"We'd get it eventually," she says. "The husband may be entitled to the money."

"We'll research him," Knolls says. "Maybe they were never legally married."

Back at the squad room, the detectives prepare for an interview with Anna, a friend of Luda's from Kiev who now lives in Los Angeles.

Luda's mother provided Krumer with Anna's number and he asked her to stop by.

McCartin is surprised that Anna is so straightforward. She immediately volunteers that Luda admitted to her that she was a prostitute, and once even turned a trick while Anna was visiting. "She asked me to wait on the balcony," says Anna, who seems more titillated than embarrassed. "She said it would be very fast. And it *was* very fast. Ten minutes at most."

McCartin asks her whether Luda ever confided that she was in danger.

"She told me she paid to bring some girls over here. She said she was receiving threats because of these girls. I went to Western Union with her once to send two thousand dollars to her family because she didn't want to have cash around the house. She was frightened. I told her to move. But she thought these people were only after her money. Not her life."

While she rattles off a few sentences in Russian to Krumer, Knolls enters the room. An FBI agent involved in a counterintelligence investigation has just called. He told Knolls he has a Russian asset—spy jargon for "informant" or "snitch"—who has heard something about the murder. Excited, Knolls interrupts the interview and motions for McCartin to follow him into a hallway. The FBI has just learned, Knolls says, that Boxer confessed to a friend: "I left Luda's child without a mother."

"That's a hell of a tip," McCartin says. He returns to the squad room, quickly concludes the interview, and then calls the agent, whom he knows, for more information. The asset told the FBI agent that Boxer is a Russian immigrant whose name is Alexander Gabay. He apparently confessed to a friend when he was drunk. Boxer's girlfriend is Oxana, one of the girls Serge and Luda smuggled into the country. She did not want to work as a prostitute, so Luda might have pressured her to either turn tricks or pay the $6,000 for her passage. This dispute, the asset said, might have provided a motive to kill her.

McCartin and Knolls know that snitches are frequently unreliable, but the FBI's asset sounds legitimate. And the detectives are familiar with Gabay: his photograph was among those that the FBI provided them of Russian underworld figures.

"If Gabay's involved, why is Serge pointing to Armenian Mike?" Knolls says, more to himself than McCartin.

"Maybe he wants to protect him because they're friends," McCartin

says. "Maybe he wants to eliminate his competition. Maybe he wants
to do both."

The detectives review the various suspects. Gabay, acting alone,
could have killed Luda. Gabay might work for Mher, and the two of
them might have killed her. If Armenian Mike is not Mher, Armenian
Mike might have killed Luda because he believed she reneged on a
business deal.

"The homicide game is not always about trying to *identify* a suspect," Knolls tells Krumer. "Sometimes you first have to *eliminate* a
suspect."

Serge calls and tells the detectives that he has convinced three of the
Ukrainian prostitutes to cooperate. The girls are afraid of police sta-
tions, Serge says, so he suggests the detectives wear plain clothes and
conduct the interviews at a Starbucks near Luda's apartment in Studio
City. The detectives are elated when Serge informs them that one of
the three is Olena, the girl he had said was raped by Armenian Mike.
At the very least, they will determine today whether Mher is Armenian
Mike.

On a blistering early September afternoon, the detectives climb into
Knolls's unmarked blue Caprice and drive to the Valley. The temperature hovers at 100, and the sun glares overhead in the burnt-out
white sky. Knolls and his passengers are disgusted when they discover
the air conditioner is broken. As the Hollywood Freeway snakes over
the foothills, the temperature rises and the detectives curse the city for
providing such an unreliable car. When they roll down the windows,
a dusty, searing breeze blows through the car. As they drop into the
Valley, the smog thickens and the temperature reaches a scorching
105 degrees. The car feels like the inside of a dryer.

They cool off in a deli, where they order pastrami sandwiches and
strategize. They decide not to press Serge about Boxer's alleged confession. They want to see whether he volunteers the information. Serge
is attempting to curry favor by rustling up the girls, and they plan to
fully exploit his services as an intermediary before they browbeat him
about Boxer.

Outside Starbucks, Serge waits with three pretty young women,
who slow traffic and turn heads with their skimpy, low-cut tops, skintight lycra pants, and high heels. Serge points to Knolls's Hawaiian
shirt, McCartin's polo shirt, and their jeans. He grins and says, "So
this is how cops dress when they don't want to look like cops."

Starbucks is too crowded and noisy for interviews, so Knolls walks across Ventura Boulevard to a sprawling, faux-rustic establishment called the Sportsmen's Lodge. The name evokes the agricultural roots of the San Fernando Valley. During the 1930s, the actors Noah and Wallace Beery owned a trout farm on the site. After World War II, a new owner created a French-country-inn motif and filled the ponds with water lilies and swans. In its latest incarnation, the restaurant resembles a mountain lodge. The entrance features a huge archway hewn from thick trunks of timber, boulder pillars, and a splashing wooden water wheel, which appear somewhat farcical on this bustling city street.

The Lodge's manager agrees to let Knolls and McCartin conduct the interviews in the dim, quiet bar, which will afford some privacy. The detectives intend to talk to each girl without Serge hovering over them, so McCartin positions Olena beside a stone fireplace, while Knolls chats with Serge and the others at a table in the corner of the bar.

Olena, who is eighteen, wears white jeans, high heels covered with silver sequins, and a black tube top that reveals so much cleavage the bartender frequently cranes his neck to catch a glimpse. Olena, who wears no makeup, has flawless porcelain skin, high cheekbones, and almond-shaped eyes of the palest blue. She speaks no English, so Krumer translates for McCartin. All the girls worked as secretaries in the Ukraine, she says, barely surviving on their pay of $50 a month. "There's no hope in the Ukraine," Olena says, sounding like a rehearsed but distracted narrator in a grim documentary. "Nobody has any money. Everyone's afraid they won't be able to pay their rent and will get thrown out of their apartment. Hunger is a problem. Two-thirds of the people I know have no jobs."

A Ukrainian travel agency obtained the girls' visas and passages to Mexico, where they met Serge. Then they boarded a trawler in Rosarita Beach with about twenty other Ukrainians—mostly couples—on the night of July 4. A good night for smuggling, Olena adds, because so many people were out on boats watching fireworks. In the United States, the women were forced to work as prostitutes to pay off their $6,000 passage. Luda sold Olena to a madam named Lana, who took away her passport and who lives in a high-rise on Wilshire Boulevard—the same apartment building the detectives visited earlier in the week, McCartin realizes.

After Olena had paid off half her debt, she slipped away and contacted Serge. He did not care that she had run off, because he had already been paid for the smuggling operation. He arranged for her to stay in a friend's apartment, along with Helen, another of the missing Ukrainian girls.

Olena tells McCartin she was not angry with Luda for selling her to Lana. She even socialized with Luda occasionally. The arrangement, after all, was mutually beneficial, and it allowed her to stay in the United States. The Saturday before the murder, she attended Luda's birthday party, she says, along with Mischa, Ivan, and Leyla.

"I genuinely want to help you," Olena says, turning toward McCartin, looking earnest. "Luda had a young daughter. It's not right that she was killed."

At some point, Olena says, Lana found her cell phone number. She called to demand the rest of the money owed her and told Olena she was "playing with fire." When Olena refused to pay, Lana's associate—an Armenian man named Michael—called. He wanted to know if Olena and the other girl who disappeared were now working for Luda. Olena denied working for anyone else.

"He told me that if I didn't come back and go to work he was going to have my whole family in Kiev killed." She drops her chin and adds, so softly that Krumer cranes his neck to hear, "He threatened to rape me."

"Did he rape you?" McCartin asks.

She puffs up her cheeks and slowly exhales. Krumer chats with her quietly for a few minutes in Russian. Although a decade older, he looks about the same age as Olena, and she seems to trust him. Finally, Olena admits that Michael did rape her. She closes her eyes for a moment and shudders. "I was afraid he would have me killed if I didn't submit."

McCartin shows her Mher's picture. Now, at least, he will learn whether Armenian Mike is Mher. "Is this him?" McCartin asks.

She looks at Krumer and says, *"Nyet."*

"Can you describe him?"

"Early to mid-thirties. Grew up in Russia. Been in the U.S. about ten years. Brown hair. Starting to grow bald."

"Did he kill Luda?"

"I don't know." She pauses and then begins again, gesturing with both hands as Krumer translates. "If he did, maybe it was to show everyone that a new regime is taking over. He thought Luda might be hiding the other girls who disappeared. He thought they were working for her."

"Were they?"

"I don't know, but Michael and Lana thought so. Luda told me that Michael and Lana came to her apartment. They accused her of encouraging the girls to run away to work for her instead. They threatened her, told her not to get involved in the business. Serge told me that Luda called him one night, crying. They told her she had two days to leave Los Angeles. But at her birthday party she didn't seem that afraid."

McCartin shows Olena a driver's license photograph of Alexander "Boxer" Gabay. He has a shaved head, eyes as cold as embedded marbles, and a thick, muscular neck. Olena explains that Boxer met Oxana—one of the Ukrainian women—at a party and they now live together.

"Oxana and Luda didn't have a good relationship," she says. "Oxana owed Luda money, but refused to pay."

McCartin asks whether Boxer has a gun. She knows he has a gun, she says, but does not know what caliber.

After the interview, he escorts Olena back to Serge's table. Then McCartin confers with Knolls, who questioned the other girls, and discovers that they confirm much of Olena's story. They decided to talk to the detectives in the hopes that the police will help them gain legal residency. None can identify Mher, but they all know Boxer. They met him in San Diego, shortly after their boat docked. He is a good friend of Serge's, they say.

After Serge and the girls drive off, the detectives gather in the bar's courtyard, which is laced with ponds, winding paths, wooden bridges, and waterfalls. The night is sultry, with a full, luminous moon. Pine and cedar trees border the ponds, casting silver shadows on the water. The patio feels a world away from urban Los Angeles.

The detectives decide their two leading suspects are Armenian Mike and Gabay, with Mher a distant third.

"I'm going with Armenian Mike," McCartin says. "We gotta track down Lana and squeeze her ass so she tells us where we can find him. For Gabay, I need a stronger motive."

"Maybe he was pissed at Luda for turning his girlfriend into a prostitute," Knolls says. "Maybe, like Olena says, he's pissed because Luda keeps hitting on her for the rest of the money she owes her."

"I don't like it when a case goes in two directions," McCartin says. "I had a South-Central case once that split into *five* different directions. We never cleared it."

The following Tuesday morning, Knolls and Krumer arrive in the squad room and find McCartin at his desk, smiling. "I have some good news," he tells them.

FBI agents, who have access to more sophisticated technical equipment than LAPD detectives, have spent the past few days examining the videotape recorded outside the door of Luda's apartment building. McCartin has just finished talking on the phone to an agent.

"At nine oh-three, on the morning of the murder," McCartin says, "the tape shows Gabay and his girlfriend Oxana entering the building. It shows them leaving at nine twenty-three."

Detectives are by nature pessimists. Witnesses recant. Suspects devise last-minute alibis. Juries free guilty men. But after tracking this convoluted, bewildering case for a month, Knolls allows himself a moment of elation. He raises a clenched fist and claps McCartin on the back. "That's great! We'll get their prints, and if we're real lucky they'll match up with prints at Luda's place. We'll get them in here and if they deny being at her apartment that day, they're bought and paid for."

"I'm psyched," McCartin says. "This corroborates what the asset is saying."

"A little bit more, and we'll have him," Knolls says. "I'm concerned, though, about coordinating the interviews with Gabay and Oxana. We'll have to get them in at the same time."

"There's no rush," McCartin says. "Let's finish up the peripheral stuff first. Since Gabay's in the naval reserve, let's talk to navy criminal investigators and see what they've got on him. Maybe Gabay's got a forty-five that was issued by the navy."

He turns to Krumer and says, "This has brought us a lot closer, but you can't get tunnel vision."

The detectives have taken an interest in Krumer. Knowing that he plans to apply for a detective spot in a year or two, they attempt to teach him the basics of homicide investigation. "The asset could be full of shit," McCartin tells him. "There could be a reason besides murder why Gabay and Oxana visited Luda. Maybe the asset has his own reason for spinning all this. Serge may be trying to save his ass and his friend's ass and leading us off the trail. He owed Luda fifteen thousand bucks, so maybe he condoned the murder and even set it up. Maybe Serge is being so helpful so he can find out where we're at." McCartin strokes his chin and says, "What's the saying? 'Keep your friends close, but your enemies closer.' "

Although the investigative spotlight has shifted to Boxer, Mher still might be involved, McCartin explains. He reminds Krumer that another Russian asset had heard that Mher was in the apartment when Luda was killed. And since Mher was Luda's pimp, he might have had a motive to kill her.

Even if Mher and Armenian Mike are innocent, Knolls now tells Krumer, they still must not definitively rule them out. If they do, a defense attorney could "bite them in the ass." He could accuse the detective of railroading his client while ignoring important leads that pointed to other suspects. Failing to pursue all plausible suspects—even ones you believe are innocent—could provide a jury with enough reasonable doubt to free a killer.

On Thursday afternoon, a jittery Mher arrives for the interview McCartin had arranged. Looking like a caricature of a Russian mobster, he wears a gray leather jacket, a gold Gucci belt, and a garish pink, black, and white silk shirt.

"We know all the shit you're involved in, but we don't care," McCartin says, confronting Mher immediately. "We don't work vice. We just want to give you a quick polygraph exam to see if you're being truthful about this murder."

Mher reluctantly agrees. They march him up to the fourth floor, and the examiner hooks Mher up to the polygraph equipment. He sits stiff as a board, his hands tightly clasped.

"Are you employed?" the examiner asks.

"No," Mher says. "Not right now."

Knolls, monitoring in another room with McCartin, snorts derisively and mimics Mher: "I'm temporarily unemployed because my prostitute's dead."

Asked how he met Luda, Mher says he rented the apartment in Studio City because he had planned to lease his house for $2,700. When that deal fell through, he was stuck with the apartment. After he met Luda in a restaurant, he sublet the unit to her.

Knolls and McCartin study the monitor as the examiner asks Mher a series of questions including: "Were you inside Luda's apartment at the exact time she was attacked?" "Did you shoot Luda?" "Do you know for sure who caused Luda's death?"

A few minutes later, the examiner hurries into the monitoring room, announcing excitedly, "I think he's your guy!"

Krumer jumps to his feet. McCartin claps. Knolls whistles.

"You really think so?" Knolls asks.

"He's deceptive," the examiner says. "I think he was in the room or he pulled the trigger."

Part II

5

On a Thursday afternoon in September—the last day of summer—a woman and a child are discovered lashed together beneath a commercial fishing boat in the Los Angeles harbor. Initial speculation is that they are kidnap victims, possibly foreign nationals. A Harbor Division lieutenant, already overburdened with homicides and sensing the complexity of the case, calls Captain Jim Tatreau to ask if Homicide Special will take over. The fresh homicide galvanizes the squad room, generating an adrenaline rush in detectives and supervisors.

John Garcia and Rick Jackson, the first team listed on the on-call board, head south on the Harbor Freeway at about two o'clock. Because one of the victims was a child, the detectives quickly intellectualize the grim scenario. Already they are intrigued by the case's possibilities.

"How deep under the water you figure they were found?" Garcia asks.

"Probably ten to twelve feet," Jackson says. "We'll need to get a dive team out there. Definitely bizarre. I never had anything even close to this."

"Could be drugs," Garcia says.

"Maybe a payback," Jackson says. "Maybe domestic shit."

As they drive south toward the ocean, the temperature drops, a film of fog veils the horizon, and offshore winds kick up swirls of dust on the frontage roads. Garcia pulls off the freeway in San Pedro, about twenty miles south of downtown. Speeding by the waterfront, past

cruise ships and tankers, he realizes he is heading in the wrong direction and whips around. Moments later he crosses the Vincent Thomas
Bridge, a graceful emerald-green suspension structure spanning the
main channel of the harbor and leading to Terminal Island. The car
passes a convoy of huge trucks. From dawn to dusk, trucks rumble
across the artificial island, picking up loads from the massive container
vessels from Asia that have recently docked. Garcia slows down to
traverse a grimy jungle of warehouses, loading docks, shipyards, and
shuttered tuna canneries.

"What a fucked-up spot," he says. "A perfect place for a dump
job."

Terminal Island and the harbor area are part of Los Angeles—
which was founded on a river, not on the sea—because in the late
nineteenth century, the city's business magnates realized the city
needed a port if it was to prosper. Collis Huntington, who headed the
Southern Pacific Railroad, proposed Santa Monica, about fifteen miles
west of downtown, because he had purchased much of the waterfront
property there. But the powerful Chandler family, which owned the
Los Angeles Times, preferred San Pedro, partly because they believed
that if the port was located in Santa Monica, Southern Pacific would
monopolize transportation to the area. Several panels of engineers
appointed by federal committees also picked San Pedro. They contended that the porous cliffs surrounding Santa Monica would provide
insufficient solid ground for port facilities and property development,
and that the bay offered no shelter from the pounding surf.

The Chandlers prevailed. The federal government approved about
$3 million for the harbor. The city annexed a half-mile-wide corridor
to the ocean, bisecting a string of cities. San Pedro and its neighbor
Wilmington were "consolidated" with Los Angeles in 1909. (State law
prohibited "annexation" of one incorporated city by another.)

The shallow harbor was dredged and deepened, and the city finally
had its port. Los Angeles soon surpassed San Francisco, which has a
fine natural port, as the economic engine of the West.

Garcia screeches to a stop at Fish Harbor. A half-dozen patrol cars
are parked near a long ribbon of yellow crime-scene tape that keeps
a gaggle of reporters and camera crews at bay. In the harbor, rugged
commercial fishing boats flank a cracked asphalt dock speckled with
bird droppings. A gray navy frigate and a few freighters cruise in the
distance, silhouetted against a skyline of spired cranes. A brisk breeze
carries the scent of seawater laced with diesel fumes. The only sounds

are the thrumming of boat engines and the squall of gulls. A late-afternoon burst of sunshine burns off a layer of fog, and bright patches of blue bleed through the mist.

Garcia and Jackson are met at the harbor by three other Homicide I detectives; a fresh homicide means reinforcements. In addition to the five detectives, Captain Tatreau and Lieutenant Clay Farrell—who heads Homicide I—are gathered on the dock with a coroner investigator. Farrell, who is forty-four, red-haired, and lanky, is the antithesis of the stereotypical officious LAPD command officer. Self-deprecating and easygoing, with an off-the-wall sense of humor, he leads through conciliation, not confrontation.

Many of the detectives in Homicide I and II reflect the personalities of their lieutenants. Farrell's men joke more often and seem to spend more time fraternizing in the squad room, comparing notes on cases. Lieutenant Hartwell is soft-spoken and reserved, and his Homicide II detectives—who tend to be younger, and newer to the unit—often spend entire mornings quietly hunched over their murder books. Homicide I detectives usually head downstairs for coffee breaks, where they gossip and swap stories.

Tatreau, who is tall and slender, with graying red hair, supervises Homicide Special, as well as RHD's other units. Although clearly ambitious, Tatreau, who is fifty-one, has engendered much loyalty because he is not afraid to challenge LAPD brass and back up his detectives when they need his support.

As the group gathers for a briefing, a Harbor Division detective describes the discovery of the bodies. A diver was checking the brass fittings beneath a fishing boat this morning, when suddenly he spotted two feet. Then two legs. Then two bodies bobbing beneath the hull. He called the port police, who notified the LAPD about noon.

A harbor patrol boat pulls up beside the dock, and the coroner investigator and RHD crew climb on the vessel. The coroner investigator lifts a royal blue tarpaulin to reveal a woman and a young girl bound face-to-face by a weighted nylon scuba-diving belt. The woman's left wrist is tied to the girl's right wrist by an elaborate binding of what appears to be telephone cord. The skin of both victims is mottled and slightly decomposed. A tattered yellow sundress drapes the woman. The girl, who looks about four or five, wears a green dress with purple daisies. Tiny toes peek out of her pink and powder blue sandals.

The detectives study the intricate binding and debate whether the case is a double murder or a murder-suicide. "If the mother wanted to kill herself and her child, why bind the hands?" Jackson asks.

"To prevent them from escaping," Garcia says.

"You figure she'd think that far ahead?" Jackson asks.

"Maybe not," Garcia says. "The diver's belt bothers me."

Crouching beside the bodies, another detective studies the binding and says, "That ain't no fucking suicide. To be bound up like that doesn't make any sense."

"The autopsy will determine if they were alive *before* they hit the water, by the absorption of water into the lungs," the coroner investigator interjects. "That will tell us if it's a murder or a body dump."

"Either case, there's at least *one* murder," Jackson says. "No five-year-old girl decides on her own to jump overboard."

The victims are not Caucasian, but the detectives cannot determine their race or ethnicity. One detective, convinced the woman and child are Asian, bets another, who believes they are Latino, a Code 7—the police code for a meal break. The detectives then argue over whether the victims were dumped beneath the boat or killed elsewhere and carried by the current to Fish Harbor. They also speculate on how long the victims have been dead. The coroner investigator estimates that gases in the bodies would have buoyed them to the surface after about ten to fourteen days.

The detectives climb back onto the dock and Tatreau tells them to send out a Teletype to law enforcement agencies. Farrell suggests that Detective Eric Mosher call the department's missing persons' bureau and check incident reports at the Harbor Division station. Detective Wally Tennelle interviews the captain of the boat where the bodies were found. Another detective, Mike Berchem, a single father, asks Tatreau whether he can slip away for an hour to meet with his daughter's clarinet teacher at school. Farrell tells Tatreau he has to attend the Back to School Night festivities at his son's school. Tatreau, who looks bemused, tells them the Homicide Special old-timers, who used to work until midnight and then drink until the bars closed, would not recognize the detectives today.

Although the other investigators at the harbor will provide assistance, Jackson and Garcia head the investigation. Jackson, forty-eight, is burly and bald, with a florid face and a bushy gray mustache. Voluble, with a line of patter and a wisecrack for even the bleakest occasion, he truly seems to love the work and revels in the challenge of piecing together the random clues, the disparate leads, the wisps of evidence. Smaller and stocky, Garcia, forty-one, is a flashy dresser, one of the few detectives who departs from the squad's investment banker uniform. He wears a tan suit, a lime-green shirt, and a matching green silk tie.

The detectives, who exude the ease of veteran partners, immediately divide the duties and split up. Garcia slowly circumnavigates the harbor, gazing downward, searching for evidence. He stops occasionally and interviews forklift drivers, crane operators, and fishing boat crews. Waiting for the dive team to arrive, Jackson chats with an officer whose metal nametag identifies him as Sergeant Mays.

"Any relation to Willie?" jokes Jackson, a rabid baseball fan.

"He's my second cousin."

"Seriously?" Jackson asks, taken aback.

The sergeant explains the family connection and says, plaintively, "Whenever I'd play ball they'd always stick me in center and expect too much."

Mays, who tells Jackson he is half black and half Japanese, asks how the woman and young girl were bound. "Mother-child suicide is not uncommon in Japan," Mays adds. "But that kind of binding is more consistent with the Chinese culture."

When the sergeant who heads the dive team arrives, he and Jackson—who are old friends—shout in unison: "Yo, man!" They laugh and shake hands. After Jackson briefs the dive sergeant, he confers briefly with the other divers before they leap off the dock and into the water to search for evidence beneath the boat where the bodies were found.

The glassy water undulates as the divers descend. As the languid summer twilight lingers, the setting sun tints a bank of low clouds coral and crimson. The bellow of a freighter working its way out of the harbor shatters the calm. Atop the warehouses, cranes, and shipyards, lights gradually flicker on, streaking the water with flashes of gold as the sky fades from violet, to deep blue, to black.

Leaning against a patrol car, Jackson tells a few officers the significance of the "Yo, man" greeting. He was a young detective, and the dive team sergeant was a patrol officer. "A guy was playing Pac-Man at a 7-Eleven," Jackson says. "Another guy walks into the store and says, 'Yo, man.' The guy playing Pac-Man turns around and shoots him: Bam! Bam! Bam! Just like that. The victim staggers around, spits up blood, and finally collapses." Jackson pauses for effect, then continues.

"You know what I found interesting? When I got there, the owner of the 7-Eleven was doing a brisk business. He never even closed the store."

The shooting stemmed from a "pimp versus pimp dispute," Jackson explains. He has a wealth of stories from his days as a homicide detective in Hollywood, a division famous for its bizarre and varied cases. Jackson, who enjoys holding court, has an engaging manner and a performer's instinct that suggests he was well suited to his old beat.

Jackson knew he wanted to be a detective when he was a junior high school student in Lakewood, a working-class suburb about ten miles north of Fish Harbor. He read all the Hardy Boys books, and for a junior high school career project, he wrote to the FBI. When Deputy District Attorney Jack Kirschke was arrested for the murder of his wife and her lover in 1967, Jackson, who was in high school, avidly followed the case and pored over all the lurid newspaper stories, fascinated by the detectives.

A few years later, he enrolled at San Jose State University, one of the first schools in the state to offer a major in criminal justice. Jackson, whose father was a plumber, was the first person in his family to graduate from college. When an LAPD hiring freeze was lifted, he joined the department, with the homicide unit as his goal. Six years later, while he was working as a robbery detective in Hollywood, the homicide unit was overwhelmed and Jackson was drafted to assist during busy stretches.

The head of Hollywood's homicide unit was Russ Kuster, a legendary detective known for his exacting standards and scrupulous attention to detail. Kuster saw that Jackson was bright and hardworking and had an aptitude for talking to people from all strata of society. In 1983, he hired him.

Homicide investigation was Kuster's life and he expected the ultimate effort from detectives investigating the ultimate crime. "This report may go before the U.S. Supreme Court!" he would rage, tossing a misspelled document back to an embarrassed detective. "Do it right!" In part because of Kuster's zeal, Hollywood Homicide always had one of the highest clearance—or solve—rates in the city. Many nights, when Jackson awoke from a deep sleep and wearily picked up the ringing phone, he heard Kuster murmur, "Are you naked?" Someone had been murdered and it was time for Jackson to go to work. These were some of the happiest days of Jackson's life. Every case seemed like an adventure, an escapade of the unexpected. And, unlike some L.A. homicide units, Hollywood had great camaraderie.

When Kuster was still a bachelor, he and a roommate worshiped the country singer Roy Acuff and started calling each other Roy, an inside joke. Soon Kuster was addressing all his detectives as Roy. They knew whom he was talking to—when he called out "Roy!" or "Roy?" or *"Roy"* or just plain "Roy"—by his tone of his voice. So many Hollywood alumni were promoted to RHD that the custom spread. Now, even Homicide Special detectives with no connection to Hollywood often address one another as Roy.

Practical jokes were a staple of the Hollywood Homicide squad room. On Jackson's first day of work, an old-timer slipped a motel key into his suit pocket, so his wife would find it when he returned home. Jackson soon devised his own repertoire of practical jokes. Once, he even targeted Kuster himself. Knowing that Kuster had recently undergone a comprehensive physical examination, he managed to obtain a sheet of official stationery from the medical clinic. He wrote: "Complete results of the tests are still pending, but a preliminary analysis of your stool sample detected a parasitic larvae. Although not yet a serious intestinal problem, if this condition goes unchecked, you probably will detect, for the next seven to ten days, a persistent itching in your rectal area. Please contact me as soon as possible." After signing the name of the doctor who had actually performed the physical, Jackson mailed the letter to Kuster at home. Kuster was at his desk in the squad room when he nervously called the doctor and inquired about the parasitic larvae. The doctor laughed. When he told him that the letter was a fake, Kuster folded it up, buried it in his pocket, and, without saying a word, quietly returned to his paperwork. Jackson never let on to Kuster that the prank was his.

After five years at Hollywood Homicide, Jackson was promoted to RHD. On call one night shortly after joining the unit, he was awakened by a detective who told him that someone from Hollywood Homicide had just been shot. "You know him," the detective told Jackson. "It's Russ Kuster."

Kuster had been off duty, drinking at a Hungarian restaurant's bar, when a belligerent customer argued with the owner, who demanded that he leave. The customer returned with a nine-millimeter pistol and flashed its laser-beam sights at patrons. Kuster identified himself as a police officer and attempted to convince the man to drop his weapon. But the gunman opened fire. Wounded in the knees and chest, Kuster crumpled to the ground. But before he died, he managed to fire seven rounds, hitting the gunman three times. The final bullet entered the gunman's chin and shattered his skull.

Now as Jackson studies the patch of inky water where the divers descended, he says, "Seeing this water reminds me of a case in Hollywood where a guy was stabbed ninety-nine times. It was kind of disappointing. I was kind of hoping it would hit triple digits." The patrol officers laugh. "It was a bizarre sight. The pathologist circled each stab wound with Wite-Out and numbered them."

Finally, the dive team sergeant emerges from beneath the boat and climbs onto the dock, panting. "We did a thorough hull search. No hair found where the body was discovered. Couldn't really find much of anything. I checked the whole boat. I wanted to do a quick once-over before the tide changes. We'll have a more thorough search tomorrow when we've got daylight."

About nine P.M., the detectives climb into Garcia's Dodge Intrepid and cruise through Terminal Island's darkened maze of streets on their way back downtown. Jackson and Garcia agree that this is a singular case.

"I never had a water caper before," Garcia says.

"I never had one where people were tied together like this," Jackson says.

"I doubt this is a mother-child suicide," Garcia says. "All that extra tying and binding. And the diver's belt bothers me. What are the chances of this woman knowing anything about diver's belts?"

"If it's a murder," Jackson says, "I hope it's a gunshot. Strangulation might be hard to see because they've been in the water so long."

"We could go a long time without an ID," Garcia says.

"Might have to get an artist down to the coroner to draw a composite. But that could prove to be a pain in the ass. Could generate jillions of calls."

A detective pages Jackson, who calls him back on his cell phone. After hanging up, he tells Garcia that a composite might be unnecessary. A Thai Airways boarding pass has been discovered in the mother's pocket. The victims flew from Tokyo to Los Angeles fourteen days ago. IDs may be possible when the airline opens tomorrow.

At the coroner's office, the detectives wait by a counter for the investigator. Jackson points to the aquarium by the back wall and asks a clerk, "You feed the fish any scraps from the autopsies?" The clerk, gnawing on a large ear of corn, ignores Jackson. He has heard the joke before.

A coroner investigator leads the detectives to the room where the official autopsy will be conducted tomorrow. Splayed on a metal gurney, the victims are still bound together. Their bodies are face-to-face, streaked yellow and green, like tarnished brass. Wedged between them is a small pink-and-white checked purse with MICHELLE printed along the side.

From a distance, the figures look like a sculpture in a traditional mother-child pose: the woman is on her back, head turned slightly to the side, one arm draped protectively around the neck of the little girl, whose head is buried beneath the woman's breast, a tiny hand reaching out, fingers extended.

Garcia studies the victims' hands and determines that, although they have been in the water for almost two weeks, the ridges on their fingertips have sufficient definition for fingerprinting. On the back of the girl's head, Garcia studies a perfect circle, the size of a dime. "Is that a gunshot?" he asks.

"I think you'd see some eggshell fracturing," the investigator says. "But we'll know for sure at the autopsy."

Jackson points to the metal weights on the dive belt. "If someone else strapped them together, maybe we can get prints off the buckle. We'll have to go with vacuum metal deposition." This sophisticated, high-tech procedure is probably the only hope of recovering a fingerprint from a metal weight that has been submerged in the ocean. Evidence is placed in a steel vacuum chamber and a thin layer of gold is applied. Microscopic specks of oil from the fingerprints absorb gold fragments. Zinc is then spread over the surface. The two metals vaporize when they are heated in the chamber. The zinc coats the entire surface, except the fingerprints, which become visible as a contrasting image.

Garcia and Jackson examine the cord binding the victims' wrists, scrutinizing the intricate pattern of swirls and knots.

"It's kind of a loose binding, so maybe she could have done it herself," Jackson says. "But it's not like it's just wrapped around. It's wrapped and woven and twisted and turned."

"That's what bothers me," Garcia says. "Could the woman do that with one hand?"

"It would be pretty damn hard," Jackson replies. He asks the investigator if the woman could have tied the binding herself.

"Possible," the investigator says. "Not plausible."

Another investigator speaks up: "I think Mama did it for cultural reasons."

"Or maybe someone wants us to *think* she did it for cultural reasons," Garcia says. "Something about this situation stinks."

The next morning, the squad room is abuzz. Homicide Special detectives are so jaded by sudden and violent death that they often approach even the most brutal homicide in a blasé manner. But this one is unusual enough to capture their interest. Detectives who sit near Garcia and Jackson pepper them with questions: Could the woman have tied the knots with one hand? If no vehicle was recovered, how did the pair get to Fish Harbor? Did they die beside the fishing boat, or did the current carry them there? Finally, every question leads to the critical one: Is this case a murder-suicide or a double homicide?

By midmorning, Thai Airways provides the IDs: Yuriko Taga, thirty-eight, and her four-year-old daughter, Megumi. "Is that a Japanese name?" Garcia asks Ron Ito, a Japanese-American detective, who nods.

The case is moving fast, so Lieutenant Farrell calls a meeting. Garcia, Jackson, and four other detectives gather with Farrell in Captain Tatreau's office, which serves as the unit's conference room when he is gone. Farrell dispatches one detective to the Japanese consulate and another to search driver's license data. A third heads to LAX to pick up the manifest from Thai Airways and interview other passengers on the flight. Garcia will attend the mother's autopsy while Jackson coordinates the investigation.

Back in the squad room, a detective who grew up in India tells Garcia and Jackson that mother-child suicide is not uncommon in Asian cultures. "In India there have been a number of cases where mothers have burned or drowned their kids," says the detective. "In Ventura, a mother killed her kid and the Indian community rallied behind her because of the cultural thing. The Japanese even have a name for it."

The detectives soon learn that *oyako shinju,* parent-child suicide, has a long history in Japan, where suicide is not considered a sin. A woman who leaves her child behind, however, is regarded as a cruel mother who has broken the parent-child bond. If a Japanese mother believes herself disgraced—if her husband leaves her for another woman, for example—she might commit *oyako shinju* to expiate shame and punish him. If she survives, Japanese courts do not consider her a murderer, although parent-child suicide is illegal. The mother often is not imprisoned and is charged with, at most, involuntary manslaughter.

Garcia and Jackson recall that a Japanese woman living in Santa Monica killed her children in the mid-1980s, and the case received extensive publicity.

A thirty-two-year old housewife, humiliated by her husband's affair, waded into the ocean, her infant daughter and four-year-old son in her arms. She gulped salt water and lay facedown on the sandy bottom. After bystanders dragged the floating bodies out of the water, doctors were unable to save the children, but the woman was resuscitated and charged with first-degree murder.

More than four thousand Japanese-Americans signed a petition urging the court to grant her clemency. A Japanese sociologist who testified at a hearing for the woman claimed that there is at least one parent-child suicide a day in Japan, usually involving the mother. The woman was eventually allowed to plead guilty to manslaughter and was sentenced to one year in the county jail, which she had already served at the time of sentencing. She received five years' probation, with psychiatric treatment.

Jackson wonders if this is a variation of the Santa Monica case. But if his victims are from Japan, how did the woman know about Fish Harbor, a remote spot? Jackson asks Ito.

But before Ito can respond, Mike Berchem rushes into the squad room and interrupts. He informs Jackson that the mother had a driver's license, so he was able to obtain her address from the state Department of Motor Vehicles. Her husband, Kazumi Taga, is now waiting in an interview room. Because Garcia is viewing the autopsy, Berchem assists Jackson.

A veteran homicide detective never informs a family member that a loved one is dead until *after* the interview. Once a death notification is made, family members are usually too shaken to provide the detective with any useful information. So Jackson decides to interview Taga first and establish some basic biographical information.

Taga, who is fifty, wears jeans, a short-sleeved denim shirt, white socks, and black dress shoes with silver buckles. He sits stiffly in the chair, arms crossed, fingers tightly gripping his forearms. A thick, swirling, coal-black toupee that sits slightly askew atop his head is his most distinguishing feature.

For the past twenty years he has lived in the United States, he says in heavily accented English. He works at home, buying and selling cars for an independent dealer and shipping car parts to Japan. He met his wife about six years ago, in a restaurant bar.

Taga's statements and mannerisms are oddly disjointed and contradictory. When Jackson asks, "How is your marriage?" Taga smiles and laughs briefly. "She want to live in Japan. I want to live in United States. We were having some discrepancy or argument. Whatever you call it."

Taga explains that his wife has enrolled their daughter, Megumi, whom friends in the United States call Michelle, in a Japanese kindergarten because she wants her to be educated there. Michelle attended preschool in Los Angeles last year and Taga says he had hoped she would continue her studies here. His wife and daughter flew to Japan in July, he says, and are staying with Yuriko's mother.

"Do you know when they're supposed to come back?" Jackson asks.

"January."

"So she wants her to start school over there for a little while and see how they like it?" Jackson asks.

Taga nods.

"Were you guys talking about a divorce?"

"Not that far yet . . . we were trying to work it out." Taga tells them he last talked to his wife on the phone about three weeks ago. She asked him to send money. Next week he plans to call Japan again for his daughter's birthday. Finally, he asks: "Is anything wrong?"

Jackson has been waiting for this question. Detectives have snatched Taga up, transported him to LAPD headquarters, deposited him in an interview room, and bombarded him with questions about his wife and daughter. Jackson finds it odd that it took Taga this long to express concern.

"We'll explain everything," Jackson says. "It's just important that we get as much information as we can now."

Taga meekly acquiesces.

"Some of these questions may seem strange, but I'll explain everything in a little bit," Jackson repeats. "Let's change the subject for a minute. Do you golf, by any chance?"

"Golf," Taga asks, looking bewildered. "Used to."

"Do you have any hobbies? Do you swim? Do you fly an airplane? Do you fish?"

"Ooooh," he says, dragging out the word and slowly exhaling. "After marriage, you can't pursue the hobby so much."

After they casually discuss sports for a few minutes, Jackson asks in a matter-of-fact tone, "Do you scuba dive or snorkel or anything like that?"

Taga rubs his mouth and says through his fingers, "No."

"Okay," Jackson says. "So she isn't coming back until January, right? Did you have a lot of arguments about this?"

"Yeah, sort of. I mean, I don't know what her intention is, but she wants to try to live in Japan."

"Did your wife have any medical problems at all? Either physical or psychological?"

"Well, yes, mental . . . like depression. She doesn't want to do anything. Not sleeping."

"She wouldn't sleep much? How much?"

Taga says he does not know because Yuriko sleeps with their daughter and he spends his nights alone in the master bedroom.

"That's okay," Jackson says reassuringly. "That happens."

Jackson attempts to glean the names of Yuriko's friends, but Taga insists that his wife had no friends and rarely talked to neighbors.

Berchem has told Jackson that he discovered that several other people were staying at Taga's house. When Jackson asks about them, Taga says that a Japanese woman and her two children, friends of the family, are temporarily living with him so they can learn English. Jackson asks him about previous marriages, and Taga says he is divorced. Flashing a complicitous smile, Jackson points to himself and Berchem, noting that they are divorced as well. Taga says his ex-wife and two daughters now live in Hawaii. Then Jackson discovers that Taga has not talked to them in fourteen months, which he finds significant.

"What's your relationship with your daughter, Michelle?" Jackson asks.

"Very close," Taga says.

"Who is closer to your daughter, you or your wife?"

"She closer to me. When I come home from work, she hang around me all the time. . . ."

"What was the main problem that you and your wife had?" Jackson asks.

"Ooooh. Time to time we had, you know, some financial problems. But that wasn't a big issue, because we managed."

"Did your wife ever tell you she was definitely going to leave you?"

Taga fiddles with his watch and says, "No. No."

"Was the most recent problem her wanting to live in Japan and you wanting to stay here?"

Taga nods. When his cell phone rings to the tune of "Take Me Out to the Ball Game," Jackson uses the interruption to grab a cup of coffee and confer with Berchem in the squad room.

"He seems to be close to his daughter," Berchem says. "He's going to be really upset."

"Unless," Jackson says, "*he* killed them."

As they return, Jackson hears Taga murmur the word "sweetie" before clicking off the cell phone.

" 'Sweetie'?" Jackson says, surprised. "Who is 'sweetie'?"

"Ooooh," Taga says, looking embarrassed. "Sweetie?"

"Yeah."

"Ooooh. That's the person . . . " he sputters. "What do you call that . . . the nickname . . ." Taga finally says he was talking to Sachiko, the woman staying at his house.

"Do you have a relationship with her?"

Taga strokes his chin.

"A little bit?" Jackson suggests.

"In a sense, yes, but not, not . . . " he says, searching for the right word. "Not quite yet."

"Maybe later?" Jackson suggests.

"Well, depends. I mean, my wife . . . I don't know," Taga says, struggling. He explains that, initially, the woman's thirteen-year-old daughter was going to live with him so she could learn English. Then her mother and her young son decided to study English as well, so the family arrived from Japan in July and will leave next month.

"When did your wife find out about Sachiko staying with you?"

"Ooooh. Sometime in August."

"And how did she find out?"

Taga pauses a moment. "I mentioned it."

"What did she say?"

"She say, 'Well, that's good for you.' And stuff like that. So she can stay in Japan longer."

"Was she jealous?"

Taga insists his wife was not jealous, because they last had sex in January and she "wants me stay away from her."

"Do you have a sexual relationship with Sachiko?" Jackson asks.

"No," Taga says.

Jackson does not believe him, but he does not think Taga will reveal much more now. Jackson asks him if his wife had life insurance. Taga shakes his head.

Now is the time, Jackson decides, to tell him about the bodies found at Fish Harbor. He inches his chair closer to Taga and says softly, "Let me explain something. We're conducting an investigation that started yesterday. And that's why we have you down here to talk to us today. What I'm going to tell you is going to be bad news for you. We found two bodies yesterday—a woman and a young girl. And there was paperwork on the bodies that indicate, most likely, it's your wife and your daughter."

Taga clenches his fists. Tightly shutting his eyes, he pinches the bridge of his nose and grits his teeth, jaw muscles quivering. A minute later, his body suddenly goes slack and he collapses in his chair. "My Michelle?" he sobs.

"I believe so," Jackson says.

Taga stifles two quick cries and says, "No! They're in Japan."

"No," Jackson says sadly. "They're in the United States." Jackson asks Taga whether he knew his wife and daughter might return early.

"No," Taga says. He throws his head on the table and weeps, his body heaving. Jackson and Berchem leave the room to get him a glass of water, but Taga's sobs echo throughout the office bay adjacent to the interview room. Craning her neck, a secretary listens for a moment and asks Jackson: "When they cry like that, does that mean they're guilty or innocent?"

"With this guy, I can't tell."

Berchem tells Jackson he believes there is a chance Taga truly did not know his wife and daughter had returned from Japan. Berchem speculates that when the wife arrived at the house and saw another woman and her children, she decided to commit suicide and, to punish Taga, take the daughter with her.

A detective who overhears them says sarcastically, "This poor guy hadn't had sex with his wife since January. If I hadn't had sex with my wife since *August,* I'd toss her in the harbor."

Garcia returns from Yuriko's autopsy and explains to Jackson that the pathologist was unable to find any obvious evidence of injury, strangulation, or suffocation. The pathologist had hoped, by assessing how much water was absorbed into her lungs, to learn whether Yuriko was alive before she plunged into the harbor. But because she had been submerged for so long, and had lost so much fluid, an accurate assessment was impossible. Tomorrow, Garcia says, during Michelle's autopsy, they might have better luck.

While Garcia and Jackson mull all this over, Berchem returns to the interview room, where Taga is still crying. Scrutinizing him in a detached, clinical manner, Berchem tries to discern if Taga is truly surprised or is feigning grief. He eventually asks, "You honestly still believed they were in Japan?"

Taga lifts his head and says weakly, "The only thing she mentioned was, she might want to come back . . . early . . . because my daughter miss me."

"Do you have any reason to believe that she may have taken her own life with your daughter?"

"Well, she kept saying she's going to kill herself."

"When did she start talking about that?"

She threatened to kill herself with a knife and once cut herself on the hand, Taga says. He stares at his shoes and says, "That's part of the depression." Taga adds that in addition to threatening suicide, Yuriko "beat me couple of times. . . . She had a mental problem."

When Jackson returns, Taga says, "She mention, you know, she want to kill herself a few times, but not seriously. When she depressed she either get very violent or very self-closing."

"Very closed up?" Jackson asks.

"Yeah."

Berchem asks Taga, "What would your wife be doing down in San Pedro?" He wants to determine how familiar Yuriko was with the harbor area.

"Well, we go to Ports O' Call," he answered, referring to a waterfront tourist spot with restaurants and shops, not far from Fish Harbor.

"Is that a special place for her?"

"Well, when we were dating, you know, we go there to chat, to date."

Jackson tells Taga he is not under arrest, but that the detectives in the unit would like his permission to search his home and car. Taga agrees without hesitation.

Taga lives in Torrance, between downtown and the harbor, in a new development not far from the Harbor Freeway. Garcia and Jackson drive there along with Tina Matsushita, a thirty-three-year-old Japanese-American officer just drafted from the LAPD's Asian Crime Investigation Section to translate. Both of Matsushita's parents were born in Japan; they immigrated to Los Angeles in the 1950s, and she grew up speaking Japanese at home. Farrell and four other detectives, who will help with the search, meet the others at Taga's home.

The tidy complex where Yuriko Taga once lived with her daughter is threaded with narrow streets and lined with dozens of nearly identical two-story tan and white stucco town houses. The roofs are red tile and the postage-stamp backyards are dotted with barbecues, soccer goals, and toys. Taga's town house has plush beige wall-to-wall carpeting and is decorated simply with Danish modern wooden furniture. When he greets the detectives, he is friendly and cooperative.

"This guy's hard to read," Farrell says to another detective. "When my cat died, I was more upset than him. I was so traumatized I had to take a week off."

Jackson and Tina interview Sachiko, the woman staying at the town house, while Farrell and the others scour every room, closet, dresser, desk, bed, cabinet, and clothes hamper in the house. They examine the drains and toilets for remnants of blood and hair and even probe the vents and look beneath the toilet seats. While the detectives search, Taga plays with Sachiko's seven-year-old son. When the boy scampers out the door, Taga turns to a detective and says, "I wish he was mine."

The detectives find it curious that there is not a single picture of Yuriko or Michelle in the house. In fact, there is absolutely no hint that they ever lived here. Their clothes are not in the closets. Nothing in the drawers seems to have belonged to them. Sachiko's son and daughter have each taken over a bedroom, and the house is filled with their possessions.

Farrell pulls a thick bundle of telephone cord out of a closet and shows it to Garcia.

"That's just what was used to tie them up," Garcia says. "This is probably where she got it from."

"Or where *he* got it from," Farrell says.

After about half an hour, Jackson, Matsushita, and Sachiko, who looks shaken, emerge from the breakfast room. Sachiko, slender and pretty, is barefoot and wears jeans and a loose black blouse. Jackson motions for Garcia and Farrell to meet him in a bedroom.

"He's a fucking dog," Jackson says. "They've been sleeping together since April. He met her in an Internet chat room when she lived in Japan. He told her that he was divorced, with no contact with his wife and daughter. She's living here. *Permanently.* And remember when he told us he doesn't dive? She says that when she was in Japan, he e-mailed her that he just got back from a trip to Baja. Where he went scuba diving. I want to book him right now," Jackson says, tapping his bald pate, "so I can confiscate his toupee."

The first maxim a homicide detective learns is *Everyone lies.* Taga certainly reinforces the detectives' cynicism. But while Taga misrepresented every aspect of his personal life, Garcia and Jackson need evidence to book him for murder.

A few minutes later, a detective finds a dozen nude pictures of Sachiko in one of Taga's dresser drawers. "She looks younger than thirty-six," the detective says.

"His wife was only thirty-eight," Jackson says. "That's not much of an improvement."

"You got to do it in increments," Garcia quips.

When they finish searching the house, Garcia, Jackson, and two other detectives stop in Gardena at Guliani's, a landmark Italian delicatessen, for meatball sandwiches on the front patio.

"I don't think he whacked her," one of the detectives says.

"I disagree," his partner says. "This guy's dirty."

"You don't understand—it's a Japanese *thang.*"

"It could be a double murder *thang,*" the suspicious partner says.

Jackson interjects, "That's why I call this case the Pendulum. I go back and forth. Sometimes I think he killed them. Other times I don't know."

When they return to the office, Matsushita prepares to call Yuriko's mother. Jackson reminds her to amass as much information as possible before providing any details. After speaking quietly in Japanese for a few minutes, Matsushita places her hand over the telephone and whispers to Jackson: "The mom says the consulate called her and told her about two bodies found in the harbor. She wants to know if her daughter and granddaughter are dead or alive."

"Tell her later," Jackson says. "But first just say the investigators are doing an interview in another room and they won't be free for a while. Then dirty the husband up a little bit and get her on our side. Tell her he was living with another woman and her two kids."

She nods and continues the interview. The mother confirms that Yuriko and Michelle left Japan in early September and says her daughter was not depressed. When Matsushita asks who met Yuriko and Michelle at the airport, the mother says, "Her husband, of course." Asked if Yuriko and her husband had marital problems, the mother says, "No. They were happy. Toward the end of August, my daughter called her husband and everything seemed fine. She even bought him gifts. My daughter never talked of marital problems. I never saw any sign that she was unhappy."

Matsushita, looking drained after she has confirmed the mother's worst fear, replaces the receiver carefully. The mother said that if Yuriko discovered Taga living with another family, she never would have committed suicide. She would have returned immediately to Japan. The last comment the mother made before hanging up was, "He did it!"

The detectives ask Matsushita if she can provide any insight. "If Yuriko returned home and found another woman and children living there, I think she would have felt a lot of shame," Matsushita says softly. "Maybe she felt it was more honorable to take her life than live with the shame of her husband leaving her. In her mind, maybe the new girlfriend could never be a mother to her daughter. She might have felt it was a bigger disservice to leave the child alone than to kill her."

"She might have come back, seen the other woman and kids, and flipped out," Jackson says.

"Or he picked her up from the airport, didn't want her interfering with his new life, and did her in," Garcia says.

"The airport keeps track of all vehicles coming and going," Jackson says. "If we can show he went to the airport on the day they arrived, he's fucked."

Eric Mosher, who is hunched over a computer checking Taga's background for previous convictions, calls out, "You're going to love this, guys. He's got a manslaughter conviction."

Garcia and Jackson hurry over. "You're kidding," Garcia says.

"I am," Mosher says. "But he *does* have a GTA [grand theft auto] conviction in Florida and a couple of other minor things on his rap sheet. He's got several different driver's licenses with several different names listed."

"A flimflam man," Jackson says.

"He's a fuck stick," Mosher says.

"I think he told us she didn't have any friends because he doesn't want us talking to them," Jackson says.

"That location where she was found bothers me," Garcia says. "How'd she get there?"

Jackson waves a hand back and forth. "The pendulum's been swinging all day for Taga. I think it just swung back to guilty."

Early Saturday morning, Garcia and Jackson drive to the county coroner's office, a drab, low-slung tan building at the edge of East Los Angeles, across the street from a busy stretch of Interstate 5. As they slip on their powder blue scrub suits, booties, and masks, Jackson says, "Nothing like the smell of decomposing bodies to start your weekend."

Michelle, who is three feet six inches tall and weighs less than forty pounds, is laid out in the center of a seven-foot gurney. Surrounded by the expanse of steel, she looks tiny, forlorn, and poignantly alone. Her toes are too small for the usual toe tag. Instead, a yellow tag is tied around her ankle.

The gurney is lined up at the edge of the autopsy room, a large gray industrial chamber with a brown tile floor and huge fluorescent lights that hang from the ceiling. On one wall is a vast trough studded with chrome faucets. Another is lined by a countertop, covered with scalpels, scales, trays, and rulers, where pathologists measure, weigh, and log internal organs.

It is a busy summer Saturday, following a murderous Friday night. The room is bustling as pathologists work on half a dozen other corpses. Michelle is flanked by a man with a mountainous belly and a tattooed gangbanger with a gaping bullet hole in his chest. The gangbanger shot a policeman with an AK-47, a pathologist says, but fortunately his assault rifle then jammed and the cop's partner dropped him with a single shot. He died facedown in a box of cat litter. Above his right nipple is a tattoo: ME SO HORNY.

"How'd you like your daughter to bring home a guy with *that* on his chest?" Jackson asks Garcia.

Detectives often informally grade their victims. They will search for the killer of a gangbanger or a drug dealer, but, perhaps, not with much investigative zeal. Detectives who work the ghetto often say, "Today's suspect is tomorrow's victim." But victims who are not criminals, who are not complicit in their own deaths, are referred to as "good victims" or "innocent victims."

There is no more innocent victim than a four-year-old child.

The pathologist carefully examines Michelle before the autopsy and concludes that there are no obvious bruises or signs of trauma or sexual abuse. After a victim has been strangled or suffocated, red hemorrhage specks—petechiae—often are visible around the eyes and inside the eyelids. But because Michelle's body has been decomposing for the past two weeks, the pathologist says, petechiae are difficult to discern.

The pathologist conducting the autopsy on the gangbanger makes a huge Y-shaped incision from his shoulder to his lower abdomen. An autopsy technician, employing a tool that resembles a pair of gardening shears, crunches through both sets of ribs, and removes the sternum. The pathologist lifts the rib cage, like a door on a hinge, exposing the internal organs.

Michelle is so small that the shears are not necessary; the pathologist simply opens up her abdomen with a scalpel. He points to her ribs—"There's no evidence of injury or old injuries"—then removes her organs, including the heart, lungs, liver, and kidneys. After examining them for trauma, he weighs them and prepares samples for microscopic examination and future testing.

When petechiae cannot be discerned, pathologists can sometimes confirm strangulation by examining the hyoid bone, which is just above the throat. "Take a look," the pathologist says to the detectives. He holds up the U-shaped bone, covered in reddish tissue, and manipulates it to show the detectives it has not been fractured. But a child's hyoid is flexible and pliant; the bone grows more brittle with age. Someone Michelle's age could have been strangled, the pathologist says, but still have an intact hyoid bone.

Before an autopsy, all bodies are X-rayed to locate bullets, fractures, and other injuries. The gangbanger's chest X ray, posted on an illuminated viewing box just above Michelle's, reveals a white smudge: the bullet embedded in his body. Michelle's tiny X ray, dwarfed by the gangbanger's, reveals no major injuries.

A few serpentine lines thread the image of her skull. "We'll soon see if those are hairline fractures," the pathologist tells the detectives. He points to a perfectly round circle in the back of Michelle's head. "We'll also see if that's a bullet hole."

While two technicians are needed to move the gangbanger, the pathologist easily turns Michelle onto her stomach. She is so slight, he might be flipping a doll. After he hoses off her head, the detectives study the hole. Next the pathologist makes an incision with a scalpel, peels away her scalp, and studies the bare gray skull. It is as slick as an egg, except for one small indentation.

"It's most likely postmortem," the pathologist says. "She could have knocked it while under water. Or it could have been a fish."

He points to several faint cracks in Michelle's skull: "Those aren't fractures. She's so young, her skull's still mending, still coming together."

An autopsy technician zips off the top of Michelle's skull with a device that looks like a power saw, and Jackson and Garcia avert their gazes. After the pathologist removes the brain and weighs it, the detectives quickly leave the room and strip off their scrubs.

"I hope I never have to see another autopsy of a little girl," Garcia says.

Jackson groans. "Brutal."

On Monday morning, Knolls and McCartin continue tracking Luda's killer. Despite Thursday's seemingly decisive polygraph, the examiner later withdrew his opinion: because Mher lied about every aspect of his relationship with Luda, from how he met her to why she lived in the apartment he rented, and was so evasive about his own criminal activities, the results of the exam, he decided, were skewed. Later that afternoon, Mher finally leveled with detectives, describing his pimping operation and explaining truthfully how he met Luda and how she came to work for him. At the end of the interview, Knolls and McCartin believed that while Mher might have some insight into why she had been killed, he was not involved. They are now certain that either Alexander "Boxer" Gabay or Armenian Mike was the shooter.

While still trying to track down the two suspects' addresses, Knolls and McCartin continue to talk to peripheral players in the hopes of learning something that will focus the investigative spotlight on one of the two suspects. The detectives surmise that word has circulated among local Russian criminals that several pimps and prostitutes have cooperated: the people they interview are more compliant now.

In the early afternoon, a woman involved in smuggling Russian prostitutes, who knew Luda well, agrees to stop by RHD. Thin, nervous, and birdlike, the woman—who is in her forties—speaks no English, so Krumer translates. She tells the detectives that Luda branched out from prostitution to smuggling because she was desperate to earn enough money to bring her daughter to Los Angeles. The woman cannot identify Armenian Mike, but she does know Boxer and

Oxana, who now live together, she says. She confirms that Oxana owed Luda money and was supposed to work as a prostitute to pay her back, but refused. Boxer, she says, frequently works for Serge.

"Serge always has people who owe him money, and Boxer beats up people to get the money," she says through Krumer, who performs with his usual unflappable efficiency. "General strong-arm stuff."

"What's the deal with Oxana?" McCartin asks.

"Luda once mentioned to some friends in Kiev that Oxana wanted to kill her," she says. "People I've talked to in Kiev consider her a possible suspect."

McCartin presses her to identify the friends in Kiev, but she is reluctant to elaborate. He then asks her to describe Oxana.

"Serge talks a lot about her. He says she's oriented like a man. Very tough. Not afraid of anything. He considered making Oxana a captain of one of his smuggling boats. I said, 'A woman?' and he said, 'You don't know her.' Serge once said to me that if you told her to kill someone, her hand wouldn't even shake."

When McCartin asks her if she thinks Boxer or Oxana killed Luda, she says she does not know. The detectives, however, are intrigued by what Luda told friends in Kiev about Oxana and by Serge's description of her.

If Boxer is the shooter, the detectives speculate, perhaps he did not act alone.

The next morning, three FBI agents, three detectives in the LAPD's organized-crime unit, and Knolls and McCartin meet in a conference room at the department's Central Division, located in a shabby downtown neighborhood. Luda was killed five and a half weeks ago, and this summit has been called so that the two agencies can share updated information. McCartin and Knolls describe their progress and recount their recent interviews.

"Mher failed the poly, but that's because he lied about everything beforehand," Knolls says. "Luda was brought over by Mher's organization and she worked for him. He may have made threats to Serge, via Luda, but we don't think he killed her."

Boxer might be the leading suspect, Knolls says. And Serge might be their conduit to him. "Boxer, apparently, does strong-arm work for Serge," Knolls says. "So if we get Serge in and pressure him, he may lay out Boxer. If he's facing a lot of time, maybe we can flip him."

"Oh, he's facing a lot of time," an FBI agent says. "He's involved in smuggling girls and cars, laundering money, white slavery."

Later in the afternoon, the detectives pull up in front of a fashionable three-story apartment building in West Los Angeles, just south of Wilshire Boulevard. When they identify themselves, they are buzzed in to an airy, loftlike apartment with wood beam ceilings, Picasso prints on the walls, and sweeping views of the Hollywood Hills and the downtown skyline.

They are greeted by a stylish, attractive blond madam in her late thirties. "I've been expecting you," she says. "I heard you were asking around and talking to people." The detectives, Krumer, and the woman gather around the dining room table. "We're here to investigate the murder of Luda and we need your complete honesty," Knolls says. "If you're not honest, we can make life much more difficult for you." Knolls glances at the madam's teenage daughter, who is padding around the apartment. He whispers, "It might be difficult for you with her here."

The woman waves a hand dismissively. "That's okay. She knows all of it."

She tells the detectives she did not know Luda well and had only two conversations with her, the second a week before her murder: Luda wanted to talk to her about some girls she had recently smuggled into the country.

"So they could be prostitutes for you?" McCartin barks.

She swallows hard and says, "Yes." She adds apologetically, "All I do is answer the phone."

"*And* send them clients," McCartin says coldly.

"Yes," she acknowledges.

Knolls chats with her amicably for a few minutes about her prostitution operation. He shows her a photograph of Boxer but does not identify him.

McCartin asks her, "You ever hear of Armenian Mike?"

She smiles nervously and downs half a glass of water. "Yes. He works with Svetlana." She explains that Svetlana is also known as Lana.

"I heard Lana is using him to get control over the girls," McCartin says.

"I heard he's very dangerous," she says. "He's an enforcer."

"We heard," McCartin says, "that a few days before the murder,

Lana and Armenian Mike went to see Luda and threatened her because she went out on her own and was trying to take girls from Lana."

"I don't know about the details. But, yes, I think they did threaten her. Mike and Lana also went to one of their girls and Mike said to her, 'You heard about the girl who was killed. It'll happen to everybody who doesn't go along.' "

"You know where we can find Armenian Mike?" McCartin asks.

She nods. "I have his phone number." She leaves the room in search of her address book.

Knolls shakes his head in amazement. They have been searching for the elusive Armenian Mike for more than a month, and now, after one quick question, they have his phone number. He grins and says to McCartin, "When she comes back you'll probably ask her who killed Luda and she'll have that for you, too."

As McCartin drives back toward downtown, the detectives agree that the investigation is finally taking shape. The interviews with the smuggler and the madam have confirmed their sense that the case boils down to either Armenian Mike or Boxer. And if Boxer is their shooter, they speculate that Oxana might have assisted him.

The squad room is empty except for Rick Jackson. He takes a break from the Taga murder book, crosses the narrow aisle from Homicide I, and asks Knolls and McCartin whether he can see their crime scene photographs.

Knolls spreads the pictures out on his desk and points out the three slash marks on Luda's neck and face. Jackson studies the pictures for a moment and then turns them upside down for a different perspective.

"What do you think?" Knolls asks

Jackson strokes his chin thoughtfully. "I think she's dead."

"Thanks, Sherlock," McCartin says.

Jackson examines the bullet hole above her left nipple. "Contact wound?"

"No," McCartin says.

"What kind of gun?" Jackson asks.

"Forty-five," McCartin says.

"Looks like he got her right in the heart," Jackson says.

"What's up with *your* case?" McCartin asks.

"One day we think it's a double homicide and the next day we think it's a murder-suicide," Jackson says. "They were in the water about two weeks. There's so much decomposition the coroner can't determine a cause of death. Without that, all we've got is a circumstantial case."

Jackson pulls out the crime scene photographs.

"How much weight on that belt?" McCartin asks.

"Twenty-two pounds."

"That's enough to sink both of them."

"Hopefully we can get prints off it."

Knolls points out the binding on their wrists. "That would be hard for the mother to do."

"But not impossible," Jackson says. "This guy's a total sleaze. While his wife's in Japan on vacation, he's got another family living with him. We found a bunch of nude pictures of the girlfriend." Jackson purses his lips. "Of course," he says primly, "I didn't look at them. I didn't think it would be right. I felt it was personal."

"How'd she look?" McCartin asks.

"She looked good," Jackson says. "If you like girls."

Jackson snaps the murder book shut. "I'm going to book this guy tomorrow morning." He pauses a moment and adds, "For possession of a bad toupee."

At eight o'clock on an overcast morning, the squad room is filled with the dissonant fusion of Russian, Japanese, and English. Krumer is on the phone questioning a friend of Luda's in Kiev; a few feet away, Matsushita interviews Yuriko's mother in Osaka. The mother describes what Yuriko and Michelle were wearing when they boarded the plane in Japan—the same clothing their bodies were found in.

Garcia buys coffee and Jackson picks up tea at the downstairs snack bar. They join a few other Homicide I detectives who are sipping coffee out of foam cups outside Parker Center. The key question, Jackson tells the detectives, is what happened when their victims arrived in Los Angeles. Did Yuriko return home, spot the other family living in her house, and become so suffused with shame that she killed herself and her daughter? Or did Taga pick them up at the airport, suffocate them, and dump their bodies?

Last night, Garcia says, he enlisted his wife and a four-year-old neighbor girl and attempted to re-create the murder scenario. After describing the intricate pattern of swirls and knots that bound Yuriko and Michelle, he handed his wife a bundle of telephone cord and asked whether she could tie her left wrist to the girl's right.

"She couldn't duplicate it exactly, but it was pretty close," Garcia tells the other detectives. "That made me realize Yuriko could have done it with one hand. When I add that to the absence of trauma or wounds on either of their bodies, it makes me think it's suicide. Taga's dirty for something. And he's a real scammer. But I'm not convinced he did them both."

Garcia—everyone calls him Johnny G.—grew up in a small apartment with his single mother in a Mexican immigrant neighborhood a few miles west of downtown. This was an era before Rodney King, O. J. Simpson, and the Rampart scandal, and his favorite television show was *Adam-12,* which lionized cops and celebrated the LAPD. He was intrigued by the exploits of the street cops, the way they helped people in peril, but it was the detectives he identified with, the detectives who captured his imagination. He was mesmerized by the dangerous dance between cop and killer, the way detectives used not just their night-sticks but also their intellects to stay a step ahead of criminals.

When his mother found a job as a security guard and started wearing a uniform every day, Garcia vowed to progress to the next step. He decided to become a cop. After high school he enrolled at a community college and majored in police science. But, married at eighteen, he became a father a year later and ended up driving a truck for UPS. His plans to join the LAPD soon devolved into a distant dream. When he turned twenty-two, however, he told his wife that in ten years he did not want to be sitting on a loading dock, complaining to his buddies. Although she knew the job was dangerous, she reluctantly supported his decision to join the department.

After a few years as a street cop, Garcia joined a gang detail. At twenty-nine he was promoted to homicide detective in South-Central's "Shootin' Newton," one of the busiest divisions in the city. In five years he personally investigated more than one hundred murders—more homicides than most American detectives track during an entire career. In 1996, Garcia was promoted to Homicide Special.

About a year later, at five A.M. on a January morning, Garcia was awakened by a call from his lieutenant, who said, "You got one. Bill Cosby's kid was shot." By the time Garcia arrived at the scene—a dark shoulder parallel to the San Diego Freeway near Bel Air—reporters and camera crews were already clustered behind the yellow crime-scene tape. Garcia crouched in the dirt and examined Ennis Cosby's body, which was splayed beside his Mercedes.

He attempted to envision the murder scenario: Cosby was still clutching a pack of American Spirit cigarettes. Garcia assumed that he had been taken by surprise. Stippling—pinpoint abrasions caused by hot gases and microscopic gunpowder and metal particles emitted from a gun's muzzle—was clearly visible on Cosby's right temple. Garcia knew he had been shot at close range. Cosby was a twenty-seven-year-old doctoral student at Columbia University's Teachers College. Garcia figured it was not likely that he had been involved in a crime. Cosby had $800 in his pocket and an expensive Rolex on his wrist. Garcia did not believe that robbery was the motive. But a witness at the scene described the gunman as extremely pale. Garcia speculated that he might be a drug addict who had intended to jack Cosby for another fix, but was scared off before he could snatch the cash and watch.

The witness—the only witness—was a flamboyant red-haired woman who wore a fur coat and high heels. A colorful Hollywood character who had been married six times, she had recently attempted to sell a manuscript about courtship, entitled "Every Trick in the Book." She told Garcia that she had only recently met Cosby, who was on his way to her apartment when his car blew a tire, careening off a freeway exit and onto a dirt road. In the darkness, Cosby was unable to change the tire. He called the woman on his cell phone, asking her to meet him so she could illuminate the area with her headlights.

About fifteen minutes later the woman arrived in her Jaguar and parked behind Cosby's car. The two chatted as he changed the tire, but the night was cold and misty and she was chilled, so she climbed back into her car and waited for Cosby to finish. Suddenly, a man with a complexion so white his skin appeared almost phosphorescent emerged out of the darkness, banged on her window, and shouted, "Get out of the car or I'll kill you." Frightened, she sped off, but after driving several hundred feet she whipped her car around to check on Cosby and spotted the suspect sprinting away. Cosby was crumpled on the ground beside his car. The woman gave Garcia and his partner a detailed description of the killer. A police artist drew a composite, but it did not lead to a suspect.

The murder sparked an international media feeding frenzy. Garcia and a team of Homicide Special detectives investigated more than fifteen hundred leads, but they hit a dead end. Still, the pressure mounted to clear the case. Bill Cosby frequently conferred with the LAPD brass, and the media continually carped at the LAPD, hinting that another O. J. debacle was in the works. Many nights, after working late yet again, Garcia downed beers after work at a dive bar called the Shortstop, an LAPD hangout, and he thought about the case. He thought about it until he went to sleep and he thought about it the moment he awakened. The LAPD command staff constantly asked for updates. Garcia attended a seemingly endless series of meetings, strategy sessions, and conferences. And the clues kept on coming.

Some were red herrings—calls from psychics, dog psychologists, dream interpreters. The plausible but fruitless ones were even worse because they were so time-consuming. Desperate for leads, Garcia even took Ennis Cosby's blown-out tire to a California Highway Patrol laboratory, where accident reconstruction experts performed an "autopsy" to determine if it had been intentionally punctured.

Then, almost two months after the murder, an anonymous man called a tabloid tip hotline, asked whether Cosby had been killed with a .38, and left his beeper number. Garcia was intrigued because the killer had indeed used a Smith & Wesson .38-caliber revolver. But the caller had abandoned his pager and left a trail of aliases with the pager company. Finally, detectives tracked him down. He was a man in his thirties, and he told a mesmerizing story that led to Cosby's killer:

In late January, a teenage Asian friend had asked the caller for a favor, a ride to the Valley to visit a Russian he had once served time with at a juvenile prison. The Russian, the teenager told his friend, hung out with Hispanic gang members. They met the Russian—a tall, slender, very pale young man—at a gas station. He did not have a car and asked to be taken to a rest stop near the San Diego Freeway, where he and the Asian teenager disappeared into the brush. When they returned and lingered beside the car, the driver overheard the Russian say, "I shot a nigger. You'll hear about it all over the news."

After the driver dropped the Russian off at his mother's apartment, the Asian teenager explained that the two of them had searched the brush unsuccessfully for the weapon, which the Russian had tossed in a panic after the shooting and wanted to bury.

Garcia and his partner immediately recruited teams of police academy recruits to search the rugged, brushy area. After only five minutes, one of the searchers told Garcia he had found something and pointed out a dark knit cap beside a tree. Lifting the cap with a branch, Garcia spotted the butt of a .38-caliber pistol. Now they had to find the Russian.

The informant did not know his name, but he knew that the Russian and the Asian teenager had been cellmates at a juvenile prison in the San Bernardino Mountains. The prison records included no Russian names, but there was a Ukrainian one: Mikail Markhasev.

While detectives searched for Markhasev, Garcia pondered a mystery surrounding the bank of pay phones at the rest stop, near where Cosby was shot. Immediately after the murder, Garcia and his partner had worked with a multiagency task force that uses computers to track, trace, and collate phone records for law enforcement agencies. The task force logged every phone call made at the pay phones on the night of the shooting, but not one provided any leads. Garcia was troubled, however, by two brief calls to a Long Beach candle shop, made moments after the murder. Why the killer would call a candle shop at 1:30 on a Thursday morning, Garcia could not imagine.

One afternoon, a member of the task force casually mentioned that the phone booths were near the dividing line between two area codes: 310 and 818. The candle shop had a 310 area code. Garcia wondered if the killer could have entered the wrong area code by mistake, so he traced the same number, but with the 818 area code. This led him to a house on Mulholland Drive, not far from the crime scene. Interviewing a woman at the house, Garcia heard a scream. Then a moan. Then a groan. He peered out a window and spotted two people grappling in the backyard. He soon realized that they were not grappling. They were having sex. And someone was filming them.

Garcia discovered that the residents made porno movies. After he convinced them that he was not interested in shutting down their business, they tipped him off to a young couple who had visited the house on the night Cosby was killed. That couple eventually admitted to detectives that Markhasev had also been at the house early that evening, drinking and snorting cocaine. The couple and Markhasev left but returned to the area late that night, stopping at a phone bank near the San Diego Freeway to call a drug connection who lived at the house. If he was not home, Markhasev planned to slip inside and steal his drugs. But a Mercedes with a flat tire distracted Markhasev. "I'm going to jack that guy," he told his friends.

A few minutes later he returned. "Let's get the fuck out of here. I just shot the guy. He didn't move fast enough."

The day after Markhasev was convicted of first-degree murder, Garcia was at home playing with his daughters when Cosby called and thanked him for catching his son's killer. Cosby asked how Garcia was doing. He mentioned that his mother had been recently diagnosed with leukemia. Cosby instructed his personal physician to call Garcia to discuss his mother's condition.

One afternoon at the hospital, Garcia's mother hung up the telephone, turned to a nurse, and asked, "Guess who just called me to see how I was feeling?"

"Who?" the nurse asked.

"Bill Cosby."

Garcia and the other detectives continue discussing Taga as they finish their coffee, walk through the Parker Center lobby, and ride the elevator back to the squad room. Wally Tennelle, a detective who helped Garcia and Jackson at the crime scene and at Taga's town house, spots an enlarged California driver's license photograph of Yuriko on Jackson's desk. She has shoulder-length hair and small gold hoop earrings. Her mouth is slightly pursed and her riveting gaze and wide, troubled eyes reveal a deep melancholy, even in this picture.

"This woman looks so depressed," Tennelle says. "I think suicide is certainly possible."

During the next hour, the detectives are continually interrupted by the phone. "Every rinky-dink police department in the county has voice mail—except us," Lieutenant Farrell complains. "Just once, I'd like to come in to work and not have to play receptionist."

He leaps to his feet and yells across the room to Tennelle, "You ready to go out and kick some Crip ass?" Tennelle stands up and pats his .45, and he and Farrell swagger out the door. "Kicking Crip ass" is Farrell's code phrase for a different kind of mission. He and Tennelle are on a Starbucks run to pick up a couple of café lattes.

Later in the morning, Garcia, Jackson, and Farrell meet in the captain's empty office to plot strategy. Jackson compiled a sixty-one item to-do list on the commuter train this morning. The list includes "follow up on diving equipment; vacuum metal deposition on diving belt buckle; search warrant for Taga's credit card and computer; check ocean currents; reinterview girlfriend; interview ex-wife in Hawaii; talk to knot expert; flag Taga's passport; check insurance." Jackson explains to Farrell that there is no national insurance clearinghouse that lists policies. To find out whether Taga had recently insured his wife they will have to interview his business associates and friends or wait until the insurance company contacts the police.

"You mentioned *his* computer," Farrell says, "How about the girl-friend's computer in Japan? Might be helpful to check the e-mails she got from him when she was in Japan." Farrell then asks about Yuriko's friends.

"Taga told us she didn't have any friends," Garcia says, "but he also told us where Michelle went to preschool. We're going to talk to the people there and see if they can give us a few names."

The purple-and-blue stucco preschool is in a residential neighborhood not far from Taga's Torrance town house. Inside, Garcia and Jackson pass dozens of yellow smiley faces, a large aquarium, and a grid of cubbyholes stuffed with lunch boxes. In the school office, Garcia and Jackson deliver the bad news to the school's director, a cordial, matronly woman, who covers her mouth as her eyes fill with horror. "This isn't something," she says, "that we've ever had to deal with at this school before."

The director tells them she rarely saw Michelle's father. "The mother almost always picked her up. She seemed a very traditional Japanese woman, you know, always bowing. She didn't speak much English."

She sifts through Michelle's file and finds that her last day of summer school was supposed to be August 11, but that Yuriko had decided to depart for Japan a few weeks earlier. This corresponds with the time line Taga provided.

The director lets them inspect Michelle's file, and Jackson removes a sheet of paper. He waves it in front of Garcia, and beams. At the top of the sheet is the heading "Additional Persons Who May Be Called in Case of Emergency." Three women with Japanese names are listed, with their telephone numbers.

Two days later, Jackson meets one of the friends, a plump soft-spoken woman, at a Torrance restaurant. She had said she was not comfortable inviting the police to her house, and Parker Center was too far for her to drive. Garcia has been called to court for another homicide, and Matsushita is unavailable to translate today. Detective Ito, who speaks passable Japanese, has volunteered to accompany Jackson.

The woman covers her eyes and cries for several minutes when Ito informs her of the deaths. When she regains her composure, she says that she met Yuriko about six years ago, when they both worked at a

Japanese restaurant in Gardena. Yuriko met Taga, who was a customer. She became pregnant and they married.

"She was very quiet and reserved," the woman says to Ito, glancing at Jackson and wiping her eyes. "After she got pregnant, she worked as an office clerk. Since Michelle was born, she's been a housewife."

After the wedding, the woman says, she used to visit Yuriko about once a month. Jackson, thinking of how the town house was devoid of any trace of Yuriko and Michelle, asks her whether she ever saw any family photographs.

"On the walls," the friend says. "Family pictures, school pictures of Michelle. Everything."

Yuriko had told her friend that she would probably return from Japan in August. She even registered Michelle for kindergarten in Torrance. Two weeks ago—in mid-September—the woman was concerned because she still had not heard from Yuriko, so she called the town house. No one picked up and the answering machine was not on, which was unusual. Looking at Ito with a quizzical expression, the woman collects herself and says, "Something strange happened that night." A few hours after she phoned Yuriko, Taga and a male friend showed up at the restaurant where she works and ordered yakitori—grilled chicken on skewers. She asked whether Yuriko was home yet; Taga replied that Michelle was attending kindergarten in Japan and the two would probably not return to California until January. She does not know whether it was simply a coincidence that Taga stopped by the restaurant that night, or whether he knew she had called.

Jackson asks whether Yuriko had been depressed. The woman nods: Yuriko had been very worried about her family's financial problems and had planned to look for work when Michelle started kindergarten, because Taga had switched jobs several times and had operated a number of businesses that had failed. At times, Yuriko had been so distressed and angry about what she considered her husband's "shady business dealings" that she had considered divorce. Yuriko's friend does not know what kind of business Taga owns and was afraid to ask.

"She eventually decided to stay with him because she wanted them together for Michelle and she still had affection for her husband," the woman says. "She thought he was a good father, so she was trying to stick it out."

"Did the husband have a girlfriend?" Jackson asks.

"I never heard her complain about a girlfriend," the woman says.

Jackson asks whether she thinks Yuriko could have committed suicide.

"I don't think so, but if she did there's a possibility she'd take Michelle with her because she loved her so much," the woman says. "But she never mentioned suicide to me."

The woman drops her head and sobs. Slowly, she straightens up and says softly, "Please find out what happened."

After the interview, the detectives return to Terminal Island. Jackson wants to study the area in daylight. A briny breeze blows across the water, rustling the palm fronds at the edge of the harbor and buffeting the sails of the boats at sea. A few barefoot Vietnamese fishermen sit cross-legged on the dock, mending nets. Others repair equipment or eat lunch in the bright sunshine.

"If it's suicide, this is a pretty strange place to do it," Jackson says.

The streets that ring Fish Harbor, Ito explains, once housed a thriving Japanese fishing village. Maybe the area's history, he suggests, drew Yuriko here.

Terminal Island was originally a sand spit in San Pedro Bay known as Rattlesnake Island. In the 1890s, a fashionable resort called Brighton Beach opened where Fish Harbor now is. When the Terminal Railway constructed a rail line from Los Angeles, the area was renamed Terminal Island.

Tourism was destroyed in 1916 when landfill projects scarred the beaches and the port of Los Angeles continued to expand. The idyllic vacation spot was transformed into gritty Fish Harbor, where tuna boats lined the dock, canneries ringed the island, and the shipyards thrummed. The hotel was abandoned and the wealthy sold their beach bungalows to Japanese fishermen and packinghouse workers. Many of the approximately 2,500 residents were from Wakayama prefecture on the southwestern coast of Japan. They planted bonsai trees in front of their cottages, built a Buddhist temple, and created a Japanese garden at the public school.

On February 25, 1942, two and a half months after the Japanese attack on Pearl Harbor, the village was extirpated. Within two days all residents of Japanese descent, including American citizens, were expelled at gunpoint. Most were transported to relocation centers. Their boats were stolen or repossessed and their homes were looted and bulldozed.

After the war, the canneries and shipyards thrived, but few Japanese returned to Terminal Island. By the 1970s and '80s, most of the canneries, seeking cheaper labor, moved their operations to Puerto Rico or American Samoa. Still, the container terminals, a federal prison, a U.S. Customs station, busy commercial harbors, and a ship-yard keep the area bustling.

At a market near the harbor, the detectives order fried-fish sand-wiches, eating in silence as they mull over the interview. Finally, Jackson says, "That's pretty interesting, the way the husband shows up at the restaurant the night she called. Maybe he's got caller ID."

"This woman says Yuriko planned to enroll Michelle in a Torrance kindergarten in September," Ito says. "But Taga stops by the restau-rant and tells her she won't be back until January. Why?"

"Because he's a murdering asshole," Jackson says. "What do you think—murder or murder-suicide?"

"Taga's acting kind of crazy," Ito says. "And it seems like Yuriko had some affection for the guy. She had problems in the marriage, but was going to stick it out. . . . I'm leaning towards murder."

After lunch, Jackson walks about the harbor and studies the spot where the bodies were found. A few feet away, on the dock, there is a small shrine. Paper plates filled with Japanese pears and persimmons ring a bouquet of flowers. Bits of burned incense fleck the tops of four empty soda cans.

Jackson picks up a pair of rubber gloves and an envelope from the trunk of his car. He crouches by the shrine and tells Ito, "I'm going to print the cans."

The Taga investigation is Jackson's third homicide investigation with Japanese victims. In the first case, a fashion importer visiting from Tokyo told police that his wife had been shot and killed by two Latino robbers while they snapped photos downtown. The importer, it turned out, was having an affair and had murdered his wife to collect her life insurance. In March 1994, to celebrate the end of the suc-cessful investigation, the Japanese consulate hosted a dinner for Jack-son, several other detectives, and police and prosecution officials visiting from Tokyo. As Jackson left the dinner, he was paged. Two nineteen-year-old Japanese exchange students, who attended a local university, had been shot in a supermarket parking lot. They later died. The case generated national news and an international incident. President Clinton called the victims' parents. The governor of Cali-fornia and the American ambassador to Japan issued statements. After several weeks of investigation, Jackson and his partner solved the case, finding the gangbanger who had shot the two during an attempted carjacking.

Jackson was at the pinnacle of his profession. He loved the variety of demanding cases at Homicide Special and was proud of investigating some of the most challenging murders in the city. His wife, however, hated Los Angeles. In the mid-1990s, he quit the LAPD, moved with his family to a small town in Maine, and found a job investigating theft for an airborne delivery firm. He was miserable. He and his wife eventually divorced, and he returned to Homicide Special in 1999. Jackson is gratified to be back, but he misses his daughters—one is in high school, the other in college—and speaks about them often in the squad room.

Jackson and Ito meet Garcia in front of a large condominium complex in Torrance where another woman on Michelle's emergency contact list lives. Many of the approximately quarter-million Japanese in the Los Angeles area reside in the South Bay beach communities not far from the harbor. The area is popular among businessmen and their families sent to the United States by Japanese companies. Many of the women, like Yuriko's friends, speak no English.

Although in her thirties, this woman looks like a teenager. She cries for several minutes when Jackson tells her the news. She is less than five feet tall, wears wire-rimmed glasses, and is too shy to look at Ito when she answers his questions. Much of what the other woman said, she confirms: Yuriko was depressed about the family's financial state, but planned to look for work when Michelle enrolled in kindergarten. Because Yuriko was always broke, she explored Torrance for free events and sometimes went to festivals at the local park.

When asked if she thought Yuriko would commit suicide, the woman says, "She was strong-willed. I don't think she'd do that."

Like Yuriko's other friend, this woman recently encountered Taga. While eating dinner at a restaurant with her family last week, she confided to her husband that she was worried about Yuriko and Michelle: they should have returned from Japan; she should have heard from them by now. She had called the town house repeatedly, but no one ever answered. After dinner her husband said, "If you're so worried, let's stop by."

They spotted a light on in the town house, so her husband knocked on the door. Taga said that his wife was still in Japan. "My wife wants to get hold of her," the husband said. Taga told him he did not have the phone number in Japan, but he promised the husband that Yuriko would call his wife.

When the friend's husband returned to the car, he described the conversation, which disturbed him. If Taga did not have Yuriko's phone number, how could he contact her and tell her to call? The husband also had spotted a little boy scampering about inside Taga's house, which seemed odd to him.

"He was really acting strange," the husband said when he returned to the car. "Something's not right."

After this interview, Garcia and Jackson decide that the time has come for them to question Taga again—this time as a murder suspect.

As they drive back toward the freeway, Jackson and Garcia suddenly realize the significance of the date, September 29. It is Michelle's birthday. She would have been five years old today.

Knolls and McCartin are still searching for Alexander "Boxer" Gabay. They have more evidence against him than against their other suspect, Armenian Mike, so they hope to interview Boxer first. He is a member of the navy reserves, but has been AWOL for months, according to his commanding officer. A phone number the officer provided is obsolete, and the address listed with the navy appears to be an uninhabited commercial warehouse. Knolls and McCartin have checked traffic-ticket records for the past decade, but the address Boxer listed on several of the tickets appears to be outdated.

McCartin shuts the murder book with a snap, turns to Knolls, and says, "I sure hope he's not in the wind."

A few minutes later, across the narrow aisle that separates Homicide I and II, Jackson tells Lieutenant Farrell that he has finally found a definitive motive for the murder of Yuriko and Michelle. "Michelle's birthday was last Friday, and her mother's birthday was last Wednesday," Jackson says. "That's why Taga did it. He wanted to save money on birthday presents." Farrell snorts and swivels around in his chair.

Although Garcia and Jackson both have daughters and are troubled by Michelle's murder, they use humor to maintain some perspective. But as Garcia removes a photograph of Michelle—a standard headshot taken on school picture day—from the murder book, he looks distressed. She is an adorable little girl with a pageboy haircut, wearing a pink top adorned with green leaves. He places it on Farrell's desk and says, "What kind of asshole could kill this kid?"

Eleven days after picking up the case, Garcia and Jackson arrange for Taga to stop by for an interview late in the morning. If they are able to break him down, this could be a long day, so they decide to eat before he arrives. Like many detectives, both men live so far from downtown Los Angeles that they have to rise by five to get to work at eight. By midmorning they are ready for lunch. Garcia pulls up in front of Uncle John's, located in a dreary section of downtown, on a street lined with sooty turn-of-the-century hotels with rusty fire escapes, dingy lobbies, and clerks ensconced in clear plastic booths. Uncle John's is a narrow shotgun strip of a restaurant, consisting of a dozen swivel stools filled with cops and city workers. The counter faces a smoky, aromatic griddle sizzling with hash browns, eggs, ham, and chow mein. A sign in front advertises CHINESE AND AMERICAN FOOD.

After Garcia and Jackson order, they prepare for the upcoming interview. As they polish off heaping plates of chow mein, Garcia entertains Jackson with some condescending advice given to him when he was first promoted from South-Central. His partner warned Garcia that in the ghetto he had investigated cases with a machete, but now he would have to learn to use a scalpel. Jackson chortles and says, "Let's get out our scalpels and get ready to open up Taga."

They meet Taga back at the squad room. He is wearing the same outfit he had on the first time they interviewed him, jeans and a short-sleeved denim shirt. He appears nervous, picking at a cuticle and licking his lips. He agrees immediately to a polygraph, so the two detectives escort him up a flight of stairs, deposit him in a room, and brief the examiner, Jesse Delgado. As is customary, Delgado interviews Taga before the exam, while the detectives move to another room and watch on a video monitor. Taga tells Delgado that his first name is Kazumi, but friends call him George. He immigrated to the United States twenty-one years ago and lived in New York and Florida for five years before moving to California. When Delgado asks Taga if he is currently taking any medication, he looks embarrassed and acknowledges that he occasionally pops a few Viagra pills.

"Roy," Garcia says to Jackson, "nothing is real with this guy. He takes Viagra so his new girlfriend will think he's a stud. He's bald, but wears a toupee. He's married with a child, but pretends he doesn't see them. He says he runs an auto business, but he's a flimflam man."

Taga then recounts the story he told the detectives last week, again insisting that he had not seen Yuriko and Michelle since they left for Japan. Delgado hooks Taga up for the test and says, "I'm going to ask you a math problem. The reason is, I want to see how you react when you're thinking about something."

"The math question," Jackson quips, "should be: If Taga drove seven miles to the harbor at a speed of thirty-five miles per hour with two bodies in his trunk, how much faster could he drive, using the same amount of engine power, after he dumped the bodies into the water and drove home?"

After Delgado tells Taga to add 65 and 65, he asks him a number of questions: "The last time you saw Michelle and Yuriko, were they alive?" "Did you tie anything around the arms of the victims?" "Did you place the victims' bodies into the harbor?" Delgado asks the same set of questions four times.

Taga sits rigidly, tightly gripping the arms of his chair, looking like a terrified passenger in a plummeting airplane. After the exam, he asks, "How did the test come out?" Delgado tells Taga he will know in about ten minutes.

In the observation room, Delgado spreads the printout on a table and detectives study the results. "He's lying big-time," Delgado says. "This is textbook." He turns to the detectives and asks, "You want me to go after him?"

"The sympathetic approach is the best way," Jackson says.

"Give him an out," Garcia says.

Delgado nods and returns to the polygraph room. He explains to

Taga that there are three results of a polygraph exam: truthful, inconclusive, and "deception indicated." He tosses the exam on a table, points to the result, and tells Taga, "Read it to me."

" 'Deception indicated' . . ." Taga reads. " 'Probability of deception is greater than ninety-nine percent.' "

"What is greater than ninety-nine percent?" Delgado asks.

"A hundred percent," Taga says weakly.

Delgado nods. "George, one hundred percent you failed this polygraph test. . . . Now, I don't know why you did this to her. Maybe she threatened you. You said she attacked you. . . . Maybe this was self-defense. . . . The truth is going to come out with the evidence. It's just a matter of time. So what I need to know, George, is why this thing happened? Because you're not a bad person. . . ."

Delgado stares at Taga, whose legs and arms are tightly crossed. He bends slightly, into an upright fetal position.

"Okay," Delgado says, "did she threaten to kill you? Is that why you did this?"

"But I didn't *do* this," Taga pleads.

"That determination has already been made—"

But Taga interrupts: "You not a policeman, though, right?"

"No . . . but I can go back and explain to the detectives why this thing happened. . . ."

"Okay," Taga says. "So you want me to tell the truth."

"I want you to tell me the truth."

"Not to Rick?"

"Well, I can explain it to Rick. Why did this happen, George?"

"Why?" Taga asks, canting his head to the side. "Well," he says, pausing for a moment. "Because they wanted to die."

Jackson and Garcia stare at the monitor for a moment, dumbfounded. Then they leap to their feet. Jackson throws an arm around Garcia.

Garcia points excitedly at the monitor and says, "He's talking some serious shit!"

"They wanted to die?" Delgado asks, attempting to hide his surprise and retain his equanimity. "So they came back to the house? Tell me what happened.

"No," Taga says, shaking his head. "It wasn't at the house."

"You picked them up at the airport?"

"In fact, I did," he says casually.

"Okay. And what did they say to you?"

"Well, I explained I don't want to live with them and, you know, we had a long conversation. And I don't know what happened, but they just took some kind of poison. So when I came back to them, they passed away. . . . And what happened is, you know, they didn't want, when die, to be separated. They don't want nothing to do with me. And they brought something from Japan . . . and they drink something."

"Where do they drink it at, George?"

"I don't know. Okay? Because I wasn't there. . . . I went to the rest room. We were talking at the harbor, in San Pedro . . . at Ports O' Call, where the restaurants are."

Delgado holds up a palm. "Okay, George, wait a minute. You picked her up at the airport and then you took her and Michelle from there to Ports O' Call?"

"Yeah. And we stayed in the parking lot and then talked quite a bit. And then I park. But by then I should have reported to the police. . . ."

"Where did you get the telephone cord from, George?"

"From the airport."

"Okay. So did you give her the poison?"

"No!" he says emphatically.

"After they took the poison, you wrapped their arms?"

"No. After they took poison or whatever they took, I just check the pulse and there is no pulse there. . . . Because I went to the public bathroom that's there in the parking lot. When I come back, they are gone."

"Were they still inside the car?"

"Yeah."

"And then what did you do?"

"Well, she was talking about she was going to kill themselves. If she die, please put her in the water. . . . I didn't want them, you know, separated. That's why I . . . tied them up."

"Where did you take them to?"

"The harbor."

"What did you put on them to weigh them down?"

"A weight."

"Did you feel bad?"

"Of course I feel bad," he says defensively.

"George," Delgado says, "how did Michelle take the poison?"

"Mom giving them or some kind. I don't know. I just know they're gone."

"I need you to be up-front with me, okay? . . . George, did you give the poison?"

"No."

"Where did she get the poison from?"

"I don't know. . . . Actually, I was going to kill myself too, but . . ." He drops his chin and his voice trails off.

"George, how come you didn't say this before?"

"Because . . . nobody knows, you know, how they die. . . . Because I'm the responsible."

"Feel bad?"

Taga nods. "Feel bad."

Garcia and Jackson confer before confronting Taga, who they realize is more clever—and more devious—than they had anticipated. Tying the bodies together, face to face, and dumping them in the harbor was, the detectives suspect, an attempt to throw investigators off his scent by creating a plausible Japanese mother-child suicide scenario. They decide the solicitous approach will be most effective. Jackson is known as an excellent interviewer and Taga seems to trust him, so he will take the lead.

In the interview room, Jackson hands Taga a 7UP, then reads him his constitutional rights so his statement will be admissible in court. Taga agrees to recount what happened the day Yuriko and Michelle returned from Japan. He had expected them back in September, he admits, not January, and Yuriko called him when she arrived that morning. Taga picked her up at the airport; he eventually told her he had a new girlfriend, who was living at the house.

"We drove to . . . Ports O' Call. . . . And we park in parking space and we talk, talk, talk, talk," Taga says. "She said she want to . . . to take the life away." She asked him, Taga says, "to put me to the water and don't let anybody know how I died."

Yuriko climbed out of the car and walked about the parking lot as she described her plan. "And so I'm getting hungry, you know," Taga says. Jackson and Garcia share an almost imperceptible look of disbelief. Taga says he asked Yuriko if she wanted to eat. She told him he could pick up dinner while she waited with Michelle. Taga visited the men's room first; when he walked out, he glanced at the car.

"They weren't there. So I looked at it a bit closer. They were laying in the backseat." He closes his eyes for a moment and shudders. He checked their pulses. They were both dead, so there was no point, he says, in calling an ambulance. "At that point I should have contact, you know, the authorities, but I didn't. . . . And then I waited until evening."

Taga does not have the demeanor of the stereotypical murder suspect. He is extremely polite and agreeable, without a hint of defensiveness. He may be lying through his teeth, but he is almost obsequious in his desire to appear cooperative.

When Jackson asks about Yuriko and Michelle's luggage, Taga explains that he dumped the suitcases off at a storage facility, where earlier he deposited the family pictures. Jackson, thinking ahead to trial, is attempting to demonstrate that Taga was not a bereaved husband but a cold-blooded opportunist. He asks whether Yuriko had any cash in her purse. Taga acknowledges that he found $90, pocketed the money, and then threw the purse away.

Taga tells the detectives that Yuriko carried a yellow plastic bottle with her on the plane. He holds his hands a few inches above his 7UP can to indicate the size. She and Michelle, he says, both drank a "strange-smelling" poison from the bottle. The detectives know that the coroner's preliminary toxicological tests revealed no poison residue, but the bodies were submerged for so long that a poison could have dissipated. More sophisticated tests eventually will be conducted.

Taga says he returned home at about three P.M. and transferred the bodies to his van. Holding his palms together, he demonstrates how he tied them up. He grabbed a weight belt from the garage and strapped them together.

"Where was Sachiko when this happened?" Jackson asks. "Was she in the house?"

Taga nods, but says she had no idea what he had done.

"Did you do anything else, or did you stay home until you left that evening?" Jackson asks.

"I don't remember," Taga says. "I might have gone out. I'm not sure . . . I was just, you know, gone . . . mentally." At eight P.M., he transported the bodies to Fish Harbor, he says, "and slipped them in the water." He told Sachiko he had to work that night.

Garcia and Jackson know that while Taga's story might contain a modicum of truth, it also includes numerous inconsistencies, elisions, and outright fabrications. But they are reluctant to confront Taga now, to home in on his falsehoods and challenge him. As long as he is in a cooperative mood and does not ask for an attorney, they hope to beef up their case. They decide to present an unusual request to him. Jackson asks Taga if he will accompany them to Fish Harbor and Ports O' Call tonight and demonstrate how Yuriko and Michelle died, how he tied them up, and how he dumped their bodies in the water.

Taga cheerfully agrees, seemingly under the impression that because Jackson asked him to accompany them to the crime scene, he accepts his version of events.

Taga waits in the interview room while Jackson and Garcia look for help tonight. When a murder case comes to fruition, the squad room instantly mobilizes. Half a dozen detectives volunteer and Garcia and Jackson, aided by Lieutenant Farrell, deploy them. A few are enlisted to write search warrants for the storage facility where Taga claimed he put the luggage, and for the town house, where they will search for vials, prescription bottles, poisons, credit cards, and home computers. Others agree to remain on call in case they are needed. Jackson, flushed with excitement, recounts how Taga transported the bodies in the van from his house to Fish Harbor.

"I have one critical question, Roy," a detective tells Jackson. "Because he had the two bodies in the back of the van, did he use the carpool lane?"

Jackson and Garcia are cackling as they walk back to the interview room. They usher Taga down the elevator and cross the street to the Parker Center parking lot.

"Will I be charged for assisting the suicide?" Taga asks.

"Obviously you haven't been truthful with us," Jackson says, stalling for time. "So we'll just have to see."

The detectives and Taga pile into Garcia's Dodge at about six o'clock and head south on the Harbor Freeway. "When did your first marriage end?" Jackson asks, as they snake through rush-hour traffic.

"Eight or nine years ago."

"Why'd you get divorced?"

"She found out I had a girlfriend."

Jackson turns around, wags his finger at Taga, who sits in the backseat, and says, "You never learned. You should be like Johnny here," Jackson says. "His motto is 'Home to work. Work to home.' "

"I was like that for one day," Taga says somberly. Jackson and Garcia laugh and Taga, seeing their amusement, laughs too.

Garcia is unfamiliar with Terminal Island, so Taga, eager to be helpful, provides directions to Fish Harbor. "I should have brought some flowers," he says, staring out the window. They arrive at dusk and walk to the dock. The searing heat of September has passed, and the muted, honeyed light heralds the subtle Southern California fall. The sky is streaked purple, pink, and orange, a watercolor palette. There are only a handful of boats in the harbor tonight and the silence is occasionally broken by the ping of water against the steel hulls and the occasional flutter of seagulls' wings as they pass overhead.

"What made you pick this spot?" Jackson asks.

"We used to date near here," he says, pointing across the harbor to Ports O' Call.

Jackson asks him where he dropped the bodies. Taga leads them down the dock and stops. His body sags. His face crumples for a moment. "Here."

"Did you step out of the van?" Garcia asks.

"No," Taga says. "I stay in van for about ten minutes. I kind of meditate and say *sayonara*." He demonstrates how he shoved the bodies out of the van and into the water. His lower lip trembles. He clasps his hand over his mouth. "After splash, I put hands together and . . . and . . ." He searches for the word.

"Pray?" Garcia asks.

"Yes. Pray."

"Were there any boats around?" Jackson asks.

"No. This peaceful spot. Very quiet. Dark. Stars and moon."

"Did you ever think they'd be found?" Jackson asks.

"Not for long time."

They return to the car and cross the Vincent Thomas Bridge. Taga directs them to Ports O' Call. As Garcia cruises through the parking lot, Taga points to a public rest room. Garcia screeches to a stop, and they climb out of the car. The first stars flicker overhead as the light fades above the hills.

Taga says he parked near here and then talked with Yuriko while Michelle played. He then decided to pick up some food at a nearby restaurant. But first he used the rest room. When he walked out, he could not see his wife and daughter in the car.

Garcia asks why he did not simply walk from the rest room to the restaurant. Why did he leave the rest room, walk all the way around to the other side, and check on his wife and daughter?

"I wanted to ask them something."

"What?" Garcia asks.

Taga looks confused, as if the question has stumped him. He finally says, "I want to see what they want to drink. But I don't see them. I think maybe sleeping." Taga then crawls into the car and lies down on the seat to demonstrate Yuriko's position. He taps the floor to show the detectives where Michelle was curled up. He shows how he picked her up, shouted her name, and shook her lifeless body. His manner is curiously devoid of emotion.

"Anything unusual about their bodies?" Garcia asks.

"Their eyes open. They smell funny."

"Then where do you go?" Garcia asks.

"Home."

"When you got home, did you transfer the bodies to the van right away?" Garcia asks.

"Yes. But didn't put diving belt on them until evening." Taga explains that the van he used to transport the bodies is parked at a Torrance garage that a business partner owns.

They drive north on the Harbor Freeway, past the glaring lights of the oil refineries that stink of burnt rubber and spew clouds of white steam, vivid against the night sky. They pull into a cinderblock garage, past oil-stained parts and several cars in various states of repair. Taga motions toward a large white Ford van.

He then directs them to the nearby storage facility where he dumped Yuriko and Michelle's suitcases and stored the family pictures. Taga tells them that the blanket he spread out in the van before he transported the bodies is also in the facility. "Even though dead bodies, not appropriate to put on floor. I use blanket."

Jackson asks Taga where he keeps the key. He fishes in his pocket and hands it over. Garcia parks in front of the building, flips on his cell phone, and whispers into the receiver. Jackson turns around and faces Taga, who sits primly in the backseat, hands folded on his lap.

"Let me explain something," Jackson says. "You lied about some crucial things. We have two people dead and the way they died, according to your story, is highly unlikely. Even if poison was used, it's also highly unlikely they'd be dead in five minutes, like you explained. Johnny and I have been doing this kind of work a long time. To be very honest, we suspect they died in another way. So we have to arrest you."

"For murder?" he says, surprised.

"Yes."

Taga massages an earlobe and says, "Even if you find poison, I still be charged?"

"Yes," Jackson says.

"So you really think I need to be arrested?" he asks.

"No question," Garcia says.

When two Homicide Special detectives pull up behind Garcia's car, Jackson opens the back door, gently guides Taga onto the street, and cuffs him.

"Any weapons?" Garcia asks.

Taga laughs, but his eyes are flat. "No."

The detectives who just arrived lead Taga into the backseat of their car. Jackson thanks them for working late and agreeing to book Taga at the county jail. One of the detectives says he is happy to earn the overtime. "October collars," he whispers, "mean Christmas dollars."

Garcia and Jackson sit in the car for a moment and stare out the windshield as the detectives drive away with Taga. They then turn toward each other and somberly shake hands. "If he hadn't copped out, we'd be in trouble, Roy," Garcia says. "We went from no case to a murder case."

"What a bastard," Jackson says.

"I really feel for that little girl," Garcia says.

"If you can't trust your father," Jackson says, "who can you trust?"

At about ten o'clock that night they meet their translator, Tina Matsushita, at Taga's town house. They want to interview Sachiko before Taga has a chance to call her from jail. The detectives follow her to the dining room table. Taga's place is still set for dinner. The rice and soup bowl are facedown, flanked by chopsticks and a dish of tofu. Pictures of Sachiko's children line the fireplace mantel. Sachiko is barefoot, her hair is damp, and she wears loose black pants and a gray T-shirt. The detectives are taken aback when they spot her T-shirt. Emblazoned on the front, in large block letters, is the word WHY?

"We have some bad news for you," Jackson tells her, as Matsushita translates. "George has admitted doing a number of things that are very serious."

"What kind of things?" she asks in a high-pitched little-girl voice.

"We can't get into details," Jackson says. "But he disposed of his wife and daughter's bodies. We just arrested him for murder."

She slaps her hand over her mouth and stares, wide-eyed, at Jackson. For about ten seconds she sits stock-still. The detectives hear the dryer tumbling on the back porch.

"We're very sorry and I know this is very upsetting to you, but we have to ask you these questions," Jackson says. "If he told you anything about what happened, it's important for us to know."

She sniffles and nervously bites a finger. "He hasn't said anything."

The detectives ask her questions about the night of the murder, but she recalls very little. He parked the white van in back of the house on several occasions, but she says she cannot remember the dates.

"This is a very serious case," Jackson says. "A four-year-old girl is dead. If he calls you from jail, it's important to tell us what he says. You understand?"

She quickly nods several times. "Is he coming home?" she asks.

"We'll know in a few days," Garcia says. "After we talk to the district attorney."

Garcia and Jackson hope to quickly bolster their case before they present it to the DA, who has to file charges within forty-eight hours of an arrest; otherwise, the suspect is released. So the next day, a group of detectives search the storage facility and the town house and monitor the LAPD criminalists who scour the van for evidence. Others check with airport officials to confirm when Taga picked up his wife and daughter. Another detective escorts Taga from jail to the RHD interview room. He still has not asked for an attorney, so the detectives hope they can pry a few more details out of him and, perhaps, a *full* confession—without the self-serving details that limit his culpability. Taga's toupee was confiscated at the jail and today the hair above his ears flares out like mini-wings and unruly strands swirl atop his head. He looks like an Asian Einstein.

Jackson is writing the lengthy arrest report, so Garcia will conduct the interview, assisted by Mike Berchem, who established a rapport with Taga when he first picked him up outside the town house. Taga tells Garcia and Berchem an elaborate—and possibly apocryphal— story of how he and Yuriko ripped off a Japanese businessman for

$300,000. After discovering the scam, the man demanded the money back and threatened to kill Yuriko because it was "her account and her signature" on all the business documents, Taga says.

Taga and Yuriko were so despondent they discussed suicide, he says. "We thought about it, how we going to kill ourselves." Eventually, Taga says, he researched poisons on the Internet.

Berchem asks sarcastically, "What did you look under, 'poison dot com'?"

Taga chuckles. "Something like that." He found a "recipe," he says, for a particularly deadly poison, and mixed ferrocyanide with water and sulfuric acid. After boiling the compound for twenty minutes, he added ice water for the "cooling stage" and transferred the mixture into a "receiving tank," which contained calcium. Then he measured the poison into four small vials.

After Taga enthusiastically describes the process, he diagrams his step-by-step approach on a piece of paper, providing the detectives with the name of the laboratory where he purchased the chemicals. He explains that he found the poison recipe on a CD-ROM he ordered over the Internet called *The Poor Man's James Bond*.

"You drink it, you sniff it, you gone," Taga says.

But instead of committing suicide, Yuriko fled to Japan with Michelle, taking two vials with her in case she decided to commit suicide at her mother's house, Taga says. Challenging him, the detectives insist it would have been impossible for her to slip the vials past Japanese and U.S. Customs and airport security. But he sticks to his story.

When the detectives question him further about his family's finances, Taga says Yuriko had no life insurance, but she owned their town house and had $100,000 equity in the property.

At first, Garcia did not believe that Yuriko and Michelle had taken poison. But Taga has been so specific that Garcia now believes it is a possibility. Still, he is certain that Yuriko and Michelle did not ingest the chemicals voluntarily.

During the summer, Taga says, he and Yuriko decided that when she returned she would carry the two vials, he would bring one from home, and the family would commit suicide. The detectives angrily tell Taga that his story is nonsensical: Why would she return to the United States to commit suicide? If she had the two vials with her, why didn't she simply drink the poison in Japan?

Taga sips his coffee. "She want all of us to die, three of us . . . together." After their conversation in the Ports O' Call parking lot,

Yuriko asked him, " 'Will you put us into the water together?' That's it. . . . I should have saved her. . . . I walked away. . . . So in the sense, I killed them. . . ."

After listening to Taga's implausible, mutable tale, Garcia is angry. He jabs a finger at Taga and says, "Let's stop playing these little touchy-feely games. You know, the financial this and the depressed that. It's all baloney. I don't believe it. . . . All you're doing is digging a bigger hole for yourself. And it's making things bad for you. You keep changing it because it's not the truth."

Taga scratches his pate with a curious expression, as if searching for the toupee that is no longer there. Eventually, however, he acknowledges that he did not get the telephone cord at the airport, but brought it from home *before* he picked up Yuriko and Michelle at the airport. Taga also says that he made it easy for Yuriko and Michelle to ingest the poison. He opened Yuriko's two vials, set them on the front seat, and walked away. Months ago, Taga says, he tested the poison on a rat, so he knew it worked fast.

If Yuriko was intent on committing suicide, the detectives ask, why didn't he simply leave a vial for her and save his daughter?

"My wife . . . no want to be separated from Michelle . . ." Taga says. "That was Yuriko's choice. . . . I can't control her. . . . She need Michelle to go with her."

As Garcia and Berchem are concluding the interview, the detective assigned to search airport records discovers that Taga lied about picking up Yuriko and Michelle in the family car: he picked them up in the van. Garcia and Jackson are elated—they believe this means that Taga *planned* to kill his wife and daughter and dispose of their bodies. Because the act was premeditated, Taga could face first-degree murder charges and possibly the death penalty.

The detectives who searched his house have been successful, too. They have discovered three empty vials, wrapped in tinfoil, buried under a stack of receipts in a dresser drawer. In the drawer they also find a vial of Rohypnol, the "date rape drug." Garcia and Jackson suspect that Taga slipped the Rohypnol into a drink and gave it to Yuriko and Michelle at the airport. When they were unconscious, he might have pulled out the vials and poured the poison down their throats.

Garcia uses the new information to set a trap for Taga. "After you left . . . Ports O' Call . . . after they were dead, you took them to your house and *then* you placed them into your van, right?" Garcia asks.

Taga nods.

"What would you say if I told you that's not true?"

"The van?" Taga looks confused.

"What if we have cameras, and all the license plates are recorded that come and go out of that airport?" Berchem interjects. "And we can say on September seventh at such-and-such a time that *van* was there to pick up your daughter and your wife. And you *did* pick them up in the van."

"I can prove it, George," Garcia says. "We do our homework."

Taga crosses his arms and stares vacantly at the interview room wall. His hands tremble.

"George," Garcia calls out. "You all right? . . . You trying to think of a story to tell us this time, or what? . . . So what do you have to say to what we just told you, George? Help me understand, how did that van get in the airport?"

"Okay, so let me see. I, I go in the van," he acknowledges.

"And you picked them up in the van so nobody would see them in the back . . . because you knew what was going to happen," Garcia says.

Finally, Taga says, with a hint of irritation, "All right. I drove the van, okay? I had the van." He explains, as the detectives stare at him skeptically, that he was embarrassed to admit he picked them up in such a beat-up, grease-stained vehicle because it would appear that he was disrespectful.

Garcia and Berchem press Taga further. He admits that his wife did not carry two vials with her from Japan. *He* brought three vials from home, the same three vials the detectives discovered in his dresser drawer. The final point that the detectives hope to establish is that Taga did not simply set the vials inside the van and walk away.

"Well, I gave them the . . . vials," Taga acknowledges. "I walked. I couldn't see them take it."

"But you *gave* them the vials," Garcia says.

"Yeah, I gave it to them . . . just hand it to her."

The detectives keep grilling Taga, but he will make no further admissions, instead repeating segments of his story in a monotone as if he has memorized them. The detectives realize the interview is coming to a close. They allow Taga to recount his final minutes with Yuriko and Michelle; he adds a few new wrinkles in this version.

He gave Yuriko the vials. "She said, 'How I take this?' I say, 'Just drink it.' No pain. Then I said good-bye to Michelle. Michelle said,

'Papa.' Taga chokes on the word and emits a sudden sob. He covers his eyes and cries. He drops his hands limply to his sides. "I closed the door. I was crying. When I came back my wife was laying sideways. So I picked up Michelle and I opened the window to let the air in a little bit. Then I drove back home. And I went inside the house. . . . I pray. I was crying. . . . I wish they are going to come back. . . . I was looking outside hoping they'd come back . . . as some kind of ghost or something."

Garcia and Berchem look at Taga with disgust. "It's hard to come back," Berchem snarls, "with thirty pounds of weights on you in the bottom of the ocean."

Garcia and Jackson spend Thursday morning at the district attorney's office. When they return to the squad room, shortly before noon, they announce that the DA has agreed to file murder charges against Taga. Several detectives exchange high-fives with them. A detective asks if the DA charged Taga with two counts of murder. Garcia nods. The detective claps him and Jackson on the back. Captain Tatreau shakes their hands and says, "Good job, guys."

A detective calls out to Jackson, "Hey, Roy, the DA's going to put out a press release and get all the glory."

"They always do," adds another detective.

Homicide Special detectives contend that whenever they screw up, their mistakes are magnified and the criticism in the press unrelenting. But when they do their job well, they believe, reporters pay little attention.

"Call press relations," Captain Tatreau tells Garcia and Jackson. "Let's get our *own* press release out."

The detectives have been at their desks by six every morning this week. They are exhausted now, but giddy with the excitement following a cleared case.

At 3:40 in the afternoon, Garcia drives to Carrow's, a chain coffee shop just north of downtown. He finishes off a French dip sandwich and Jackson bolts a fried chicken salad—their first meal of the day. As Jackson pushes aside his plate, he tells Garcia that he investigated his first poison case when working Hollywood. Like all good homicide detectives, Jackson has an excellent memory for names, addresses, and bizarre details.

"A radio call came through and patrol was sent to an apartment on Sierra Vista, off Santa Monica and Western," Jackson recalls. "Two women were rushed by an ambulance to the hospital. Both were unconscious. One of them, Dorothy Green, had recently had a dispute over money with a man who used to live in the apartment building. Later, the man stops by the building carrying a gift box with a bottle of gin inside. He gives it to a friend of Dorothy's and says, 'Let her know I'm sorry.' Witnesses say Dorothy pours a shot for her and her friend. Dorothy takes a big gulp and says, 'Something's wrong with this gin.' She collapses. The friend, being brilliant, takes a sip and says, 'Yeah, tastes bad.' The friend is still conscious and she calls 911. Turns out the gin was spiked with cyanide. Dorothy ends up almost a vegetable—blind, can't talk.

"We can't identify the man because he lived in the building under an AKA. But two weeks later, the patrol officer who responded to the poisoning cruises by the apartment building and calls in on his radio: 'Attempted murder suspect at location.' He'd recognized the suspect by the description—male black, shaved head, beard, early forties. This suspect found out the second woman was released from the hospital. Maybe he returned to finish the deal. Anyway, patrol brings him to the station.

"We go through his wallet and find his real ID. In his wallet we find a to-do list on notepaper. It says, 'Get cyanide,' and lists the names of some lab companies. The guy goes to prison. Then two years later, Dorothy Green dies as a result of the poisoning. A jury convicts him of murder. The DA starts digging into his background for the penalty phase of the trial. They discover he attended Los Angeles City College twenty years earlier. A DA tracks down his chemistry teacher and asks if he remembers the guy. The teacher say, 'Matter of fact, I do. He was very smart. He had to do a project at the end of the class. He wanted to do an experiment—with cyanide.' "

The day after Taga is charged with two counts of first-degree murder, Garcia and Jackson arrive at work rejuvenated and enormously relieved that the case is cleared. Still, there is hard labor ahead before the preliminary hearing and trial. Taga has made numerous admissions, but this is still a circumstantial case, with no eyewitnesses. Taga continues to insist that Yuriko took the poison voluntarily and administered it to Michelle. Because the prosecution might pursue the death penalty, even the most minute aspect of the case will be scrutinized. The detectives still have many leads to follow to buttress the case.

Garcia and Jackson want to update Lieutenant Farrell, but he is not at his desk. "He took a few days off," a detective explains. "His wife's sick."

Another calls out, "He probably stole some of Taga's cyanide at the search warrant and slipped it into her Cheerios."

Knolls and McCartin walk across the squad room and congratulate Garcia and Jackson. "When you going to hook up your Russian?" Jackson asks.

"First we have to find him," Knolls says.

Another detective walks up to Jackson and points to the captain's office, where a summary is kept of every Los Angeles homicide case from the turn of the century until recent years. "That poison angle," the detective says, "is one for the books."

The century-old binders in the captain's office catalog a vast array of human frailty, the same litany of sins and motives and methods that keeps homicide detectives busy today. The earliest murders, listed in the first dusty blue binder, typed on yellowed paper, the letters faded with age, include:

> *May 31, 1900: Copeland, A. R., Private Watchman. Held up and shot in back of neck by 2 highwaymen; 6th and Union, 8:45 this p.m.*

> *July, 15, 1900: Mitchell, Elmer, Fireman Santa Fe R.R. . . . Shot last night by C. C. Tilley, grocer, for being intimate with his, Tilly's wife.*

> *Oct. 19, 1902: Brag, Andrew. Old man conducted small restaurant, 617 N. Alameda St. Found dead in his restaurant about 7 this a.m. . . . Brag had been stabbed 17 times. Believed to have been done by Mexicans; purpose robbery.*

> *July 28, 1904: Smith, William. About 3 this p.m. . . . Smith (colored) became involved in a fight with Bud B. Green and Jim Green near the Pickwick Club on San Pedro St. . . . Fight started in a conversation relative to Smith's ability as a chauffeur. . . . Green stabbed Wm. Smith in the left side, the point of the knife entering the left ventricle of the heart.*

During the next few decades, the burgeoning murder rate matched Los Angeles's population boom. By the 1930s, the LAPD, however, was not much of a bulwark against this criminal tide. Already, it was known as one of the most corrupt departments in the country, where police officers often obtained their detective stripes by paying off downtown politicians or buying answers to promotion exams. Officers routinely used rubber hoses, which leave no marks, to beat suspects during interrogations. Vice detectives padded their salaries with payoffs from madams, con men, bookies, and bootleggers. As a result, crime flourished; and by the late 1930s, Los Angeles had about 1,800 bookmaking operations, 600 brothels, 200 gambling dens, and 2,300 illegal slot machines. When police raids were planned, the LAPD's Central Vice Squad frequently tipped off the targets ahead of time. A madam named Lee Francis was famous for chilling bottles of French champagne and preparing dishes of Russian caviar for officers while she awaited an imminent raid.

Business owners also paid LAPD officers handsomely for their after-hours work, storming picket lines and busting the heads of union strikers. During the Depression, LAPD officers deputized by counties bordering Arizona formed the infamous "bum blockade." They met Oakies and Arkies at the state border and roughed them up, discouraging them from looking for work in Los Angeles.

Some civic leaders, clergymen, and businessmen were so outraged by the pervasive corruption in the LAPD and at city hall that they formed an organization called Citizens Independent Vice Investigating Committee (CIVIC) to eliminate graft in the city. The head of CIVIC and several other members of the Los Angeles County Grand Jury issued a report that stated: "Los Angeles Police work in complete harmony and never interfere with . . . important figures in the underworld. The police investigation squad is spending its . . . budget . . . not on the investigation of crime, but to build up a file of dossiers designed to intimidate respectable citizens whose only crime consists of their unswerving opposition to the present city administration."

On the morning of January 14, 1937, Harry Raymond, a private detective working for CIVIC, climbed into his car and turned the key. The car exploded, destroying his garage and peppering Raymond with 125 pieces of shrapnel that almost killed him. Investigators soon discovered that Captain Earl Kynette, the head of LAPD intelligence, had been tapping Raymond's phone and monitoring his activities from a house across the street. Kynette, investigators suspected, had been ordered by Police Chief James Davis to follow enemies of Mayor Frank Shaw's administration. Kynette and his lieutenant were eventually convicted of the bombing and sent to San Quentin prison. Voters elected a new mayor, Fletcher Bowron, who during his first year rid the LAPD of its police chief, almost fifty corrupt policemen, and about twenty high-ranking officers.

During the 1940s, the five Los Angeles newspapers, instead of filling their front pages with the latest LAPD scandal, now trumpeted the many lurid crimes that plagued the city. Gangsters, including Benjamin "Bugsy" Siegel and Al Capone's brother, Phil, had gained a foothold in the city, but Los Angeles was simply too spread out geographically for mobsters to be able to control it as they did some East Coast cities.

After World War II, 10,000 people a month descended on Los Angeles, and precipitated even more crime. By the late 1940s, when the city had more than a hundred murders a year, the lawyer Bernard

Potter wrote: "Los Angeles has become the dumping ground for the riffraff of the world. Racketeers of every type, bootleggers, bookmakers, black market operators, thugs, murderers, petty thieves, procurers, rapists, fairies, perverts, reds, confidence men, real estate sharks, political carpetbaggers and opportunists. Ask for any violator of the law and we can promptly fill the order."

The most complex cases—baffling, sometimes sadistic crimes that challenged the resources of divisional investigators—were transferred to the Homicide Bureau, located on the ground floor of city hall and manned by a crew of seasoned detectives with citywide jurisdiction. If a case was more intricate than a "Ma and Pa Kettle murder," it was sent downtown.

These detectives soon developed a cachet that set them apart from the other officers in the department. Most accepted into the unit were big, burly World War II combat veterans. They dressed in double-breasted suits, florid silk ties, and expensive snap-brim hats; they wore gold ID bracelets and flashy gold rings, and they jotted notes with gold mechanical pencils. They were able to afford their stylish clothing and jewelry because they were privy to valuable information. There was an acute housing shortage after the war, and homicide detectives were the first to know when a body was shipped off to the morgue and an apartment suddenly was available. Some detectives supplemented their income by tipping off rental agents, who expressed their gratitude with envelopes of cash.

These Homicide Bureau detectives were made famous—and in some cases infamous—in the movies and pulp novels of the noir years. The apogee of this era was 1947, when the city's demimonde and detectives dominated the headlines. On January 15, every investigator in the Homicide Bureau was called into action when the mutilated body of Elizabeth Short, the Black Dahlia, was discovered at Thirty-ninth and Norton streets. The city's most notorious unsolved murder prompted thousands of fruitless tips and more than a hundred false confessions during the year.

Three months later, a matronly woman named Louise Peete captured the city's curiosity when she was executed in San Quentin's gas chamber. Peete, whose first three husbands supposedly committed suicide, had served eighteen years in prison for murdering a Los Angeles boyfriend. After her release, she killed again—this time, the wife of a Pacific Palisades man she was trying to swindle.

In July, the gangster Benjamin "Bugsy" Siegel was lounging on a sofa at his girlfriend's Beverly Hills house when a hit man, aiming through the living room window, knocked him off with nine blasts from a .30-.30 carbine—a grisly capstone to the mobster era in Southern California. A number of other sensational murders mesmerized residents that year, establishing Los Angeles as a crime capital equal to New York and Chicago—and as a locus for corrupt cops.

The LAPD's road to reform began in 1950, when William H. Parker, a decorated army captain during World War II, was named chief. Rooting out corruption, Parker created an aggressive, efficient, militaristic organization. Officers who stole money and took bribes were immediately fired. Visitors from other cities, accustomed to slipping $20 bills under their driver's licenses, were stunned when LAPD patrol officers returned the money with a lecture.

Parker, a law enforcement innovator who emphasized technology, was one of the first chiefs in the country to establish a division to analyze crime patterns. But what he gained in efficiency he lost in community relations. This was an era when many police departments assigned officers to walk neighborhood beats, getting to know residents and merchants. Known today as community-based policing, this approach is now recognized as a good way to fight crime and defuse tension in the inner city. Ever vigilant against police corruption, Parker wanted his officers to regularly rotate assignments so they would not become too familiar with the people they were policing or with one another. Gradually, Parker ordered his men off the street and into squad cars, where they would be mobile and aggressive, and make more arrests. Parker felt it was important to discourage criminal activity before it happened. He called this proactive policing.

While Parker regarded this style of policing as aggressive, residents in black and Latino neighborhoods, who bore the brunt of proactive policing, considered it harassment. Many LAPD officers believed they had the authority to stop anyone, at any time, for any reason. When minorities entered white neighborhoods, they were routinely tailed, stopped, and searched. They also complained that they were often bullied, intimidated, and beaten in their own neighborhoods. Outrage against the LAPD, department critics contended, ultimately ignited the 1965 Watts riots. When it was over, after six days of mayhem, thirty-four people were dead, more than a thousand had been injured, and the damage was estimated at almost $200 million.

While patrol officers and divisional detectives contended with the explosion in street crime and gang problems, the downtown Homicide Bureau remained above the fray, investigating select cases such as mob hits, killings that captured headlines, and the sadistic sex crimes of predators such as Harvey Glatman, known as the Murderous Momma's Boy.

Then, in 1968, the LAPD was overwhelmed by an assassination that changed the course of the nation's history. Shortly after midnight on June 5, Robert Kennedy, who had just won the California presidential primary, was following a maître d' through the pantry of the Ambassador Hotel after addressing supporters. A Palestinian immigrant named Sirhan Sirhan jumped off a tray rack, yelled, "Kennedy, you son of a bitch," and jammed a .22-caliber revolver near the senator's ear. Then he pulled the trigger.

Although Sirhan was apprehended with the pistol still in his hand, LAPD leaders feared a debacle like the botched investigation by the Dallas Police Department of the John F. Kennedy assassination. They assured the public that there would be no enduring conspiracy theorizing or interminable second-guessing after they wrapped up their case.

Now, for the first time, there was a murder case of such vast scope that the Homicide Bureau's resources were inadequate. The LAPD created a massive task force called Special Unit Senator. Fifty detectives drafted from the Homicide Bureau and other divisions throughout the city launched an immense investigation and eventually compiled a ten-volume report, chronicling almost five thousand interviews, which concluded that Sirhan had acted alone.

At the end of the year, Deputy Chief Robert Houghton, who headed the task force, decided that in an era of political assassinations and serial killers, the Homicide Division was understaffed and overburdened. Detectives handled troublesome cases from throughout the city, but they were also responsible for the more mundane murders in the downtown area, since Central Division, at the time, had no homicide investigators.

Houghton envisioned a specialized unit, with adjoining squad rooms, combining robbery and homicide specialists who would investigate only the most difficult cases in the city. Many murders are robbery-related, so Houghton figured the two units could benefit by sharing information. Because this new unit would have more detectives than the old Homicide Bureau, investigators could handle a mammoth case like the Robert Kennedy assassination without a special task force.

In 1969, Robbery-Homicide Division was created. A few weeks

later, Homicide Special detectives were called out on a case that immediately taxed the resources of the new unit. Roman Polanski's twenty-
six-year-old pregnant wife, Sharon Tate, and four others were found
slashed and slaughtered on Cielo Drive in an exclusive canyon estate
off Benedict Canyon. A single word had been scrawled in blood on
the front door: PIG.

The Manson Family murder investigation was an inauspicious
beginning for this new unit.

The next night another team of Homicide Special detectives was
called out to investigate the murder of a Los Feliz couple. There were
a number of obvious parallels between the two murders: both sets of
victims had been stabbed many times; there was no evidence of robbery; ropes had been wrapped around the necks of two victims on
Cielo Drive, and cords had been wrapped around the necks of the
Los Feliz couple. Finally, at both murder scenes, there was bloody
writing. At Los Feliz, DEATH TO PIGS and HEALTER (it should have
been HELTER) SKELTER was scrawled inside the house. Yet Homicide
Special detectives decided that the two cases were not connected.

A Homicide Special detective also made another critical error the
day after the Cielo Drive murders: he dismissed a tip from Sheriff's
Department investigators, which could have quickly solved the case.
The sheriff's investigators mentioned that for the past week and a half
they had been tracking a similar murder in Malibu in which the victim
was stabbed to death and the words POLITICAL PIGGY had been printed
on a living room wall in the victim's blood. They had arrested a man
who was wearing bloody clothing, driving the victim's car, and had
also hidden a knife in the car's tire well. The suspect was in custody
at the time of the Cielo Drive murders. Still, he could have had accomplices. When the sheriff's investigators mentioned that the suspect
lived with a group of hippies who followed a guy called Charlie, the
Homicide Special detective insisted that hippies were not involved in
his case. The Cielo Drive murders, he contended, were the result of
a major drug deal.

Although detectives did not link the three murder cases until
months later, the press was unaware of their foul-ups at the time. And
at trial, the LAPD's mistakes were overshadowed by the bizarre cast
of characters and their lurid testimony.

A few years later, a unit called Major Crimes was created and the
detectives were assigned to investigate all police officer killings, split
the high-profile murders with Homicide Special, and track other com-

plex crimes that were a priority of the police chief. Eventually, the unit was disbanded, and its detectives were absorbed into Homicide Special.

Detectives managed to escape the criticism that was increasingly directed at the LAPD from the late 1970s to the early 1990s, the era of Police Chief Daryl Gates. Gates, Parker's former driver, was another enthusiast of proactive policing. While he led the department, Los Angeles was regularly among the nation's leaders in settling excessive-force lawsuits. The LAPD routinely fired corrupt officers, but brutal cops were coddled. Even officers who had been repeatedly sued for excessive force—and had lost—were treated leniently, given feeble warnings, and allowed to return to the streets.

Gates claimed that his officers had to be aggressive because they were outmanned. Los Angeles had the lowest officer-to-resident ratio among the nation's six largest cities. Overwhelmed and overworked LAPD officers had to patrol a vast, sprawling city with a swelling crime rate and the worst gang problems in the country.

Los Angeles voters had rejected several bond measures that would have increased police funding, and the city council kept the department's annual budget and staffing levels well below those of other major cities. The politicians and white, middle-class residents had a Faustian agreement with the LAPD: the police would keep order, in their own way, at a bargain price, and residents and politicians would not ask too many questions about how they did it.

This agreement, department critics believed, led inexorably to the March night in 1991 when—while their sergeant and a group of more than twenty officers looked on—two LAPD officers pummeled Rodney King, a drunk African-American motorist who led police on a high-speed chase before he finally pulled over. The officers, wielding aluminum batons, fractured King's cheekbone, cracked his right eye socket, broke his ankle, and broke eleven bones at the base of his skull. Suddenly, the LAPD was at the epicenter of a national law enforcement scandal that presaged the worst decade in the department's history.

In 1992, the all-white Simi Valley jury's acquittal set off the most deadly riot of the century. Fifty-one people died and about $1 billion worth of property was destroyed. The LAPD was again denounced, this time for its disorganized and poorly prepared response to the unrest.

Two years later, after O. J. Simpson was arrested for the murder

of Nicole Brown Simpson and her friend Ronald Goldman, the LAPD
was again the subject of intense criticism. But this time it was not the
patrol officers who were denounced. It was Homicide Special detectives.

Supervision of the crime scene was abysmal, and the evidence was
treated carelessly. Detective Tom Lange, for example, covered Nicole
Brown Simpson with a blanket taken from inside her home when
television cameramen focused on the body. This was a gracious ges-
ture, but a rookie mistake: it enabled O. J. Simpson's defense attorneys
to argue that the blanket could have contaminated the crime scene.
The detectives' problems were compounded when they obtained a
blood sample from Simpson at the jail and instead of booking it into
evidence, Detective Philip Vannatter delivered it later that day to a
criminalist collecting evidence at Simpson's house. That dubious decision enabled defense attorneys to suggest that police had planted
Simpson's blood on his white Bronco, at his home, and at the crime
scene. While Vannatter was hamstrung by the LAPD's burdensome
evidence booking policy, he could have avoided transporting the blood
to Simpson's house.

The interview with Simpson at RHD—about thirteen hours after
police found the bodies—was also considered amateurish. This was
the detectives' sole opportunity to question him, but the interview was
brief—Lange and Vannatter ended the questioning after only thirty-
two minutes—and superficial. On numerous occasions, when it was
obvious that Simpson was lying, Lange and Vannatter failed to ask
trenchant follow-up questions. "It was about as hardball an interrogation as a celebrity interview with Larry King," wrote Hank Goldberg,
a member of the prosecution team, in *The Prosecution Responds*.

A number of current Homicide Special detectives are, privately,
critical of the investigation. They agree that the interview with Simpson was inadequate and that detectives made errors during the crucial
initial stages of the investigation. But they also contend that the case
was weakened by numerous prosecution errors, by the racist statements of Mark Fuhrman—a detective in the West Los Angeles Division—and by the inadequate funding of the department's crime lab
and the poor training of its personnel. Despite the problems with the
case, Homicide Special detectives believe that Lange's and Vannatter's
investigation would have convicted Simpson had he not been a famous
former athlete wealthy enough to hire a team of lawyers with unlimited
resources. Even the much maligned interview, which prosecutors

ignored during the criminal trial, helped the plaintiffs' attorneys during Simpson's civil trial impeach him and destroy his alibi.

During the decade before the Simpson case city officials routinely denied requests for crime lab funding and new equipment. This bureaucratic parsimony and neglect was exploited during the trial by defense attorneys, who portrayed the facility as a "cesspool of contamination." Since then, the crime lab has added more than two dozen new employees, spent about $500,000 on training programs, and invested $3 million in upgrading the facility. The department's Scientific Investigation Division is still understaffed and underfunded—detectives frequently complain about long waits for results—but at least the technicians are now better trained, have more sophisticated equipment, and give more persuasive testimony during trials.

During the mid-1990s, Homicide Special solved a string of murders and LAPD patrol officers managed to steer clear of scandal. But in 1997, after rap star Biggie Smalls was murdered, a few journalists contended that high-ranking LAPD officials orchestrated a cover-up to protect dirty black cops. Then, a year and a half later, the LAPD was battered by its worst corruption scandal since the 1930s. Police Officer Rafael Perez, who had pleaded guilty to stealing eight pounds of cocaine from the LAPD property room, agreed to a reduced prison sentence (five years) in exchange for identifying other corrupt officers, who were later charged with beating and threatening unarmed suspects, planting weapons and drugs on them, and lying in court.

Perez was a member of CRASH, the antigang unit in the Rampart Division, a gritty, congested neighborhood west of downtown with a large Central American population and numerous warring gang factions. Because of overcrowding at the division, CRASH moved to a substation almost two miles away. Officers there, free of supervision, created their own rules, Perez told investigators. CRASH evolved into a police department within a department, an insular, hyperaggressive unit that took proactive policing to a new and felonious level. Officers viewed their confrontations with gangbangers as urban warfare, and they considered themselves the occupying army. Rampart members created their own patches, including a skull wearing a cowboy hat. These cowboy cops routinely roughed up drug dealers and gave plaques to officers who shot gangbangers.

Perez implicated about seventy other antigang officers, claiming they were involved in or knew of crimes or misconduct. He told investigators that he and his partner Nino Durden shot an unarmed gang member and later framed him for assaulting a police officer. After the scandal erupted, the man was freed from prison.

In addition to Perez and Durden, seven LAPD officers were charged with crimes and more than two dozen were fired or resigned for misconduct or corruption. About a hundred convictions were dismissed, and city officials anticipate spending $100 million to settle lawsuits stemming from the scandal.

In the wake of Rampart, police officials assigned new duties to Homicide Special. In the past, if a cop was shot at but not hit, or if an officer fired at a suspect but missed, divisional detectives conducted the criminal investigation. Rampart officers, however, had been involved in questionable shootings, and the follow-up investigations were considered inadequate. So LAPD officials decided that to prevent another scandal the city's elite homicide detectives should roll on all police shootings. Now Homicide Special, instead of the divisions, is called out up to a hundred times a year for shootings and threats against officers.

Some veteran detectives are so irritated by the callouts, which take precious time away from their murder investigations, that they are considering transferring or retiring. Detectives consider themselves specialists, and they want to focus on their specialty. They believe that detectives in a unit as storied as Homicide Special, detectives who frequently face intense scrutiny by the press and the public because of their high-profile cases, detectives who are considered the finest in the city, should be allowed to do what they do best: investigate homicides.

9

On a Tuesday morning in mid-October, Knolls, McCartin, and David Krumer decide to try their luck and see if they can catch Alexander "Boxer" Gabay at home. They are still not certain he killed Luda, but the evidence against him is more persuasive than their case against Armenian Mike. First, there is the video of Gabay and Oxana entering Luda's building at 9:03 on the morning of the murder and leaving twenty minutes later. Then there are Gabay's supposed confession to the FBI informant and the money that Oxana owed Luda, which supplies a motive.

But informants are frequently unreliable and the couple may have a plausible explanation for visiting Luda that morning. Today may reveal all. Or nothing.

Gabay's commander in the navy reserves provided the detectives with an address, which turned out to be a commercial warehouse. McCartin contacted the building's owner, who told him that Gabay is a welder and works out of the warehouse. The owner has been trying to track him down, also, because he is two months behind on his rent. Knolls and McCartin have obtained a search warrant for the warehouse: if Gabay is the killer, he may have stored evidence there.

"If this guy's a welder," McCartin says, "he could have hit her with anything."

"He could have *made* the weapon that imprinted those unusual marks on her," Knolls says.

"Maybe today's our lucky day," McCartin says, as he pulls up in front of a crumbling gray cement building at the edge of the downtown produce district. The street is lined with deep loading docks stippled with shreds of lettuce and broccoli. "This could be our killer, boys," McCartin says. "Let's do it right."

He bangs on a heavy metal security door, waits a beat, then bangs again. He presses his ear against a wall. Seconds later, a dog barks. "Anyone there?" McCartin shouts.

Finally, a bare-chested man with a buzz cut wanders out of the dim warehouse, wearing shorts and sneakers. The man, whom the detectives realize is Gabay, looks like a middleweight—thick neck, sinewy arms, barrel chest—ready to go twelve rounds. Unshaven, with a pitted complexion, he stands in the doorway, cigarette dangling from his lips, squinting into the bright sunshine.

McCartin introduces himself and says casually, "You probably heard we've been talking to friends of Luda. We're just trying to touch base with everyone who knew her. We'd like to talk to you and Oxana." McCartin and Knolls, who do not know where Oxana lives, hope Gabay will lead them to her.

"Oh, you want to talk to Oxana, too?" asks Gabay in a Russian accent. "Well, she's here, fixing lunch now."

"There's no rush," McCartin says, feigning patience. "We'll come back when you finish. Say, about one o'clock. You can follow us over to the station, where we can talk. It shouldn't take more than an hour."

Gabay agrees—fortunately, because there is not enough evidence to arrest him. At this point, the detectives need his cooperation.

Knolls and McCartin decide to break for lunch themselves. Speeding down First Street, McCartin crosses a sturdy cement bridge built in 1929—a portal to East Los Angeles—spanning the dry, concrete bed of the Los Angeles River. McCartin cruises past Mariachi Plaza, where musicians gather on Saturdays waiting for gigs, past *tiendas* (stores), *carnicerias* (meat markets), *taquerias*, and other Mexican businesses. But he parks in front of Otomisan, a modest Japanese restaurant consisting of four small booths and a counter with five stools. Paper lanterns and Japanese scrolls adorn the walls. Otomisan is the last remnant of the once thriving Japanese community in Boyle Heights, a neighborhood now almost entirely Latino. The detectives order shrimp tempura and prepare for the interview.

After lunch, McCartin drives back across the First Street bridge. The downtown skyline rises in the distance, the glass office towers gleaming. During the past few days, a bone-dry Santa Ana wind has gusted across the Mojave Desert, down the mountains, and through the city, blowing the smog to the sea, raising temperatures to the high eighties, and coating the streets with dust. The San Gabriel Mountains are clearly visible today, etched against a faded blue sky. McCartin closes his window and flips on the air conditioner. He and Knolls are keyed up: they have worked long hours, spent many nights away from their families, chased dead ends and false leads, interviewed countless peripheral players. Now, finally, they sense a payoff. Still, they are apprehensive. They fear Gabay might have hopped in his car and fled. And they hope they are not walking into an ambush.

As McCartin parks in front of the warehouse, he says to Knolls, "If things go right, we can clear this friggin' case today." Then he takes a deep breath, exhales, and climbs out of the car. He knocks on Gabay's metal door. There is no answer. The dog barks. He knocks again.

"Anyone there?" Knolls shouts, pounding on the door.

A minute later, Gabay opens up. He has changed and now wears jeans and a tight gray T-shirt. "So where'd you have lunch?" he asks.

"Japanese," McCartin says. As they chat about downtown lunch spots with a strained conviviality, Gabay's two fearsome-looking pit bulls bound through the door. The detectives stiffen.

"Don't worry," Gabay says. "They're chickens."

While Gabay leads the dogs back inside the warehouse, Oxana finally appears and glances at the detectives warily. She is twenty-three, the detectives know—fourteen years younger than Gabay—and pudgy, with stringy blond hair. She wears pink lipstick, faded jeans, black boots, and a tight powder blue top. McCartin is relieved when the two hop in their car and follow him to Parker Center, which is about a mile north.

Cruising up Alameda Street, he says, "That was easier than I thought."

Five minutes later, as the detectives walk from the police parking lot to Parker Center with Gabay and Oxana, McCartin asks her whether she speaks English. She shakes her head.

"Neither does he," Knolls says, jerking his thumb toward McCartin.

"I only speak New Yorkese," McCartin says, grinning.

Knolls scrutinizes Oxana and tries to discern if she is as cold and calculating as people have said. He decides that the descriptions have been accurate. For a young woman, new to the country, suddenly hustled into a police station, she does not appear particularly concerned. When Krumer ushers her into one interview room, and Knolls and McCartin lead Gabay into another, she seems not frightened but miffed, as if the separation is an inconvenience.

The detectives decide to interview Gabay first. "You're free to go at any time," McCartin tells him. "You're not under arrest."

"I want to help you guys," he says earnestly.

But McCartin and Knolls ease into mentioning the murder. Sipping inky squad-room coffee, Gabay tells the detectives in his heavily accented English that he grew up in Moscow and immigrated to the United States with his parents as a teenager. He studied architecture in college, but for the past year and a half he has worked with a construction battalion in the navy reserves. He also creates kinetic steel sculptures—"They move on their own," he explains—in the front of the warehouse and lives with Oxana in a loft in the back.

The detectives are taken aback. For months they had been tracking this spectral suspect alternately described as a thug, a boxer, an intimidator. They had not expected a sculptor enthusiastically expounding on form and function like an art critic.

When McCartin asks about his boxing background, Gabay says that although he has bulked up during the past decade, he once competed as a lightweight and was ranked number one in Moscow. He fought throughout the Soviet Union, including one bout in Siberia.

When McCartin asks if he knew Luda, Gabay nods and says he met her at a party a few days after Oxana and the other girls were smuggled into the country. All the girls, Luda, Serge, and "a bunch of Russian guys" were there, Gabay says. When Knolls asks whether he recalls the date, Gabay shakes his head, and says he only remembers that it was on a Friday or Saturday night, a few days after July 4. Knolls sets a calendar on the interview room table and Gabay studies it, trying to figure out whether the party was held July 7 or July 8.

McCartin shows Gabay pictures of the five other girls who were smuggled into the country with Oxana. He confirms that they were the girls at the party. "Some of the girls started stripping and if someone went to the bedroom . . . well . . ." Gabay smiles slyly and shrugs.

"How late did you stay?" McCartin asks.

"Oh, about one-thirty or two."

"One of those nights, huh?" McCartin asks, flashing him a sympathetic look.

"Yeah," Gabay says.

McCartin is uncharacteristically genial and Gabay seems increasingly at ease as the interview meanders along. But just as the last lingering sense of tension has faded away, McCartin decides that the time is right to ask Gabay the critical question. If Gabay denies visiting Luda's apartment on the day of the murder, or if, better still, he denies *ever* entering the building, the detectives have bolstered their case significantly. If, however, he acknowledges dropping by the apartment on August 17, the video—the detectives' best piece of evidence— cannot help them.

Finally, McCartin asks offhandedly, "After the party, when was the next time you saw Luda again?"

Without hesitation, Gabay says, "I never saw her again."

"You *never* saw her again?" McCartin repeats, poker-faced.

"No."

"You never saw her at her apartment?" McCartin asks, assuming control as Knolls's attention heightens.

"No."

"Not with Serge?"

"No."

"When did you find out she was dead?"

Gabay sips his coffee. "About two months ago. I heard about it the next day because all the girls were scared."

Gabay leans forward, his body tense. He tightly grips his chin with a hand.

"What did you hear about the murder? Anything?" McCartin asks.

"I heard mafia."

"Like Russian mafia?" McCartin asks.

"Yeah. That's what people thought."

"What do *you* think?"

"I have no idea."

"Hear anything else about her death?"

"I heard some Armenians. At first I heard it was mafia. Then Armenians. You know how rumors are."

"Did Luda pay to bring the girls over?"

"I don't know, but I wouldn't be surprised."

"Was Oxana ever a hooker in Russia?"

Gabay waves a hand. "No."

"Here?"

"No. I support her."

Nonchalantly, McCartin says, "There's one thing we usually do in cases like this. We put people on the polygraph when they're done."

Gabay blanches, fixes McCartin with a hostile stare, and says, "No."

"Serge took one," McCartin says.

"No," Gabay says coldly. "I don't want to take a poly."

"It's just for our peace of mind," McCartin says in a mollifying tone. "We just want to ask you some basic questions—"

"No. I don't want to." Gabay points to McCartin's notes. "Everything I told you is there."

The detectives meet Krumer in the squad room and McCartin says, eyes shining with excitement, "We got him! He denies *ever* being at her apartment." Krumer raises his fist in the air.

But to ensure that the district attorney files charges against Gabay, they need more. They decide to confront Oxana with the videotape first: despite her self-assurance, they believe she is more vulnerable than Gabay. If she folds, they will confront Gabay and attempt to play him off against her. If one of them turns against the other, the detectives will have what they need.

"If she starts going off on a tangent, cut her off," McCartin tells Krumer. "Right now, it's do or die."

Knolls opens by asking Oxana—Krumer translates—about her journey from the Ukraine to the United States. She leans back in her chair, crosses her legs, and coolly assesses Krumer and the two detectives. Appearing satisfied, she says flatly that the trip was hard and tiring— from Kiev to Warsaw to Amsterdam to Mexico City to Ensenada to Tijuana. Then on July 4, she and about twenty other men and women boarded a boat in Tijuana and slipped into San Diego. Luda brought her and another girl to Los Angeles and they stayed at Luda's apartment for a few days.

"How did you think you'd earn the money to pay your passage?" Knolls asks.

"At first I thought it was an escort service," she says. "In Mexico, I learned what they meant by *escort* service. . . . I thought . . . some agency. But I figured . . . I could always take off."

McCartin asks if Luda forced her to work as a prostitute.

"No," Oxana says forcefully, looking Krumer squarely in the eye. "She never forced us, ever. . . . I *never* worked as a prostitute. . . .

Luda paid for the girls and had us sitting around and didn't know what to do with us. . . . She wanted to resell us, to get rid of us quicker and collect the money so that we would not be on her head."

Another girl staying at Luda's contacted Serge. He picked up the two girls and took them to his friend's apartment in the Valley. The friend was in Russia for two months and Serge said they could live there temporarily. Oxana moved in with Gabay maybe a month later.

"After you moved out of Luda's apartment, did you see her or call her?" McCartin asks.

"I didn't talk to her."

"So when was the last time you saw Luda?" McCartin asks.

She tilts her head back, puffs up her cheeks, and studies the ceiling. McCartin and Knolls study her while trying to appear blasé.

When Oxana tells them she last saw Luda at the party, McCartin decides that she and Gabay have coordinated their stories. Luda "was drunk and happy," Oxana says. She casually mentioned the money that Oxana owed her, but did not pressure her.

"Did you ever see Luda again?" McCartin asks, obviously impatient as he waits for Krumer to translate.

Immediately, without hesitation, she shakes her head.

"Ever talk on the phone after that?" he asks.

"No."

"Ever visit her apartment?"

Clenching her purse strap, she says, "I have no reason to visit."

"Do you remember when . . . and who told you she was killed?" Knolls asks.

One of the other girls told her about the murder, she says.

"Okay," Knolls says. "Let's take a break."

In the squad room, McCartin says, "Okay, we got 'em both denying they visited the apartment. But I don't think it's enough to file on them."

"Show her the video," Knolls says. "If we're going to break her, it's got to be now."

Moments later, they ask Oxana once more to tell them about the last time she saw Luda. After she repeats her story, McCartin says, "This is a very serious matter, so it's very important that you tell us the truth."

"I *am*," she insists.

"We don't believe you," McCartin says.

Oxana purses her lips into a tight frown. She then acknowledges that she stopped by Luda's apartment once to pick up some clothing and a pair of sneakers. The detectives disguise their distress; if she admits stopping by the apartment on August 17, their case could be endangered.

"This was when . . . approximately?" McCartin asks.

She studies her nails for a moment. "I think middle of July."

Knolls's eyes reveal barely discernible relief as McCartin asks Oxana a few more questions to pinpoint the date. Then Knolls lays out on the metal table two pictures—still photographs from the security video from Luda's apartment building entrance. One shows Oxana and Gabay entering the building at 9:03 A.M. on August 17; the other shows them leaving at 9:23 A.M.

"Is that you?" Knolls asks.

She studies the photos with a queasy expression, appearing concerned for the first time. "It looks like me, but it couldn't be me at that time."

"You better tell us the truth," Knolls snarls.

"We know you were there," McCartin says.

"If you don't tell us what happened, it will look like you're involved in the murder," Knolls says.

She sighs heavily and drops her elbows on the table. "What day was Luda killed?"

"The same day and time these pictures were taken," McCartin says.

Oxana, biting her lower lip and hugging herself, looks panicked, quickly glancing from Krumer to McCartin to Knolls.

"This is very serious," Knolls says.

The detectives sense that their onslaught is working, that Oxana is close to confessing. After months of clashing and crossing signals, Knolls and McCartin have finally developed an interviewing rhythm as partners. They now seem to read each other intuitively. When McCartin established a rapport with Gabay during the interview, Knolls let him ask the questions. When Knolls attempted to penetrate Oxana's reserve by asking her about the journey to Los Angeles, McCartin did not interrupt. Now Oxana is weakening under their unrelenting enfilade, so they continue seamlessly alternating questions.

"If you didn't know this was going to happen, let us know," McCartin says.

"We know Luda demanded the money that you owed her," Knolls says.

"She did not demand, she *reminded* me, but did not demand," Oxana says.

"You have to take care of yourself," Knolls says.

"Tell us why you were there," McCartin demands. "We need the truth."

Oxana drops her head and locks her fingers under her chin. "We didn't go inside," she says softly, looking defeated. "We were inside the building, but not inside the apartment."

This is what the detectives had been waiting for. Now they move in to fully exploit the crack in her story.

"We *know* you were inside the apartment," McCartin says.

"We *know* you were there," Knolls adds.

"We need for you to tell us what happened that day," McCartin says.

Knolls taps a finger on the still photographs. "You were there twenty minutes," he says. "What happened?"

She licks her lips and swallows hard. "I heard someone in the apartment. Luda was arguing and we decided not to go inside."

McCartin stares at her skeptically. "It's too late for that. We have people who *saw* you going inside the apartment," he says, bluffing.

"We were just standing in the hallway, deciding whether to go in," she says.

"We know you were in the apartment," McCartin says. "A lot of people go to work at that time. They saw you."

"We didn't go into the apartment that day," she says. "Nobody could have seen us."

"Did you know you were being videotaped?" McCartin asks.

"No," she acknowledges.

"Then how do you know no one saw you enter the apartment?" McCartin asks.

"People saw you through their peepholes," Knolls says.

McCartin shouts, "The way it looks now, you're involved in a murder! If you can't tell us what happened, it's going to be a problem for you."

She fiddles with her purse strap, wrapping it around her wrist. The detectives can hear the clacking of a secretary's typewriter and the World Series game blaring from a television.

"Can I see Sasha?" she asks, referring to Gabay.

"Sasha can't help you," McCartin says. "You need *our* help. You're a young girl. You don't need to be involved in this."

"This is the most important thing that's happened to you in your entire life," Knolls says.

"Can I have a smoke?" she asks.

"No," McCartin barks. "We need this right now."

She clenches her fists and rests her chin on them.

"We know you didn't come here for this to happen," Knolls says.

"You came here for a better life," McCartin says. "You tell us what happened and you can have your smoke."

"Can I see Sasha?"

"It's too late," McCartin says. "He can't help you."

"I just want to see him. . . ."

Employing a tactic he learned investigating gang murders in South-Central, McCartin slaps a picture of Luda on the table and shouts: "You killed this girl!"

She pushes the photo away, but McCartin moves it right back. She hangs her head and pleads, "I want to see Sasha."

"What happened, Oxana?" McCartin murmurs. "We know you want to tell us."

"If we allow you to see him, will you tell us the truth?" Knolls asks.

"Maybe." She refuses to answer any more questions until she sees Gabay.

Knolls is exasperated. He turns to Krumer and asks, "Does she want to *talk* to him or just *see* him?"

"She doesn't believe he's here," Krumer says. "She says she just wants to see him. . . . She says she'll talk to us after she sees him."

The detectives confer in the squad room. "She's a tough friggin' cookie," McCartin says. "I don't know if we should let her see him."

Another detective, who has followed the discussion, says, "She's trying to control the interview."

Knolls asks Krumer, "What's your spin?"

"I think he'll crack before her."

They escort Gabay back into the interview room. "We talked to Oxana," McCartin says. "She gave us a lot of information. She's scared."

"Of course she's scared," he says angrily.

"So the last time you saw Luda was at that party in July?"

"Yes," he says.

"You know, Oxana gave us a lot of information," McCartin says.

"We need your side. What happened on the day of the murder at Luda's apartment?"

Gabay grips the side of his chair and jolts forward. "What?"

McCartin spreads out the photographs again. "We have video of you going in and out of that apartment on the day of the murder."

Gabay strokes his chin.

"What happened that day?" McCartin asks.

Gabay gulps his coffee and says, "We just had to pick up some of Oxana's stuff."

"Tell us the sequence of events," Knolls interjects, deciding to double-team Gabay.

"We just picked up some clothes and shoes and left."

"Did you wake her up?" Knolls asks.

"No. We quickly talked to her and left."

"When you went in there, did you sit on the couch?" Knolls asks.

"No. We just came in. Oxana talked to her and got some stuff and left. They talk: 'Hi, hi. 'Bye, 'bye.' That's it."

McCartin fixes him with a withering stare. "After you talked to her, she ends up dead. How did that happen?"

Gabay tugs on his index finger. "I don't know. . . ."

"We had someone tell us you were crying in your beer because you left Luda's child without a mother."

"I didn't do it," Gabay says angrily. "That's the bottom line."

"We have a video of you there," McCartin says. "We have neighbors see you going in there. We have the coroner telling us you were in there at the time she died."

Gabay grips the edge of the table. "Oxana and I came there. We talk about, 'How's this, how's that.' We left. She closed the door behind us."

"That's not what happened," McCartin says. "You want to take a poly?"

"No."

"That's because you're lying," McCartin says.

"You were trying to protect Oxana from white slavery," Knolls says.

"They wanted her as a prostitute," McCartin says.

"No, that's not it," Gabay says.

"Oxana was being threatened," Knolls says. "If you were trying to protect Oxana . . . I need to know it."

"Tell us what happened," McCartin says. "Did Luda pull a gun on you?"

"I didn't do it. I didn't kill her, and that's the final line."

"When you go to prison," McCartin says, "*that* will be the final line. . . . You pulled the trigger and killed that girl."

"Oh my God!" Gabay cries, his face flushing. "I did not."

"What do you think Oxana told us?" McCartin asks.

"I don't know and I don't care."

"You don't care if she laid you out?" McCartin asks.

Gabay stares at them, eyes smoldering.

The detectives handcuff him in the squad room and take him down to the first floor and into a stuffy holding cell. They slip off his belt and shoelaces and pat him down.

Staring straight ahead, Gabay mutters, "If that's the way you want to play it."

"We're not playing it," Knolls says.

"You're trying to pin it on somebody!" Gabay shouts.

Back in the squad room, the detectives decide there is only one way to break Oxana. They escort her to the hallway outside Gabay's holding cell where the two exchange a sad, lingering glance. Oxana steps toward Gabay and appears as if she is about to speak to him, but McCartin quickly leads her down the hallway. While Knolls finishes booking Gabay, McCartin accompanies Oxana back to the interview cubicle.

He tells her, as Krumer translates, that Gabay has confessed and implicated her. "He said enough for us to book you, too," McCartin says. "Tell us what happened. Then we will have your side."

Krumer points to McCartin and says confidentially, "He's giving you the opportunity to say something for yourself."

She mutters a few unintelligible words. "Let me smoke and I will talk."

McCartin nods.

After lighting a cigarette, she says, "It's not easy."

"I know it's not easy," McCartin murmurs. "Just tell us what happened."

The night before Luda's death, she called Oxana and said she had to tell her something. "I told her to say it over the phone," Oxana says, sounding as if she is improvising. She says that Luda demanded to see her. When Oxana and Gabay slipped into the building, the door to Luda's apartment was open. Oxana spotted Luda's body on the floor of the bedroom. She was already dead. Oxana insists she does not know who killed her. She then takes a few quick drags of her cigarette, squinting as a cloud of smoke hangs under the fluorescent lights.

McCartin knows she is lying. Gabay told them Luda was alive when they left the apartment. Oxana contends she was dead. McCartin does not chastise Oxana, but says in a soothing tone, "We appreciate you telling us a little of what happened. But we need the truth."

She taps her cigarette butt on the side of her cup until it is extinguished.

"You've come this far," McCartin says softly. "We need the whole truth."

She cradles her head in her palms.

"You just have to go that extra step," he says, gazing at her sympathetically.

She covers her eyes.

"It's always tough, Oxana, but you just have to go that extra step." McCartin holds his thumb and forefinger an inch apart. "You're this close. Let's go all the way."

She asks to see Gabay again.

After she tells him the entire story, McCartin says, he will allow her to sit with Gabay and chat with him.

She folds her arm on the table and lowers her head. For several minutes the room is silent.

Finally, McCartin asks, "So what happened? Was there an argument, a fight?"

Slowly lifting her head, she emits a long sigh, as if relinquishing all resistance. Nodding weakly, Oxana says she will tell them what happened at the apartment.

She asked Luda for the number of one of the girls smuggled into the country with her. Oxana had heard that the girl had become addicted to drugs and that her pimp beat her up. She was worried. She just wanted the number, but Luda laughed at her and said, "Find it yourself."

Krumer quickly follows up. "Then what happened? Sasha wanted to help? He began yelling at her to give the number?"

She nods. While Gabay waited in the living room, she and Luda argued in the bedroom. Then Gabay stormed in. "Luda was baiting us," Oxana cries, "making fun, saying mean things. . . . We were all arguing. . . ."

"What happened in the bedroom?" McCartin asks in a hushed tone.

Oxana stares into space. After McCartin studies her quietly for several minutes, he says, "Someone hit someone. Sasha got angry and hit her. What happened?"

Oxana throws an angry punch in the air. "He hit her one time and she fell," she says in a monotone.

"Did he hit her with his fist? Or did he have something in his hand?"

"He didn't have anything in his hand. . . . After she fell, I left the room because I couldn't bear to watch. . . . Then we left."

"What else happened? We're *this* close." McCartin leans toward Oxana, nodding compassionately. "Let's finish it. . . . You know what happened. It's too late to lie. . . ."

"I heard one sound," she says, her eyes glazed. "Like a door being slammed real hard."

"Could it have been a gun?"

"I don't know exactly what a gunshot sounds like."

"Did *you* hit her with anything?"

"No . . . I peeked into the bedroom for a second. . . . She was on the floor . . . on her back."

"What did he say about what happened?" McCartin asks. "Was he upset?"

"Of course he was upset," she says angrily. "He said it happened foolishly. . . . It was not supposed to happen like that. . . . He has a kind heart. . . . Do you promise I'll be able to see him again?" she sobs.

He nods. But before McCartin ends the interview, he wants to know about the marks on Luda's face and neck. "We know he's a metal worker," McCartin tells Oxana. "We know he makes things. Have you ever seen him carry any metal pieces as protection, like a key chain or anything metallic?"

"No," she says. "He makes sculpture. He makes beautiful things."

A few minutes later McCartin ushers a handcuffed Gabay from the jail to the interview room. They kiss and Oxana asks whether Gabay can smoke. Krumer gives him a cigarette.

McCartin and Knolls chat in the hallway. "I think the reason Oxana wanted to see him so bad," McCartin says, "is because she knows she may *never* see him again."

McCartin knows that later he is going to search the warehouse, so he asks Gabay, "Do your pit bulls bite?"

"They will if I'm not there," Gabay says.

"We're getting animal control to deal with them," McCartin says.

"Don't hurt them," Gabay says.

"That's why we have animal control. If it was just us, we'd shoot 'em," he jokes.

Gabay glares at McCartin. "Do you always have that KGB personality?"

"I've got nothing to do with the KGB," McCartin says, looking amused. "I'm Irish."

At 10:30 P.M., the detectives strut out of Parker Center, elated. McCartin is in a particularly good mood. Knolls has given him so much grief about his manner with suspects, but tonight with Oxana, he showed that he can shift his style to suit the circumstances. Krumer tells him that his interview was a virtuoso performance.

"With some people, you gotta get in their face," McCartin says. "With others, you gotta be sympathetic."

McCartin and Knolls thank Krumer for his contributions and tell him he aided the investigation immensely. But, they add, the night is not over. They still have to transport Oxana to the Seventy-seventh Street Division in South-Central, which houses the nearest women's jail. The desert winds have died down and the heat has dissipated. Mist cloaks the downtown skyline. A cool breeze blows in from the ocean. A typical fall night in Los Angeles.

They drive to the station in silence, guide Oxana through the jail, and hand her over to the booking officer. The cells are filled with black and Hispanic crackheads and hookers, scooped up during the night's vice sweep. Oxana, a blond, blue-eyed white girl, is a novelty.

"What's she in for?" the booking officer asks.

"Murder," Knolls says.

"Ooh," the officer says, jerking her head back in surprise. "She looks so, so"—she struggles for the right word—"so *nice.*"

Speeding north through the deserted city streets at midnight, the detectives explain to Krumer that Oxana was booked for murder because she might be a coconspirator or an accessory. They may believe some of her story, but do not buy the idea that she and Gabay visited Luda just to obtain a phone number. The detectives suspect that they stopped by to intimidate Luda at the very least, to persuade her to forget about the money Oxana owed. The detectives anticipate that Oxana's attorney will get her a deal to testify against Gabay, and, they speculate, he might eventually turn on her and claim she actually fired the gun.

"We'll let the DA sort it out," Knolls says.

They cruise by the downtown flower district, passing a vendor stacking sheafs of bloodred roses on the sidewalk. As McCartin heads west, past the produce district, glaring lights above warehouses illuminate men unloading crates of lettuce and oranges from the backs of trucks. When they pull up in front of Gabay's place, they are happy to see two animal control officers waiting for them. Armed with long poles with loops on the end, they tentatively enter the warehouse as the detectives observe. When the pit bulls charge them, the officers deftly slip the loops over their necks and guide them into the back of their truck.

Knolls and McCartin are soon joined by Lieutenant Farrell—who is on call tonight—and several other detectives, who help search the warehouse. Although Gabay described his living quarters as a loft, the place is just a dim, windowless warehouse with a small stove, refrigerator, and dining table in front. In the back is a wooden platform with a bed and dresser. Gabay's sculpture workshop, flanked by an oxygen tank and drill press, is set up by the front door. The oppressive smell of unwashed dogs pervades the warehouse. Gabay is not much of a housekeeper. The dining table is strewn with newspapers, bottles, plates, and Coke cans. Shirts and pants cascade out of dresser drawers and hampers, and dirty clothes obscure the unmade bed.

The detectives find a nine-millimeter pistol on the bed, under a pillow. The murder weapon, however, was a .45. Later they spot a box of .45 ammunition and two empty .45 semiautomatic magazines. At the end of the warehouse, a thick slab of wood speckled with holes attracts their attention. Gabay must have used it for target practice. The detectives will transport the wood to the ballistics unit so technicians can dig for a .45 slug they can link to the murder weapon.

"We have a problem here," Farrell shouts. "He couldn't have done it!" He points to a shelf near Gabay's bed. In a small wooden frame is a picture of a cat. "Anyone who likes his cat *this* much couldn't be a killer," says Farrell, who lovingly nursed his twenty-one-year-old cat, Napoleon, in the pet's declining years.

The detectives cart off boxes of ammunition, a shotgun, a few other weapons, and all of Gabay's shoes and boots to test for Luda's blood. Seeing Gabay's heavy bag and workout equipment, they figure he is a kick boxer and examine the soles of his boots. There is the distinct possibility that Gabay could have slashed Luda's face and neck with a few jarring kicks.

Shortly before dawn, Knolls, McCartin, and Krumer linger in front of the warehouse in the mist, which has thickened since they arrived. The downtown skyline is almost completely obscured now, the lights glowing dimly through a scrim of fog. An open-bed produce truck grinds to a halt at a nearby warehouse, and the pungent smell of onions wafts down the street.

"What's next?" Krumer asks.

"We go to the DA and present the case."

"Any chance they won't file against Gabay?"

McCartin sniffs the air and grimaces. "Any time you have a witness who is also a suspect, there's a chance."

The next morning, Knolls and McCartin are the focus of attention. Detectives flash them thumbs-up signs, or shake their hands, or kid them that their murder was a "self-solver." Rick Jackson, who has spent the past few days studying poisons, jokes that since his killer is Japanese and theirs is Russian, they can solve the two countries' intractable dispute over the Kuril Islands, which border the two countries.

"Let's let Gabay and Taga in here and let them fight it out," Jackson says. "The winner's country gets undisputed ownership."

Jackson minored in geography in college and his joke might be a bit abstruse for the squad room. McCartin and Knolls flash him perplexed looks.

Later, at the district attorney's Van Nuys office, they prepare to file the case.

"This is more interesting than your usual drive-by with Flaco and Spanky as your suspects," Knolls tells a deputy district attorney who listens avidly.

"I like it," she says. "You're right. It's a sexy one." She agrees without hesitation to file murder charges against Gabay and Oxana.

There is no time for a celebratory lunch—the detectives still have to write the arrest report and complete stacks of paperwork—so they stop by Cupid's, a Valley hot dog stand where Knolls hung out as a teenager. After finishing their chili dogs and Cokes, they bask in the hazy sunshine. Krumer is in a bittersweet mood. He is thrilled at having had the chance to investigate such an interesting case and learn so much from two experienced homicide detectives, but he is not looking forward to returning to night shift patrol. Knolls and McCartin appreciate having been allowed to spend the past two months working solely on one case. While other detectives were frequently called out in the middle of the night to investigate officer-involved shootings, Knolls and McCartin have remained exempt. Now it is back to the on-call roster.

"I'm not looking forward to that next OIS call," Knolls grouses.

"Neither am I," McCartin says. "But I'm not going to worry about that now."

The detectives have had little time recently with their families. Tomorrow, McCartin says, he will ask for a day off and take his two children to an amusement park. He imitates a popular commercial that features winning Super Bowl quarterbacks plugging Disney World.

McCartin stands up and says, "I'm going to Legoland."

Part III

WEST L.A.

10

A few weeks after the district attorney filed two murder charges against Kazumi Taga, Rick Jackson spends an afternoon in the city archives, researching an old homicide. Flipping through a cardboard box, he discovers a dozen misfiled folders from another antiquated case. Jackson recognizes the name of the victim—Stephanie Gorman—and recalls that he recently overheard an RHD detective discussing the case.

He flips on his cell phone, calls Detective Dave Lambkin and tells him he has found some of the missing Gorman files. Lambkin is exultant. Investigating a cold case is always daunting and unusually bad luck and LAPD incompetence have dogged Lambkin since he reopened the Gorman investigation a few months ago. He is far from the superstitious type, but he tells Jackson that his discovery of the missing files may be a propitious sign.

Cheryl Gorman, Stephanie's sister, first approached the LAPD in the mid-1990s. She called a homicide detective in the West Los Angeles Division and told him that her sixteen-year-old sister had been murdered in 1965. Cheryl, nineteen at the time of the crime, had spent the intervening years attempting to expunge the murder from her memory. Now she finally felt strong enough to confront the truth. She wanted to know why her sister had been murdered and what the investigation had uncovered before it was abandoned. Cheryl knew that detectives had many new scientific tools at their disposal. Maybe they could now find the killer.

The West L.A. detective was brusque. "This is too old a case," he said, sounding impatient and inconvenienced. "The files have been destroyed." Discouraged, she abandoned her quest. But five years later, she summoned up the courage to try again. Fortunately, she knew a woman who was dating Mike Mejia, an RHD detective, and after Cheryl told him her story, he searched the city archives and discovered that the Gorman files had not been destroyed. He exhumed a box of documents compiled by the original detectives and, from the reports, concluded that the case had never been cleared. Mejia was well aware that many cold cases across the country had been solved because of advances in DNA technology and automated fingerprint systems. He believed—and his supervisor concurred—that the Gorman murder should be reopened. But because the case was so old and so complex, Mejia realized that a sexual assault specialist was needed.

Rape Special is located in a narrow anteroom adjacent to the Homicide Special squad room. A thin wall, connected by an open passageway, divides the two units. The single window at Rape Special is covered with a ragged brown drape, and mismatched desks and a few metal filing cabinets line the galley office.

Every sexual assault–murder in the city is investigated by Rape Special. Divisional detectives no longer handle these cases because so many rapists roam the city, crossing jurisdictions. The most effective way to pursue these predators, RHD officials decided, was to form a centralized unit to investigate sexual assault–homicides, serial rapes, and rapes involving high-profile victims.

Dave Lambkin, the supervising detective of Rape Special's downtown unit, has investigated more than a thousand sexual assaults and many homicides. He teaches LAPD investigators the nuances of sex crimes at the department's detective school, lectures throughout the state, and advises many agencies, including the FBI. Mejia is convinced that no one in the LAPD knows more about sex crimes than Lambkin. So in March 2000, Mejia presented the Gorman case to him.

Fascinated, Lambkin immediately concluded that DNA was the key to solving the murder. But Mejia delivered distressing news: all of the evidence that might have connected the killer to the crime through DNA was gone.

An LAPD computer periodically generates "disposition cards" for all criminal cases. Depending on the crime, detective supervisors can, because of space limitations, authorize the destruction of evidence if a case has been cleared. The evidence connected to a homicide—particularly an unsolved homicide—is *never* to be destroyed. But in 1989, after scanning the Gorman disposition card, a detective supervisor in Van Nuys mistakenly authorized the destruction of the evidence. Mejia told Lambkin that he had questioned the supervisor, who could not remember the case and was now retired. No disciplinary action against him was possible.

What was less important, but still distressing, was that a number of critical files were missing, too. Some evidence remained, however, Mejia assured Lambkin, including a number of fingerprints that were lifted at the scene and never identified. (At the time of Stephanie's murder, detectives had to "manually" compare fingerprints with those found at a crime scene. Today detectives looking for a match can enter anonymous fingerprints into automated identification systems, whose databases include the fingerprints of millions of felons.)

Lambkin was enraged that the evidence had been destroyed. He felt sure that with a scintilla of DNA he could solve the murder, because the killer fit the profile of a repeat offender. But fingerprints are dicey. A suspect cannot equivocate about why his semen or hair remains on a victim, but there are many innocent explanations for the presence of fingerprints at a crime scene. Houses are filled with smudges from multifarious people, including repairman, furniture movers, family friends, and, sometimes, previous tenants. Even if Lambkin matched an unidentified print and managed to track down the person, he knew it would be difficult to prove when the print was left at the scene.

But Lambkin did not want to abandon the case. Something about the murder troubled him—perhaps Stephanie Gorman's innocence, or the brutality of the attack, or his conviction that the perpetrator should be punished. He picked up four boxes of files from Mejia, arrayed them around his desk, and began to read. This murder, he had decided, would be the greatest challenge of his career.

Dave Lambkin does not have the mien, the manner, or the background of a typical cop. In the small Wisconsin town where he attended high school, he was considered alienated and rebellious. He had shoulder-length hair, played guitar in a rock band, and rode a 1953 hard-tailed Harley-Davidson chopper.

At the University of Wisconsin–Stephens Point, Lambkin majored in political science and theater. Passionate about plays, he enrolled in acting, dance, and ballet classes. During a semester abroad in England, Lambkin grew enthralled with punk rock (which he still enjoys listening to in the squad room, to the horror of other detectives). He also enrolled in a photography class at the Tate Gallery. At the end of his semester abroad, Lambkin believed he had found his life's work: fashion photography. The field seemed glamorous and he believed it would allow him artistic freedom. After finishing college, he moved to Los Angeles and enrolled at Art Center College of Design. By the end of his second semester, however, he had grown disillusioned. Photography lost its allure when he studied it intensively. And the chance of succeeding in such a competitive field, he decided, was minimal. So he dropped out of art school.

At the time, Lambkin lived with his sister and her husband, an LAPD officer. Police work seemed interesting, the pay was decent, and the hours were flexible enough to allow him to pursue his many outside interests. But Lambkin knew his personality and his background were quite different from those of most of his brother-in-law's friends. While he contemplated police work, he enrolled in a criminal justice graduate program at California State University, Los Angeles. One of his professors was a retired FBI agent who was also one of the nation's leading sex crimes investigators. Lambkin was fascinated by the agent's cases because they were so varied, so complex. When he discovered that the majority of all serial murder cases were sexually motivated, he was even more enthralled. Lambkin decided that he would join the LAPD, get promoted to detective as soon as possible, specialize in sexual assaults, and work in Hollywood, which had the most diverse cases in the city.

In 1978, Lambkin entered the LAPD academy; he made detective four and a half years later, a meteoric rise. In the mid-1980s, he was promoted to the sex crimes unit at the Hollywood Division station. Lambkin, who frequently attended seminars and read widely on the subject, soon became known as an expert. He joined advisory boards for victims' advocacy groups, trained counselors at rape crisis centers, and advised the state Department of Justice on investigative procedures.

At most police stations, rape victims are questioned in the same bare, sterile interview rooms where suspects are interrogated. In Hollywood, Lambkin consulted with the department psychologist, who advised him on color scheme and design, and then he spent a few weekends and about $350 of his own money transforming one of the interview rooms into a setting where the victims would feel more at ease. Lambkin covered the walls with designer paneling, hung soothing pictures, painted the doors and baseboards powder blue, and installed blue-gray carpeting. Instead of a sofa, Lambkin acquired white uphol-stered chairs with casters so victims could control how far they sat from detectives. The Los Angeles Commission on Assaults Against Women named him its Humanitarian of the Year in 1989.

After almost seven years in Hollywood, however, Lambkin ended up leaving the sex crimes unit. He was depressed, disillusioned, and burned out. Frustrated by the size of his workload and the lack of resources, he joined the Hollywood homicide unit, which had many more detectives. From 1991 to 1996, he compiled a legendary inves-tigative record: a 100 percent clearance rate. Actually, there were a few murders Lambkin did not clear, but he had also solved a handful of old cases that had been gathering dust on the shelves, so he was awarded the perfect clearance rate.

For a year, Lambkin supervised the unit, and then, in 1998, he transferred to Rape Special, where he was named supervising detec-tive. Because he is bald, stocky, sharp-featured, and eccentric, some of the other detectives call him Uncle Fester. But they respect his intellect and investigative skills, so the kidding is good-natured. While many in the squad room are avid hunters, Lambkin is a vegetarian. He is not fond of children, but is devoted to his two dogs. He and his wife live in the city, in a fashionable hillside house. He has eclectic interests, including blues guitar, architecture, film, and wine collecting. At a Beverly Hills wine shop he stores more than a hundred vintage Burgundies. He subscribes to several cooking and architecture maga-zines and has collected more than a thousand blues and rock CDs. A film buff, Lambkin seems to see almost every movie released, no matter how obscure, and spends his weekends cooking gourmet meals and going to small blues clubs.

When Lambkin was working Hollywood Homicide, he noticed a gang officer by the name of Tim Marcia at a number of crime scenes. Marcia's astute observations and enthusiasm impressed Lambkin. Young cops are often intimidated at homicides and lurk in the shad-ows. Lambkin noticed that Marcia was aggressive, displayed initiative, and frequently gave the homicide detectives valuable information. When Marcia was named Officer of the Year in Hollywood, Lambkin considered the honor well deserved.

Years later, after Marcia had been promoted to detective in the

Hollywood sex crimes unit, he briefly worked on a case that was transferred to RHD. Lambkin ensured that Marcia never returned to Hollywood. They are now partners.

Marcia, who is thirty-six, and Lambkin, forty-seven, are a study in opposites. A former college baseball player, Marcia wears a crew cut and a neatly trimmed mustache and lives in a distant suburb. He has two children and coaches his son's baseball team.

Many police officers enter the academy idealistic, but during their years on the street turn cynical. Marcia, however, has retained an almost ingenuous optimism and enthusiasm for the job.

He grew up in a large, Catholic family in West Los Angeles. When he was seven years old, his Indian Guide troop visited an LAPD station, where the boys toured the facility and were shown an episode of *Adam-12*. Marcia vowed to his best friend that he would be a policeman one day. The next week they visited a fire station. The friend told Marcia he wanted to be a fireman. Thirteen years later he joined the fire department and Marcia entered the LAPD academy.

He was raised in a religious home where his parents emphasized that the essence of Catholicism is to serve people and society. Police work, Marcia believed, was his path for helping others. A family friend, an LAPD sergeant, once told Marcia, "The police are the closest form of government most citizens will ever encounter." During his years as a patrolman, Marcia tried to remember his responsibility. But years later, after the shame of the Rodney King beating and the Rampart corruption scandal, Marcia was frequently hurt when people assumed he was corrupt or brutal simply because he was an LAPD officer.

Marcia recently investigated the rape of a black woman who distrusted the LAPD. When she stopped by the station one afternoon, she asked Marcia why the composite drawing of the suspect in her case was posted above his desk. He told her that the drawing was a daily motivator, a reminder to solve this case.

She wrote a letter to Marcia's supervisor: "I want you to know from the beginning that the detectives . . . on the scene that morning have treated me with the utmost respect and concern. . . . Detective Marcia (and the other investigators) have made me confident that the person, will, in time, be apprehended. . . . I truly believe that they want to help me bring that person to justice."

A year after the rape, Marcia and his partners arrested the suspect, who was convicted.

Unlike Lambkin, who distances himself from his work with his many interests and enthusiasms, Marcia cannot forget a case at night. He often brings files home with him, and hunkers down in the family room and writes reports, listens to interview tapes, and scans the Internet for research material. His wife recently established a house rule: *No crime scene photos in the family room.*

While the two detectives have disparate interests and backgrounds, they have been compatible partners for more than two years and are considered a highly effective team. When Marcia heard about the Gorman case, he agreed with Lambkin. This homicide, he told his partner, is a career case.

Stephanie Gorman was a most unlikely murder victim. An A student, she had just been voted junior class vice president at Hamilton High School in West Los Angeles. Her father, Edward, always told her that with her intelligence, looks, and savvy, she could be America's first female president. The Gormans lived on Hillsboro Avenue in Beverlywood, an upper-middle-class West L.A. neighborhood. Edward was a prominent attorney, the president of an L.A. County lawyers association; he eventually became a Superior Court judge. Her mother, Julie, spent her days at a nearby country club, playing tennis and bridge. Her sister, Cheryl, attended UCLA.

Stephanie had spent the morning of August 5, 1965, attending summer classes at Hamilton, about a mile south of her house. After school, at 12:30 P.M., a girlfriend dropped her off by the back gate. Five and a half hours later, Edward and Cheryl—she worked in their father's law office during the summer—returned home. Their lives would never be the same.

The original Homicide Investigation Report described the scene:

> *Cheryl went into her room and discovered . . . Stephanie, in a hunched-down position at the foot of a twin bed. . . . There was a quantity of blood visible on her semi-nude body. Cheryl ran from the room and notified her father. Mr. Gorman entered the room and lifted Stephanie from the floor and placed her on the bed. He then covered her nearly nude body with a quilt and bits of clothing he gathered from the closet. Stephanie Gorman was dead when discovered by her family. . . .*
>
> *There was no evidence of a forced entry. The back doors of the*

house were unlatched, as a general practice, when any member of the household was at home. . . . There was no evidence of ransacking, and a thorough search of the house by the family members indicated that nothing was missing. . . .

After school that day, the detectives deduced,

Stephanie Gorman went to her bedroom, put her school books and purse on the book shelf. She then went into the kitchen and had something to eat, probably cookies and milk. . . .

It is evident that the suspect entered the house with a [handgun] and a quantity of chalk line [rope] with the intent to have sexual activity with some person inside the house. The crime occurred . . . probably prior to 3 p.m. . . . It is possible that he had designs against Cheryl, Stephanie's older sister. Both girls wore the same clothes and were similar in appearance. . . .

The existing evidence indicates that the suspect hit the victim in the mouth. . . . Both her upper and lower lips bore deep lacerations caused by pressure on her teeth. . . . It is believed that the victim was then dragged or carried into Cheryl's bedroom. Brush burns on the right hip and slight abrasions to the left elbow indicate that at some time the victim was dragged across a surface, probably a rug.

Victim was probably unconscious or at least helpless from the blow to the mouth. . . . It is believed that the assailant rendered the victim helpless, tied her to the bed, stripped her lower body, threw the clothes on the floor. . . . It is the opinion of the autopsy surgeon that the victim had been raped. . . .

It is evident that the victim struggled violently against her bonds. Deep indented marks on both wrists attested to the pressure put against them. Evidently, her struggles broke the chalk line. . . . The other end of the line was still attached to the bed leg. It then appears that she got off the foot of the bed. . . . At this time she was shot. . . . It can be assumed that the suspect . . . walked out of the house through the sliding door into the den and out onto the patio . . . then proceeded out onto Sawyer Street by way of the back gate. . . .

The aforementioned sequence of events is a logical reenactment of the crime by the investigating officers, based on evidence and knowledge of the personal habits of the victim and her household.

In the middle of that afternoon, a neighbor heard a girl scream at the Gormans' house. She later told police that she thought Stephanie and her sister had been playing. Only one witness was listed in the 1965 homicide report:

Between 1 p.m. and 2 p.m., George Iwasaki, a Japanese gardener ... parked his truck just north of the Gorman residence. As he got out of his truck, he observed a ... person who appeared to be looking into the bedroom window. Iwasaki described the suspect as follows: male Caucasian, Latin type, 43 to 45 years, 5-7, 140 pounds, sallow cheeks, unshaved, unkempt hair. He was wearing uniform type cotton twill shirt and trousers. ... Clothing ... was light blue in color. ... The location where the suspect was observed is between the houses and it would appear to be highly irregular for any person on legitimate business to be there. ... The suspect gave him a menacing look. ...

Lambkin and Marcia spent weeks perusing the dusty files, studying clues, the autopsy report, suspect lists, ballistics data, and summaries of interviews. Lambkin concluded that the original investigation had been meticulous and exhaustive. Stephanie was killed during an era when the murder of a young girl in Los Angeles still shocked people, when detectives had the time and resources to investigate cases thoroughly. Less than a week after the murder, however, the Watts riots erupted. Lambkin and Marcia suspect that the riots derailed the investigation during its first, crucial weeks. Still, the LAPD, which had transferred the case from West L.A. to the downtown homicide unit, did establish a task force of about twenty-five detectives and police officers.

George Iwasaki, the gardener, worked with a police artist who sketched a composite portrait of the suspect, which was circulated across the country. More than a hundred people were interviewed. Detectives questioned students whom Cheryl had dated, friends of Stephanie's, neighbors, teachers, school counselors, members of the Gormans' country club, relatives, appliance repairmen, and even the boys who sold candy door-to-door in the neighborhood. The Gorman task force checked the record of every student at Hamilton High School and discovered that about 250 boys had been arrested—for crimes including indecent exposure, masturbating in front of children, peeping into windows, burglary, car theft, and petty theft. Each student who had been arrested was questioned and several were given polygraph examinations. More than sixty lewd-phone-call reports in the city were investigated in the hopes that detectives could establish a link to the Gorman murder. Detectives compared the fingerprints of about a thousand sex offenders to those lifted at the crime scene. Even the fingerprints of the mass murderer Richard Speck, who killed eight student nurses on a single night in 1966, were eventually obtained for comparison.

The original murder books chronicle dozens of pages of clues and tips that the original detectives investigated:

> *Mr. Lockwood stopped in a bar on the morning of August 6, 1965. A person . . . at the bar . . . made the following statements: "You will read all about the murder in the morning paper. My time is running out. Everybody thinks I'm a clown." The person then left by taxi.*

> *Miss Fitzgerald called and said in Jan. 1965 . . . a gas man came to her residence and made several attempts to rape her. . . . She thinks this man is worth checking out for the Stephanie Gorman homicide.*

Two days after the murder, an anonymous caller told a *Los Angeles Times* phone operator: "Did you do a story on Stephanie Gorman? I'm Bill Lancaster and I know what happened that night." The caller was disconnected as the operator transferred him to an editor on the city desk. The detectives tracked down every Bill or William Lancaster in Los Angeles, including the son of the actor Burt Lancaster. But after extensive questioning, the investigators determined that none of the men were connected to the crime.

The task force detectives also investigated a man, Michael Goldsmith,* who had graduated from Hamilton High School a few years earlier.

The day after Stephanie was killed, Goldsmith had told West Los Angeles detectives that on the afternoon of the murder he had stopped by the Gormans' to visit a friend whose family had previously lived in the house. Goldsmith claimed he was not aware at the time that his friend's family had sold it to the Gormans.

* This is a pseudonym.

The detectives later discovered that Goldsmith's friend had not lived in the house for four years. "Officers felt that possibly the telephone call was made to cover up the fact that his car could have been seen at the Gorman residence at the time of the crime," they wrote.

During an interview, Goldsmith told investigators, "I went to the home sometime in the afternoon. I believe that it was about 2 or 3 P.M. I remember that I was out of work and I went to that house after I had gone to the employment agency. . . . I pulled into the driveway and honked the horn. No one came out, so I left. I thought I saw someone peeking out of the window. I called police because I thought I might have some information that might help them."

The detectives interviewed Goldsmith's friend, who said his family had sold the house on Hillsboro Avenue to the Gormans in 1961, moved to a house nearby, and then . . . moved again. "Yes," he told detectives, "he [Goldsmith] knew where I lived. After we moved from Hillsboro, he had my address and telephone number because he came to both addresses. . . . I know that he knew where I lived before 1965."

After investigating Goldsmith's background, the detectives discovered that when he was a juvenile he was arrested for a "lewd or lascivious act with a child under the age of fourteen." They asked him to take a polygraph exam, but he "flatly refused," the detectives wrote. He then called back and agreed to take the test. But a few minutes before the scheduled appointment, he called back again and canceled.

The detectives wrote, "The suspect's mother and brother were contacted prior to interviewing [Goldsmith] and his brother stated, 'I don't know why you want to talk to him. He told me that he was at the Gorman house two hours before it happened.' " A detective scrawled three question marks beside this statement.

In June 1966, Goldsmith was arrested for the murder. He agreed to take a polygraph exam, which he passed. During a lineup, the gardener was unable to identify him, and his fingerprints did not match those at the scene. "Further investigation failed to reveal any new evidence against this suspect," the detectives wrote. "At this time the suspect was released."

Lambkin and Marcia did not believe it significant that Goldsmith had passed the polygraph because the equipment during the mid-1960s was relatively primitive. Also, the killer could have worn gloves and not left fingerprints at the scene. Lambkin and Marcia were distressed because they knew that had the DNA evidence not been destroyed, they might have been able to determine in an instant whether Goldsmith was Stephanie's killer. Now, even if they re-interviewed him, they had no way to connect him to the crime—no leverage, no way to force a confession.

So, in the fall of 2000, Lambkin and Marcia returned to the evidence that remained and to their files, retracing the original detectives' investigation. The files were a jumble, and a number of folders were missing entirely. Lambkin spent days photocopying hundreds of pages and then reorganized the entire record. But he and Marcia could work on the case only in their spare time: they were assigned a spate of sexual assaults in the fall.

After Lambkin had thoroughly familiarized himself with the case, he turned his attention to the best evidence that remained: the fingerprints. Several fingerprints lifted at the crime scene had never been identified. When Lambkin submitted them to LAPD technicians, he was informed that there were no "hits." But feeding old prints into the new automated system can be tricky. The technology has since improved, but in 2000, a technician had to trace photographs and manually feed them into the computer. Sometimes the process had to be repeated, so Lambkin asked a technician he trusted to do it again.

A few days later, he arrived at the station in the late afternoon after spending all day on another case. On his desk he spotted a note from a Homicide Special detective: "They got a hit on your case." Lambkin was elated—and desperate to learn the suspect's name—but he could not reach the detective, and all the fingerprint technicians had already left. So he called his partner and his lieutenant at home and delivered the good news. That night, he and his wife dined at an elegant Italian restaurant to celebrate. The next morning, he leaped out of bed, sped to work, and immediately called the fingerprint technician. "Didn't the detective tell you?" she asked. "The hit we got was on a police officer who was at the scene."

The detective's note had been a practical joke. Lambkin was not amused; without a fingerprint match, the odds were negligible that he would ever solve the murder. He tried a statewide automated fingerprint identification system, without success. Finally, he sent the prints to a system that scans the western United States. Again, no hits.

There was only one option remaining: the FBI's new state-of-the-art computerized system had almost 50 million fingerprints on file. Lambkin mailed the crime scene fingerprints to Washington. After six weeks he still had not heard from the FBI, so he called an agency analyst.

"I don't know if the prints I sent were ever processed," Lambkin said. "You got any good news?"

"Well," the analyst said, "I do have a hit for you."

A fingerprint belonging to a man named Vincent Rossi* had been lifted from the doorway leading to the bedroom where Stephanie was killed. Lambkin told himself to stay calm, to temper his enthusiasm. First, he quickly determined that Rossi was not a policeman. Then he checked the field interview cards filled out by patrol officers, which name everyone present at a crime scene. Rossi was not listed. Lambkin wanted to know whether there was any legitimate reason for Rossi to visit the Gormans' house. After studying the voluminous files and checking the name of every person questioned, every suspect investigated, every friend and family member, Lambkin still could not find Vincent Rossi's name.

Next, Lambkin and Marcia devoted themselves to learning everything they could about their suspect without tipping him off. Searching Rossi's criminal history, they discovered that in 1971 he had been arrested for burglary and pleaded guilty to receiving stolen property. But there was something else interesting: in the early 1990s, a young relative had accused him of a sexual impropriety, although the case was never prosecuted. Lambkin had hoped Rossi's record would be more extensive—and violent—but was still encouraged, because many rapists have criminal histories that include burglary as well as sexual offenses. The detectives then checked gun records in the hopes that Rossi had once owned a pistol of the same caliber that killed Stephanie Gorman. The gun check, however, was negative.

Lambkin and Marcia were startled by Rossi's driver's license photograph, which bore a strong resemblance to the composite portrait of the suspect. Rossi, in his sixties now, was heavier and a bit more jowly than the drawing, but his features appeared quite similar. Swarthy and Italian, he fit the general description—"male Caucasian, Latin type"—that the gardener provided. The momentum was building.

The detectives spent a few days in courthouses and the county recorder's office, searching for Rossi's marriage, property, and tax records and employment history. He had obtained numerous professional

* Also a pseudonym.

licenses—as a real estate agent, a security guard, a notary public—and had held a series of jobs such as property manager and garden tool salesman. There were several federal tax liens on his property and he owed more than $50,000 in unpaid taxes.

His employment and tax history revealed an encouraging instability. In the early 1960s, according to his marriage records, Rossi had worked for an insulation company. The gardener had told investigators that the man he saw on the afternoon of the murder was dressed in a light blue uniform, which was consistent with what an insulation worker would wear. The detectives also determined from Rossi's children's birth certificates that, like the Gormans, he lived on the West Side at the time of Stephanie's murder.

When the detectives returned to the office, they began investigating the criminal histories of Rossi's children. A daughter, they discovered, had been arrested dozens of times in Hollywood for prostitution. This, too, intrigued Lambkin: many prostitutes were victims of sex crimes at home.

Despite the heartening developments, Lambkin was haunted by the feeling that the case would have been solved by now if the DNA evidence had not been destroyed. He was also furious about the half-dozen missing files, which contained not only summary reports that could serve as a blueprint for the present investigation, but interviews, evidence lists, the crime scene floor plan, and results of the suspects' polygraph examinations.

The loss of the DNA put Lambkin at a tremendous disadvantage. The absence of half a dozen of the most critical files was almost an insurmountable hurdle to the investigation of a thirty-five-year-old case. So on that November afternoon, when Rick Jackson discovered the missing files, Lambkin felt a crucial step closer to catching Stephanie Gorman's killer. He now hoped that he might, one day, be able to answer her sister's questions and ease their family's enduring burden.

11

A week after Jackson's call from the city archives, Lambkin and Mar-cia decide to visit the house where Stephanie was murdered. Marcia cruises west on the Santa Monica Freeway on a hazy November morn-ing, with a fusion of smog and fog shrinking the horizons. Pulling off the freeway, he drives through Beverlywood—about a mile south of Beverly Hills—a placid, upscale neighborhood with manicured lawns and carefully pruned shrubbery. The Gormans bought their house here in the early 1960s for $65,000. Now many houses in the neigh-borhood sell for more than $700,000.

Marcia pulls up in front of the place where Stephanie was mur-dered, a three-bedroom, brown stucco and clapboard home with white shutters. The detectives have spent months studying reports and rec-ords and files. Now, gazing at the residence from the street, they can truly visualize the murder for the first time. Lambkin remembers read-ing that the family used to leave their back door unlatched when they were at home. Today he sees that the house has thick bars outside the bedroom windows, a heavy iron mesh door in back, and a security system sign posted on the lawn. The house is on a corner, which Marcia finds interesting: corner houses are burglarized more often because passersby are not as noticeable.

"Maybe because this house is on a corner, the crime might have been opportunistic rather than preplanned," Marcia says.

"I don't think so," Lambkin says. "Look what the guy had with him—a gun, rope, a cutting instrument for the rope. And there was no financial motive. Nothing was taken. I think it was preplanned."

Lambkin recalls that when Cheryl and Edward Gorman returned home, and before discovering the murder, they noticed that the back gate was open. While he gazes at the gate, Marcia reminds him that Mrs. Gorman discovered a doll with its head torn off a few days after the murder. They walk to the side of the house and Marcia says, "This must have been where it was found." The detectives, who are unsure if the doll is significant, walk back around to the front.

"The first time I saw the Eiffel Tower, I was not that impressed," Lambkin says. "I'd seen so many pictures of it. Being here now is a different kind of feeling. The impact of the case really hits me."

Marcia is also moved. Staring at the house, lost in thought, he re-creates the murder in his mind, from the knock on the door, to the punch, to the rape, to the shot.

When the detectives finish looking around, Lambkin sifts through the murder book while Marcia drives to a cavernous West Los Angeles hardware store where his father, a painting contractor, once bought supplies. The detectives hope to learn more about the binding that the killer used, but it was destroyed along with much of the other evidence. Fortunately, the crime scene photographs, which clearly show the victim and the rope, do still exist.

The original homicide reports stated that Stephanie was bound with chalk line—used by carpenters to mark a straight line between two points—but the crime scene photographs reveal a thicker cord. The detectives hope that identifying the type of binding will help establish the profession of the killer. Marcia shows the hardware store clerk a detail of the crime scene photograph. "Is this chalk line?" he asks.

"Chalk line's thinner," the salesman says. "That's definitely not chalk line." He leads the detectives to the rope aisle. "Here's some nylon rope that appears similar."

"This picture's from 1965," Lambkin says. "We're looking for cotton."

The salesman proceeds down the aisle, grabs a section of cotton rope, and compares it to the photograph.

"That's it," Lambkin says.

"It's mason line," the salesman says.

As they walk to the car, Marcia says, "We need to find a bricklayer, someone who was building walls in the neighborhood."

"I think I recall from the files that there was a construction site on the corner," Lambkin says. "I'll try to find it, but there are so many damn pages to sift through."

Marcia and Lambkin head south, toward the cemetery where Stephanie is buried. Lambkin wants to photograph her headstone. The picture, he believes, might be an effective prop for his interview of Vincent Rossi.

Lambkin spots a liquor store in the distance and tells Marcia, "When I was a probationer in Rampart my training officer stopped at a liquor store one afternoon. While I was waiting outside, a little kid came up to me and said, 'I want to be a police officer when I grow up.' I felt great. I asked him why, because I thought he'd say because he wanted to help people. But he tells me, 'So I can get stuff for free.' Turns out this guy regularly stopped by the store to pick up free cigarettes. Other cops used to stop by and get free booze."

Marcia chuckles, but his mood turns somber when he pulls off the San Diego Freeway, enters the cemetery, and turns onto a narrow lane bordered by olive trees. They climb a hill and locate Stephanie's grave. A chilly breeze rustles the leaves of the magnolia tree that shades the grave in the watery autumn light. Freeway traffic thrums in the distance like the sound of the surf. Crouching beside Stephanie's flat marble headstone with roses engraved on the border, the detectives read:

STEPHANIE GORMAN

1949–1965

BELOVED DAUGHTER AND SISTER

WHO TOUCHED THE HEARTS OF ALL

WHO KNEW HER

Next to Stephanie's headstone is her father's:

THIS WAS A MAN

EDWARD I. GORMAN

JUDGE OF THE SUPERIOR COURT

1921–1987

Marcia gently sweeps the leaves off the headstones with a palm frond. As the sun flashes in and out of the clouds, Lambkin photographs the grave, deftly changing lenses and shifting positions with the panache of a professional. He mutters to Marcia that at least his year studying photography was not a total waste.

As they return downtown, Marcia says, "Her father died while the case was still unsolved. That's a brutal thing to live with."

"I usually don't get emotional about my cases," Lambkin says. "But I'm getting emotional about this one."

Back in the squad room, Rick Jackson wanders over and asks Lambkin about the Gorman case. Eventually, they begin reminiscing about their days in Hollywood Homicide and the bizarre things they saw. The other detectives half-listen as they work through the chatter.

"We had one case at this club," Lambkin begins. "There was this comedy act and a guy was running around popping balloons on people's bodies. Then the comedian tripped and planted the knife right in the middle of this guy's chest. He killed him."

As Lambkin cackles, Jackson says, "I've always liked the Stove Top Stuffing murder. A woman is walking down the street in Hollywood and runs into a guy she knows. She's in her fifties and he's in his sixties. They talk about dinner. He says he's making turkey with Stove Top Stuffing. She says that it's lousy stuffing. He doesn't want her bad-mouthing his dinner, so he starts to leave. She gets mad and slams him with her purse. The guy falls down, has a heart attack, and dies."

Lambkin asks Jackson, "You remember that big buff cop who dated a porn star? He had a brain aneurysm and woke up in the hospital. He thought his name was Carlos and he owned a flower shop in Hawaii."

Jackson walks back to his desk, laughing. Lambkin and Marcia return to the murder books. They have to get ready for an interview with Stephanie's mother and sister.

A few days later, Lambkin and Marcia drive to the West Los Angeles office of Cheryl Gorman, now a psychologist. The murder shattered her family. In 1969, after twenty-four years of marriage, Edward and Julie Gorman divorced. The detectives know this sad history and they plan to approach the family delicately.

When the detectives arrive at Cheryl's office, Julie is fidgeting in the waiting room. Nervously rubbing her thumb and index finger, she appears absorbed in her thoughts, and her eyes have a grim, faraway look. She wears a red pantsuit and her hair is carefully coifed. As she chats with the detectives she seems uncomfortable. The detectives know she was not happy about her daughter's decision to reopen the case. She remarried decades ago and says that dredging up old feelings is simply too painful.

"You either kill yourself, or you go on," Julie says to the detectives. She sighs heavily. "It's so hard to relive this. You know, I always worried it was someone we knew. I kept looking at everyone."

After a few minutes, Cheryl, who has a determined expression, steps into the lobby and leads the detectives and her mother into her office. Cheryl was a nineteen-year-old college student when her sister was murdered. Now she is woman in her mid-fifties, married, with a grown child. All these years, her need to know what happened has never waned. Slender, youthful looking, she wears lavender pants and a green sweater.

Lambkin explains that they have located a suspect, Vincent Rossi, whose fingerprint matches one lifted from a door frame in a hallway. Now, he says, they need to find out whether Rossi had any connection to the family or was ever employed as a workman at the house. If he had a legitimate reason to be in the house, he might be eliminated as a suspect. If not, there is a good chance he was the killer. Neither woman recognizes the name.

"We've been trying to gather as much information as we can without him knowing," Lambkin says. "We don't want him on notice. If he knows we're coming, it could be deadly, especially if he still has some evidence. These kinds of offenders sometimes keep something to reminisce about the crime."

"Is *all* that original evidence down the drain?" Julie asks, horrified.

"No," Lambkin says. "Just some of the physical evidence, so we can't use DNA. That's why the interview with him is so critical."

Lambkin tells them that he and Marcia have obtained Rossi's criminal record, his two marriage certificates, his tax records, his employment history, and the birth certificates of his children. Cheryl and Julie are unfamiliar with the names of his ex-wives and his children, but they do find it interesting that Rossi's mother has a Sephardic Jewish name and that he married his first wife in a synagogue. The Gormans are Sephardic and both Cheryl and Julie were married in Sephardic temples. Still, they cannot think of a connection to him. Lambkin lists his employment history, to help determine if Rossi had ever visited the house.

"On his marriage certificate, he listed his occupation as an engineer for an insulation company," Lambkin says. "Did you ever have any walls ripped up?"

"No," Julie says.

"On one of his children's birth certificates he gave his occupation as salesman for a garden tool company," Lambkin says. "Does that ring a bell?"

Julie glances at her daughter with a quizzical expression. They both shake their heads.

"He worked as a property manager once," Lambkin tells Julie. "Did Mr. Gorman's law practice have anything to do with real estate?"

"No," she says.

"Was there any brickwork done at your house?" asks Lambkin.

"No," Julie says. "We had all flagstone."

"Any brickwork done nearby?"

"I can't remember," she says.

Finally, Lambkin reveals the composite of Rossi. Julie picks up the picture and a flicker of recognition flashes in her eyes.

"There's something about him that's familiar," she says.

Cheryl studies the composite. "He looks Sephardic to me."

"We blew up his profile," Lambkin says. "It's almost identical to the composite."

Julie shakes her head. "I just can't place him."

Lambkin tells them that in 1971, a dozen typewriters were stolen from a Hollywood business and Rossi was arrested after reselling one of them for $200. He claimed that he did not know the typewriter had been stolen, and eventually pleaded guilty to receiving stolen property.

"We'd prefer if his burglary was a hot prowl or had some sexual overtones," Lambkin says. "But what's really interesting is that the business was in Hollywood, but the man who owned the business lived only three blocks from your house."

Lambkin provides them with the address and the names of the other two people arrested in connection with the burglary. "Ring a bell?"

"No," the mother says.

Marcia then tells them, for the first time, about Michael Goldsmith. "He's a bizarre-looking guy. Longhaired and kind of crazy-looking. He stopped by the house on the afternoon Stephanie was killed and actually called the police himself. He said he visited the house to see a friend and didn't realize the friend no longer lived there. But the friend told the detectives that he hadn't lived in the house for years and the guy should have known it."

"That story doesn't make sense," Julie says.

"It's very odd," Cheryl says. "This is the first we've ever heard of that story."

"He was eliminated on prints," Marcia says.

"What time was the murder, do you estimate?" Cheryl asks.

"It would have been around the same time period he showed up at the house," Lambkin says.

"That's one of the weirdest things I've heard," Julie says.

Lambkin tells them that Goldsmith graduated from Hamilton High School a few years before the murder.

Cheryl appears alarmed and says, "Then he would have graduated with me! And don't forget, I was supposed to be at home that day." Cheryl hugs herself and says, "About a week or two after it happened, I got several calls. They were horrible. Someone said: 'You're next!' " Staring at a wall, she adds, "I had to get away from it. It happened in August. I moved into my sorority in September. I didn't want to come home. It happened in my bedroom."

"We led a quiet life," Julie says. "My husband spent a lot of time at home. He had rheumatic fever and had two heart operations. I just played tennis and bridge at the club."

"Stephanie went to the club a lot," Cheryl says. "I wasn't athletic, but she was a great athlete. She played tennis every day."

"I just gave her money so she could be on the drill team," Julie says, staring into the middle distance. "The tennis pro was crazy about Stephanie. Everyone was." She grips the sofa and adds, "I wanted to leave the club and go home, and I was just walking out, but they begged me to fill in so they could play doubles. This has been on my mind for years. Why? Why did I stay to play? I didn't even want to. Maybe I could have saved her. Or maybe I would have been killed, instead of Stephanie."

After a minute of silence, Julie says, "I have a feeling about that guy who pulled in the driveway."

"I agree," Cheryl says. "Why'd he stop by that particular day?"

"Why'd he call police?" Julie asks.

"Maybe he thought someone spotted him," Lambkin says.

Lambkin agrees that Goldsmith's story is suspicious, but he tells her that he believes Rossi is their primary suspect. "The more I look into him the stronger I feel about it."

Lambkin tells them Rossi's daughter has been arrested many times for prostitution and that a young relative accused him of a sexual impropriety. "This is consistent with a sexual offender. His lack of a criminal record bothers me. But there are explanations for that."

"Is it your gut feeling that you've got the right guy?" Cheryl asks.

"I just can't see any legitimate reason," Lambkin replies, "for this guy's prints being in your house."

12

Yuriko Taga's mother and brother, who have come from Japan to settle her financial affairs, want to visit the spot where she and Michelle were killed. They also hope to discuss the case with Garcia and Jackson, who are eager to question them.

The detectives believe they have solved the murder, but not the mystery. Many aspects of the case are not yet accounted for, and they still know very little about Taga or Yuriko. In the next month, they hope to interview several people who may provide them—and ultimately the jury—with insight into the killer and his victims.

The detectives, Tina Matsushita, and Deputy District Attorney Gary Hearnsberger meet Toshiko and Satoshi Kuno in the lobby of the New Otani, a Japanese-owned hotel downtown. Toshiko is a tiny woman, a few inches under five feet, who wears black pants and a black silk top with a floral pattern. Her son, about five and a half feet tall, is dressed in a brown suit, a taupe shirt, and a striped brown tie. They are waiting, expressionless, in the busy lobby with two Japanese embassy officials. When the officials introduce them to Garcia and Jackson, they bow.

After a few awkward moments, arrangements are made for the trip to the harbor. The embassy officials, who will chauffeur the mother and brother in their Toyota van, will follow Garcia. In the car, the detectives and Hearnsberger discuss the preliminary hearing. Garcia tells Hearnsberger that although a vial of Rohypnol, the "date rape drug," was found at Taga's town house, there was no trace of it in the victims' blood. The tests for poison were also negative, Garcia says, possibly because the victims were so badly decomposed. The coroner wants to send the samples off to another lab for more sophisticated testing.

When they arrive at Fish Harbor on this ash gray afternoon, the fog has rolled in and there is not a hint of wind. The dusky water is as sleek as a pane of glass. The detectives lead the group to the edge of the dock, near a rusty trawler. Toshiko carries a bouquet wrapped in a large purple nylon scarf. The embassy official, translating for Toshiko, points to the water and asks, "Is this where she died?"

"Pretty close to here," Jackson says.

Toshiko and Satoshi briefly bow their heads and pray as the detectives stroll down the dock to allow them some privacy. Suddenly the water appears to explode. Waves crash against the hull of the trawler. Salt water splashes the dock. Everyone jumps back. Toshiko's eyes widen in fear. The detectives seem unnerved. Finally, everyone spots the sea lion that has burst through the water. When Toshiko regains her composure, she unties the scarf and slips out a dozen orchids and pink and red roses. Bowing her head again for a moment, she tosses the flowers into the water. The sweet scent of roses lingers in the air.

Toshiko and her son study the petals floating on the water. Occasionally a beam of sunlight pierces the fog and illuminates an oil slick, reflecting a rainbow prism of colors. Although it is only about 3:45, a hint of dusk darkens the sky on this late fall day, adding to the somber mood. Finally, after the last rose petal sinks from the surface, the mother and son climb into the van and everyone heads back to RHD where they gather in the captain's empty office. Toshiko answers questions about her daughter's background, tightly clasping her hands and staring at the table.

Yuriko grew up in a small town not far from Osaka and, after high school, worked as a bookkeeper. When she was in her early twenties she decided to attend school in the United States and enrolled at a community college in Washington state, where she earned a degree in marketing and business accounting. For about ten years, Yuriko worked at a Seattle bank.

"What brought her to L.A.?" Garcia asks, as Matsushita translates.

"Seattle was too cold," Toshiko says quietly. "She wanted warmer weather."

Her daughter, she says through the translator, moved to Los Angeles in 1994 and a month later met Taga. They married the following year and bought the town house, which Yuriko had proudly described to her mother during her recent trip home.

"Do you know who made the down payment and how they financed the house?" Jackson asks.

"My daughter paid for everything," Toshiko says with a frown.

"The down payment, too?" Jackson asks.

"Yes."

Toshiko says she attended the wedding, where she met Taga for the first time.

"What was your opinion of him?" Jackson asks.

"He was very quiet," she says. "A studious kind of guy."

"Did you like him?" Jackson asks.

"I kind of liked him." Looking hesitant, Toshiko removes a wedding picture from her purse and places it on the table. Yuriko, bathed in sunshine, wears a full-length white dress with a veil and clutches a bouquet of white roses in both hands. She stands on a stone pedestal with BE THY KINGDOM COME engraved at the base. This is the only picture the detectives have ever seen of Yuriko in which she is smiling. Taga, who stands in the shade beside her, is sans toupee. Dressed in a tuxedo, he grins at the camera.

Jackson asks if Toshiko thought it odd that her daughter would leave her husband alone for several months during her recent visit back to Japan.

"Her husband said he was going on a lengthy business trip," Satoshi says, through the translator, breaking his silence.

"In Japan, did she talk about any problems she was having in her marriage?" Jackson asks.

Toshiko shakes her head.

"Did Yuriko ever tell you Taga might be involved with another woman?"

"No," Toshiko says adamantly.

Hearnsberger asks how she would describe Yuriko's personality.

"Quiet and shy," Toshiko says. "But she was fun-loving, too."

He then asks what her granddaughter was like.

"Active. A good little girl. Helps people all the time."

Jackson asks, "Anything seem to be bothering Yuriko during this trip?"

"No," Toshiko says. "She acted normal. She just talked about wanting to come home early. . . . The child got bored and wanted to return and play with her friends."

"During her stay with you in Japan, how many times did Yuriko speak to Taga?"

"Three times . . . Michelle acted so happy and would tell me that she just got a call from her father."

Pulling a small notebook and pencil out of his suit coat, Satoshi studies a page for a moment and asks Jackson through the translator: "Do you feel it's a single suspect or multiple suspects?"

"We have nothing to indicate that anyone did this other than Mr. Taga," Jackson says.

"What was the motivation?" Satoshi asks. Tears well in his eyes and a neck vein pulsates.

"Another woman was involved," Jackson says. "Your sister didn't know. He lied to her."

"When he put the bodies in the ocean," Toshiko asks, "were they dead or alive?"

"Taga said they were dead already," Jackson says. "But he lied so much we just don't know."

"You think he hired someone to kill them?" Toshiko asks.

"I don't think so," Jackson says.

"I hope it wouldn't be rude or improper of me to ask," Hearnsberger says, "but I'm interested in what it meant to you and what your thoughts were when you put the flowers in the water?"

"It's basically saying good-bye," Satoshi says. "We pray like Christians pray. It's very common for Japanese to do this. If we didn't go to the water, we'd regret it for the rest of our lives."

Two days later, Garcia and Jackson fly to Hawaii to meet Taga's ex-wife. In Waikiki, they check into a beautiful oceanfront hotel. The room rate here far exceeds their per diem, but a Secret Service agent in Honolulu, someone Jackson once worked with, secured them a discount. After dropping their luggage off in the room, they stroll along the beach. Garcia, who has never visited Hawaii, wears black cowboy boots, jeans, and a button-down shirt. He looks uncomfortable and out of place as he strides across the sand, stepping over sunbathers. Jackson appears more at home in his Dockers, polo shirt, and deck shoes.

Although it is early December, the temperature is in the eighties and the detectives are soon sweating heavily. They stroll through a few hotel lobbies to cool off. The images of Christmas in the tropics are disorienting: poinsettias beneath the palms; tiki torches and Christmas lights; hibiscus and holly, the smell of pine and plumeria; snow-men with leis; Christmas carols and hula music. Atop a beachfront hotel, Garcia and Jackson find a comfortable bar with an expansive vista of the serrated surf and the razor-sharp horizon line where the sky meets the sparkling turquoise sea. They order beers and relax beneath the plantation fans. Admiring the view, Jackson says to Garcia: "I'll bet they've got some interesting homicides here."

"I wonder how many a year they pick up," Garcia says. He sips his beer and begins reminiscing about the first case he solved at Homicide Special—the murder of Haing Ngor, the Academy Award–winning actor who starred in *The Killing Fields.*

Although Ngor's father, wife, and several other family members died during the Khmer Rouge's regime of slaughter, which claimed more than a million Cambodian lives, Ngor escaped to Thailand and eventually reached the United States. He spent years lobbying tirelessly for an international tribunal to prosecute Pol Pot and other leaders of the genocide.

On a Sunday night in 1996, after Ngor had parked his car behind his apartment, he was shot in the chest and killed. Robbery was not considered a motive because the killer did not take the $1,500 in Ngor's pocket, or his wallet. The Cambodian community in Los Angeles was certain Ngor had been murdered by a Khmer Rouge hit man.

Thrust into what quickly became an international incident, Garcia and his partner met frequently with FBI agents, State Department Cambodian experts, and antiterrorist specialists. They collected reams of data about Cambodian history, the Khmer Rouge, Pol Pot, and expatriate Cambodian communities throughout the world. Garcia spent his nights studying and his days at the crime scene, while trying to make time for State Department briefings and FBI conferences.

"The pressure to clear the case was phenomenal," Garcia tells Jackson, who was living in Maine at the time. "The O.J. trial had just ended. The unit was being overhauled. I was new. There was huge pressure to perform."

Garcia had never worked a case with international implications, but he had investigated countless street killings. Since he knew the streets, that is where he started. Ngor lived in a Cambodian neighborhood on the edge of Chinatown, and many of his neighbors spoke no English. Garcia and his partner recruited a Cambodian-speaking officer and together they knocked on every door within a four-block radius of the crime scene. One young man, who lived less than two hundred yards from the alley where Ngor was killed, said that he had not seen or heard anything unusual that night. The man spoke only Cambodian, but Garcia suspected he was hiding something because of his defensive body language—he kept his arms and legs crossed—and the way he occasionally averted his gaze.

After an intense three-hour interview, the man finally broke down. He told the detectives that he had seen three young men running down an alley from the direction of Ngor's apartment. He provided a description of the suspects, young Asian men. Garcia picked up a second clue a few weeks after the murder, during an interview with Ngor's niece, who said she wanted to pick up her uncle's property, including his $6,000 gold Rolex watch—the single luxury item he purchased after *The Killing Fields*—and his 24-karat gold chain with a locket containing a picture of his late wife. Garcia had stared at the woman for a moment, startled. After weeks of frustration and confusion, the niece's comment sparked an epiphany for Garcia.

When Ngor's body was found sprawled in the alley after the shooting, there was no Rolex on his wrist or gold locket around his neck. Garcia suddenly realized that this was not a political hit but a street robbery gone bad. The killers were probably Asian gangbangers looking for a quick score, and they might have been scared off before they could grab the cash and wallet. Garcia no longer felt out of his depth. He had worked dozens of gang-related murders and solved many of them. This was his métier.

Garcia and his partner determined the three suspects were members of the most violent gang in the neighborhood—the Oriental Lazy Boyz. They eventually tracked down a former member who admitted that he had partied with three gangbangers hours after Ngor was killed. They told him they had "robbed and shot some guy in an alley." Garcia and his partner arrested the suspects, who were later convicted of murder.

The three Oriental Lazy Boyz had smoked crack that night and were searching for someone to rob so they could buy more drugs. They spotted Ngor under his carport and noticed his Rolex. One gangbanger whipped out a gun and grabbed Ngor's watch. When he tried to steal the chain and locket, Ngor resisted. The picture of Ngor's wife inside the locket was his most treasured possession. He was willing to die for it. And he did.

The day after arriving in Hawaii, Garcia and Jackson drive through the pink Pacific twilight to the Honolulu Police Department. Ragged ribbons of coral-colored clouds mass over the mountains behind the city.

The police station is a blocky tan building with a memorial in front for the thirty-five officers killed in the line of duty during the department's history. Garcia and Jackson check in with the desk officer and wait beside the "Aloha Grotto"—a ceramic underwater seascape—until two Hawaiian investigators, whom they have worked with before, escort them to the squad room.

"If this was South Dakota, we'd probably just do the interview by phone," Jackson says. The Hawaiian detectives laugh.

They chat for a few minutes, until Taga's first wife arrives. She is slender and attractive, with shoulder-length hair, and the detectives are taken aback by how much she resembles Yuriko.

"We should be done in about seven or eight hours," Jackson says.

The woman looks petrified, but when she sees Jackson smile, she realizes he is kidding and manages a nervous half smile. She tells the detectives that although she is deathly afraid of her ex-husband and uncomfortable talking about the most unpleasant chapter of her life, they can count on her cooperation.

"I feel it could have been me," she says in a thick Japanese accent. "I feel I owe her. She took my place. I want to do whatever I can. I want to help you."

Taga grew up in Saitama Prefecture, a few hours north of Tokyo, she says. In his twenties, he moved to Miami, worked as a bartender at a Benihana restaurant, and enrolled in English classes. Taga also attended pilot's school in Florida, but ended up dropping out: that was typical, she says with a sad smile. There were many failed plans and schemes.

They met in the early 1980s, she tells them, at a meeting of a Buddhist organization. Like him, she had recently moved to Miami from Japan. Growing up in a sheltered Japanese home, she was not worldly enough to suspect his motives. Taga told her he was in the import-export business, but he never seemed to earn much money, so he drove a cab at night. In many ways, he seemed on his own in the world. His parents were dead and his sister lived in Japan. She never learned much else about his family, she says.

Later, he started a business in San Pedro, which eventually foundered, exporting sea urchins to Japan. Because of his reckless spending, they were always in debt and faced foreclosure on their house. "All five of our credit cards were charged to max," she says. "They were all in my name. . . . I was in debt for about thirty thousand dollars."

After about ten years of marriage, she and their two daughters visited her parents, who lived in Thailand at the time. Taga, she says, stayed at home and had an affair. "When we were gone . . . she moved into my house," the ex-wife says. "She stole towels, sheets, my clothes, quilts. It was terrible."

"How'd you find out?" Garcia asks.

"He called me in Thailand and said, 'Someone wants to talk to you.' She said, 'Your husband's not happy with you. He's intimidated by you. He wants to leave you.' This girl had friends in a motorcycle gang. . . . He bragged she was in Hell's Angels."

Her parents had given her more than $25,000, which she kept in a private bank account, but Taga attempted to filch the money while she was in Thailand. After she explains how bank officials thwarted him, Jackson asks about Taga's relationship with his two daughters.

The first year after the divorce, Taga saw his daughters two or three times, she says. "He kept making promises he would visit on other times. But he didn't show up." Five years passed during which he never once visited his daughters. Then he stopped by to drop off a child support check and stayed for ten minutes. The next year, before she moved to Hawaii, he visited a final time. He and Yuriko took his daughters to a juice bar for an hour.

"At first . . . he had a good relationship with older girl. . . . The second girl, he didn't seem to care for her. When he'd feed her milk bottle, he put her on edge of his leg. She was almost falling off. I knew he wasn't good person. . . . It was very hard for older daughter when she didn't see him. She couldn't understand it. She felt it was her fault."

After the divorce, Taga never contacted his daughters on their birthdays and never sent a single present. He paid child support only sporadically. "I finally went to court so he would pay $750 a month," she says. "He'd say, 'I put money in your account.' But it wouldn't be there. It was like nightmare. He worked for places, but he always had problems."

"What kind of problems?" Garcia asks.

"Integrity problems." She drops her head, clasps her hands, and mutters, "So many lies. So many deals."

"What did he like to do in his spare time?" Jackson asks.

"He liked to drink beer. . . . He liked to go to parties." She stares at her nails and appears embarrassed. "I hate to say it, but there was a pervertedness about him. I'd find porn . . . porno magazines and videos." She places a hand on her heart and says, "I hate to tell you this, but my definition of him is low life."

When she learned that Taga had killed his wife and daughter, she says, she was not surprised. "It's hard for me to say this to you. But when I live with him I can feel it. It could be possible. He has no scruples. No respect for people. He's a very cold person. You have to be a person with very little loving in your heart to cut off your children." Looking alarmed, she asks the detectives whether her daughters are in danger.

"I don't think so," Jackson says. "But he may feel that resuming contact could help him. Maybe he'll think having the girls and his ex-wife at trial may help him."

Jackson asks if she is going to tell her daughters the truth about their father.

"My dad says definitely not. What do you recommend?"

"Let me answer that," Garcia interjects. He leans forward and says in a confidential tone, "When I was a young boy, eight or nine, someone lied to me when I asked about my father. I would have dealt with this issue a lot better if I knew the truth."

After the interview, Garcia is subdued. His thoughts have returned to his own past.

His mother was sixteen years old and unmarried when she gave birth to him. When he pressed her about his father, she was evasive and told him he lived far away. Growing up, he always felt dejected when he thought about the father he had never met. When Garcia was in his late twenties, his mother finally told him the truth. She said that she knew one day they would have this conversation.

It turned out that Garcia had known his father, who was a family acquaintance, for years. He contacted the man, who was uninterested in forming a relationship.

Garcia admires and respects his mother. She often worked long hours of overtime, and sometimes two jobs, to clothe and feed him. But he believes that her decision to keep the identity of his father secret was a mistake. His advice to Taga's former wife comes from the heart. One day her daughters will learn about their father. Garcia does not want them to experience the confusion and anguish he once felt.

By the time the detectives walk to their rental car, Garcia's contemplative mood has passed and he is in high spirits. Now he and Jackson can prove that Taga's behavior during his second marriage—including moving a girlfriend into the house—fits a pattern.

"The DA's going to love this stuff," Garcia says. "The jury will see who Taga really is. This woman will be devastating at the trial."

They linger beside their car on this sultry Honolulu night, considering the interview. Taga's struggles to make his child support payments after the first marriage, they believe, may have influenced his decision to kill his third child.

"The way he treated this lady and his daughters shows a pattern," Garcia says. "She seemed classy. Sheltered. Very nice. Just the type for him to victimize."

"Taga's just a con artist," Jackson says.

The detectives drive to a dim, dank bar where Honolulu detectives hang out after work. The two investigators who set up the interview greet them at the door. The small bar features two cracked red leather booths, with an enormous boar's head and dartboards on the walls. Dusty venetian blinds cover the windows. Fans whir above.

Over the next few hours, while Garcia and Jackson talk shop with the two Honolulu detectives, cops arrayed around the bar send over rounds of beer. The owner serves heaping platters of tempura, shrimp wrapped in bacon, and sashimi.

"What kind of cases you been working on?" Garcia asks.

"We had one where the guy gets in his boat and dumps his wife into Pearl Harbor," a Honolulu detective says. "But he ran out of gas and needed a tug. While he's stuck out there, the body comes up."

"It's a good thing some of these guys are so stupid," Jackson says laughing, "because we're not that smart."

"How many murders you have this year?" Garcia asks.

"Only about twenty-five," the Hawaiian detective says. "It's been slow."

"We have a serial murderer," his partner says. "He killed two in Kauai and maybe three here."

"How?" Garcia asks.

"Knife in Kauai and strangled here."

The detectives commiserate about the frustrations of the job. They complain about staffing limitations, overtime cutbacks, and politics interfering with police work. After a discussion of memorable autopsies, a Honolulu detective asks, "Was the trip worth it?"

Garcia downs his beer and says, "The interview sunk our guy. We just nailed him."

On a Monday morning, not long after the detectives return from Hawaii, a man named Kato calls Garcia and introduces himself as Taga's former business partner. "I should have told you this before," he says, "but Taga tried to poison me a year ago."

A few days later, Kato arrives at RHD for an interview. He is in his late thirties, with long, shaggy hair and grease-stained hands. No translator is available, so the detectives try to make sense of his fractured English. When he sits down in the interview room, he drops a bottle of Goo Gone, encased in a plastic bag, on the table.

"What's that?" Garcia asks.

"Evidence," he says, flashing a conspiratorial look.

He starts by explaining that Taga bought three or four used cars a month from an auto rental company. Kato repaired them at his garage and Taga sold them to Japanese customers in Southern California. One afternoon, at Taga's office, Kato mentioned that he was thirsty.

"He grab Styrofoam cup, put water in it," Kato says. "He give it to me. It tastes like lemon. I say, 'Something wrong.' Ten, fifteen minutes later I vomit. I sick four days. Real upset stomach. I have to go to doctor. . . . Mr. Taga tell me he give me this toilet bowl cleaner"—he points to the Goo Gone—"by mistake. But I don't think so."

The detectives attempt to determine why Taga poisoned him, but Kato says he does not know and is still perplexed.

Before they were partners, he tells the detectives, Taga worked with someone he referred to as Mr. Ikeda, a Japanese businessman who had purchased three Dodge Durangos. Mr. Ikeda paid Taga to ship the vehicles to Japan. The vehicles never arrived in Japan, Kato says, because Taga sold them in Phoenix. When Mr. Ikeda discovered Taga had ripped him off, he tried to seize his town house.

Two days after Taga spiked the drink with Goo Gone, Kato says, "he used cyanide gas to try to kill Mr. Ikeda in Long Beach."

"How do you know this?" Garcia asks.

"Mr. Ikeda told me."

Taga picked up Mr. Ikeda in a Lincoln Continental whose door handles he had jury-rigged so they would not open from the inside. After driving around awhile, Taga stopped and told Mr. Ikeda that he had to get something, Kato says. Taga then reached into the backseat and suddenly punctured a can of cyanide, which he had bought at a nearby chemical plant. Using a screwdriver, Taga slipped out of the car while Mr. Ikeda struggled with the door. Eventually Ikeda managed to escape.

"Why'd you wait so long to tell us this story?" Garcia asks.

Kato picks up the plastic bag and stares disconsolately at the Goo Gone.

"Before he was arrested, were you afraid?" Garcia asks.

"Yes. Very afraid. Afraid for two years." After the incident, he called a county sheriff substation, but the officers, he says, never investigated the poisoning.

The detectives ask Kato what Taga told him about his family. After Yuriko and Michelle flew to Japan, Kato says, Taga mentioned that they would not return. A week later, Sachiko arrived. "I say, 'My goodness, only one week?'" According to Kato, Sachiko owned property in Japan worth $100,000. Taga had expected her to sell the property and bring the cash to the United States when she moved in with him. He was disappointed when she decided not to.

On September 7, Kato says, he and Taga sold a car to a Japanese woman and her daughter, a student at an American college. When Jackson hears the date, he perks up. "How'd you remember it was September seventh?"

"I remember from the news. . . . He kill his wife on September seventh." Kato explains that during the afternoon, "he ask me to help them with the insurance. He too busy." But that evening Taga joined the woman and her daughter for dinner at a Gardena sushi bar.

Now that Kato explained how Taga spent the day, the detectives are confident that at trial, the DA can shock the jury with a description of Taga's cold-blooded manner. Taga sold the car, then picked up his wife and daughter at the airport, and killed them. He parked the van at home, with the bodies inside, then enjoyed a festive dinner at the sushi bar. Afterward, he waited until dark, drove the van to Fish Harbor, and dumped his wife and daughter into the water.

When they step out of the room for a moment, Jackson says to Garcia, "Don't be so hard on Taga. Everyone deserves a dinner break."

Later, Kato tells the detectives that he recently visited Taga in jail. "He ask me if Tora, his cat, is doing okay. . . . He want me to feed it. . . . That's all. Amazing. Never say anything about his wife and child."

Taga is even more devious and complex than the detectives had realized. They speculate that unraveling his story may lead to other victims. More immediately, however, Kato's tale sends them back to the murder book to review the various poison possibilities.

A detective who helped with the search warrant has scrupulously examined the hard drive of Taga's personal computer. One file had sparked the interest of Garcia and Jackson because it included a recipe for ricin, a castor bean extract so toxic that Bulgarian secret agents used it to kill a defector in London in 1978. An agent stabbed the victim with a specially rigged umbrella that shot a ricin pellet into his leg.

A county pathologist, however, does not believe ricin killed Yuriko and Michelle. Ricin precipitates a slow, painful death that might take several days. Taga's wife and daughter died within hours of their return from Japan. When the detectives check back with the pathologist, he repeats that he is "leaning toward asphyxiation as a cause of death."

The detectives feel they cannot ignore the ricin recipe in the computer file. While they are frustrated that no conventional tests can detect ricin, antibodies to the poison can be found with very specialized equipment. Neither the coroner nor the FBI has sophisticated-enough equipment, but the detectives know of a military lab on the East Coast that can conduct the test. They hope the coroner will send Yuriko's and Michelle's tissue samples there. If ricin antibodies are detected, the DA may be able to file—in addition to the two murder counts—two charges of attempted murder against Taga, which could buttress their case for the death penalty.

Later, one of Yuriko's friends calls the office. After the woman tells a translator that she suspects Yuriko was poisoned in June, and she describes the symptoms, Jackson's interest in ricin intensifies. He decides to question her in person. Rick Ishitani, a young police officer who grew up speaking Japanese at home, drives Jackson to the interview. Tina Matsushita is off today and Garcia is busy preparing another case for trial.

Jackson, who is almost twenty-five years older than Ishitani, talks to him in an avuncular manner about the case and about homicide investigation. He tells Ishitani about the 1944 movie *Laura,* in which a detective falls in love with a murder victim during the course of his investigation. Ishitani looks skeptical.

"It can happen," Jackson says. He tells Ishitani that Yuriko Taga was so beautiful, so compassionate, and so devoted to her daughter that he finds himself attracted to her.

"That's weird," Ishitani says.

When they arrive at the apartment, Yuriko's friend, a middle-aged Japanese woman named Kazuko, who speaks no English, greets them at the door and asks that they leave their shoes in the hallway. She wears a baggy green jogging suit, and her short black hair is highlighted with blond streaks.

While Ishitani translates, Kazuko paints a grim picture of Yuriko's last year. Because of Taga's shady business, Yuriko was constantly pursued by creditors and under tremendous stress. While Taga always had enough money to fund his schemes and trips, Yuriko bought all her clothes at the Salvation Army and scoured the city for free activities for Michelle. Sometimes, when creditors waylaid her at home, she fled with Michelle to a friend's house in Huntington Beach and stayed there for a few days.

"I asked her why she didn't divorce the guy," Kazuko recalls, as Ishitani translates. "Yuriko said she didn't want to because of her daughter. . . . She told me she'd always had bad luck with men. She hoped her luck would be different when she married Taga."

"Was she ever so distraught she wanted to kill herself?" Jackson asks.

"Never," Kazuko says. "But in June, she got food poisoning. Afterwards she told me, 'You know, I almost thought I was going to die.' "

Jackson, who has been waiting for the woman to bring up this incident, nods, encouraging her to continue.

Kazuko says that after eating a steak dinner that Taga prepared, Yuriko was violently ill for several days. But neither Taga nor Michelle was sick. Yuriko could not afford to visit the hospital, she told her friend, because she had no medical insurance.

Jackson thinks immediately of the ricin recipe. The symptoms of ricin poisoning are almost identical to Yuriko's: diarrhea, severe nausea, stomach pain, vomiting.

About a week later, Kazuko called Yuriko, who told her she had had food poisoning again, this time after eating sushi. "Yuriko said the symptoms were the same," she recalls, as Ishitani translates, his eyes grave with concern. "She was throwing up for two to three days and couldn't get out of the bathroom." Again, neither Taga nor Michelle was sick.

"I asked Yuriko who bought the sushi," Kazuko says. "She said,

'Actually, my husband did. He went to a restaurant with friends and purchased it to go.' "

Kazuko crosses her arms and tightly grips her shoulders. "Yuriko would never mention that her husband would do such a thing. But I mentioned it. I confronted her." She then recounts the conversation:

"Isn't this weird?" Kazuko asked. "Do you have life insurance?"

"Are you trying to say my husband is trying to kill me?"

"That's not what I'm trying to say. But it's something you have to think about."

A few months after the food poisoning incidents, Kazuko says, she received a frightening phone call. When she tells Ishitani about it—in Japanese—he nervously rubs his face with both hands. "Oh shit!" he exclaims. "Whew."

"Now you've really got my curiosity," Jackson tells him. "What's going on?"

"During the first week of September, she gets a phone call and a hang-up," Ishitani says. "Shortly after that, the phone rings again. She picks it up and hears a female voice screaming. I mean *screaming*! A few seconds later, she hears a click. She thinks this woman was trying to talk, but someone came in on her. . . . She was so shocked, she went downstairs and told her boyfriend."

A few weeks later, when Kazuko heard about the murders on the news, she was horrified because she had had a premonition about Yuriko's death. "I have a characteristic inside me almost like a psychic. I think something, I'm usually right."

When Jackson presses her for the date of the call, she leaves the room and searches for her phone bills. It seems, from what she can piece together, that the frightening call came after Yuriko's death.

As they drive back to the freeway, Jackson assures Ishitani that, quite often, even people who are certain about dates later realize they are mistaken.

"When she told me about that call, I got goose bumps," Ishitani says. "If Yuriko was calling for help, and Taga got to her, that would be pretty damn chilling."

13

Lambkin and Marcia are back at their desks after a week off following Christmas. Marcia spent the holiday with his wife, children, and large extended family. Lambkin joined his sister and her husband for an early dinner at a fashionable restaurant. Like Lambkin, his sister is childless, but passionate about her pets. They bought gifts for each other's dogs and exchanged them on Christmas night.

The detectives are hunched over their desks, with the twenty-two Gorman murder books stacked up beside them. The books' headings include "Suspects A–K," "Suspects L–Z," "Phone Threats," "Crime Reports," "Hamilton High School Data." A dozen photocopied newspaper articles about the crime are taped to the wall. The murder was covered extensively, and the headlines included: "Honor Student, 16, Found Slain in Home"; "Father, Sister Find Body of Victim"; "Police Seek Clues in Sex Slaying of Girl, 16"; "Beverlywood Slayer Still Hunted"; "Security Patrol Begins Job in Beverlywood."

Marcia is called out to help detectives search for a man who raped three young girls in a South-Central alley, so Lambkin will conduct the interviews this week without him. He drives to the west Valley, to visit one of the last people to see Stephanie Gorman alive. Illene Jackman was sixteen years old and living with her family a few blocks from the Gormans, when she dropped Stephanie at home after summer school. Now fifty-one, she lives in a spacious, ranch-style home and has a daughter in college.

Lambkin joins Illene, her husband, and their daughter at the dining room table. He tells her that the handwritten statements compiled during the interviews in the original investigation are gone. All he has now are the synopses of interviews conducted in 1965. "All I know from the summaries is that you dropped her off at twelve-fifteen and you were with a male."

Illene explains that her companion was a high school friend. They let Stephanie out in front of her house and watched her walk through the backyard, to her back door. Then Illene drove off.

"And that's the last time I saw her," she says, gazing out a window. She turns toward Lambkin. "I don't remember much else about that afternoon."

The car she drove that afternoon, she says, was a 1965 Mustang, which she'd won in a radio contest. "It was a very simple time. Our neighborhood was our world. We didn't drive far, maybe to Beverly Hills or Westwood. It wasn't like kids today, who drive everywhere."

Illene says she will never forget Stephanie's funeral. One of the Gorman relatives ran up to her shouting, "You could have saved her!"

Lambkin removes photographs of Stephanie and other girls from the murder book. The pictures are grouped under the heading "Phi Delts."

"Was that a sorority?" Lambkin asks.

"It was more like a high school club."

The girls in the photos smile demurely and are neatly dressed in cashmere sweaters and skirts. They wear headbands, and their shoulder-length hair is lacquered, with perfect flips at the ends.

Lambkin pushes aside the photographs and asks, "What would have been her nature if she was confronted by someone in the house?"

"She was very athletic," Illene says. "But she'd be in total shock. I don't see her putting up a big fight."

"Do you know if she was sexually active?"

"No," she says, firmly. "Not too many of us were then."

"Do you recall any major work being done on the house?"

She shakes her head.

Lambkin drops a picture of Rossi on the dining room table. "He look familiar?"

"No," she says.

He then places the 1965 suspect composite beside Rossi's picture.

Illene's daughter, who has quietly watched her mother during the interview, studies the two pictures and says, before anyone can respond, "They look exactly alike."

Back in the squad room, Lambkin studies two of Michael Goldsmith's old arrest reports that Marcia recently unearthed. In 1986, a vice officer scanning an underground paper discovered an odd personal ad: "For Women Only. Male Outcall." When a woman officer called the phone number listed, Goldsmith told her he charged $75 an hour for a "date." Two days later, the officer met Goldsmith at a San Fernando Valley restaurant.

The arrest report documents the conversation:

"What do I get for seventy-five bucks?" the officer asked Goldsmith.

"Are you into spanking, fetishes, or bondage?"

"No, I'm just a normal person."

"Then I'll give you straight sexual intercourse."

Goldsmith was booked for prostitution. After waiving his rights, Goldsmith told officers, "Yeah, I run my own outcall service. Mine is for women only. But I do have four whores working for me."

Because Stephanie was tied up with rope, Goldsmith's comments about bondage pique Lambkin's interest. He locates the second arrest report, which details Goldsmith's arrest for spousal abuse. According to the report, Goldsmith's wife told the officers, "Take him away. He's beaten me up."

"Yeah, I hit her," Goldsmith responded. "She's banging everyone in the building."

Lambkin calls an LAPD psychologist, who suggests that Goldsmith "might have been a goofy kid who interjected himself into the case for attention." Still, Lambkin continues to feel uneasy about Goldsmith. And that casual comment, "Yeah, I hit her," interests Lambkin.

Lambkin continues scouring files, thinking through each new bit of information from every perspective. His attention grows more intense when he learns that the friend Goldsmith claimed he intended to visit, Robert Gelf, told detectives that his family had sold the house to the Gormans four years before the murder.

Lambkin tracks down Gelf and stops by his West Side house on a late Thursday afternoon. Goldsmith's friend is bald now, with just a fringe of gray hair. He wears a thick gold chain around his neck, and a matching gold bracelet. Lambkin asks him about Goldsmith and shows him his picture.

"I don't remember knowing someone this odd-looking," Gelf says.

"You remember *any* relationship with him?" Lambkin asks.

"No. He just looks vaguely familiar."

"At the time, you told police he should have known you didn't live there."

"That's probably right. I just can't remember it," he says apologetically.

"His story just doesn't hold up," Lambkin says. "It's one of those bothersome things in the case."

"I wish I could remember more." Gelf studies the ceiling for a moment and says, "I hope you catch this guy. I remember being really flipped out about the murder, totally shocked. If it was a few years earlier, it could have been *my* sister."

Lambkin asks Gelf about the provenance of the real estate. Although highly unlikely, Lambkin knows it is possible Rossi could have left his fingerprint in the hallway before the Gormans lived there. Gelf says his family moved into the house in about 1950 and sold the property to the Gormans eleven years later. Lambkin then lists Rossi's various jobs to find out whether he had ever had a reason to visit the house.

Gelf shakes his head.

"This is a long shot, but I want to see if there's any possibility that you might know him." Lambkin shows him the composite and a picture of Rossi.

Gelf slips on a pair of reading glasses. "It's a very common-looking face. But no."

As Lambkin walks out, he notices a Salvador Dalí print on a wall. "I love Dalí," Lambkin tells him. "I've got a number of them at home."

Gelf, who seems surprised that an LAPD detective is a Dalí aficionado, shows him a few other prized pictures, including a Picasso print. Lambkin rhapsodizes about the Picasso museum in Barcelona.

Later in their conversation, Gelf mentions that his sister works for a woman's fashion design company in Los Angeles. Lambkin is familiar with the name.

"How do you know that?" Gelf asks.

"Since I was in high school, I've subscribed to women's fashion magazines," Lambkin says. "I came to L.A. to become a fashion photographer."

On Monday morning, Lambkin studies a Gorman murder book while listening to the English punk band 999 on his CD player. As Marcia ambles into the office, the song "I Believe in Homicide" is blaring.

Marcia rolls his eyes. "That's worse than what my kids listen to."

"You need to broaden your taste in music," Lambkin says. "This song will get you in the right frame of mind to do your job."

Lambkin flips off his CD player and the detectives head for the parking lot. At Nate 'n Al's, a Beverly Hills delicatessen, they meet George Smith, an eighty-two-year-old lawyer with whom Stephanie's father, Edward, worked in the 1960s and '70s. Larry King holds court at a corner table.

Just to be thorough, the detectives want to learn whether Gorman ever handled any criminal or divorce cases, which sometimes generate vengeful clients. But Smith says Gorman specialized in business law and estate planning before being appointed to the bench. He assures the detectives that it is highly unlikely Gorman ever had a client or an adversary who sought revenge.

"It's hard to convey to you people what a decent, nice person he was," Smith says. "He was a person of the highest caliber—honest, with integrity, and very capable."

He lifts his spoon from his oatmeal, his eyes opaque with a distant memory. "I'll never forget where I was when I heard the news. I was driving. I heard it on the radio. I had to pull over. It was like someone punched me in the gut. You read in the paper about three hundred people being killed. It doesn't mean anything. But I knew those Gorman girls. We'd bring our kids to bar conferences then."

He pushes his oatmeal aside. "I thought this would kill Ed. At the time, he had a heart problem. I really thought it would kill him."

Lambkin and Marcia tell him about Vincent Rossi and show him the composite and the current photograph.

"I have no recollection of such a person," Smith says. "My memory's not that good. I'll be eighty-three in March. I do remember that, at the time, I heard a relative did it—a demented cousin who got in the house. But there were a lot of amateur sleuths, a lot of theories going around."

Smith mentions that he still heads the Stephanie Gorman Memorial Scholarship Fund at Hamilton High School. But the account has dwindled to $9,000. "I doubt the kids there know who she is now," he says. "She's probably just a name to them."

He launches into a long reverie about Los Angeles, a paradise lost. "My dad used to take me for drives and I could smell the fragrant orange groves. It was a wonderful city then. You never locked your door. I used to let my kids sleep in the yard. We were a decent city then. We could take walks at night. I wouldn't dare do that now."

He extends his hands toward the detectives. "I really appreciate what you're doing in this case. It would be an absolute miracle if, after all these years, you were able to run this down."

Lambkin and Tim Marcia finally locate—with the help of an LAPD pension clerk—the last surviving detective assigned to the Stephanie Gorman murder task force. When they discover he lives in a Santa Monica convalescent hospital, they are elated. After months of studying records and files and interviewing peripheral characters, they will finally be able to talk to someone with firsthand knowledge of the case. The detective, Lambkin and Marcia believe, could be an invaluable resource, so they leave a message for him.

The detective's wife returns the call. "My husband won't be much help," she says. "He suffers from severe dementia. He doesn't even remember being a police officer."

A few days later, a dispirited Lambkin discusses the case with an FBI profiler in Washington to gain insight into the killer and his crime. Profilers specialize in psychological portraits of serial killers, sexual predators, and sadistic murderers. A profile consists of the probable personality traits, characteristics, motivations, and compulsions of an offender. Profiling—officially known as criminal investigative analysis—provides detectives with a kind of psychological fingerprint that helps them focus on the most likely suspects.

The profiler talked extensively with Lambkin and thoroughly familiarized himself with the case. Then, drawing on personality disorder studies, statistics, computer tracking, and the Stephanie Gorman crime scene files, and guided by instincts honed from studying hundreds of rape-murders, the profiler offered Lambkin his assessment:

The killer probably did not know the Gormans personally. Because the family did not keep a regular schedule, the situation was "high risk" for him. The suspect approached the door with his gun concealed, the profiler speculated, talked briefly with Stephanie to find out whether anyone was home, and then employed the "blitz approach," punching her in the mouth to subdue her. While she was dazed, he tied her to the bed.

The suspect probably entered the house with a "preconceived sex fantasy" and did not plan to kill Stephanie. But when she managed to free herself, he panicked. It is possible that the murder "scared the hell out of him," the profiler said, to the extent that it ended his criminal career. Rossi's checkered job history, tax problems, and obvious instability might be an indication of the incident's impact.

Even after the conversation with the profiler, Lambkin and Marcia are still troubled by Rossi's minimal criminal record. But, as Lambkin knows, sex offenders are not *always* recidivists.

"Whatever this guy's criminal record is, if he denies ever being in the house, we're in business," Lambkin tells Marcia. "That's the key to our case, right there."

The detectives have exhausted their interview list. Now they prepare for their confrontation with Rossi. As they discuss strategy, they keep in mind the advice of the profiler who suggested that Lambkin raise Rossi's anxiety level by letting him know the LAPD has spent months on the case. Lambkin and Marcia now spend long nights meticulously creating props that look as professional as court exhibits.

Lambkin, who has never lost his love of the theater, has perfected his use of props over almost two decades. When he worked Hollywood Homicide, a prop helped him solve a cold case, the stabbing of a man on the steps of a church. After studying the old files and interviewing a few people, Lambkin and his partner thought they had identified the killer, a man who was in prison for another crime. Lambkin knew he needed convincing evidence to persuade the suspect to talk. So he bought a button that looked similar to the ones on the victim's coat, and obtained the suspect's fingerprint card from a previous case. Lambkin duplicated the fingerprint on the button, using his own blood, to make it look as if the killer had left it there. He then bluffed, telling the man that new technology had been used to trace the print to him. Presented with the "evidence," the suspect asked, "How do I know that it's *my* print?"

Lambkin showed the man his fingerprint card and said, "You compare."

The suspect eventually confessed.

The key to the confession, Lambkin knew, was his extensive preparation: if you are going to lie to a suspect, you had better be ready to back up your lie. He remembers this lesson when he plans for the Rossi interview.

Rossi, of course, does not know that the DNA evidence is gone. Lambkin and Marcia decide to exploit this advantage. They recently assigned an LAPD undercover surveillance unit to follow Rossi, and an investigator has managed to surreptitiously photograph him eating soup at a Chinese restaurant. A few days after receiving the photos, Lambkin and Marcia buy a bowl and spoon similar to those in the photographs and place them in a plastic bag labeled as a container for DNA samples. They also mount a photograph of Rossi at the Chinese restaurant.

Next, they choose a detective with straight black hair—like Rossi's hair in 1965——and slip a few strands between some glass lab slides. Beside a photograph of the bed where Stephanie was killed, the detectives draw yellow arrows and print, "Where the suspect's hairs were found." Lambkin and Marcia also create an official-looking document, laminated in plastic, that reads: "DNA hair analysis . . . primary DNA profile of hair matches DNA profile from second source (soup spoon). . . . Vincent Rossi has been identified as the donor of the primary DNA source (hair)."

From Marcia's late father's painting business, the detectives obtain a yellowed invoice form that they plan to fill out. It will be used to create the impression that the Gormans painted their house just a few months before the murder, so Rossi will not be able to claim that he left his fingerprint on the wall years earlier. In their final act of showmanship, the detectives will mount mason line—similar to the rope that was used to bind Stephanie—on a board, beneath the heading: "FBI Rope Analysis."

Lambkin and Marcia plan to secure a search warrant for Rossi's house, perfect their props, and devise a few others. Then they will knock on his door.

Part IV

THE CANYON

14

On the morning of January 11, while Lambkin and Marcia put the finishing touches on their props, Homicide Special picks up its first case of the new year. This is another cold case of sorts. The murder took place three weeks ago—an eternity for homicide detectives.

The victim was Susan Berman, and she had a premonition that she would die a violent death. At the age of thirty-five, twenty years before her murder, she wrote: "I am never secure and live with a dread that apocalyptic events could happen at any moment."

Her father, Dave Berman, was a notorious gangster whose FBI file described him as a "trained killer" and a "stickup man." Arrested during the Depression for kidnapping a mob bootlegger, Berman eventually served seven years in Sing Sing. A New York City detective called him "the toughest Jew I ever met."

During the early 1940s, Berman headed a gambling empire in Minneapolis–St. Paul, but when Mayor Hubert Humphrey shut down the illegal clubs, Berman headed for Las Vegas. He helped run hotels and casinos for Mafia bosses—Meyer Lansky, Frank Costello, Lucky Luciano. Berman also was a business partner of several gangsters, including Bugsy Siegel. After Siegel was knocked off in 1947, Berman and his partners took over his project, the Flamingo Hilton. Eventually, Berman would own parts of several other hotels, including the Riviera.

Susan Berman grew up on the Las Vegas Strip as a Mafia princess. When she was four, her father taught her to play gin rummy so the three bodyguards who lived with the family could keep her occupied. In third grade she learned math when her father gave her a slot

machine and a roll of nickels. She finished her homework every afternoon in a casino counting room. Liberace sang "Happy Birthday" to
her when she turned twelve.

Yet, Berman was unaware of her father's extensive arrest record
and organized crime connections. He was always nattily attired in a
tie and business suit with a monogrammed white handkerchief in the
pocket, and she believed he was simply a hotel owner. Berman was
told that the three men who lived with them were simply her father's
"friends." Her mother, a former tap dancer, referred to the family's
occasional late-night trips to Los Angeles during mob wars as "vacations." Decades later Susan finally realized that the reason the windows
in their custom-built house were set so high was to prevent assassination attempts from the street.

Her childhood abruptly ended shortly after her twelfth birthday
when Dave Berman died during an operation. The threat of violence
that permeated the family's life in Las Vegas rapidly destroyed Susan's
mother, who suffered a series of nervous breakdowns and was insti-
tutionalized. A year after her husband's death, she died of an overdose
of barbiturates. Some friends believed she had been murdered to prevent her from inheriting a share of her husband's Las Vegas hotels.

Susan was sent to live with an uncle in Lewiston, Idaho. Chickie
Berman was a bookie and a compulsive gambler who had dodged
several contracts on his life. A sharp dresser with a rakish charm, he
smoked English Ovals and always wore silk shirts and French cologne.
Susan adored him, but he could not run a gambling operation while
caring for a young girl, so for the next five years, she was shuttled off
to several exclusive boarding schools. During holidays and summers,
she stayed with Uncle Chickie.

She attended UCLA, a serendipitous choice because the Westwood
campus was less than an hour from the Terminal Island federal prison,
where Chickie had been sentenced to six years for stock fraud. On
her regular visits, Susan wore Chanel No. 5, as Chickie requested, so
"he could smell the real world." When Susan told him she planned
to pursue journalism as a career, he said, "You'll be the first Berman
to break into print legitimately."

She earned a master's degree in journalism at UC Berkeley and
spent the next decade working as a reporter. In her memory, her father
was a devoted, loving family man who always protected her, but when
she was in her early thirties, she vowed to finally learn the truth. After

obtaining her father's FBI files, traveling to Las Vegas and the Midwest, where he was raised, and interviewing relatives, former business associates, and aging mobsters, she wrote a memoir: *Easy Street: The True Story of a Mob Family.* The book was published in 1981, to excellent reviews. She sold the film rights for $350,000. Berman was at the apex of her career. Although eccentric, with numerous phobias, she had a charismatic personality and an acerbic wit, and was a spellbinding storyteller. She lived in Manhattan and wrote regularly for *New York* magazine and frequently lunched at Elaine's with writers and actors.

Since Berman had been orphaned at a young age and had only a few distant relatives, she felt extremely close to her friends. And when her friends were in trouble, Susan invariably came to their aid. Shortly after *Easy Street* was published, one of those friends, Robert Durst, needed her help. They had met at UCLA and, although they'd never been romantically involved, they were extremely close; he is mentioned in the acknowledgment section of her book.

While her family was infamous, his was merely famous: the Dursts own one of New York's largest real estate empires, including ten of Manhattan's most prominent skyscrapers. When Robert Durst's wife, Kathleen, disappeared in 1982 under suspicious circumstances, the couple's difficult marriage attracted extensive press coverage. Defending him unequivocally, Berman served as his unofficial press spokeswoman. In a sworn affidavit, she supported Durst's version of events. Kathleen's disappearance was never solved, and during the next few decades the case was dormant. Robert Durst led a reclusive life, but kept in touch with a few close friends, including Berman.

After the success of *Easy Street,* Berman moved to Los Angeles to pursue a career as a screenwriter. Two months later she met a man while standing in the Writer's Guild script-registration line. He was more than a decade younger than she, but he quickly moved into her home and they later married. Robert Durst, assuming the traditional paternal role, gave her away. This was the happiest day of her life, she told friends. She purchased an elegant home in a fashionable Brentwood neighborhood and hoped to have children. Her exhilaration, however, did not last long.

The marriage failed after a year, and a short time later her husband died of a drug overdose. Although they had already split up by then, Berman had hoped for reconciliation. Her life spiraled downward, into depression and despair. She spent several years living off her savings. Although Berman's father had left a trust fund for her, she was convinced that the money was a pittance compared to what she was owed. She knew her father had owned a share of several Las Vegas hotels, and she believed that Meyer Lansky and other mobsters had cheated her and her mother.

In the late 1980s, she dated a man with two children, and the family eventually moved in with her. She and her boyfriend attempted to produce—using her money—a Broadway musical based on the Dreyfus affair. The project was a disaster. She ended up broke, was forced to sell her house, and the relationship failed.

Although she lost everything after the musical debacle, Berman felt she had gained the family she desperately wanted. She had become a mother to the two children—a boy and a girl—and when she moved into a West Hollywood condominium, the girl lived with her for five years. But Berman still hoped to have a baby. She considered, she told friends, becoming a single mother and asking Durst to father the child.

Berman wrote two mystery novels, but neither was as successful as her memoir. Struggling to pay private school tuition and expenses, friends said, she contacted her old friend Robert Durst, who sent her $20,000.

In 1996, her dormant career was resurrected when she returned to the subject she knew best: Las Vegas. She wrote a four-hour television documentary called *Lady Las Vegas* and then completed a book to accompany the project. Her name, she discovered, still meant something on the Strip. She called publicity-shy entertainers and hotel moguls, said sweetly, "I'm Davie Berman's daughter," and convinced them to appear on camera. The infusion of cash and acclaim the documentary brought her—she was nominated for a Writer's Guild award—delivered her from a deep depression.

During the late 1990s, however, several screenwriting projects failed, and she found herself in dire financial straits and months behind in her rent. A cable television station rejected a Las Vegas project she had suggested. She had just completed a book proposal that she was trying to sell, a memoir about growing up wealthy and ending up broke. Desperate, she again wrote Durst, asked for a loan, and described several writing projects she expected would succeed—proof that she planned to repay him. Durst never responded. In the fall of 2000, however, shortly after New York authorities had reopened the investigation into his wife's disappearance, he sent her $25,000—a gift, he emphasized, not a loan. Berman immediately repaid her landlady.

In November 2000, she wrote Durst a chatty note, effusively thanking him for the money. She assured him that during the past thirty years, he had been "a wonderful friend . . . like the brother I never had." She emphasized that their friendship "was never about money," and apologized for her impoverished state. She described herself as "waif thin and on Prozac from the lack of security and no feeling of well-being about the future." But she also emphasized that she still felt "strong and I work every day trying to turn this around."

About a month later, New York investigators began trying to arrange an interview with Berman about the disappearance of Durst's wife (the body had never been found). They were too late.

On Christmas Eve, Berman was found shot to death at home.

The first major storm of the year batters Los Angeles during the second week of January. Countless traffic accidents snarl the morning commute, and power outages plague the city. Inexplicably, the squad room's air-conditioning is blowing full blast and the detectives huddle at their desks, still wearing their suit jackets, while rain clatters against the windows. On Thursday morning, the LAPD brass informs an RHD lieutenant that Homicide Special has just been assigned the Susan Berman murder. He apprises the on-call team, Paul Coulter and Jerry Stephens.

Stephens, who will turn fifty-five in the spring, is the second-oldest detective in the unit and plans to retire before the end of the year. He spent twenty-five years as a detective, fifteen of them at RHD. He joined the LAPD in 1967, after two tours in Vietnam on a destroyer escort. For a few years he worked as a motorcycle officer, enjoying the cachet and the freedom of the job. Detectives, he believed, were nerds, drudges who spent their days examining bloodstains and bullet trajectories and poring over dry documents in the office. But after a few years on the motorcycle he tired of flagging speeders and drunk drivers. For the first time, the intellectual challenge of detective work appealed to him.

After being promoted to detective, Stephens was assigned to the Hollywood rape unit, where his work attracted the attention of Russ Kuster, the legendary detective in charge of Hollywood Homicide who hired Rick Jackson and was later killed in a shootout. Kuster trans-

ferred Stephens to homicide after less than six months. He was scheduled to begin on a Monday morning. But on the previous Friday
afternoon, before Stephens had a chance to leave the station after
finishing his last shift in the rape section, Kuster sent him out on his
first murder. A female bartender had invited a man home, and he slit
her throat. Stephens eventually identified and arrested the man—an
ex-con on parole—because he had left a fingerprint on the woman's
back—in blood.

Hollywood detectives were considered among the best in the city,
and many alumni had come to RHD. They vouched for Stephens.
Since he was transferred downtown in 1986, he has helped solve a
number of major cases, including several murders of police officers;
the Koreatown stabber, a paranoid schizophrenic who killed six transients and wounded seven, all with the same kitchen knife; and the
William Leasure case. Leasure, once dubbed "the most corrupt cop
in L.A.," eventually pleaded no contest to setting up the murders—
for cash—of two people.

Stephens is one of the few detectives remaining in the squad room
who was assigned to Homicide Special during the O. J. Simpson case.
Stephens was one of several detectives who arrested Simpson and
booked him into county jail after he led police on a nationally televised
low-speed chase with a friend at the wheel of his white Bronco. Deputy
District Attorney Christopher Darden described Stephens in his autobiography as "raucous and friendly . . . one of those guys who could
stand still at a bar for twelve hours and never pull his wallet, one of
those guys you never minded buying a drink."

While Stephens is gregarious and confident and enjoys swapping
insults in the squad room, Coulter, forty-six, is reserved and soft-
spoken. His mother is Latino and his father is from Tennessee.
Although Coulter was raised in Venice, near the beach, he has retained
some of his father's southern mannerisms. If he slipped on a pair of
sunglasses, he would bear a strong resemblance to the stereotypical,
big, barrel-stomached, slow-talking, slow-moving southern cop.

By the time the lieutenant finishes briefing Coulter and Stephens
and they slip on their trench coats and trudge across the street to the
parking lot, the rain has subsided. Ominous clouds still darken the
eastern horizon, but in the west, toward the ocean, shafts of sunlight
filter through the mist.

"They gave it to us because they couldn't solve this piece of shit
in three weeks," Stephens says.

Another detective, who overhears the discussion, calls out, "West L.A. is probably down to their last fucking clue. Nobody wrote on the wall 'I did it,' so they're cutting it loose."

Coulter, driving a blue Ford Crown Victoria, snakes through the heavy traffic and exits the San Diego Freeway on Sunset Boulevard. He cruises east through Bel Air, past the estates of Beverly Hills, and then heads straight up Benedict Canyon, climbing the slick, sinuous road past clouds of pink and white oleanders beaded with raindrops, and crimson bougainvillea cascading over fences. They speed past steep olive-drab hillsides, sheathed in chaparral, studded with live oaks.

The homes abut the canyon roads and the backyards are bordered by towering bluffs, shaded by cypress, sycamores, and an occasional redwood, ringed with thick stands of bamboo, banana plants, or yucca. Canyon living offers the best of Los Angeles. The drive down to the city is a short cruise, but the canyons are rural respites where the smell of sage wafts through bedroom windows, where houses hover above the smog and feature mountain vistas, where foxes timidly sip from backyard swimming pools, where coyotes roam the foothills and howl at night.

Benedict Canyon is popular among successful actors, directors, and musicians. Berman's modest house, however, is an anomaly in this fashionable district. A rustic wood-shingle cottage, squeezed between a busy road and an overgrown hillside, it seems distinctly out of place at the edge of Beverly Hills.

Coulter and Stephens stand in the middle of Berman's weed-choked lawn, which is bracketed by desiccated hydrangeas and withered Japanese boxwood, listening to the cars roaring down the canyon and the wind rustling the oaks. The air is pungent with wet eucalyptus.

"This isn't what I expected," Coulter says.

"What a dump," says Stephens, a dapper dresser with styled silver hair, who wears a chocolate-colored Jones of New York suit, a pale green shirt, and a green silk tie.

Coulter wears a rumpled gray suit and generic white shirt.

Berman's house, which is about a mile from the estate where Sharon Tate and four others were killed by Manson Family members, has not been heated for several weeks and is bitterly cold. Her living room is a jumble of unopened Chanukah presents, books and magazines, and Christmas cards taped to the walls. In the center of the room, a computer and printer are perched atop a chipped white table.

A Liberace ashtray, shaped like a piano, with a few crumpled butts, is lined up beside the keyboard. Nearby are Berman's framed book jackets, a Writer's Guild award, and magazine covers featuring her articles—mementos of a better time. Fingerprint dust streaks the walls and doorknobs.

Throughout the living room, Berman has hung pictures of her parents. One wall is covered with newspaper photos of her mother tap dancing, her parents at Las Vegas banquets, a World War II army photograph of her father, a shot of him in the casino, and one of his Wanted posters, which reads: "Reward $8,000. Wanted for hold-up and post office burglary. Dave Berman—alias Dave the Jew." Another wall features a 1950s photograph of Susan in a party dress, posing with Jimmy Durante, who wrote: "To Susan, I love you. Uncle Jimmy."

Stephens studies the pictures and says to Coulter, "She's living in the past, Roy."

Berman dined on a plastic card table—flanked by two mismatched folding chairs—in the corner of the kitchen. Her freezer is empty and the refrigerator contains only a few items: a carton of milk, a half-stick of butter, a jug of cranberry juice cocktail, and a package of cheddar cheese.

The bedroom is shabby and cluttered, the room of a woman running out of hope. The floor is a bare cement slab. The windows are covered with tattered blankets. The bed is unmade.

"She's a writer down on her luck," Coulter says.

"I don't care *how* down on her luck she is," Stephens says. "I've been to better crack houses in the south end. A rookie cop has more stuff than her."

The original investigators from West Los Angeles arrive and lead Coulter and Stephens to the spare bedroom, where Berman was killed. One of her three wire-haired fox terriers, which did not get along with the other two, was kept here, a West L.A. detective says. Empty, except for a stripped bed and mattress and a metal cage, the room reeks of dog hair, urine, and mold. Faint winter light bleeds through the window and illuminates a few brownish-red commas of blood and a single bloody paw print that gleams with an enameled sheen.

Stephens crosses the room, crouches, and studies a chipped door jamb. Flecks of paint dapple the hardwood floors. "Looks like a struggle by the door," he says. "Maybe she was thrown against it or she struggled to get away."

Berman was found, the West L.A. detectives say, barefoot, dressed in a white T-shirt and purple sweatpants. A single bullet casing was discovered next to her body. She was shot once in the back of the head.

At the West Los Angeles station, off a hectic stretch of Santa Monica Boulevard, Coulter and Stephens meet with the two detectives and their supervisor, Ron Phillips, in an interview room. Phillips and Stephens were partners decades ago, at the old Highland Park station.

"Any grandkids?" Phillips asks Stephens.

"Yeah," Stephens says. "Two."

Phillips shakes his head. "Where have all the years gone?"

Phillips opens up the murder book and begins. "The press really pushed this one. They kept running all those stories about Berman's connection with the mob. It got all the higher-ups interested. Everyone kept calling me: the commander, the press, RHD brass. I didn't want to lose the case. But, finally, after I got four calls one morning, I said, 'Okay. Everyone wants this case to go downtown. Let 'em have it.' "

On the morning of Christmas Eve, Phillips says, a neighbor of Berman's was concerned: one of her dogs was wandering down the street, her back door was wide open, and nobody answered when he rang the bell. He called police. Two patrol officers arrived at the house, discovered Berman, and spotted a pool of blood beneath her head. When homicide detectives arrived, the front door was closed, but unlocked. All the windows were secured with the screens in place. There was no sign of a break-in. The interior did not appear to have been ransacked. Berman's purse lay on the kitchen counter with her credit cards and a small amount of cash, so robbery was not an obvious motive. The coroner determined that Berman had been dead over twenty-four hours.

She was discovered on her back, arms to the side, which defies the laws of physics. Since she was shot in the back of the head, she should have crumpled forward. The detectives reasoned that the killer had flipped her over for some reason. While they examined the crime scene, Berman's cousin called and agreed to meet them at the station. She told detectives that Berman was security conscious to the point of neurosis and always peered out a window before opening her front door. So the detectives figured that the killer had to be someone she knew well. The relative said that Berman had only one enemy—the landlady. She had attempted to evict Berman several times because she had not paid her rent.

During the next week, the detectives interviewed a dozen friends and relatives, most of whom mentioned the tension between Berman and her landlady. Several suspected she had killed Berman. One relative recounted numerous heated arguments between the two. Berman had told several friends that the landlady packed a gun and threatened to kill her dogs. The landlady, she complained to another friend, "showed up at all hours of the day and night demanding that she get out."

The detectives obtained several letters Berman wrote to the landlady during their eviction dispute. "Please," said one, "don't ever threaten me again, saying that if I didn't pay the rent 'something bad is going to happen to you and your dogs,' or that you'll 'come up here and throw my ass on Benedict Canyon.' I take such threats seriously." In another letter, Berman quoted the landlady threatening her and her boyfriend's daughter, who used to live with her: " 'Something very bad is going to happen to you and your daughter and your dogs. I have a key.' "

Phillips tells Coulter and Stephens that shortly after Berman's body was found, the Beverly Hills Police Department received a brief letter informing them that there was a corpse at Berman's address. The detectives believe the killer wrote the letter because it was mailed before the body was found. The stamp was submitted for DNA testing, but the laboratory was unable to extract a sufficient saliva sample.

"We figured maybe the landlady didn't want a rotting corpse ruining her hardwood floors and smelling up the house," Phillips says. "Another thing that interested us was that the landlady left on a vacation right after the murder and was driving a rental car. When we talked to her, she told us the vacation was preplanned and her car was being repaired. But it still seemed odd."

Berman's friends and relatives steered detectives away from Robert Durst; they did not believe he was involved. Berman and Durst had once been so close that their relationship was almost like siblings, friends said. Berman had always insisted that Durst did not kill his wife. Even if she had known something about Kathleen's disappearance, friends told detectives, Berman never would have spoken out now, especially after keeping silent for eighteen years. Perhaps because of her upbringing, friends said, Berman believed in the Mafia code of *omertà*—silence. She would never roll over on one of her closest friends, a man who had been so generous to her. Durst, Berman's friends contended, was fully aware of her loyalty.

"Will Durst talk to us?" Stephens asks.

"I asked his attorney that," one of the West L.A. detectives says. "He said, 'That's an interesting question. I'll have to talk to my client. We're handling things gingerly.' "

The detective thinks it is highly unlikely that Berman was killed because of her father or her Mafia writing projects, a theory popular in the tabloid press because she was shot once in the back of the head, the signature of a mob hit.

"These mob guys would have no reason to knock her off," Phillips interjects. "The stuff she wrote about happened too long ago."

A man who paid Berman to edit his screenplay stopped by her house twice a week but, Phillips says, he seems harmless. Another suspect West L.A. has discounted is a stalker whom Berman's friends mentioned, an older man who sent her love letters.

"Have you talked to him?" Coulter asks.

"We don't have a clue who he is," a detective says. "But she was so security conscious I don't think she'd ever let this old man in the door."

Initially, West L.A. focused on the landlady, questioning her and obtaining a search warrant for her house, which yielded very little. And the writing samples they found did not appear to match the letter sent to the Beverly Hills Police Department. They now believe it is unlikely that she killed Berman.

"If landlords started killing people over arguments like that," Stephens says, "we'd have thousands of murders a year in L.A."

The West L.A. detectives tell Coulter and Stephens that one of Berman's close friends finds it curious that Durst sent the $25,000 check shortly after the *New York Times* published an article reporting that police had reopened the investigation into his wife's disappearance.

"That's a hell of a coincidence," Phillips says. He believes that Durst is a viable suspect, but Stephens is skeptical. "I'm not ruling anyone out at this point, but I don't think the two cases are connected," he says. "Eighteen years is a long time. If she were going to say something now, she probably would have mentioned it to a friend. But she never said a word about it, according to all the people you talked to."

Phillips tells Coulter and Stephens that Berman's friend, a writer from the East Coast, also provided another possible direction for the investigation. Berman had a close, platonic friendship with Nyle, her manager. He runs a small agency out of his house and represents mostly actors. Berman was his only writer client.

Berman's friend told the West L.A. detectives that Nyle had behaved in a strange manner since the murder and uttered some disturbing comments. He had cared deeply for Berman, but she was such a difficult woman that he was often angry and frustrated after spending time with her, Nyle told the friend. Then he added that now, after her murder, he was "dealing with a lot of anger," and felt "pissed off."

Nyle also told the friend that on Christmas morning, he climbed through one of Berman's windows because he heard that her relatives were unable to contact her. He noticed soot on the walls, so he assumed there had been a fire. When he played the messages on her answering machine, he heard a neighbor say that he had found one of Berman's dogs. Nyle said that he walked next door and the neighbor said that Berman fell, hit her head, and died. "That makes sense," he told the friend. "Susan was such a klutz."

The friend later discovered that the neighbor told Nyle that Berman had either been killed or had fallen. She found it curious that Nyle did not mention the possibility that Susan was a murder victim. He later told the friend, "It seems very much like a professional job. It was very quick." She wondered how Nyle came to that conclusion when he told her, initially, that he believed she had died after a fall.

The friend also told the West L.A. detectives that a few weeks before the murder, Berman underwent eye surgery. Nyle had taken care of her during the next week, but he resented the imposition. Berman fell down once on the street and instead of helping her, Nyle appeared embarrassed and shouted at her.

"I didn't think much about him at first," one of the West L.A. detectives says. "Then I talked to that friend of Berman's and I got interested."

"He's weird," the other detective says. "He was acting hinky when we talked to him. Then he settled down." The detective taps his finger on the murder book. "There's something funny about him. He and Berman supposedly talked all the time. But before the murder he said he hadn't been in touch with her. And there were no messages from him on her answering machine."

"He have any criminal record?" Coulter asks.

A detective shakes his head.

"You run him for guns?"

"No guns."

After Phillips hands over copies of his notes and reports to Stephens, they reminisce about the old days when they were rookies. "Remember that old guy who felt young cops couldn't do anything right the first time, so he'd tear up all our reports?"

"He raised hummingbirds," Phillips says. "The way to get on his good side was to read up on hummingbirds and talk to him about them."

"One day I was working day watch," Stephens says, "and I saw this young officer crying. Tears were running down his face. The old guy had just told him, 'You're too dumb to be a police officer! Give me your badge and gun and go home.'

"Two weeks later someone calls the kid at home and asked, 'What happened to you?' The kid said he'd been fired. The guy on the phone said, 'No, you haven't. Come on back to work.' "

The rain kicks up again as Coulter and Stephens drive back downtown on the cold, windy night. The mist drifts through the beams of their headlights, and colors from the traffic lights reflect off the puddles in the street.

Coulter and Stephens discuss what needs to be done next. They plan to obtain a search warrant for Berman's phone records, so they can identify the last people she talked to. They also will request that LAPD technicians employ more sophisticated methods and search for additional fingerprints. The chemical ninhydrin, often used on porous surfaces such as paper, wood, and walls, reacts to the amino acids in the fingers' sweat patterns, leaving a purple residue. The detectives will ask technicians to apply ninhydrin to the walls near where Berman's body was found because the shooter might have braced himself for balance after firing the shot.

"Fingerprints in the house probably won't mean much—unless they're in blood—because she knew her killer well," Stephens says to Coulter. "But we might as well give it a try."

Coulter points out that the killer might have left a print on the shell casing—found in the room where Berman was killed—while loading the gun. A method using ordinary superglue is effective on many surfaces, including metal, so the detective will request that technicians use the process. The casing will be placed in an enclosed chamber, where the glue's vapor might adhere to—and illuminate—the oil and moisture of a fingerprint. The detectives also plan to submit the casing to the FBI database and hope the gun can be traced.

They stop for dinner at Philippe's, a downtown landmark restaurant with sawdust on the floor, where customers line up at the counter and order French dip sandwiches from waitresses in starched uniforms and aprons. The detectives pick up their sandwiches, ten-cent-a-cup coffee, and pie and sit on wooden stools and eat at a long wooden table. The restaurant's walls feature numerous articles about how the founder, a French immigrant named Philippe Mathieu, invented the French dip. In 1918, while preparing a sandwich for a policeman, he accidentally dropped the sliced French roll into a roasting pan filled with drippings. The officer enjoyed the sandwich so much that he returned the next day with a group of cops and ordered more au jus–dipped sandwiches.

The manager of Philippe's greets Stephens warmly and they chat for a few minutes. He knows her well, because when her son was murdered, it was Stephens who arrested the killer and sent him to San Quentin's death row.

When the detectives finish their dinner, Stephens says, "Why was Berman on her back when she was found?"

"It's almost like someone cared for her and turned her over because they wanted to make her more comfortable," Coulter says. "I don't think the landlady would have the strength to move the body like that."

Stephens stares at his coffee. "I would have liked to have picked up this case from the beginning."

"We're at a real disadvantage, Roy," Coulter says.

Coulter and Stephens grouse that the West L.A. detectives never requested a coroner's criminalist, who would have collected hair and fibers from the body at the scene. Instead, Berman's body was transported to the coroner's office, where her clothing was packaged. Hairs and fibers eventually will be collected, but the process is not as efficient. A criminalist, using a standard "sexual assault kit," also could have checked to determine if Berman had been raped, although the crime scene suggests that it was highly unlikely. By the time an autopsy is conducted it might be too late.

The detectives are also stunned that Berman's fingernails were never clipped and examined. When victims struggle and scratch, their fingernails sometimes scrape microscopic skin samples that yield the assailant's DNA. Berman had no defensive wounds, but checking a female victim's fingernails is a standard procedure. After a body has been washed during the autopsy, however, many criminalists believe it is too late to gather evidence from the nails.

"Maybe because she was shot in the back of the head, nobody thought it was necessary," Stephens says. "But the coroner should have done it anyway. Especially when you consider all those paint chips by the door jamb."

"It was Christmas Eve," Coulter says. "People got sloppy."

15

At 6:15 on a chilly January morning, Tim Marcia parks in front of Dave Lambkin's house, which is nestled on the side of a canyon, not far from Mulholland Drive. Today they will discover whether Vincent Rossi killed Stephanie Gorman.

Stars still dot the sky and the clouds are rimmed with moonlight. The air smells of acorns and damp hillsides. Marcia bangs on the door, setting off a cacophony inside. A crazed Schipperke, a breed better suited for guarding Dutch canal boats than roaming a Los Angeles home, barks furiously, evading Lambkin's attempts to corral him in a back room. When he finally lets Marcia inside, Lambkin grumbles about his Schipperke's high-strung personality. His toy Manchester terrier is a model dog, he boasts.

The décor in Lambkin's house is eccentric. On the wall hang Salvador Dalí prints and lithographs; and frightful Day of the Dead skulls and skeletons—which his wife collects—are scattered about. First editions of Stephen King and Anne Rice line the bookshelves.

Marcia hops into Lambkin's maroon Cutlass and they head down to the freeway. The rising sun illuminates the ridges along the canyon with the smoky light of dawn, and a vast sea of lights glimmers below, from the foothills to the sea.

"I know we've done everything possible," Marcia says. "We've left no stone unturned."

"I think when he sees us at the door, he'll say, 'I've been waiting thirty-five years for you guys,' " Lambkin jokes. "He'll break down and confess."

He pulls off the freeway in West Los Angeles, and Marcia picks up a dozen doughnuts at Primo's, where his family once breakfasted every Sunday before church. After nervously negotiating the rush-hour traffic all the way to Orange County, Lambkin parks at a police station near Rossi's residence. Waiting inside are the lieutenant of the Rape Special section, Debra McCarthy; two detectives who will help search the house; and two members of an LAPD undercover unit who have tailed Rossi and his wife for the past week. As the group munches on doughnuts in the parking lot, the undercover officers report that Rossi's wife usually departs at midmorning. Rossi generally stays home until lunchtime.

"We want to play it a little Colombo-ish, a bit dimwitted," Lambkin tells McCarthy. "We'll tell him we reopened the case last year, his name came up and we want to see if he has any connection. We'll try to get him over here, where we've got an interview room arranged. We want him away from his house as soon as possible, to get him out of his comfort zone. We'll tell him we want him to look at some pictures."

The key to the interview, Lambkin says, is to ensure that Rossi denies ever visiting the Gorman house. They are hoping for a confession because the district attorney might be reluctant to file a case based on a single fingerprint.

"I get the feeling he's a deviant of some sort," one of the undercover cops says. "The way he moves. The way he looks at people. He gives them hard looks."

Encouraged by the insight, Lambkin and Marcia, along with McCarthy and the other two detectives, drive off to a nearby mall parking lot. The undercover officers will watch Rossi's house, and when his wife leaves, they will notify Lambkin. As the detectives wait in the parking lot, McCarthy, who is about six months pregnant, asks Marcia for another doughnut. They talk about children.

"I'll show you a picture of my daughter, but I won't bother showing Dave," she says, laughing. "I know he doesn't like kids."

Lambkin and Marcia become increasingly anxious as they wait for the phone call. They pace beside their car in silence.

McCarthy says she thought about the case all night and slept fitfully. She dreamt that Rossi denied knowing the Gormans, which is a favorable omen, she believes. She tells one of the detectives that she joined the police department partly because of the murder of another young girl: her sister. "It was sixteen years ago, back in Rhode Island.

He was a neighbor. It was a stalking, *Fatal Attraction* type thing."

"What happened to him?" the detective asks.

"He did fifteen years and got out. My family was totally flipping out. I said, 'Stand by. He'll screw up.' And he did. He developed a drug habit in prison. He was violated his second week out. He peed dirty. He was thrown back in prison."

At 10:15 A.M., Lambkin's cell phone finally rings. The detectives hop in the car and cruise through Rossi's modest neighborhood to his small white house with blue trim, ringed by palm trees. When Rossi opens the door, Lambkin is surprised. In his 1971 booking photo, he looked like a thug, a cast member of *The Sopranos*. Now, standing in his doorway, the detectives see nothing menacing about him. Pudgy and gray-haired, he is dressed in a beige polo shirt and polyester slacks. He looks like an amiable grandfather who spends his days puttering in the garden.

Lambkin and Marcia introduce themselves and shake Rossi's hand. "We've reopened an old murder case and we just need a few minutes of your time," Lambkin says, smiling reassuringly. "We have some names we'd like to run by you."

Rossi, who appears composed, invites them inside. Lambkin sits on the sofa and Marcia pulls up a chair. Rossi remains standing. His house is immaculate and the walls are covered with pictures of his children and grandchildren.

"This is a very old case," Lambkin says.

Rossi scrunches up his face in a baffled expression, which encourages the detectives.

"It was in West Los Angeles," Lambkin says.

Rossi says he is not familiar with any old West L.A. murders.

Lambkin and Marcia are elated. They have obtained a crucial denial. Now all they need is a confession.

"But I was the property manager of sixty properties at that time," Rossi says. "They were on the West Side."

Lambkin thinks, *He's already making excuses.*

"The name of the victim is Stephanie Gorman," Lambkin says.

Rossi, still standing, walks over to the kitchen counter and writes her name down on a business card. Then he turns toward Lambkin and asks, "Is this about that sixteen-year-old girl who was killed?"

"Yes," Lambkin says.

Rossi crosses the room and sits on the L-shaped sofa beside Lambkin. "How is it that you've come to talk to me now?"

"We saw your name listed in the original investigation," Lambkin says. "There were hundreds of people interviewed, but we discovered you never were."

Rossi explains that on that day in 1965 he stopped by the Beverlywood home of a doctor friend from New York. The doctor was not home from work yet. While Rossi waited for him with his wife, a frantic woman came to the door, pleading for the doctor.

"I went back to the house with her to see what I could do. I'm not a doctor, but I could tell the girl was obviously dead. I was only there a few minutes."

"Did anyone ever interview you?"

"No," Rossi says. "The cops told me to get out. So I did."

Lambkin feels as if he has been punched in the stomach. For a moment, he cannot breathe. He recalls Stephanie's sister saying that she ran to the doctor's house to get help, but the doctor was not home.

Rossi's voice is measured. His hands are steady. He sits right beside Lambkin on the sofa, calmly answering his questions. No killer is that good an actor.

After a few more minutes of desultory conversation, Lambkin and Marcia stagger out the door and drive to the mall parking lot.

"I feel sick to my stomach," Marcia says.

"Three months of work down the drain," Lambkin grumbles.

"What are the fucking chances of him looking so much like the composite?" Marcia mutters.

At the parking lot, Lambkin says to McCarthy, "Just shoot me." He recounts the conversation with Rossi. Marcia leans against the car, looking like a whipped dog.

"I could never imagine the case going this way," Lambkin says. "Over twenty-five detectives and officers worked this case. They tracked down hundreds of people, even the kids selling candy in the neighborhood. Why couldn't they track this guy down?"

Lambkin is angry because he has wasted so many months, invested so much in the case—unnecessarily. If the DNA evidence had not been lost, he could have cleared Rossi in an afternoon. He had thought that the lost evidence was the only snafu in the case. Now he discovers another egregious LAPD blunder. One of the most elementary rules police recruits learn is "Secure the crime scene and secure the witnesses." Patrol officers are required to fill out "field interview cards," which identify everyone at a crime scene. This enables detectives to contact all prospective witnesses. Also, their fingerprints can be compared against all those at the crime scene, for the specific purpose of preventing the kind of debacle that has befallen Lambkin and Marcia.

McCarthy attempts to comfort the detectives. She tells them their investigative work was excellent and their preparation superb. The props they devised will be a model for future cases. The abortive investigation was not their fault. The detective supervisor who destroyed the evidence and the patrol officer who failed to identify Rossi sabotaged the case. She tells Lambkin and Marcia they are among the best detective teams she has ever supervised. She hugs them and says, "I feel sorry for the family. And I feel sorry for you guys. I know how much work you've put into the case."

"With all the physical evidence, it would have been so simple," Lambkin says.

"If the patrol officer had identified him, it would have saved us months of work," Marcia says. "They ought to use this at the academy when they teach recruits how to handle a homicide scene."

After a session of cathartic complaining, the detectives call the doctor whom Rossi visited. He confirms Rossi's story. They then deliver the bad news to Stephanie's sister, a call they had been dreading.

Lambkin tells McCarthy and the other detectives, "The day is shot. I'm not really hungry, but we might as well eat lunch." He is familiar with a nearby beachfront restaurant that serves one of his favorite dishes: pumpkinseed-crusted three-cheese chiles rellenos with papaya salsa.

Lambkin drives along the Pacific Coast Highway, toward the restaurant. The storm that battered Southern California the past few days has moved east and the cloudless sky now is a dome of radiant blue. The beach is desolate on this crisp winter afternoon and the ocean glitters in the sunshine. A faint onshore breeze kicks up patches of frothy surf.

At the restaurant, nobody has much of an appetite. McCarthy and the detectives pick at their food. They stare glumly at the sea. After lunch, as the detectives head back home, Lambkin says he is going to take his wife tonight to an appropriate setting: a blues club. He will drink a bottle of wine with her and drown his own case of the blues. Marcia intends to spend the rest of the afternoon playing baseball with his son.

Lambkin snakes along in the afternoon rush-hour traffic. The detectives sit in silence for a half hour. Finally, Lambkin says, "This is fucked."

After another stretch of silence, Marcia tells Lambkin that at least they still have one suspect—Goldsmith.

"From the beginning, I had an uncomfortable feeling about him," Lambkin says.

"His story sucks," Marcia says.

"But if he tells us to pound sand, we can't do anything," Lambkin says. "The problem is, we have no leverage on him."

"*He* doesn't know that," Marcia says. "That bondage thing with him bothers me. He seems like a sexual predator. He's a good suspect."

Marcia strokes his chin. "He's looking better and better now."

16

The day after the Vincent Rossi disaster, Lambkin and Marcia recuperate at home. The next morning they reluctantly return to the office.

"Great police work," Otis Marlow tells Lambkin. "You cleared another suspect."

Lambkin laughs. He copes with the disappointment by joking with the other detectives and sardonically recounting the case's litany of errors, from the lost evidence, to the missing files, to the failure to identify Rossi at the crime scene.

Marcia is too morose to chat. He spends the day staring into a computer screen, studying Goldsmith's prior arrests, searching for juvenile offenses, scanning the reports for accomplices.

Rick Jackson commiserates with Marcia. "Ninety-nine percent of the time, they'd have identified your suspect," Jackson says. "You couldn't have been more thorough. This scenario is so remote."

Marcia nods in agreement, but without much enthusiasm.

Cheryl Gorman calls the detectives and thanks them for all their hard work. "But I still don't see," she says, her voice tinged with frustration, "how they could have failed to identify the guy at the time."

The detectives have no answer.

In the adjacent squad room, Coulter and Stephens pore over crime reports, autopsy results, and interview statements; they make copies and compile their own murder book. Stephens sits next to Otis Marlow, another veteran, and the two frequently trade barbs. Marlow stands up, peers over Stephens's shoulder, and says, "You've already had that Berman murder for a few days, Roy. Why haven't you solved it yet?" Marlow, who overheard Stephens discussing the case, offers his assessment: "Durst's wife's dead. New York detectives are coming out to talk to Berman about the wife's murder. Now *she* turns up dead. I may not be much of a detective, but Durst is the first guy I'd smack in the forehead."

Stephens explains that Durst is guarded by a phalanx of high-priced New York lawyers who probably will not let him talk. Eventually, he says, they will need to find a way to interview him. "But I'm not so sure he's our guy. Nobody coming out from New York to kill her would send that letter to the Beverly Hills police. And why would he want her dead? She'd always backed him up."

Stephens and Coulter have assiduously retraced the investigation of the West Los Angeles detectives. Now they are ready to conduct their own case. They plan to reinterview some of the people who were already questioned and will also attempt to unearth other friends and relatives who have not yet been contacted. When they are familiar with the details of the case and the habits of their eccentric victim, they will then pursue their suspects.

Coulter tells Stephens, who can be charming and is known for his sense of humor, that because he is a "people person," he should conduct the interviews. Coulter will assume responsibility for the evidence, the murder book, and the daily chronological record of the investigation.

Coulter was a Wilshire Division homicide detective when he first met Stephens. He was not impressed. When Stephens dropped by the division to check on a case, he worked the room like a comedian, joking with everyone, keeping up a steady stream of patter, laughing with the detectives. Coulter considered him a lightweight.

When they were named partners at Homicide Special a few months ago, Coulter was initially dismayed. Now, Coulter respects Stephens and realizes that his exuberant personality is an asset: witnesses, and even suspects, loosen up around him. Stephens may be an acquired taste, but Coulter now enjoys his partner's sense of humor and light-hearted approach.

Stephens sets up an interview with Berman's ex-boyfriend's son. During the early 1990s, he and his father and sister lived with Berman and she considered him the son she never had. Now in his mid-twenties, he works in the music business and has distinctive, waxed, spiky, blond-tipped hair. As the detectives lead him from the squad room to an interview cubicle, one of the older investigators in the unit mutters, "Can't anyone lend that kid a comb?"

The young man tells Coulter and Stephens that after Berman and his father split up, he continued to visit her at least once a week. She named him the beneficiary of her modest Writer's Guild insurance policy.

"How often did you talk on the phone?" Stephens asks.

"Constantly. We were very close," he says as Coulter jots notes on a yellow legal pad.

"Did she generally keep the house locked?"

"Yes. I'd have to knock on the door. She'd check the window. I'd say, 'It's me.' Then she'd let me in."

"Did she mention having any problems with anyone?"

"The landlady was a point of great contention."

"What was the problem?"

He explains that the landlady tried to evict Berman on a number of occasions because she had not paid her rent. During several court hearings Berman argued—successfully—that she was withholding the rent until repairs were made to the house.

"The landlady wanted the rent when she wanted it. She told Susan that she owned a gun. She threatened her dogs. Susan always felt threatened. She even said, 'If I ever turn up dead, it was her.' "

But last year, he tells Stephens, Berman visited the landlady in the hospital after she had had an auto accident. She brought flowers. The detectives also know that Berman sent her a Christmas card and scrawled a friendly message. The two women must have managed to come to a détente. The detectives no longer believe that the landlady, who is in her seventies, is a suspect.

Stephens asks about his father's relationship with Berman.

"Susan blamed him for losing her money," he says.

"You ever see him violent?"

"No."

"Did he have any weapons?"

"No, he's an ex-hippie."

"What was her daily schedule?"

"She'd get up and read the paper. The rest of the day was spent writing and in meetings."

"Did she do much socializing?"

"She invited very few people to come over, because she was embarrassed about her poverty and the condition of her house."

He and Nyle, her manager, were the only friends she allowed to regularly visit. The detectives are intrigued by Nyle, and Stephens hopes to learn more about him.

"She had a"—he languidly waves a hand—"*relationship* with him, sort of. . . ."

But the relationship was never romantic, he says. They went out to movies and dinner, and Nyle often drove Berman to business meetings or doctor's appointments because she had numerous phobias, including a fear of heights. Berman refused to go higher than the second floor of a building unless Nyle or another friend accompanied her.

After the murder, the young man says, Nyle visited Berman's house, picked up her mail, and opened her bank statements. Apparently, she owed Nyle money. She told Nyle that Durst had loaned her $15,000. Nyle later heard that the sum was $25,000 and attempted to confirm the amount by taking Berman's bank statements home with him to examine.

"I went off on him and he returned the bank statement to me."

"Anyone else she might have had problems with?"

He sighs. "Nobody that she mentioned to me. . . . Anyone she had problems with she'd clear out of her life."

Stephens asks him whether he thinks Robert Durst was connected to the murder.

"That's idiotic. She already proved her loyalty to him eighteen years ago. And if he *did* do it, he wouldn't pull the trigger himself. He'd send someone, and Susan *never* would have let anyone in the house she didn't know."

He drops his elbows on the metal table and leans forward. "Bobby Durst called me. He offered his condolences. He offered to pay for a private investigator. He offered to pay for the funeral."

After the interview, the young man asks Stephens, "How optimistic are you of solving this?"

"We solve most of our cases," Stephens says matter-of-factly. "Something will turn up."

A few days later, on a frigid winter morning, the air-conditioning in the squad room continues to blow, despite repeated entreaties to the Parker Center maintenance department. While Coulter and Stephens shiver in the draftiest corner, other detectives loudly complain all morning about their primitive working conditions. They have no voice mail because the department will not buy the equipment. The building is crumbling. They spend many days responding to officer-involved shooting calls, which diverts precious time from their homicide investigations. At the very least, the detectives grumble, they should not be forced to work in a meat locker.

A detective calls out to Stephens, "When you finally going to retire?"

"I'm not leaving," Stephens says, "until the LAPD can do two things—heat this building and give us voice mail."

Coulter and Stephens are eager to solve Berman's murder, which is now almost a month old, and have worked until almost midnight every day during the past week, studying the West L.A. detectives' paperwork. Stephens believes one element of the case that demands urgent attention is Berman's three dogs. "We've got to check on those dogs," he tells Coulter. "If nobody picks them up, they'll kill them."

One neighbor is caring for Lulu and another has the other two, Romeo and Golda. Stephens wants to be sure that they will adopt the dogs and not dump them off at the pound, where they may be euthanized. Berman was killed in Lulu's room—the spare bedroom—and the dog is now apparently traumatized because she witnessed the murder, the neighbor told Stephens. She spends all day in the backyard, her nose stuck in the fence, trembling and gazing at Berman's house.

"Dogs are very sensitive," Stephens tells Coulter. "My miniature dachshund, Molly, gets real upset if I don't play with her for fifteen or twenty minutes when I get home from work. She doesn't like to go outside much because it's too cold. So I built a little patio in the backyard so she'll be more comfortable."

Another detective asks, "What is it with these single women and their dogs? They treat 'em like kids."

"It's not just *single women*," Stephens says, sounding offended. "A lot of people are very attached to their dogs. They're very humanlike in their emotions."

Berman's will named a friend who works for an animal rescue agency to care for her dogs. The detectives decide to interview the friend next. But first they stop off at a city salvage warehouse. In its dank basement they poke through discarded desks, chairs, file cabinets, and an assortment of defective office supplies, finally unearthing two battered metal space heaters. If the LAPD is unable to heat its building, Coulter and Stephens decide, they will assume responsibility for their chilly corner of the squad room. The detectives then drive to the Criminal Courts Building. They drop off a search warrant for Berman's phone records at a judge's chamber.

"This is the so-called mobster's daughter case," Coulter says.

"You got anything?" the judge asks.

"Of course not," Stephens says, laughing. "That's why they gave it to our unit."

"Any insurance policy?" the judge asks.

"Yeah, but it's not much," Stephens says.

The detectives ride the courthouse elevator up to the district attorney's office because Stephens has to pick up some files from another murder he recently solved.

"I heard about that New York connection," says a deputy district attorney who is a friend of Stephens's. "Sounds like a mob hit."

"Don't believe everything you read," Stephens says.

"One shot?"

"Yeah," Stephens says reluctantly.

"To the back of the head?"

"Yeah," Stephens says.

He flashes Stephens a smug look and says, "I told you." He then asks, "Did he leave any casings?"

"Yes, he did," Stephens says cheerily. "You know the Mafia uses revolvers. And a hit man never would have left a casing."

The deputy district attorney looks deflated.

"You have a dog?" Stephens asks him.

"A golden retriever. Why?"

Stephens tells him about Lulu, how she witnessed the murder and now trembles all day. "That's pretty pathetic, don't you think?" Stephens says. "You have room to take in another dog?"

"I can't put my family at risk," the deputy DA says solemnly, "and hide a witness to a murder at my house."

Laughing, the detectives set out to interview Berman's friend who works for the animal rescue agency. She lives high atop a mountain canyon, not far from Berman's house, in a fashionable neighborhood where homes have sweeping city and valley views. On unusually clear days, residents near the peaks can see the ocean.

Inside the house, the detectives sit on a chintz sofa, flanked by antique lamps, in an elegant living room with gleaming hardwood floors and open-beamed ceilings. As the friend serves them mugs of tea, Stephens pets the woman's dog and tells her he is remarkably well behaved. "I must be doing something wrong, I can't train my dog to sit, shake hands, or anything. How'd you do it?"

The woman, who appeared nervous when the detectives knocked at her door, seems more relaxed now that she knows one of them is a dog lover. After she describes a few training techniques, and runs her dog through a series of tricks, Stephens asks her how she met Berman.

"My husband's a film producer and she pitched a few ideas to him in '83 or '84. He thought we'd get along. A few years ago she was flying somewhere, called me, and said, 'If something happens to me, will you take care of my dogs?' I said, 'Of course.' I'm an artist, but I do a lot of animal rescue work. . . . I thought Susan's dogs were very maladjusted, very hard to deal with. But if anything is needed with the dogs, I'll do it."

Several years ago, the woman says she lent Berman $1,000. "She told me she had to fly somewhere and needed money for a plane ticket. She said, 'I thought this deal would go through, but it didn't.' " The typical Hollywood conversation, the friend says with a sad smile.

"But I haven't seen her a lot recently," she adds. "One reason is that she could be very confrontational in public, very difficult to be around. She had a lot of food allergies. One time we were at a restaurant and she said to the waiter, 'I'm allergic to eggs. There are no eggs in this dish, are there?' The waiter said no. But she went into the kitchen and confronted the chef. She shouted, 'I'm wearing a tag and I'll *die* if I eat eggs! I'll *die!*' I told my husband I didn't want to go to a restaurant with her again."

During the past few years she chatted with Berman only a few times, she tells Stephens. Once Berman said something negative about her landlady, but she cannot recall the details. When the friend says she knows nothing about Berman's relationship with Durst, Stephens quickly shifts the conversation to Nyle.

"I think she had a crush on him," the woman says. "That's one of the only names she ever mentioned. I think she was very lonely. She had a hard life."

The interview does not advance the investigation, but Stephens is reassured that Berman's dogs will not be put to death. If the neighbors abandon the dogs, this friend will care for them.

As the detectives prepare to leave, the producer's wife tries to talk Stephens into adopting a dog she recently rescued. When he tells her that Molly demands all his attention, she asks Coulter whether he has a dog.

"I *had* one, a border collie named Sarge." Coulter adds that Sarge recently died of cancer. "I stayed up with him that last night. He was so weak he couldn't lift his head up. He just whimpered. In the morning, me and my daughter took him to the vet to be put down." Coulter is flushed and his voice catches. "I was blubbering like a fool."

As the detectives drive back down the canyon, Coulter continues to talk about Sarge.

"Sounds like you haven't got over the dog yet," Stephens says.

"I haven't."

"Well, *get* over it. I'm sick of hearing about him," Stephens says, suppressing a smile. "Since that lady was a dog trainer, I was embarrassed to tell her that Molly sleeps in bed with me. She keeps crawling into bed and won't go to sleep unless I let her in." He shakes his head. "Her dog was so well behaved. I can't even get Molly to shake hands. She just won't do it."

The detectives walk out to their car in the gloaming. On this cold winter evening the crest of the mountains is tinted pink in the waning light and a single star sparkles in the lavender sky. As Coulter heads down the canyon road, he and Stephens attempt to pinpoint when Berman died. Patrol officers found her body at one P.M. on Christmas Eve. The day before, neighbors found her dogs wandering on the street.

"Someone whacked her, left a door open, and the dogs got out," Coulter says.

"So whoever let the dogs out is our shooter," Stephens says. He mutters to himself, "Who let the dogs out?" He turns to Coulter, punches him playfully on the shoulder, and sings, parroting the popular song "Who Let the Dogs Out?" He sings again, "Who, who, who, *who* let the dogs out?" and ends with four loud barks.

Stephens strolls into the office singing the refrain. He explains to the other detectives that when he answers this musical question, he will solve the case. Soon, Stephens, Otis Marlow, and a few other detectives are singing and barking along to the song.

At eight the next morning, Stephens lugs a boom box into the office, slips a CD into the slot, and blares "Who Let the Dogs Out?" as the other detectives sing or bark or boogie to the beat. Every half hour until lunch, Stephens plays the opening to the song as investigators in other units, attracted by the music, scurry down the hall and, looking mystified, peer through the squad room door.

In a placid San Fernando Valley neighborhood, an elderly couple have been stabbed and slashed to death and their home set on fire. The woman might have been raped, so Lambkin and Marcia have been assigned the case. They are forced to set aside the Gorman investigation. People living near the victims are terrified; hundreds pack churches for Neighborhood Watch meetings; reporters press the detectives about the progress of the investigation. A headline in a local paper reflects the mood: "Neighborhood Swept Up in Fear." Stephens, who worked with Lambkin in Hollywood, walks over to Rape Special and tosses the article on Lambkin's desk.

"Maybe we haven't solved our homicide, but at least the neighborhood where *our* victim was killed is not swept up in fear," Stephens jokes.

Later in the afternoon, one of the few people Berman allowed into her house stops by, as arranged, for an interview. An aspiring writer, he visited Berman twice a week and paid her $75 an hour to edit his screenplay. Stephens has to leave the office briefly, so Coulter interviews the man, who carries a bottle of Evian into the small, monastic interview cubicle.

"You mind if I drink?" he tells Coulter. "I'm very nervous."

"Relax," Coulter says.

"How can I relax in a room like this?"

The man, who is in his mid-forties, has a mustache and goatee and his hair is flecked with gray. Jittery, he continually runs his hands through his hair.

"Didn't Wambaugh work here?" he asks.

"No," Coulter says. "He worked at Hollenbeck Division."

"Didn't the LAPD have a five-time *Jeopardy!* champion?"

"Yeah. He's a sergeant."

Steered back to the case, the man tells Coulter that during the past six months he usually visited Susan Berman every Tuesday and Thursday. "If I ever wanted to change the time, she'd spend thirty minutes excoriating me. Then she'd tell me, 'I can't trust you. I feel threatened.' Just because I wanted to change the time. . . . She was brilliant but crazy."

He sips the water. "This whole thing gives me the willies. She said she owed me a session and told me to come the Saturday before Christmas. I was going to come from one to three, but I needed a break. What if I'd have come? If I was there I'd be toast." He hyperventilates and says, "There were times when I was at her place and I thought, 'If anyone wanted to kill Susan, I'd be stuck here.' "

Coulter looks surprised. "What made you say that?"

"She'd always say, 'The only time I feel safe is when you're here.' Paranoia is contagious."

Coulter mentions that he heard a man was stalking Berman.

"One day she got a letter and ripped it up," the man says. "She said, 'Someone is stalking me.' " But she never mentioned the stalker again. He tells Coulter he does not know much about Berman's relationship with any of her friends, including Nyle.

"Who do you think could have done it?" Coulter asks.

"*I* could have killed her," the man says.

Coulter stares at him for a moment. "Did you?"

"No, no, no," the man says, laughing nervously. "I have receipts up and down San Vicente where I was doing Christmas shopping."

Coulter smiles and says, "I had to ask."

The man gulps the rest of his water and says in a conspiratorial tone, "About three weeks or a month before she died, I came to the door and she says, 'I just got the worst news. My best friend got charged with murder for something that happened eighteen years ago. I can't talk about it.' She got hysterical and disappeared into another room, where she talked on the phone."

During the next few sessions, instead of sitting with him in the living room, Berman huddled in a back room, making surreptitious telephone calls. He tells Coulter he believes that Robert Durst killed Berman. "My girlfriend doesn't believe it because she doesn't think Bobby Durst would kill his friend. I said, 'Honey, you're so naïve.' "

When Stephens returns to the room, the man, a former high school teacher, tells the detectives that when he attempted to determine who had cheated on a test he examined three variables: "Motive, opportunity, and history. That was my philosophy when I was a teacher. That's why I thought Bobby Durst did it. If he's connected this could be huge. It could be as big as that case in Boston involving Claus von Bülow."

While he rambles from topic to topic, Stephens cuts him off and asks, just to assess his reaction, if he is willing to be polygraphed. The man readily agrees.

"You know what's really weird," he tells the detectives. "I returned to her house to get my stuff. And on a bookshelf in the back bedroom, above a bloodstain, you know what the first book I saw was? *A Place of Execution.*"

The man pulls Berman's autobiography out of his briefcase and reads in a stentorian manner, like an English teacher lecturing a class of eleventh-graders: "There are scars within me that will probably never heal; I have uncontrollable anxiety attacks that occur without warning. Death and love seem linked forever in my fantasies and the Kaddish [the Jewish mourning prayer] will ring always in my ears."

He snaps the book shut and says, canting his head, "That's Susan."

After the interview, Coulter points out to Stephens that this man was the first friend of Berman's to finger Durst. Her other friends and relatives have dismissed him as a suspect. Of course, the man bases his supposition on the behavior of high school cheaters, not exactly overwhelming evidence.

In the afternoon, the detectives drive through the drizzle to West Los Angeles and interview one of Berman's aunts and a cousin, neither of whom suspects Durst. The aunt tells the detectives, "Everyone loved Susan. Only one person had a problem with her: the landlady. Susan told me that the woman had a gun. She threatened to harm her dogs."

The cousin dismisses the mob angle. "That Mafia princess stuff really makes me mad. The Mafia couldn't have anything to do with this. That's ridiculous. Those guys she wrote about are probably a hundred years old now, if they're still alive."

Later, Stephens attempts to circumvent the landlady's attorney and question her. He and Coulter knock on her front door, but she is not home. On their way back downtown, Stephens suggests they canvass a few more of Berman's neighbors. And while they are there, he says with a sheepish smile, they might as well check on Berman's dog Lulu.

When the dog's caretaker answers the doorbell, Stephens immediately asks, "How's Lulu doing?"

"Much better," the neighbor says. "We got a crate for her to sleep in. We lined it with a blanket. She seems much more secure in there. That helped a lot."

Stephens looks genuinely relieved.

Stephens, who has obtained Durst's cell phone number from one of Berman's friends, calls him and leaves a message. Durst surprises him by calling back. Stephens does not want to press Durst too hard and prompt interference from his high-priced attorneys, so just to keep him talking, he asks Durst how he met Berman. After describing their friendship at UCLA, Durst acknowledges sending Berman several checks during the past decade. "I lent her a lot of money," he says. "But it's no big deal because I have more money than I can ever spend." Durst says he has a house in Northern California, "but I can't stay there. I keep getting pestered by the press. Even when I get off the plane I'm followed. So I'm in New York now. No one knows me here anymore."

When Stephens slips in a few questions about his whereabouts during the weekend before Christmas and the last time he saw Berman, Durst's tone changes. "I can't talk about that now. But I don't mind speaking with you later, after I've had a chance to talk with my attorneys." Durst agrees to a formal interview next week, when he comes to Los Angeles to attend Berman's memorial service. After the service, Stephens will attempt to fingerprint Durst, obtain his handwriting sample, and ask him if he is willing to take a polygraph exam.

Stephens then calls the landlady. She is reluctant to talk without her attorney, but he keeps her on the line by explaining why the police have been unable to release the house to her yet. After he has schmoozed with her for a few minutes, she opens up to him.

After he hangs up he tells Coulter, "She said, 'Yeah, I was concerned about the rent because that's what I live on.' She said she was in a bad auto accident last year and was in a nursing facility for a while. Berman had a friendly visit with her there and later at home."

The landlady said Berman—apparently after receiving the check from Durst—had paid her rent until March and had agreed to move out in June, which the detectives confirm after talking to a few of

Berman's friends. The landlady told Stephens she had had no contact with Berman since November because her rent was paid.

"The landlady denies threatening the dogs," Stephens says. "Whether she did or not, I don't think she's a suspect. She's just a crusty old lady." He looks discouraged. "This is a tough one."

"And we're not even getting involved in the mob angle," Coulter says.

Stephens leans back in his chair, kicks his feet onto his desk, and says—it is now his signature refrain—"Something will turn up."

Beside the stage at the Writer's Guild Theater in Beverly Hills, between two enormous red floral hearts, is a large easel with pictures of Susan Berman and her parents. Her book covers, videos of her television projects, and writing awards are displayed on an adjacent table.

Coulter and Stephens hope that this February 2 memorial service will provide them with a break. An eclectic mix of writers, relatives, actors, actresses, and television executives are gathered in the theater. Nyle arrives with his aunt, and Robert Durst is also expected to attend.

A half-dozen friends deliver eulogies, all marveling at Berman's talent and mourning her loss. From childhood until death, several people say, Berman could never escape the shadow of violence. "Death lapped at Susan's ankles in a way none of us can even imagine," one friend says. "A sense of doom surrounded her."

She reads a section of Susan's memoir that depicts the day she discovered her mother was dead: " 'I was still so confused from my father's death I couldn't even comprehend it. Was it something I had done? I wondered. Could I have saved her; could I have been a better daughter? It seemed like I had been missing her all my life and now I would miss her even more. I thought I could never feel weaker than I did when my father died, but now I felt there was even less of me. Was there to be anything left?' "

The friend shuts the book and says, "In the end she had a desk, a chair, an ancient computer, and three cantankerous dogs. She was convinced her luck would change. It very well might have."

Because Berman was orphaned so young, a cousin says, she valued her small circle of relatives and treasured her friends. He closes on a portentous note. "We have to be prepared," he says somberly, "that we may *never* know why or who."

The detectives are extremely disappointed when Durst does not show up. Stephens calls his cell phone number and leaves a message, but Durst does not call back. After the service, Coulter and Stephens interview Berman's friends who have come to Los Angeles from out of town, even across the country. Several knew her for decades, and they view Durst differently from her West Coast friends.

One longtime friend, a writer, stops by RHD the day after the service. The woman, who wears a green velour top, purple pants, and clogs, says that although Berman had always professed that Durst did not kill his wife, she also always said, without elaborating, "I think his family was involved in her death."

"A man came up to me at the memorial, a guy who has known Susan for a long time," she tells the detectives. "He talked to me like he was unburdening himself. He said that Susan told him once, 'Bobby did it.' He asked her, 'How do you know?' Susan told him, 'Because Bobby told me.' "

Another writer friend of Berman's visits the squad room and tells the detectives that a mutual friend had just told her, "Susan said she once provided an alibi for Bobby Durst regarding his wife's disappearance."

A third friend reports that while Berman did not believe Durst killed his wife, she did tell him, "I think I'm the only person who knows what happened." The friend asked, "Do you mean you have a theory or you have knowledge?" Berman refused to elaborate.

The detectives find all this intriguing, but marginally useful. "That stuff might be fine for the tabloids, but how are we going to use it?" Stephens asks Coulter. "A lot of it wasn't just hearsay, it was double hearsay: Berman told all this stuff to a friend. Then the friend told another friend, who told us. That's pretty far removed from the source."

"Those New York cops still might want to hear about it," Coulter says. "They're pretty interested now in Durst's marriage and his missing wife."

In 1972, Robert Durst was working for his father, one of Manhattan's most prominent real estate developers. Kathleen McCormack, a nineteen-year-old dental hygienist from a middle-class Long Island family, lived in an apartment owned by the Durst Corporation. Durst and McCormack began dating and married less than a year later.

Durst, then twenty-eight, was eager to escape the strictures and expectations of his prominent family. The couple moved to Vermont and opened a health food store. But Durst's father was unhappy with this alternative lifestyle, and Kathleen was too ambitious for life behind a counter. Robert and Kathleen eventually moved back to Manhattan, where he returned to the family business. Kathleen enrolled in nursing school and, later, the Albert Einstein College of Medicine. The wealthy real estate executive and the aspiring doctor seemed to have an idyllic life. They had a penthouse apartment in a fashionable Upper West Side neighborhood. They were often seen at Manhattan's trendiest nightspots, where they skipped past the lines, and doormen immediately ushered them inside. The marriage was troubled, however, and in 1981, Kathleen, considering divorce, hired a lawyer. In the winter of 1982, she disappeared. Five days later, Durst contacted the police. He had not called earlier, he told investigators, because it was not unusual for him and Kathleen to spend days apart.

On Sunday, January 31, 1982, the last night she was seen alive, Kathleen attended a party at the Connecticut home of a college friend. The friend later recalled that the Dursts had argued on the telephone. Kathleen then told the friend that she was afraid of her husband and to "check it out" if anything happened to her.

That night, Kathleen drove from the friend's house to the couple's vacation home in South Salem in Westchester County. After dinner, Durst told authorities in 1982, he drove her to the train station because she planned to attend class the next day. When he returned to South Salem, he drank a cocktail with neighbors and then called his wife, who was at their Manhattan apartment. He never saw or spoke to her again.

Although he was never officially named as a suspect in 1982, investigators were suspicious of his alibi. The neighbors did not recall seeing him on the night of Kathleen's disappearance. And when investigators informed him that his telephone records would list the call to his wife, Durst said that he had called her from a pay telephone while walking his dog. But the closest pay phone had been several miles away and a wet snow was falling on that dismal winter night.

Investigators also discovered that Kathleen, perhaps in preparation for a possible divorce settlement, had obtained data about the Durst Corporation's assets and asked two friends to safeguard the papers. Both of the friends' homes were burglarized in 1982, they told detectives, and the papers were stolen.

The disappearance of a beautiful blond medical student whose in-laws owned some of Manhattan's most notable skyscrapers was headline news. Durst was hounded by reporters who had learned about the couple's unraveling marriage. At the time, Susan Berman was his stalwart ally. But the investigation eventually stalled and Kathleen's body was never found. Her family, however, was convinced that Durst knew the solution to the mystery. The year after her disappearance, in a court hearing to allocate her assets, relatives and friends filed affidavits expressing their suspicion. Kathleen's sister said that Robert's "behavior and reactions surrounding this event [her disappearance] strongly suggest that my sister may have been murdered, and that Robert Durst is either directly responsible for her death or privy to information concerning her disappearance." Several people filed affidavits claiming that Kathleen told them she had been beaten by her husband and feared for her life. Others maintained that Durst discarded some of his wife's possessions a few days after he told police she was missing.

Durst filed his own affidavit, in which he stated, "I have no responsibility in any manner direct or indirect for Kathy's disappearance. . . . I have not disposed of any of Kathy's belongings. . . . I never threatened her life or threatened her in any way or assaulted Kathy or caused her any physical harm or abuse." The couple was considering a separation, Durst claimed, and she fabricated the stories of abuse to gain "a more advantageous negotiating position."

Berman also submitted an affidavit, which supported Durst's contentions. She asserted that Kathleen was an alcoholic, suffered from chronic anxiety and depression, and needed psychiatric help. "Bob and Kathy Durst have been two of my closest friends for a number of years," Berman stated. "During the two years before Kathy disappeared, she was under a great deal of pressure. She did not handle stress well. . . . Although they argued constantly in my presence, I never saw Bobby physically abuse Kathy in any way. . . . At one point . . . she told me she had just changed lawyers in the pending divorce and that she wanted to provoke Bobby to physically abuse her in public to get a bigger settlement. . . . I want to stress that Kathy was a lovely, gentle girl who had severe emotional problems the last two years before she disappeared. . . . I hope and pray that she is alive. I miss her today."

Durst continued to work for the Durst Corporation. Since he was the oldest of three sons, he expected to take over the business when his father retired. In 1994, when he realized one of his brothers would eventually succeed their father, he resigned. For the rest of the decade Durst invested in real estate and divided his time between the East Coast and his beachfront home in Northern California.

In 1999, a New York State Police detective investigated a tip about the case from a prisoner attempting to negotiate a reduced sentence. The information was wrong, but the disappearance of Kathleen Durst piqued the investigator's curiosity. The cold case was reopened.

In 1982, the detectives were certain that Kathleen had disappeared from Manhattan, so they did not examine the couple's upstate house, which Durst had sold in 1990. But during the fall of 2000, after the case had been reopened, state police and New York City detectives, aided by dogs, thoroughly inspected the place. They questioned the retired detective who first investigated Kathleen's disappearance, and they interviewed or reinterviewed many of the Dursts' friends and acquaintances. In December, investigators were preparing to interview Susan Berman, when she was shot in the back of the head.

Although some of Berman's friends found the timing of her murder suspicious, others contended that Durst would never have killed a friend who provided unconditional support after his wife disappeared and who filed an affidavit that powerfully affirmed his version of events. Why would he kill his most reliable witness? they asked. After Berman's memorial service, a few of these friends encouraged Coulter and Stephens to look at another suspect: Nyle.

Berman and Nyle were extremely close and spent several evenings a week together. Although they did sleep together once, the friendship was otherwise platonic, Berman's friends told detectives. She pressed for a more serious relationship, but Nyle resisted.

One friend of Berman's, an East Coast writer who flew to Los Angeles for the memorial service, tells the detectives she found Nyle surprisingly cavalier about the murder. "I don't get the feeling he was sorry about her death. He was not sorry at all. . . . He seemed angry. . . . At the memorial service his face was like a mask. No emotion. I asked him to sign the guest book and he'd only print his name. . . . He shrugged and said, 'Well, I don't have anyone calling me ten times a day anymore.' "

She also reports that at the memorial service Nyle told another friend, "This was the only way it could have ended between Susan and me."

Another friend of Berman's, a heavyset woman wearing faded jeans and yellow sneakers, stops by the squad room and relates a disturbing conversation she had with Nyle. She works at a movie studio and met Berman about five years ago, when Berman was pitching a script.

"He called me on December twenty-seventh . . . and told me Susan was killed by a bullet to the back of her head. Later he told me police also were investigating suicide. I asked, 'How can it be suicide if the bullet's to the back of the head?' He didn't really answer." Her face is flushed and she nervously bites her lower lip. "After I was leaving the memorial service, what struck me was that all of Susan's friends were talking about her, telling stories. He was the only one not saying anything."

After the service, this friend continues, Nyle complained that because Berman was dead he would have to find another writer to slip him into the Writer's Guild Theater for free movies. She shakes her head, looking disgusted. "I thought that was a very harsh, unnecessary comment."

A woman who has known Berman since they were graduate students at the University of California, Berkeley also tells the detectives that she was startled by Nyle's insensitive comments. "At the memorial service . . . I said to him that Susan really loved her friends. But he replied, 'She created a web that was difficult to get out of.' I thought that was very strange."

"Was there any physical volatility in the relationship?" Stephens asks.

She quickly nods. "He pushed her once. They were out in public and he shoved her. She was very embarrassed. She told me it was over, and she wouldn't put up with that. But obviously it wasn't over."

When Coulter and Stephens finish the round of interviews after the memorial service they realize that while they have been investigating the Berman case for more than three weeks, the physical evidence had so far yielded nothing of value. The fingerprints lifted at the house did not lead to a suspect. Ballistics could not connect the slug to another weapon. The shell casing revealed neither prints nor a link to a gun. Coulter and Stephens are still waiting for the department's Scientific Investigation Division to analyze Berman's clothing for hair and fibers. DNA from a hair might identify the killer. Criminalists will later check for semen traces.

Meanwhile, they will continue to investigate Nyle. On a blustery February morning, the detectives discuss the case against him over plates of ham and eggs at Nick's, a café owned by an LAPD detective.

The squat stucco building is perched on a dusty patch of gravel north of downtown, next door to a Chinese food warehouse and across the street from an abandoned railroad yard. The roof is ringed with razor wire and a graffiti directive to the local gang is emblazoned on a back wall: "Dogtown. Please write on this side." Inside, swivel stools are arrayed around a horseshoe-shaped Formica counter.

"A lot of people said Nyle's demeanor at the memorial service was odd," Coulter says.

"Everyone in this crowd is odd," Stephens says.

Coulter nods knowingly. "They're writers."

The detectives recently discovered that the son of Berman's former boyfriend left his car parked in her driveway for a few weeks during late December, while he was visiting Europe. A friend of Berman's has suggested that the detectives should dismiss Durst as a suspect: unfamiliar with the car, he would have assumed someone was visiting Berman, and so he would not have approached the house at night. But Nyle knew the car and knew its owner was out of the country.

"I think we're ready to bring him in for an interview," Coulter says.

"We'll ask him if he'll take a poly," Stephens replies. He tells Coulter he does not trust polygraphs, and the last time he used one was fifteen years ago. "The examiner said this one guy either did it or knew who did. They were wrong on both counts. We later found the right guy."

"The equipment's a lot more sophisticated today," Coulter says.

"I still don't trust 'em," says Stephens, who is decades older than many LAPD detectives and sometimes reluctant to deviate from traditional methods. "But I'm going to ask this guy to take a poly anyway. I'd rather just question the guy myself, but with the laws the way they are, if he asks for a lawyer, we're through. This gives us another method of interviewing him."

Coulter pushes aside his plate and says, "When you ask him about the poly, I'll be very curious to see how he responds."

Paul Coulter never had any burning desire to be a cop, he tells friends, but simply "stumbled onto the job." The work appeared interesting, he admired the camaraderie he observed among the officers, and he was impressed with the pay, benefits, and job security. When he turned twenty-one he applied to the LAPD academy.

After cruising the city in a patrol car and walking a beat in Hollywood, he was promoted to detective trainee on a robbery table. As a patrol officer, Coulter had been frustrated by continually lurching from crisis to crisis, but now that he was investigating his first robberies, he enjoyed following cases from the initial crime scenes, through interviews with victims and witnesses, to arrests. Uncovering disparate clues and linking them together until they formed a coherent pattern was particularly satisfying. He knew he would spend the rest of his career as a detective.

A supervisor recruited him for Wilshire Division homicide and Coulter spent nine years there, personally investigating almost two hundred murders. During the 1990s, Coulter, like many detectives throughout the city, was unimpressed with Homicide Special. Many in the unit, he believed, were unmotivated, indolent, and arrogant. Because they handled so few fresh cases, compared to the divisional detectives, he believed their skills were rusty.

Coulter hoped for a promotion to detective grade three, the highest rank an investigator can reach, but in the divisions, D-IIIs are supervisors without their own caseloads. Coulter still enjoyed working murders. The only unit in the city that allows D-IIIs to investigate cases is RHD, so, despite his reservations, he applied.

Shortly after Coulter was accepted, he was assigned to the biggest case of his career, one of the most notorious unsolved cop killings in the history of the city.

In 1976, Los Angeles County Sheriff's Deputy George Arthur and his partner approached three robbery suspects in a bank parking lot. One pulled out a gun and clubbed Arthur in the head. Arthur's partner exchanged shots with another suspect and was critically wounded. Despite a serious skull fracture, Arthur shot and killed a suspect and managed to broadcast an "officer needs help." A second suspect was arrested and the third fled. Arthur was considered a hero in the department, a man whose bravery and quick thinking had saved his partner's life.

By 1985, Arthur had been promoted to sergeant at the men's central jail near East Los Angeles. At 9:30 P.M., on a spring night, he climbed into his Chevrolet van and headed south on the Santa Ana Freeway. Five minutes later his van crashed. California Highway Patrol officers believed that Arthur had died of massive head trauma from the crash, but during the autopsy a fluoroscope located four .25-caliber slugs in the back and side of his head.

Arthur was murdered in the city, so the LAPD assumed responsibility. The sheriff's department only has jurisdiction in certain parts of the county, but a number of sheriff's homicide detectives volunteered their services. A joint task force was created and a massive investigation was launched. Forty officers canvassed the homes and the housing project adjacent to the freeway. Dozens of jailhouse informants were interviewed.

Several witnesses told detectives that they had seen two men limping away from Arthur's van after the accident. Others, however, reported only one. "Detectives have been unable to determine when and where the suspects entered the victim's van," said a progress report. "They may have been lying in wait in the van prior to Arthur getting off duty at the jail."

Detectives focused the investigation on Arthur's work with the sheriff's department. He had been a no-nonsense sergeant, a new jail supervisor with exacting standards. Mexican mafia leaders at the jail might have targeted him, detectives speculated. He might have stumbled on a drug-smuggling scam, or on in-house corruption. Before his jail assignment, he had spent years as a hard-nosed gang officer; perhaps, detectives speculated, gangbangers had exacted revenge.

For two years, two RHD detectives and two sheriff's homicide investigators checked countless leads, clues, and potential suspects. Finally, they disbanded the task force and the detectives moved on to other cases. But in the mid-1990s, a sheriff's department homicide detective, distressed that the murder had never been solved, was permitted by his supervisors to spend more than a year investigating the case. He believed he had identified the killers. But he could not arrest them; that decision belonged to the lead investigative agency, the LAPD.

The sheriff's investigator believed that two Latino gangbangers from the nearby housing project had killed Arthur. One of the gangbangers, according to a sheriff's department document, "was seen running from the van the night of the crash by three separate eyewitnesses who knew him from the projects.... The suspects involved ... were known to have been injured in the vehicle crash. Both had injuries consistent with being in a car accident."

Although the investigator said he based his conclusion on thirteen different interviews, the Homicide Special detective in charge of the investigation was not persuaded. Many of those witnesses had offered conflicting information. He also knew that thieves from the housing projects often ran onto the freeway after crashes and relieved victims

of their cash and valuables. But the key reason the LAPD detective
distrusted the gangbanger theory was because he believed that the
killer had been injured in the crash and left specks of his DNA on the
windshield. The DNA of neither of the sheriff's investigator's suspects
matched the sample on the windshield.

The dispute was the culmination of years of acrimony between the
two agencies. Sheriff's investigators believed that after the joint task
force was disbanded, LAPD detectives had abandoned the case.
Arthur was one of their own, and they were personally offended by
what they believed was a lackadaisical approach. LAPD officers
acknowledged that the investigation had languished, but contended
that the sheriff's investigator was abrasive and contentious. They also
believed that since the O. J. Simpson case and other LAPD failures,
some sheriff's investigators had treated them in an arrogant and condescending manner.

In 1998, Captain Jim Tatreau, the new head of RHD, met with
the sheriff's homicide captain. He suggested that they form a second
task force, made up entirely of new detectives. The sheriff's captain
agreed.

Coulter was assigned to the case along with Rosemary Sanchez;
both had been recently assigned to Homicide Special. Detective Dennis Kilcoyne, who was more senior in rank, headed the investigation.
They were eventually teamed with four sheriff's investigators.

The detectives first studied the innumerable documents that delin-
eated the original investigation. After three weeks, the sheriff's detectives insisted that their colleague had been right: the killers were the
two gangbangers from the projects. But the LAPD detectives believed
that Arthur's killer had left his DNA on the windshield, which ruled
out the gangbangers.

The issue was settled when the task force detectives interviewed
several of the original witnesses and found that their descriptions of
the gangbangers were contradictory and their recollections were hazy.
This was the turning point in the investigation and forged a bond
between the two groups of detectives. They realized that if they were
going to solve Arthur's murder, they had to begin again and work
together. Coulter, Kilcoyne, and Sanchez reinterviewed every witness
listed in the original crime report. Sheriff's detectives investigated
Arthur's personal and professional life for leads and examined the
Mexican mafia's jail activities during the mid-1980s.

Eventually, the three LAPD detectives concluded that Arthur's murder was connected to his personal life, not his professional life. If a criminal or a gang member knew anything about the murder, they determined, the information would have surfaced after fourteen years: any thug facing prison time would have used it as a "Get Out of Jail Free" card.

Coulter, Kilcoyne, and Sanchez agreed that when detectives investigate the murder of an off-duty police officer, they often suffer from tunnel vision, immediately assuming that the murder was connected to police work. Sometimes, the detectives concluded, it was best to approach an off-duty-cop killing just like any other homicide and begin with the victim's private life.

Arthur and his wife, also a sheriff's deputy, had no children and had been separated for more than a year. They had recently filed for divorce, but friends said the breakup was not acrimonious. The detectives interviewed Arthur's friends and coworkers and compiled a list of every woman he had dated since the separation. They also questioned his wife extensively, and they contacted all of the men she had been involved with and attempted to obtain their DNA with saliva swabs.

But two months after the investigation was reopened, Arthur's personal life had turned up no leads. Almost every man his wife had dated had submitted a DNA swab. There were no matches. Then one afternoon, on their way to the LAPD academy, Coulter, Kilcoyne, and Sanchez stopped the car to let a priest cross the street. "This is a sign," Coulter told the others. "When I was in the Wilshire Division, I stopped to let three nuns cross the street. The next day we ID'd the suspect in a big homicide case."

At the academy, Kilcoyne's pager buzzed. One of the sheriff's investigators reported that he had put off asking a retired sheriff's deputy—an ex-boyfriend of Arthur's wife—for a DNA swab because he lived in Spokane, Washington. They finally arranged to obtain the swab, but at the last minute the retired deputy backed out and told the investigator to contact his lawyer.

The three detectives sped to the squad room and excitedly announced to Lieutenant Farrell, "We're going to Spokane tomorrow. This is the break we'd been waiting for."

The retired deputy's name was George Kirby. Arthur's wife had told the detectives that they had dated in 1985 and that Kirby was extremely disappointed when he discovered that she was not interested in an exclusive relationship.

The detectives flew to Spokane, and Coulter prepared a search warrant for Kirby's DNA. But a Washington judge refused to sign it, ruling that their investigation had not uncovered enough evidence against Kirby to supply probable cause for the warrant. The detectives decided a woman might have more success obtaining intimate details about Arthur's wife's relationship with Kirby. So Sanchez called her from Washington.

Kirby was extremely possessive, she told Sanchez, and often drove by her house late at night, lingering outside. Also, Kirby had been upset when he discovered that Arthur had balked at signing the final divorce papers. After the funeral, Kirby drove her back to the cemetery, where she had left the van that Arthur was driving the night he was killed. She had loaned Kirby the van on several occasions and he had his own key, she told Sanchez. Also, Kirby had a bandage on his head and an injured knee, she recalled. He was a triathlete, and he told her that he had fallen off his bicycle. She had expressed her suspicions about Kirby with the detectives in 1985, but "everyone blew her off," she told Sanchez.

A sheriff's detective obtained Kirby's medical and personnel records and discovered that the morning after the murder, he was treated at a hospital for lacerations to his forehead and injuries to his wrist and leg. He then spent two weeks on sick leave.

This additional information convinced the Washington judge to grant the warrant. On a Thursday in June, in a Spokane Police Department interview room, a nervous, trembling Kirby—he had a scar on his forehead, the detectives noticed—provided the saliva swab.

The following Wednesday morning, Kirby placed his wedding ring on the kitchen table, slipped off his shoes, walked into the woods, and shot himself in the head.

After the battering the LAPD had endured during the past decade, solving the Arthur case provided a much-needed boost. Sheriff's investigators thanked Coulter, Kilcoyne, and Sanchez for solving the murder. Tensions were eased between the two departments. And after a number of notorious failures, the LAPD's Scientific Investigation Division was lauded for its excellent work. LAPD criminalists had meticulously collected evidence at the crime scene and scrupulously stored it for fourteen years.

18

Stephens calls Nyle, who lives in the Valley, and sets up an interview
with him at the North Hollywood station. Despite the many witnesses
who have remarked on his strange behavior since Berman's death, the
detectives have only one piece of evidence that might help tie Nyle to
the murder: the letter sent to the Beverly Hills Police Department
alerting them to the presence of the corpse. Because it was mailed
before police found the body, the detectives believe the killer wrote
the letter. And they surmise that anyone who would write this letter,
with its bizarre touch of concern, must have known Berman well.

During their strategy session for the interview with Nyle, Coulter
and Stephens devise a way to obtain a sample of his handwriting so
they can compare it to the letter. They picked up a generic LAPD
visitor's log, which includes slots for name, signature, address, time
in, and time out. Stephens moves from desk to desk, asking detectives
to fill out the blanks on the top half of the sheet, so the log appears
authentic.

Coulter cruises toward the North Hollywood station on a cloudless
winter afternoon. The recent rains have soaked the parched foothills
and a golden winter light illuminates the velvety wisps of grass sprout-
ing in the ravines. The detectives, both a bit on edge, ride in silence.
Their clues leading to a suspect are minimal and their evidence paltry.
Of all the interviews they have conducted during the past month, this
is the most important.

Coulter and Stephens place the phony log by the station entrance and explain their plan to the desk officer. When Nyle arrives, Stephens ensures that he signs in.

Nyle is forty-five, with short brown hair, tinged with gray. He is slightly pudgy and wears jeans and a tight green polo shirt. Leaning back in his chair, he crosses his arms and stares at the detectives. Both are surprised to see that he does not appear even slightly nervous. He has a supercilious manner that momentarily unnerves Stephens.

"We work at Robbery-Homicide Division, downtown," Stephens says, "so we took over the investigation—"

"Are you starting over?" Nyle interrupts, sounding impatient.

Stephens nods.

"Right, right," Nyle says, as if he has more important ways to spend the afternoon and wants to hurry the interview along.

Although Stephens is clearly irritated by Nyle's manner, he remains cordial. "How long have you known Susan?" he asks.

"About five years. She lived across the street. We were both living in apartments then. I'd seen her walking her dogs as I walked my dogs. We waved and nodded. We finally talked one day and became instant friends."

"Are you an agent?" Stephens asks.

"I'm a manager. I guide and direct careers. But I only work with a few people, so I develop close personal relationships."

"How long after you met her did you become her manager?"

"One year. I was working with her *and* being a friend—helping her. There was always some crisis in her life. She had all kinds of phobias. She needed to have someone at her side. I kind of took over the role of manager and oversaw everything for her."

"When was the last time you were at her house?" Stephens asks.

"The Wednesday before Christmas," Nyle says. "She had a follow-up appointment with the eye doctor. She just had eye surgery. I came back that evening. We went to a screening at the Writer's Guild Theater for *Castaway*. I talked to her again on Thursday. One of her projects was not getting picked up by Showtime. She took it well."

"When you came by, were you expected, or did you just show up?"

"Expected . . . She was very needy to have someone around. Sometimes she'd call because she saw a spider and was afraid. Or she needed a lightbulb changed. I'd begrudgingly come and she'd want to talk or get a bite to eat."

"Did you have a key to her house?"

"She didn't give me a key."

"Did she have any problems with anyone?"

Nyle considers the question. He smiles faintly and says, "Well, Susan had problems with everyone."

"Serious problems?" Coulter asks.

"She was a very unusual woman. But problems to the extent that someone would do this kind of thing? Certainly not. But she'd push people to the edge. She was very demanding. I'm a softy."

"I'm sure you're aware she had financial problems."

"A few times she couldn't pay the rent. She'd cry, get hysterical, and I'd pay. But she was incredibly talented, and I really believed she'd get an answer on something and I'd get paid back. Ultimately she paid almost all of it back."

"When did you learn she was dead?" Stephens asks.

"Christmas Day."

"That's four days," Stephens says softly, attempting to muffle any insinuations. "Did you usually go that long without speaking?"

"I needed a breather occasionally. I knew if I called her, she'd want to get together. . . ."

"On Thursday evening, what did you speak about?"

"I already *told* you," Nyle snaps, losing his composure for the first time. "That the project at Showtime was not being picked up."

"What were you doing Friday night?" Stephens asks. Berman was killed late Friday night, December 22.

"Offhand, uh," Nyle stutters, "I don't know. I'd have to look it up."

Coulter asks about Saturday.

"I think I was home. I might have gone out."

"How did you find out she was dead?" Stephens asks.

"Her friend who expected us on Christmas Day told me. She said she'd gone over there, so I did the same thing. I saw packages at the front door and mail in the mailbox. There was no sound of dogs barking. I crawled in the window."

Nyle says matter-of-factly that he walked around the house, played the answering machine, and opened Berman's November bank statement. She had told him that Durst sent her $15,000. "I found it curious," Nyle says, "when I saw her deposit for twenty-five thousand. She did tell me that Durst would be sending her additional money for her eye surgery."

Finally, Nyle says, he talked to a neighbor, who told him that Berman had fallen, hit her head, and died. "Horrible," he says, shuddering. "Oh, my God. But she just had eye surgery. She was klutzy. So it made perfect sense. But . . . umm . . ." He loses his train of thought for a moment. "Anyway," he continues, "it made perfect sense. I thought, 'How awful. Being by yourself, needing help.' " He clears his throat. "It's a bad visual."

Stephens interrupts him, asking, "Did you normally open her mail?"

"She was always behind paying her bills. I helped her if they were going to turn off the lights or electricity or if she was behind on the telephone."

Stephens asks Nyle about his relationship with Berman.

"It was romantic on *her* part," he says sharply.

"I'll be blunt," Stephens says. "What's in it for *you*? She's not paying you. She's very demanding—"

"Ultimately," Nyle says, "I'm a caretaker. . . . And she was brilliant. She had the potential to make lots of money. She'd been successful in the past. I felt she could be successful again."

"When you found out from Berman's neighbor that she was dead, how'd you feel?" Stephens asks Nyle.

"Stunned. How do you process that kind of information? Fuuuck," he says, dragging out the word. "In spite of who Susan was and how she behaved, most people stuck by her. She had a real draw to her. She was a very unique person. On one hand, she could be very strong, and on the other hand, she could withdraw and be so weak and childlike. She was a woman of contradictions. She was careful, but careless. She was brilliant, but crazy."

"Any idea who could have done this?"

"I don't know. My first thought was that it was connected to Bobby Durst. But that doesn't make sense. He never indicated anything . . . like this . . . in the past. . . . She was certain she'd be getting money from him. . . ."

He clears his throat and says he always had the feeling she wanted to tell him something. "She once wrote two sentences on a card to me: 'He believed in me. He helped me out.' "

"We're asking several people, just to eliminate those close to her, to take polygraph exams," Stephens says. "Don't read anything into this, but would you be willing to take a poly—"

"Sure, sure," he interrupts.

Stephens chats with Nyle for a few minutes, then, as the detectives shepherd him out the door, asks, "Would you look in your day planner for Friday?"

"Okay," Nyle says. "Sure."

Driving back downtown, Stephens says to Coulter, "Shit, Roy, we're running out of suspects. I don't know if it's him, but if he's our guy, I'd think he would have acted more nervous."

Coulter, looking hopeful, says, "It's interesting that he can't say where he was on Friday night."

"He remembered every detail about Christmas Day," Stephens agrees. "If he has such a fucking good memory, why can't he remember Friday night?"

"I feel something about this guy," Stephens says. "But I'm just not sure."

"Let's check out his handwriting," Coulter says. "That'll give us a better idea."

Back at their desks, Stephens spreads out a copy of the letter sent to the Beverly Hills Police Department. Beside it, he places the visitor log. Nyle signed his name and address using large block letters, which resemble the printing in the letter. In fact, of eleven writing samples, the detectives agree, Nyle's most resembles the letter.

"Looks like the same 'V' to me, Roy," Stephens says.

"The 'N's look pretty close, too," Coulter says.

Stephens asks Lieutenant Farrell's opinion. "The 'N's are similar," Farrell says. "They have the same cant. But the 'R's are different."

"Maybe he was disguising his handwriting," Stephens sayss.

"How does he benefit from blasting her?" Farrell asks.

"At the very least, he'd be rid of her," says Stephens. "He was tired of her bullshit."

"Sometimes in the heat of passion you're not going to get a motive," Coulter says.

"He spent years representing her, trying to sell her projects, waiting for a big payday that never came," Stephens says. "Maybe he just got fed up."

"She was a pain in the ass," Coulter says. "He was her gofer."

Another detective asks, "Was he nervous in the interview?"

"Not really," Stephens says. "He just didn't seem that concerned."

Two days later, an LAPD examiner of questioned documents—a handwriting analyst—calls Coulter and Stephens. They bound up the stairs to the fourth floor and gather around her desk.

"You've got block printing that lacks general characteristics," she says of the letter. "The person was doing it slowly. He's making an attempt to disguise his writing—that's what makes it more difficult."

The detectives stand anxiously awaiting her decision.

"There's evidence to indicate he *may* have written the note," the analyst continues. "You're over the fifty-percent scale. Is it enough to close the jail gates? No. But it's a foot in the door."

The detectives appear relieved. Finally, they sit down.

"Even though the person is trying to mess up the note there are certain things he can't get away from. Height is one. Also, the 'N' has a double recurve at the end. That narrows it down somewhat."

Stephens says he knows the visitor log was not an ideal sample, so he will ask Nyle for an exemplar, a full handwriting sample. He places his palms on her desk and says, "Just between you and us, what's your gut feeling?"

"Oh, no, you don't," she retorts, waving a hand, indicating she is not ready to state for certain that the writing matches. But there is one way to definitively tie Nyle to the crime, she says: find the pad of paper he used to write the letter. Some of the pages might reveal an impression from the writing.

"If we can get that notebook," she says, "and do an impression . . . we'll be in business."

For weeks, the case has appeared stalled and the pace of the investigation has been discouraging. Now the detectives have a clear trail to follow. They are roused by the thrill of the hunt.

There is a scale of accuracy for handwriting analysis, from "elimination" to "identification." If the analyst had eliminated Nyle as a suspect, the detectives would have focused their efforts elsewhere. But because she said he *might* have written it, the detectives believe they now have probable cause to obtain a search warrant for Nyle's house.

"This means I'll be working all weekend," says Coulter, who knows he will end up writing the warrant.

"If he doesn't have the gun at his house," Stephens says, "maybe he'll have the pad."

Nyle knows several of Berman's close friends have been fingerprinted, so the detectives decide to try a bait-and-switch with him. Stephens will ask him to stop by for the routine fingerprinting and then casually suggest that since he is already downtown, he might as well take the polygraph. Afterward, they will serve the warrant and search his house.

Stephens leaves several messages for Nyle, but does not get a call back. Finally, the next week, Stephens reaches him at home and they set up a time to meet.

"I would have liked him to sound more nervous, but he wasn't, really," Stephens tells Coulter. "That bothers me a little bit."

On a dreary Wednesday morning in February, a winter storm blows in off the Pacific and drenches the city. Stephens and Coulter trudge to their desks, slip off their wet trench coats, and fire up the battered space heaters. Rain sluices down the windows and a pearl gray light suffuses the room. Frigid air seeps out of the ceiling vents. The gloomy mood is shattered when Stephens flicks on his boom box and blasts a few bars of "Who Let the Dogs Out?" When the detectives stop laughing, he announces, "At the end of the day, I hope to have that question answered. Our suspect is coming by this afternoon for a poly."

By midmorning, the rain has tapered off to a light drizzle. Coulter and Stephens drive to the department's Scientific Investigation Division headquarters at a technical center east of downtown. Berman has been dead almost two months, and the detectives are still waiting for criminalists to analyze her clothing for hair and fibers. Coulter decides to study the clothing himself to determine whether he should include any specific fiber or hair requests in the search warrant.

On most television crime shows, evidence is analyzed quickly and detectives often get the results the next day. But at a typical over-burdened, underfunded metropolitan police department, the timetable is much different. And the LAPD is particularly dilatory. Detectives often wait months for results—sometimes longer. SID has improved since it was humiliated during the O. J. Simpson debacle, but the crime lab is still understaffed and its processing schedule is still scandalously slow.

Today, in the evidence room, a criminalist unwraps several packages and gently sets Berman's clothing on a long wooden table covered with butcher paper. A few blond hairs glisten on the seat of her purple sweat pants, but Coulter believes they are from one of her dogs. Her T-shirt—with a Hula Girl Cigars emblem—is white with specks of blood and dirt dappling the front. The blood-soaked back and arms are brick-colored, with only a few faint white streaks. Lying in the center of the butcher paper, the shirt, which is stiff as a board and curled up at the edges, looks like a modern art sculpture displayed on a flat white pedestal. Several short brown hairs cling to the back. They are human hairs, Coulter believes, and since her hair was darker and long, they are probably not hers. If any of them contain follicles, criminalists may be able to obtain DNA samples.

Next, the detectives stop at Olvera Street—where the original Spanish pueblo of Los Angeles was founded in 1781—and order lunch. Several adobe structures still stand near the site of the Zanja Madre ("Mother Ditch") that brought water from the Los Angeles River to the first residents. Now the area, at the edge of downtown, is a faux Mexican village, a tourist attraction, but the detectives have a favorite taco stand here. As they drive back to the squad room with hefty plates of taquitos, the car is enveloped in the piquant aromas of onions, cilantro, and deep-fried tortillas.

They eat at their desks, finishing every speck. The interview with Nyle, which is scheduled for later today, may be a long one, and the detectives know they may not have time for dinner.

At about three P.M. Nyle appears, wearing black cowboy boots, jeans, and a black button-down shirt, and looking unfazed. Stephens escorts him to the second floor, where he is fingerprinted.

"Did you remember your day planner?"

"Sorry," Nyle says blithely. "I forgot it. But I checked and I didn't have anything written down for Friday."

Stephens casually suggests that since Nyle is already downtown, the examiner might as well polygraph him.

"My friends say I shouldn't because they're not reliable."

"If you're innocent," Stephens says, "you've got nothing to worry about."

The detectives fear that Nyle will ask for a lawyer. They stare intently at him, waiting for his answer, until he shrugs and nods weakly.

Moments later, Nyle is sitting on the edge of his chair in the small polygraph cubicle. As usual, the detectives monitor the exam in another room. For the first time, Nyle appears anxious. Crossing and uncrossing his legs, he nervously tugs at an earlobe.

"Look at him," Stephens says gleefully. He scratches his hands and grins. "My palms are itching. That means I'm going to solve a case."

The examiner, who had previously consulted with the detectives, asks Nyle a few key questions. "Did you shoot Susan Berman? Were you inside her room at the exact time she was shot? Were you inside her house at the exact time she was shot?"

"Let's see if that machine starts to smoke," Stephens says.

Coulter's aunt has died and he is late for the viewing, but he is reluctant to leave. Instead, he paces.

Nyle squirms and taps the tips of his boots on the floor as he answers no to all the questions. "He's fucking lying," Stephens says to Coulter. "You better get your grieving done and get back. We'll be working all night."

"I can't leave," Coulter says. "I've got to know, Roy. This is killing me."

"If my own mother died, I'd put her on ice right now until I found out if he's our guy." Looking chagrined, Stephens quickly knocks on the wooden table three times and adds, "I shouldn't say that."

After the polygraph, the examiner meets with the detectives and says, "He's not telling us the full truth. He was deceptive. I certainly can't clear this guy. . . . My gut feeling is he did this, but something's missing." Another examiner, who helped grade the results, adds, "Did he blow the test out of the water? No. Did he pluck the chicken clean? No. But something's going on."

"He doesn't seem to have much of a conscience," Stephens says.

"Maybe that's it," says the examiner who conducted the test. "The only way to find out what's going on is to hit him between the eyes. But if I *do* go for the throat and fail, he'll probably ask for an attorney."

"That's the risk we'll have to take," Stephens says.

The examiner returns and tells Nyle he failed the polygraph. Nyle blanches.

"The worst thing I could do is smile and say, 'Everything is okay,' " the examiner tells him. "How you handle this is very important. You have to cooperate."

"Is this a joke?" Nyle asks.

"When I'm joking with someone I laugh. This is the worst trouble you can face in your life."

Nyle sighs and drops his hands to his side. "This is absurd."

"This is real. This is your life. It's not going to go away. I'm still giving you the opportunity to cooperate. You have no criminal history—"

Nyle interrupts: "I'm at a loss. I don't know what you're talking about."

"I'm talking about shooting a lady to death, is what I'm talking about. . . . What caused you to shoot this lady?"

"How can you even say such a thing?" Nyle purses his lips primly.

Usually, when people are accused of murder, they will vociferously deny they committed the crime, even if they are guilty. Some jump out of the chair, shout, wave their hands wildly. Others scream at their accuser. Coulter and Stephens are amazed because Nyle shows almost no reaction. He simply stares at the examiner.

"You're like a person sinking in quicksand and I'm reaching a hand out to you. If you keep pushing the hand away, there's nothing I can do. I'm trying to get you to do the right thing."

Nyle fiddles with the heel of his boot. "I've been doing the right thing all along."

"What are you most afraid of?"

"This is absurd. I'm just flabbergasted." Nyle's voice is wavering. His lips tremble. "How can I be blamed?" But he quickly regains his composure and says angrily, "I don't believe any of this for a second."

The examiner leaves the room and tells the detectives that he sensed that Nyle was about to ask for an attorney. "I pulled back because he was on the verge of invoking. Did you ever see anyone accused of murder sit there so long without a reaction? I'd be out of that chair in a minute."

"This is one of the weirdest guys I've ever dealt with," Stephens says. He then enters the polygraph cubicle.

"Is this for real?" Nyle asks.

"It's for real," Stephens says sympathetically. "I want to be fair to you. You can talk to me if you want. I'm not going to yell at you. Will you give me a handwriting sample?"

"I should probably speak to an attorney," Nyle says.

The interview with Nyle, Stephens knows, is now over.

Coulter speeds off to the mortuary, and Stephens drives to Nyle's house, a small San Fernando Valley bungalow on a tidy, tree-lined suburban street. A jet stream from Alaska buffets the city with frigid winds ushering in a cold front. The temperature in the Valley is expected to drop to the mid-thirties tonight. Gusts have swept the skies of smog and mist and a cluster of stars shine brightly. Stephens, who stands beside his car, waiting for the other detectives, buttons his trench coat as the wind rattles the eucalyptus leaves.

Rick Jackson, John Garcia, and a few others soon join him. Stephens, who had served Nyle with the warrant after the interview, begins searching the house along with the other detectives. The house is tastefully decorated, with gleaming hardwood floors, antique mirrors, framed lithographs, and bookshelves lined with classics. Each detective scours a different room. Stephens and Coulter, who has returned from the viewing at the mortuary, focus on Nyle's office, looking for his date book and for a pad with paper similar to the note the Beverly Hills Police received. Coulter leads two LAPD criminalists to Nyle's closet, where they examine a dozen pairs of shoes for bloodstains.

"This looks kind of reddish," says one criminalist, studying a sneaker sole with a magnifying glass and flashlight. She examines another sneaker sole and says, "This might be too red. . . . But let's pheno 'em both."

On the front porch, one of the criminalists pulls a Q-Tip out of her kit and moistens it with a speck of water from a dropper bottle. After swabbing the sneaker sole, she applies drops of phenolphthalein and hydrogen peroxide to the Q-Tip and holds it up. If the Q-Tip has absorbed even a trace of blood, it will turn pink.

"I hope they find something," Coulter says. "I'm not ready for another disappointment."

The criminalists study the Q-Tip. It remains white. The test on the other sneaker sole is also negative.

After a few more hours at the house, Coulter and Stephens reluctantly admit defeat: no notepad, no gun, no date book, or anything else incriminating. Shortly before midnight, they drive back downtown.

"I'd hoped it would end tonight," Stephens says plaintively. "I'm not setting my alarm tomorrow. I'll be in whenever I'm in."

"I'm taking tomorrow off so I can go to my aunt's funeral." Coulter flicks on the heater. "This is a big letdown. Yesterday, I was writing the arrest report in my mind."

"He's a weird duck," Stephens says.

"If it's not him, we've really got a long way to go."

"We'll get his phone records," Stephens says. "That'll give us an idea of what he was doing on Friday night. Also, I'll give Durst another try and see if I can interview him."

"It ain't over yet," Coulter says.

Stephens smiles faintly. "Something will turn up."

Part V

LOS FELIZ

19

The Stephanie Gorman investigation has languished since January.
Her sister, Cheryl, has not called recently and the detectives feel guilty
because they have no news for her. Dave Lambkin and Tim Marcia
hope to return to the case, but the murder of the elderly San Fernando
Valley couple, which they picked up in February, has attracted extensive press coverage and pressure is mounting to find the killer.

Lambkin recently discovered that a local television news show runs
a regular series on unsolved homicides. He and Marcia plan to
approach the station hoping that a feature on the Gorman case may
jog a memory, unearth a clue, encourage a tipster.

On a warm Tuesday afternoon in early spring, Marcia and Lambkin
are hunched over their desks in their tiny Rape Special office, studying
stacks of pawnshop reports in an attempt to link the elderly woman's
stolen jewelry to a suspect. Marcia answers the ringing phone. His
face reddens during the brief call. "Just what we need now," he says
to Lambkin. "A sexual assault–murder in Los Feliz."

"What's the story?" Lambkin asks.

"Female in her fifties doesn't show up for work for a few days,"
Marcia says. "A coworker goes to her apartment and he finds her on
the bed. Possible blunt force trauma to the back of the head. The
woman's a doctor."

"A physician?" Lambkin asks.

Marcia nods.

Rape Special is supposed to investigate every rape-murder in the
city, but all the detectives in the unit are overwhelmed with cases.

Lambkin pages his lieutenant, explaining when she calls back that he and Marcia are still swamped with leads to track on the murder of the elderly couple. He is leaving for vacation next week, he continues, and Marcia will be tied up in court for the next few months because one of his cases is about to go to trial. The lieutenant says she will call RHD officials and attempt to work something out.

A few minutes later, an RHD lieutenant stops by and tells Lambkin that Homicide Special detectives will investigate the murder; Lambkin and Marcia, however, will have to assist at the crime scene. He adds that the victim was a prominent member of the Filipino community and a well-known physician. Homicide Special, he says, is well equipped to handle the investigation.

At the victim's apartment, Lambkin and Marcia confer with Brian McCartin and Chuck Knolls. Over the past six months they have continued to investigate Luda Petushenko's murder, working with the DA to prepare the case for the preliminary hearing. They also have been inundated with numerous officer-involved shootings and a few threats against officers. McCartin is philosophical about these cases, but Knolls has been increasingly annoyed. The early morning OIS callouts, the extensive paperwork, the time away from his homicide investigations all irrate him. Now, as he examines the crime scene, he is clearly energized by the prospect of a new murder.

The victim, sixty-three-year-old Lourdes Unson, lived in a twenty-eight-unit apartment building on a busy thoroughfare in Los Feliz, a gracious neighborhood near Hollywood. The tan stucco structure is a typical boxy 1960s-style apartment building, but it is lushly landscaped with thick stands of banana plants in front, framed with pink geraniums, red and white impatiens, and yellow rosebushes. The building's name, emblazoned on a sign in front—THE RAVENCREST APARTMENTS—evokes Raymond Chandler's Los Angeles. The units face an interior courtyard, with a lawn bordered by palm and ficus and a small pond where brilliant orange koi dart about. Flaming bougainvillea spill over railings and the first bone-white lilies of the season are beginning to blossom.

Unson lived on the second floor, in a back corner. Inside, six detectives and the two Homicide Special lieutenants move quickly and efficiently about the small one-bedroom apartment. Several LAPD criminalists dust for fingerprints, vacuum the carpet for fibers, dab the bed with tape for hair strands, and scan the bedroom with an ultraviolet light for semen traces.

The apartment, with gray carpeting, generic furniture, and plastic slipcovers on the dining room chairs, looks like a motel room. There is not a single picture on the wall, not a single framed photo on a shelf. The only personal touches are statues of Jesus, Mary, and Joseph beside a votive candle on a living room end table. The detectives are perplexed by Unson's sleeping arrangements: the living room sofa is covered with a sheet, blanket, and pillow, but the mattress in her small bedroom is stripped. There is no bedroom dresser; instead a dozen plastic garbage bags filled with clothes ring the room. Clean laundry is stacked up by a wall. A jumble of letters and bills cover a metal television table.

In the living room, Knolls and McCartin spot several empty jewelry boxes on an ironing board. They debate whether the victim was robbed. In the bedroom, Marcia and Lambkin supervise the criminalists. "He could have masturbated in another room," Lambkin tells the technician with the ultraviolet light. Confident and in his element, Lambkin turns to Lieutenant Farrell and adds, "Some of these offenders kill first and masturbate afterwards. Some of them ejaculate in unusual places. We've found semen in nostril cavities."

"Is that how *you* do it?" Farrell asks with a sly smile.

"I'll tell you after I retire."

A coroner's investigator arrives and the detectives file into the bedroom while he examines the body. The room is warm and stuffy and beams of late-afternoon sunshine seep through the closed blinds, motes of dusk flickering in the light. Unson is on her back in the center of the bed, naked from the waist down, legs spread and hands raised in a defensive position. Blotches of blood streak the insides of her thighs. Her neck is bruised, so the investigator surmises she was strangled. Dried blood dapples both ears. Her brown cardigan sweater and red-and-green striped blouse are disheveled. An expression of surprise and fear clouds her eyes. Her mouth is open in a rictus of agony, with a wad of gum clearly visible beneath the tongue.

The coroner's investigator studies the bruising along her inner thighs and shins and an abrasion above her right breast. Clotted blood mats the hair at the back of her head, and the top of the mattress is stained with brownish red blotches. "She's been dead for a while," he says, pointing to her side and the backs of her legs, which are the deep purple color that indicates lividity, or settling of the blood. He then cuts a small incision just above her waist and plunges a thermometer into her liver, which enables him to estimate the time of death: the body cools at about 1½ degrees per hour until it reaches the ambient temperature.

"This gal's been dead probably thirty to thirty-six hours," the investigator says.

The detectives figure she was attacked two days ago, on April 15— Easter Sunday. She probably died around midnight.

A coroner's criminalist clips Unson's fingernails, combs her pubic area for foreign hairs, and swabs her vagina and anus with a Q-Tip for semen. After he swabs her breasts and neck for saliva and semen, an LAPD photographer sets up his camera.

"I was watching *CSI* the other night and laughed my head off," the photographer tells the detectives. "They picked up a dead baby and didn't even look for trace evidence. There was no coroner around, no photos, no nothing. Then they barge in on the detectives, push them aside, and interview the witnesses. On another show, they picked up hairs with tweezers. Obviously, you use gloves so you don't damage the hair. One detective told me it was so bad he wanted to shoot his TV."

He is still lambasting the show when Knolls and McCartin return to the living room. Inexperienced detectives study a crime scene at eye level, swiveling their heads and searching for clues. Experienced detectives usually scan the ground, where gravity often scatters the most immediate leads. Knolls and McCartin crouch on the balls of their feet like catchers and study the carpeting for several minutes, lost in thought. They attempt to intuit the violent scenario of action and reaction.

Strewn about by the front door are a key ring, a half-filled shopping bag, and a toppled fan. The detectives surmise that Unson had just returned from the store and entered her apartment, keys in hand, when the killer surprised her from behind and stormed through the door.

They spot a chair by the front door. Beside it, there are indentations in the carpet and, nearby, a half-dozen medical magazines. They figure that Unson knocked the chair back while she struggled, which scattered the magazines stacked on the seat.

Knolls and McCartin study the coffee table, set at an angle from the sofa. Unson has bruised shins, so they assume she banged into the coffee table as she tried to escape.

Near the coffee table is a pair of glasses with a lens popped out. The detectives suspect the killer punched her in the face.

"Looks like a stranger case," McCartin says. "She sure didn't let him in the door."

Knolls nods. "He blitzed her."

Detective Ron Ito returns from the medical clinic where Unson worked and briefs Knolls and McCartin. "Coworkers said she's a very shy woman. She won't even examine men. She's very religious and goes to church all the time. Has a brother who's a priest. Doesn't drink, smoke, or have sex. Her life was work to home, home to work. Had a very regular schedule. Always on time. Before she started work she wiped her desk off with a paper towel and cleaner. Brought her lunch every day in Tupperware. She's a squeaky-clean victim. She didn't do anything to invite this. She told everyone that in two years, when she turned sixty-five, she was going to retire and return to the Philippines."

A few minutes later, a neighbor approaches and says they should investigate "a nut" in one of the ground-floor units who "runs around where he doesn't belong." Knolls continues inspecting the crime scene while Lambkin and McCartin walk downstairs to interview the man. First, however, Lambkin asks Marcia to grab a hat from the trunk of their car. He explains to McCartin that he has just called two dog handlers whom he has worked with during previous rape investigations. One of the dogs is a bloodhound, which follows scent trails. The other, a Labrador, performs "scent discrimination"—it compares scents and alerts its handler to a match.

Lambkin wants the man in the ground-floor unit to handle the hat. Then he will see if the Labrador picks out the hat after sniffing something the killer has touched. Many detectives believe that in this high-tech age, dogs are a hopelessly antiquated investigative tool. Lambkin and Marcia, however, are more innovative than the typical hidebound LAPD detectives.

McCartin knocks on the man's door and tells him he wants to question him briefly. While they chat, McCartin notices a pair of women's shoes stuffed into a trash can, which piques his interest because the neighbor told him the man lives alone. The man reluctantly follows McCartin into the courtyard. Although the evening is warm, with clear skies, he is wearing a long green raincoat. He is unshaven and stares off into the middle distance with a slightly demented expression.

Lambkin introduces himself to the man and then holds out the blue baseball cap. "Have you seen anyone wear this hat?"

The man, who tightly grips the sides of his raincoat, is reluctant to touch the hat.

"Am I a suspect?" he asks suspiciously.

"No," McCartin says with a dismissive wave of his hand. "We're talking to all the residents."

Finally, the man touches the edge of the hat and then holds it gingerly.

When they return to the victim's apartment, Lambkin grabs his cell phone and checks the man's record. He is not a registered sex offender, which disappoints Lambkin.

At dusk, the detectives linger on the deck outside Unson's apartment, waiting for the dog handlers. Palm fronds crackle in the warm breeze, which carries the scent of freshly cut grass. On the western horizon, the setting sun streaks the puffy cloud banks magenta.

Unson lived on Los Feliz Boulevard, in an apartment district, but to the north, spacious homes with red tile roofs and winding driveways dot the hills. In the classic noir movie *Double Indemnity*, the murder victim lived in this neighborhood. His elegant Spanish Revival house, which was flanked by palm trees, was an anomalous setting for such a cynical crime.

As the houses in the hills fade to silhouettes, and the clouds darken from purple to charcoal, Marcia tells a few detectives about the first time he used a bloodhound. A young girl was alone in her family's Pacific Palisades apartment when a man wearing a gas mask broke into her room, raped her, and ran off. Marcia, who was assisting the lead detectives, knew that sheriff's investigators occasionally relied on bloodhounds to track suspects. He volunteered to call the dog handler.

The bloodhound led the detectives outside the apartment, down an alley, around the block, back into the complex, and right to the front door of another apartment. Detectives questioned the tenant, a man in his early twenties who lived in the unit with his father, a fireman. He denied raping the girl. When his father returned home, however, the detectives found an identical gas mask in his car. Eventually, criminalists matched the DNA recovered from the victim's body with the son, and he was convicted of the rape.

At dark, the bloodhound handler arrives. Ted Hamm is a volunteer with the Los Angeles County Sheriff's Department, an agency that, in contrast to the LAPD, is open-minded about the efficacy of scent dogs. He runs a device that looks like a small vacuum cleaner over Unson's mattress for about a minute, drawing the suspect's scent. He then removes a five-by-nine-inch sterile gauze "scent pad" from the vacuum and places it in a plastic bag.

When the Labrador handler arrives, he arranges the blue baseball hat and several other items on the courtyard grass. The scenario is similar to a lineup: the chocolate Lab—the "discriminating dog"— sniffs the scent pad, wanders by the items on the grass, and then scampers off. "If your killer's scent had been on the hat," the dog's handler says, "he would have barked his head off." Lambkin and Marcia are convinced that the man who handled the hat is not their suspect.

Hamm sets another scent pad beneath the nose of his seven-year-old bloodhound, Scarlet, a tracker. After she sniffs it, he pats her on the side and she ambles through the courtyard, nose down, and into the apartment's parking lot. Knolls and McCartin follow and Lambkin and Marcia remain at the apartment.

The tenant who handled the baseball cap stands in the corner of the parking lot chatting with a woman. Scarlet trots right past the man without lifting her nose from the asphalt. Hamm whispers to Knolls and McCartin, "It looks like the weird guy is just plain weird. I don't think he's your man."

The dog spends several minutes sniffing about the parking lot, which is encircled by a tall chain-link fence. Finally, she follows a trail, pushes her nose up against the fence, which faces a jazz club parking lot, and barks.

"Your guy probably hopped the fence," Hamm tells the detectives. "We'll get our exercise tonight."

They walk out the apartment's front door, past the jazz club, and into its parking lot. The dog sniffs the lot and leads Hamm to a six-foot-high wrought-iron fence bordering a sidewalk. "I think the guy hopped this fence, too." They circle around the jazz club, to the sidewalk, and Scarlet picks up the trail again, straining against her leash.

The dog leads Hamm down the sidewalk, beneath a graceful canopy of avocado trees. The detectives follow, crunching across a carpet of dried brown avocado leaves.

"Stand back," Hamm tells the detectives. "She starts pissing when she's on the scent." A second later the dog urinates while she walks. Knolls and McCartin jump off the sidewalk and onto a lawn. Scarlet trots down several long blocks, past Craftsman-style bungalows, clapboard cottages, stucco apartments, and Spanish-style houses with tiled courtyards. The smell of star jasmine and mock orange lingers in the air. The dog then abruptly swings left, down a sidewalk and back to Los Feliz Boulevard. She leads Hamm into a building and, eventually, to the parking lot in back. The building is a few hundred yards from Unson's apartment and part of the same complex.

"No person who pulls anything like this goes straight home," Hamm tells the detectives. "They do a big loop. Our guy made a circle from the apartment and back to an area very near the crime scene. . . . Maybe he drove off from the parking lot. This tells me he lives right around here."

While Knolls and McCartin have been following the bloodhound, several divisional homicide detectives interview residents at the apartment building. They confirm that Unson was extremely shy and that she never had visitors. It is highly unlikely, the residents said, that she would allow a man to enter her apartment.

Knolls and McCartin plan to interview the residents themselves. But by the time they finish examining the apartment it is almost midnight, so they will wait until tomorrow. Standing outside their car, they analyze the murder before driving back downtown.

"There's a lot of broads to rape," Knolls says. "Why her?"

"Maybe he's a predator," McCartin says. "She's an easy target. Quiet and vulnerable. Maybe he was watching her."

"It's got to be someone local, probably right there in the same apartment building," Knolls says.

McCartin leans against the trunk and says, "I don't know a lot about rape, but I doubt this guy's a first-timer. Might be a serial rapist."

"We'll put the DNA through," Knolls says. "Maybe we'll get lucky."

"Here we are, a couple of ghetto cops," says McCartin, who, like Knolls, spent about five years investigating murders in South-Central before he transferred to Homicide Special. "First case we work together, we gotta learn about the Russian culture. Now we might be onto a serial rapist. It was a lot easier back in the 'hood."

On Wednesday morning Knolls attends the autopsy while McCartin peruses sex crime reports from the neighborhood. Unson is a tiny woman, only five foot one and about a hundred pounds. An autopsy technician lays her on her back, in the center of a metal gurney, among half a dozen other corpses. The room smells of disinfectant and decomposing flesh.

The pathologist begins by examining her injuries. "Bruise between third and fourth knuckle," he tells Knolls. "Abrasion by the clavicle and abrasion by the right side of the neck. Could be from a grip. There's blood in *both* ears. That's really weird."

He studies the dried blood on the back of Unson's head and then peers between her thighs. "See the abrasions?" he tells Knolls. "That'll be important to establish sexual assault." The pathologist turns his attention to her head, lifting her lips with tweezers and studying the red petechiae on the gum line. He then points out more speckling inside her eyelid and on the outer edge of her eye.

"I'm leaning toward strangulation, not blunt force trauma, as the cause of death," the pathologist says. "We'll pop her open now and get a better idea."

He grabs a scalpel and cuts a large Y-shaped incision in her chest. Using a tool that looks like a hedge clipper, he clips the ribs with a loud crunch. After lifting the rib cage, he studies the internal organs and points to the lungs, which are a vivid pink.

"Beautiful lungs," he mutters. "Definitely not a smoker."

He removes her sternum with a scalpel, then slices out the internal organs and neatly lines them up on a tray. With a metal ladle he scoops out blood and pours it into a glass vial.

"See the liquidity of that blood?" he tells Knolls. "It shows she died pretty quickly. There's no clotting."

The pathologist points out the undigested food in Unson's stomach, a viscous brown and white substance. "Looks like some meat fibers . . . maybe chicken . . . some rice, some onions." He nods thoughtfully and says to Knolls, "This should help you out with a time of death. Most people don't wake up in the morning with a full stomach. She definitely had a good meal. A meal like that would take six to eight hours to go completely through her system. That meal had probably been in her stomach for a few hours."

After the pathologist transfers some of the stomach contents to a glass bottle, he cuts through her matted black hair with a scalpel, peels back the skin, and examines the gleaming skull. He points to the streaks of purple on the sides of her head.

"There's a little hemorrhaging on the left side and more on the right side by her ear." He clenches his fist and punches the air a few times. "This woman was definitely beaten." He runs a forefinger around the skull. "No fractures, though."

The pathologist dissects Unson's neck, points out more purple hemorrhage specks on the muscle, and snips out the larynx. After removing the hyoid bone, just above the throat, he shows Knolls a jagged white edge jutting out of the purple tissue. The bone was fractured, which usually means the victim was strangled.

"I'm favoring a manual strangulation as the cause of death." He points out the purple slashes on the side of her neck. "I don't think a ligature was used, because of these uneven spots of hemorrhaging around the neck tissue. It's not circular."

Knolls tells him that nobody in the apartment building heard her scream.

"She probably couldn't speak." The pathologist holds his right hand up, fingers bent like a claw, and shakes it. "I think he got her like this, with one hand, right below the vocal cords. It was very quick. That's why nobody heard anything."

Back in the squad room, Knolls tells McCartin, Lambkin, and Marcia about the autopsy. A detective sitting nearby says, "I'll never forget my first autopsy. I was feeling real shaky and an autopsy technician came by and said, 'Detective, do you need a hand?' I turned around and he put a cut-off hand on my shoulder."

Lambkin says that he checked a California medical registry and discovered that their victim was listed years ago under a different last name, so an ex-husband might be roaming around. "Also, there's a few decent sexual offenders living in the neighborhood."

Marcia tells Knolls that the ultraviolet light found no semen stains on the bed or in the apartment. "But a lot of these guys have ED—erectile dysfunction," Marcia says. "Some can't ejaculate; some can't get an erection."

"We still need an explanation of why she slept on the living room sofa," Lambkin says.

McCartin looks baffled. "That's a pretty strange way for a doctor to live."

The detectives complain that the fingerprint technician who dusted the apartment was too cavalier. "He told me," Marcia says, "that he couldn't get prints off the bed frame because there was too much dust."

"He told me he couldn't lift prints off the door frame because it's not a printable surface," Lambkin adds, grunting with disgust. "How could the door frame be an unprintable surface? That's where we got our print in the Gorman case."

"Because she's such a loner," Knolls says, "prints might very well be the key to this case."

McCartin calls the department's Scientific Investigation Division and arranges for a new team of print technicians to dust the apartment, more assiduously this time. He also requests that they use the chemical ninhydrin to lift fingerprints on the bedroom and living room walls.

McCartin and Knolls cruise north from downtown on Interstate 5, past the graffiti-scarred cement banks of the Los Angeles River, swirling with water after the rainy winter and flanked with cattails. They pull off the freeway and head west on Los Feliz Boulevard, past sprawling 4,000-acre Griffith Park. The sun streams through the majestic deodars—planted more than eighty years ago—and streaks the sidewalk with light and shadows. At Unson's apartment, the detectives instruct the print technicians to dust for prints in a number of new areas, including the railings by the stairwell, the doors leading to the parking lot, and the back fence, which the bloodhound indicated the killer might have climbed over during his escape.

As Knolls walks through the courtyard, a tenant calls out, "You should look into some of her disgruntled former patients."

Knolls nods without raising his head.

Another neighbor informs him, "My brother's a cop. I think it was someone she knew. I guarantee that's where you should look."

The comments reinforce Knolls's belief that every man in Los Angeles believes he can do two things better than the experts: manage the Dodgers and solve murders.

He returns to Unson's apartment, finds her phone book, and notes the numbers for her priest and a few out-of-town friends. He plans to call them tonight. After scouring the rooms for clues to her ascetic life, he yells to McCartin, "Hey, we might have another Imelda Marcos here." He shows him the thirteen pairs of shoes stored inside a plastic garbage bag beside her bed.

McCartin studies her "Catholic Family Appointment Calendar." On Good Friday she circled "Fast and Abstinence," and scrawled: "Station of the Cross." Two days later, McCartin figures, she was killed. In a drawer, he discovers stacks of receipts, which reveal her circumscribed routine. Every evening after work she stopped by a drugstore and purchased water and other small items, ate at a Filipino restaurant, and then apparently returned home. There is not a single dish in her kitchen cabinets.

"It's kind of sad to die like this," he tells Knolls. "Alone, in an empty apartment, with no family around."

The next morning, a detective yells across the squad room to Knolls that Unson's brother is calling from the Philippines. The detective runs his fingers under his eyes to indicate that the man is crying. Knolls picks up the phone and confirms the brother's fears. "Yes, she was," he says softly. "I don't want to hold anything back from you. . . . No, it was strangulation. But at this point I want you to keep that to yourself. . . . I'd like to ask you a few questions. . . ."

Afterward, Knolls briefs McCartin. "All of her family's still in the Philippines. They're coming out here next week. The brother says she lived in this apartment for two years. That makes her seem even stranger because of all her stuff in boxes and garbage bags. She was a very private person and had no relationships with men. She was very frightened of the city, very scared of strangers. At the previous place she lived, she had multiple locks on the doors. The brother says her father was a decorated officer in the Philippine army. He was extremely strict. That probably accounts for her compulsive disorder and her fear of men."

"Is that your diagnosis, Dr. Knolls?" McCartin asks in a German accent.

"Okay, smart-ass, how come a lady like this had a different last name years ago?"

McCartin shrugs.

"It was a green card marriage only," Knolls says. "She never lived with him."

A detective from the division near Los Feliz calls McCartin and tells him that about five weeks ago two patrol officers responded to a "family dispute" radio call at the apartment building where Unson lived. The woman told the officers that a man who had recently moved into her apartment "forced me to have sex with him" a number of times. When the officers hauled the couple to the police station, the woman recanted. No charges were ever filed. The detectives plan to interview the woman tonight.

Later in the morning, Lambkin crosses the squad room to tell

Knolls and McCartin that crime reports for the area reveal that an accused sex offender lived right next door to the victim. The news provides the exhausted detectives, who worked until midnight the past two nights and woke up each morning before five, with a burst of adrenaline. They speed to Los Feliz and interview the apartment complex's manager.

He tells them an Armenian woman lived next door to Unson, but moved out twelve days before the murder. He was not aware that her son, who stayed with her occasionally, had been arrested for a sex crime. "But I did know," the manager says, "that he was a felon who had some outstanding warrants." The apartment has been unlocked since last Thursday, the manager says, because a handyman has just painted it and installed new carpeting.

Knolls and McCartin check in with the new crew of fingerprint technicians and discover that their persistence has been rewarded. Although the ninhydrin yielded no prints, the crew did manage to lift several more from Unson's apartment using traditional methods.

In the courtyard, an elderly man in house slippers is sitting in a plastic lawn chair, chain-smoking. He waves the detectives over and whispers theatrically, "I've got some information for you." They follow him into his musty, cluttered apartment.

Rubbing his palms together, he says, "This is what I wanted to tell you two officers. There's a lady in this apartment building who knows something. I think it might be important for you. She heard two young fellas speaking in some kind of foreign language. Very loud talking. Then she heard two screams. She said these fellas came in the front door, but she thinks they went downstairs and might have climbed the back fence."

Knolls and McCartin are intrigued because this scenario corresponds with the trail the bloodhound followed. They wonder if the language this woman heard was Armenian.

"When did she hear these screams?" Knolls asks.

"Sunday night."

Unson was probably killed Sunday night.

"I told her that I assumed she talked to the detectives. She said she hadn't. She's afraid. I told her to do the right thing."

"When did you have this conversation?" McCartin asks.

"Last night. I missed *Jeopardy!*, so it must have been between seven and seven-thirty."

The detectives ask him some general questions about the building's residents, casually mentioning the Armenian woman who lived next door to Unson.

"I didn't know her too well, but I saw her son a lot. He visited most every day."

"When was the last time you saw him?"

"Eight or nine months ago. He used to bum cigarettes from me. He was always friendly and nice to me. But the police were looking for him one time. There was some sort of warrant out for him. A detective told me, 'Stay away from him. He's a violent person.' "

After the interview, Knolls and McCartin lug their briefcases and murder book to a table in the courtyard. For a few minutes, they sit in silence, enjoying the sunshine and watching the koi, flashes of orange in the murky pond.

Finally, Knolls says, "This is how I see it. They find her body noon Tuesday. Thirty-six hours earlier would put the time of death at midnight Easter Sunday. This knucklehead is Armenian, so I'm presuming he's a Christian. Maybe he didn't know his mom moved. So he shows up on Easter Sunday to visit her, finds out she's gone, but sees the apartment is open and empty. He hangs around for a while, until Lourdes makes her nightly dinner run. Her meal wasn't digested, so she probably ate at about six or seven P.M. When she comes back, he sees his opportunity and nails her."

Later, the detectives knock on the door of the woman who heard the loud voices and the woman who claimed she was raped and then recanted. Neither is home.

On Friday, as the detectives study stacks of Lourdes Unson's shopping receipts and bank statements, Knolls makes a disquieting discovery: Unson deposited $1,783 at a bank ATM—on Monday. This means she was not murdered on Easter night, their timeline is entirely inaccurate, the coroner's estimated time of death is wrong, and the woman who heard the screams is irrelevant. Looking discouraged, they prepare to reassess the past week's work. Now they wonder whether she was abducted or followed home from the ATM machine.

The bank is just a block from Unson's apartment. The manager checks the records and confirms that Unson deposited the money on Monday. When she tells the detectives when the deposit was made— 12:59 P.M.—they are even more confused. Unson's supervisors said that she worked from ten A.M. to six P.M., Monday through Friday. She was extremely punctual and never called in sick.

"Did she withdraw a large sum on Monday?" McCartin asks the manager.

"She just got a hundred dollars cash back from the ATM."

The manager agrees to request the ATM videotape immediately, so the detectives can see whether anyone accompanied Unson to the bank.

Knolls and McCartin drive back downtown in silence. There was no money in Unson's purse at her apartment, and they found no receipts indicating she purchased anything on Monday after withdrawing the cash. They surmise that the killer pocketed it.

"This just got a lot more complicated," McCartin says.

"Yeah, but at least it narrows things down for us," Knolls says. "Now we don't have to worry about Sunday. We just have to focus on twenty-four hours—from Monday to Tuesday."

McCartin mentions that he has worked late every night this week and has not seen his children since last Sunday. Knolls volunteers to stick around the squad room tonight and review all of Unson's receipts in an attempt to track her movements on Monday. He tells McCartin to leave on time today.

Knolls stares out the car window, studies the smoggy horizon, and says, "Something's not right here. I don't know what it is. But something's not right."

20

On Monday afternoon, about a week after Lourdes Unson was killed, her two brothers and two sisters, who have just flown twelve hours from the Philippines, knock on the squad room door. The brothers look dazed, and the sisters clutch handkerchiefs and dab their red-rimmed eyes.

Knolls and McCartin usher them into the captain's empty office and explain that they will be able to investigate their sister's death more effectively if they can learn more about her personal life and habits. Cesar Unson, who serves as the family spokesman and who speaks excellent English, says he understands.

"How often did all of you talk with your sister?" Knolls asks.

"Not too often," he says. "Recently we just exchanged cards."

"We found it curious that Lourdes lived in the apartment for two years, but we couldn't even find a dish in the house," Knolls says.

"That's the way she lived. She ate out every night. She didn't like to cook."

McCartin asks where she lived before.

"She owned a house. But it was broken into. She was frightened. She moved to an apartment because she felt safer around other people."

McCartin describes how Unson stuffed all her clothing into plastic garbage bags and lined them up against the bedroom walls.

"She didn't live like that in the house," says one of her sisters. "She had a dresser."

The detectives know that Unson planned to retire and return to the Philippines. They figure that she viewed the apartment as only a way station.

"Did she have any close friends here?" McCartin asks.

"No," Cesar says. "She wasn't very sociable and she was very secretive. Even in the Philippines she wasn't too sociable." He fiddles with his ring and asks, "Do you have any suspects?"

"We have some ideas," McCartin says.

"Were you able to establish how this person entered her apartment?"

"There are some things we call 'keys,' which are details of the crime, and we have to hold off on giving them out," McCartin says.

Knolls asks them about Unson's husband.

"When she arrived in the U.S., she was holding a transit visa," Cesar says. "She married someone here—just for convenience, to get a permanent visa. I heard that the man was arrested later and my sister was a bit worried about it. Is he a suspect?"

"We're going to look into it," Knolls says.

After the interview, as the detectives drive Cesar to Lourdes's bank to close out her accounts and clear her safety deposit box, he tells them about his family's background. When World War II erupted, his father, who managed the family's sugar and rice plantations, enlisted in the army. After the war, he moved to Manila, married, and managed the farm, which was about sixty miles away. All ten of his children graduated from college. One son was the vice mayor of Manila, the oldest is a monsignor, another is a physician, and a younger son is a pharmacist. When the last child graduated from college, the parents threw a large party at the Manila Sheraton.

"They were so proud," says Cesar, who manages the family farm. "They felt that they had fulfilled their obligation."

Lourdes, the second-oldest girl, was an excellent student and a devout Catholic. She was accepted into the two finest medical schools in the Philippines, but chose the Catholic university. "She was very devout," Cesar says. "She was what you might call a prude."

For four years Lourdes was the chief resident at a Manila children's hospital. She chose pediatrics, Cesar says, because she loved children. She applied many times for an American visa, but was always turned down. Finally, in 1976, she vacationed in the United States and never returned home.

"She had no serious boyfriends in Manila, because my father was very strict," Cesar says. "But not long after she arrived here she dated a CPA. He was an ardent suitor and was ready to marry her. The problem was that he was a Protestant. She was really worried about that. And she was very devoted to her career. She was afraid that a man wouldn't understand this."

As Knolls drives north on the freeway, Cesar pauses and studies the landscape. Desert winds have blown the smog to the ocean, and the day is radiant. To the east, the San Gabriel Mountains are clearly visible, the ridges dusted with snow that glistens in the bright sunshine. The sky is an electric blue, and the puffy cloud banks that mass over the Hollywood Hills, verdant now after the winter rains, are a milky white.

"I didn't realize Los Angeles was so beautiful," Cesar says.

"This is what the city used to be like before all the sprawl and smog," Knolls says.

"In the Philippines we watch a lot of television shows about the LAPD." He sighs and says, "I never thought I'd go to your building for something like this."

When they arrive at the bank, an assistant manager leads them to a small room, where Cesar opens his sister's safety deposit box. The detectives are stunned. The deep metal box is filled with expensive jewelry. Cesar opens the boxes and small plastic bags and inspects the pieces—gold, diamonds, emeralds, pearls—while Knolls itemizes the contents on a yellow legal pad. Unson stashed away thirty-five pairs of earrings, twenty-three rings, fourteen bracelets, eight necklaces, and six pendants.

When Cesar dangles a dazzling emerald and diamond pendant, which sparkles under the fluorescent lights, the assistant bank manager shakes her head and says, "My God, this woman had some beautiful things. A *man* should have bought her all this."

Knolls says he is surprised that a woman who lived so frugally and drove a battered twelve-year-old Toyota had such extravagant tastes. Cesar says his sister did not want to attract attention because she was afraid of carjackers and robbers.

"Filipino women love jewelry," Cesar says. "All my sisters are the same way. The Spaniards influenced us. Maybe my sister bought all this jewelry because she planned to wear it when she returned to the Philippines. She felt safer there."

When the detectives drop Cesar off and return to the squad room, they attempt to learn more about the Armenian suspect. McCartin calls the Glendale Police Department, where the man was arrested a few years ago for a sexual assault. Unfortunately, a detective tells McCartin, the department does not have the Armenian's DNA sample . . . and he is currently "a parolee at large," having failed to appear in court after a stabbing. The detective explains that the sex crime he was arrested for was a kidnap-rape. But no charges were ever filed, because "the reliability of the sixteen-year-old victim was in question." Still, the suspect has a criminal record. The detective agrees to share his files on the suspect and his "running buddies." McCartin tells him he will stop by the Glendale Police Department tomorrow.

Knolls flips open the murder book and the detectives spend the afternoon struggling with the revamped homicide time line. They wait for a call from the bank manager about the ATM video, which they hope will reveal a suspect. McCartin mentions how Cesar seemed reassured when he discovered that both detectives are Catholic. Then McCartin asks Knolls, "You don't believe in evolution, do you?"

Knolls smiles. "You're going to hell."

McCartin shrugs. "Hell's more fun, anyway. That's where all the strippers and hookers are."

"Yeah, but it's hell because you can look but you can't touch."

"Hey, don't I get any bonus points for putting all those killers in prison?" McCartin asks.

"Probably not—you Irish-Jew bastard," Knolls says, laughing.

Although all four of McCartin's grandparents are Irish, a confused murder suspect once called him an "Irish-Jew bastard." Knolls finds the epithet amusing. The detectives still clash occasionally, but now that they are accustomed to each other's methods and idiosyncrasies, the partnership has developed a new ease and camaraderie.

When the bank manager finally calls, the detectives grab their phones. A security officer repeatedly studied Monday's ATM video-tape, but could not spot Unson. The officer then checked the tape for Saturday, and discovered that Unson had deposited a check and with-drawn $100.

"This is the confusing part," the bank manager says. "If you make a transaction on Saturday, they stamp it the next *business* day—which is Monday. So we've confirmed that she did *not* go to the bank on Monday. It was Saturday, like you thought all along."

"This means the lady who heard the two screams Sunday night could be an important witness," McCartin tells Knolls.

"Let's get her tonight," Knolls says.

The detectives arrive at the apartment building at dusk. Because they know the woman who heard the screams is skittish, they did not call to set up an interview; they plan to surprise her at home. Striding across the courtyard, they pass the elderly man in his lawn chair and he motions to them with his cigarette, its tip drawing iridescent streaks in the dying light. He tells them that the woman they are about to meet once borrowed $150 "from the Armenian lady with the convict son."

"This Armenian lady had a hard time getting her money back," he says. "Maybe the Armenian lady needed the cash so she then turned to the Filipino lady and borrowed money from her. Maybe she never paid her back. Maybe the Filipino lady made a big stink about it. Maybe the son got some Armenian gangs to come and kill and rob her." He puffs on his unfiltered cigarette and is suddenly convulsed by a phlegmy coughing fit. He clears his throat and says, "I was watching *Diagnosis Murder* last night on television. It gave me some ideas." He looks up at the detectives and asks earnestly, "Do you think what I said is a possibility?"

McCartin stifles a smile. As they walk off, Knolls mumbles over his shoulder, "We'll certainly look into it."

The detectives peer through the witness's curtains and are encouraged by the gray luminescence of a television screen. When she answers the door, Knolls and McCartin introduce themselves and hand her their cards. She blinks hard a few times and invites them inside. In the corner of the living room, on a wooden table, is a shrine with several statues of Jesus surrounded by Easter cards, a dozen votive candles, and rosary beads. The detectives ask a few general questions about the victim first, to put the witness at ease.

"Unson would hardly talk to anyone," says the woman, who is barefoot and wears a large silver cross around her neck. "She walked around here with her head down. At first, I thought she was a mute. Then we talked once in the parking lot. . . . We both attended the same Catholic church. She told me she wouldn't prescribe birth control for religious reasons, that it was against God's will. The last time I talked to her was by the mailbox. I told her I liked to say the rosary, and she told me she did too."

Knolls asks if she saw Unson at church on Easter Sunday.

"I saw her in church at Saturday night mass."

"Did you see her at the apartment on Sunday?"

"I can't remember. On most Sundays, I saw her doing her laundry and we'd talk. She'd also talk to the Armenian lady. That was the only other person I saw her talk to."

After they chat for a few more minutes, the woman confides that she heard something disturbing late at night on Easter Sunday. "I've been so scared. I can't sleep." She nervously shuffles the detectives' cards. "I'm *so* scared."

"Tell us what you heard," McCartin says.

"That's what's scaring me so much." She hugs herself, digging her fingernails into her arms. "I was watching TV when I heard someone walking hard. Then I heard two people walk by my door." She stands up and demonstrates, marching and pounding her feet on the carpet.

"How did you know it was two people?" Knolls asks.

"I lifted up the blinds. They stopped at the top of the stairs. They were talking in another language—very nervous and very loud. Then I heard a woman scream. It faded away. And I heard it again." She waves her hand. "It wasn't really a scream. More like this." She moans loudly.

"Was it a scream or a sigh?" McCartin asks.

"The first sound was high pitched and sharp, like a scream. The second one was lower."

"Was it a female?"

"Yes. Then I heard two men's voices, very clear. It sounded like they were arguing with each other. I thought they were speaking Armenian, because the lady upstairs is Armenian. I didn't know then that the Armenian lady had moved. I thought that these people were very rude to be talking so loud. Then someone slammed a door. I'm sure nobody came by this door. I would have heard that. If they left, it was down by the laundry room."

The laundry room is near the back parking lot, where the bloodhound followed a trail.

"When I heard the first noise I checked my watch," she says. "It was eleven-fifteen."

"What made you check your watch?" Knolls asks.

"The guys were making so much noise and it was late." She drops the detectives' cards on the coffee table and says, "I peeked through the windows, but I didn't see anything. My lights were on. Maybe when I opened the blinds . . ." She picks at a cuticle and says, "Maybe they saw me. That's why I'm scared."

"Did they sound drunk?" McCartin asks.

"No. It was like they were arguing."

"You ever hear Armenian before?" he asks.

"Yes."

"Did it sound like it?"

"Yes. The Armenian people talk loud."

"Did the Armenian lady have any other family members living with her?" McCartin asks.

"A daughter and a son."

"Did you see them lately?"

"I saw the son."

"When?"

"A few weeks ago. In the evening. I was coming home—we passed and he said hello."

"Did he and his mom speak Armenian?"

"Yes."

"You sure you didn't see these guys?" McCartin asks.

"I couldn't see anybody." She takes a deep breath and exhales loudly, shaking her head. "I can't sleep. Last night I didn't sleep at all. Should I be scared?"

"We don't think there's a predator in the neighborhood targeting women," McCartin says. "We think this is a random attack. But be aware of your surroundings. When you drive, make sure no one is behind you. When you're in the apartment, make sure your door is closed and locked."

As she walks the detectives to the door, she whispers, "I sure hope you're successful."

McCartin nods reassuringly and says, "We'll get him."

The detectives then climb the stairs to the second floor and knock on the door of the woman who claimed she was raped and later recanted. Again, no one is at home. They return to the courtyard, drop their briefcases and murder books on a metal table, and pull up chairs. The tops of the towering palm trees sway in the warm breeze and cast shifting shadows on the grass. The detectives slip off their coats and loosen their ties.

"What she said makes sense to me," Knolls says. "Unson wouldn't let out a bloodcurdling scream. She wouldn't be yelling, 'What the fuck you doing here?' I see her as the passive type. But she was so cautious. How could someone get close enough to her to get into the apartment?"

"If it's the Armenian, Unson knows his mother and knows him from living next door," McCartin says. "That could explain it."

"So what's our game plan for tomorrow?" Knolls asks.

"Let's try to figure out when she left the house Sunday and when she returned," McCartin replies.

"I'll call the priest and find out what time mass was over," Knolls says. "Let's track down where she ate dinner that night."

The detectives spend the next morning studying sexual assault statistics. They discover that during the past fifteen years, 255 women in Los Angeles were killed during sexually motivated homicides, 105 of whom were strangled. They search for cases where the modus operandi parallels that of Unson's murderer. If they find any, they will meet with the investigating detectives and compare notes.

The Santa Anas blew through the city again this morning, jacking the temperature up to 93 degrees, a record for the date. This afternoon, the winds have abruptly died and smog shrouds the horizon. The detectives climb into their car, slip on their sunglasses, and turn up the air conditioner. From her receipts, they know Unson frequently dined at a Filipino restaurant in Hollywood. They wonder if she had her last meal there. McCartin drives and Knolls, in the passenger seat, has the murder book in his lap.

The restaurant's manager recognizes a picture of Unson. She stopped by several nights a week, he says, but often asked for her dinner to go. He rarely talked to her and says he cannot recall whether she stopped by on Easter.

The detectives decide to visit the other restaurant where she was a regular. Heading east on Sunset, they pass a Peruvian, a Cuban, and a Guatemalan restaurant, a Salvadoran *pupuseria,* an Armenian market, a Russian nightclub, a Baltic crafts store, and a Cambodian doughnut shop. Finally, about a mile west of downtown, in the heart of a Filipino neighborhood, they pull up in front of the second restaurant. The stark dining room, which has tan tile floors and Formica tables, is stifling. It smells of hot oil and fried fish. A fan rattles and clicks overhead.

The detectives introduce themselves and the manager invites them to sit at a table. When they tell her that Unson has been murdered, she shouts, "Oh my God!" and clutches her stomach. "I'm so upset, my stomach hurts. I knew Dr. L. very well. She ate here often for the past four or five years, sometimes every night. She was so nice. If I wasn't feeling good she'd tell me to take this or that medicine. But I haven't seen her for a while. I thought she was on vacation."

The woman confirms that the restaurant was open on Easter, but she tells the detectives she did not see Unson that night. "A few weeks ago . . . I asked her when she was moving back to the Philippines and she said she had two more years to go before she got her pension. Then she was going to return home and live with her sister."

She peers furtively around the restaurant, and says, "Was it a gun-shot?"

"We can't tell you," McCartin says.

She makes a stabbing motion and says, "A knife?"

McCartin shakes his head.

She ties an imaginary rope and stretches it, her eyes bulging. "Strangled?"

"Again, we can't say."

"Maybe it was a burglar," the owner says. "She was a doctor. She looked like she had money. . . . Maybe someone forced entry into her apartment looking for cash."

McCartin chuckles. "You must have been a detective in the Philippines."

"You're a female Columbo," Knolls says.

"Did she dress with a lot of jewelry?" McCartin asks.

"No. She dressed simple but elegant. She looked regal," the owner says, shaking her head with admiration. "She was very neat and clean, from head to toe. She was so neat she'd clean the table herself, even if it was already clean."

"You know anyone who'd want to attack her?" McCartin asks.

"No."

"How long would she stay here?" Knolls asks.

"About a half hour. She'd eat and leave."

"Did she ever come in with anyone?" Knolls says.

"No. Always alone. She liked fish. When I'd see her in the parking lot I'd start making fried milkfish and mango." The owner extends her palms. "If you talk to the family, tell them I'm inviting them to come here. I want to do something for them. I want to make the family a meal before they go back to the Philippines."

The next morning, McCartin calls the department's fingerprint unit. He tells a technician he wants to compare a suspect's prints with those lifted at the apartment. McCartin is accustomed to the LAPD's bureaucratic inefficiency, but he is stunned anyway by the response: he will have to wait several months for the results. When he tells the technician to "put a rush" on the request, the specialist says that "every detective wants a rush for their murder," but only a captain can speed up the timetable. Like every other LAPD department, the specialist says, the print section is understaffed and overworked. McCartin and Knolls know that because there are hundreds of murders a year in the city, rush orders are usually granted only for extremely high-profile homicides or emergencies, as when detectives have evidence that a suspect plans to kill again or is prepared to flee the country.

Crossing the squad room, Lambkin overhears the detectives. "I had a rape case in the Harbor Division last year," he says. "Hairs were found in the suspect's car. I kept asking for a DNA test. Then the guy was convicted. A few days later, I got the results."

On the way to Glendale, the detectives discover the heat wave has dissipated. Ocean breezes blow a gauzy scrim of fog into the San Gabriel Valley. High clouds obscure the sun and just a faint, one-dimensional outline of the mountains is visible.

Knolls and McCartin pull up chairs beside the desks of two Glendale detectives who previously arrested the Armenian suspect. The Glendale detectives say that they recently investigated and then tailed two burglars, one of whom is related to the Armenian.

"This might get your attention," a Glendale detective says. "Our two suspects frequently cruised right by the street where your victim was killed. The other thing is that our two guys go after high-end jewelry. Your guy could have tipped them off that the lady had a lot of jewelry."

Knolls and McCartin both nod, recalling the empty jewelry boxes on the ironing board in Unson's apartment.

The other Glendale detective counts on his thumb and three fingers. "You've got a dead lady. This guy's mom lives next door. These two assholes frequently drive by the apartment. And they like jewelry. What are the odds?"

Knolls tells them about the trail the bloodhound followed.

"That makes sense," a Glendale detective says. "If they pulled it off, they'd park a few blocks away."

"Did our suspect visit his mom much?" McCartin asks.

"Oh, yeah."

McCartin asks them how long it would take to compare a suspect's fingerprints with those found at a crime scene.

"If we had both sets of prints, we'd just walk it over," the Glendale detective says. "It would take a minute or two. If we didn't have both sets, it would take a day or two."

When McCartin tells them he might have to wait months, the Glendale detectives shout in unison, "No way!"

"I know you're a much bigger department," one says, "but that's ridiculous."

McCartin then asks them if their two burglars are coldblooded enough to rape and strangle a sixty-three-year-old woman.

"You talk to these guys and they have that shark stare," a Glendale detective replies. "It wouldn't surprise me at all if they did something like this."

The other detective says, "There's a lot of coincidences involving these suspects and your murder. And when it comes to homicide cases, I don't like coincidences. I don't like them one bit."

21

The Susan Berman investigation is stymied. During the past month, the detectives have interviewed more friends of Berman's and several friends of Nyle's, examined prowler reports in her neighborhood, and attempted to track down Robert Durst. The friends have provided little new information, the prowler reports were a bust, and when Durst finally returns Stephens's call, he says he did not attend the memorial service because reporters now continually pester him. His wife's case has officially been reopened and his attorneys have advised him not to talk to detectives. "This will be our last conversation," he says and then hangs up.

The detectives recently obtained a search warrant for Nyle's phone records. Berman was killed late Friday night, after eleven P.M., the detectives know, because that was the last time a friend spoke with her. Nyle's phone records reveal that his last phone call on Friday was at 10:29 P.M. His next call was at 8:57 A.M. Saturday and he made no other calls that day. Nyle, however, had told the detectives that he spent the day in his home office, calling many people.

While the detectives found little in their search of Nyle's house, they were able to obtain about a dozen samples of his handwriting. These, they hoped, would prove that Nyle wrote the letter alerting the Beverly Hills police to the corpse. An LAPD handwriting analyst compared the new samples with the letter and concluded that a match was "highly probable." But a "highly probable" rating is not a definitive "identification." The detectives still do not have enough evidence to arrest Nyle.

Stephens walks across the aisle to where Knolls and McCartin pore over the Lourdes Unson murder book, points to them, and says, "These guys keep getting more and more evidence in all their cases, but I can't get a break." Stephens knows that in the murder of Luda Petushenko, the killer's girlfriend provided Knolls and McCartin with an eyewitness account. And DNA tests recently identified a speck of the victim's blood on a pair of the killer's shoes.

"Some detectives have all the luck," Stephens says.

McCartin grins and says, "Maybe it's not luck."

The four detectives ride down the elevator and walk across the parking lot together. Knolls and McCartin head back to Unson's apartment, while Coulter and Stephens drive to the Beverly Hills police station for yet another interview with one of Berman's friends, who lives nearby. The station occupies the top floor of a sand-colored civic center encircled by palm trees. An enlarged, autographed picture from the 1930s, of Edward G. Robinson with the Beverly Hills police chief and two other officers, hangs on the lobby wall behind the desk officer. Inside the squad room, a detective displays above his desk a signed photograph of Clint Eastwood.

Berman's friend, who is a producer, looks fresh off Rodeo Drive. His long hair is swept straight back and he is stylishly dressed in Italian sandals, tan slacks, and a bright green linen shirt. After answering some preliminary questions about his friendship with Berman, the man launches into an impassioned monologue.

"I was shocked when I heard she was murdered, but it makes sense to me." He stares off into the distance and repeats softly, as if talking to himself, "Yeah, it makes sense to me. I think Bobby Durst did it. She told me years ago that Bobby Durst killed his wife. Either he told her or she found out by investigative work. I can't remember. But I think she told me he admitted it. She's a journalist. She knew how to get information out of people."

He tells the detectives that before Berman introduced him to Durst, she said, " 'Let me tell you about Bobby Durst.' Then she told me what happened. She said Durst and his wife went to the country. They had an argument. She was going to leave him. He flipped out. He didn't mean to do it. It was a cover-up."

Berman and Durst, the friend says, were extremely close, but "on another level she had him by the short hairs."

Stephens asks, "Could you sense that?"

"That wasn't on the surface at the time. I'm projecting years later. He makes more sense than anyone else. I'm sure some would say,

'She was such a noble soul. I have no idea how anything like this could happen to her.' I'm not saying that. . . . There was plenty of good with her. She was a beautiful person in many ways. But she's someone who'd find out anything. She was bold beyond anything you can imagine. She's capable of extortion. That's not beneath her. She was getting older and running out of money. She wanted a payday. That's my opinion. I think he finished it. I may be wrong. Maybe I've watched too many movies."

"I have to tell you, I'll have to share this with the New York police," Stephens says. Although he has not been in close contact with New York authorities, Stephens has called them a few times to provide information about Durst.

The friend expresses concern because Durst is such a wealthy and powerful man. He and Berman once spent an afternoon with Durst in Manhattan, he recalls. Durst frequently pointed out buildings and boasted that his family owned them. The friend extends both arms and says, "The Dursts are as big as the Trumps in New York."

As the detectives drive back downtown, Stephens tells Coulter, "Durst might have killed his wife, but that doesn't help us solve *our* case."

"This guy thinks Durst killed Berman, too," Coulter says. "I wish he could give us more than his opinion."

Coulter and Stephens are faced with the tricky problem of how to compel Durst to cooperate with them. Unless they can obtain evidence linking him to Berman's murder, they are hamstrung.

Still, the detectives agree that Nyle is a viable suspect. "After the latest handwriting test, I gotta look at him," Stephens says. "But absent anything else, there's not much we can do. All we've got is a circumstantial case."

They are still waiting for the hairs and fibers collected from Berman's body to be analyzed. When Coulter recently called a Scientific Investigation Division technician, she listed the unit's priorities for homicide investigations: cases with court dates; cases in which a suspect is in custody; and, finally, unsolved cases. In other words, the Berman case is a low priority homicide. Because of a number of recent promotions, there is only one technician in the trace-evidence unit. As a result, the technician told Coulter, there was currently a four-month wait for results.

The detectives are accustomed to the LAPD's chronic understaffing and inefficiency. When Coulter worked at the Wilshire Division, he found a blanket speckled with blood at a homicide scene. He sent the blanket to SID and requested that the serology unit analyze the blood. He didn't hear back from a technician until four years after the killer had been convicted.

"I don't think SID's improved any since O.J.," Stephens gripes.

"I think they're better," Coulter says. "They *have* hired more people and raised their standards. But a wait this long is BS." He tightly grips the steering wheel, looking glum.

"Don't worry, Roy," Stephens says, reassuringly. "Something will turn up."

On a breezy spring evening, Knolls and McCartin return to the apartment building where Unson was killed. The complex is a mini melting pot: the residents are Jamaican, Lithuanian, Brazilian, Armenian, Mexican, Puerto Rican, African American, and Japanese. They are unified now by a common emotion—fear. So officers at the local police division have arranged a community meeting tonight to reassure them.

The tenants gather on lawn chairs and benches in the grassy courtyard and listen carefully as two patrol officers discuss safety tips and hand out crime prevention pamphlets. Knolls then provides a brief outline of the murder investigation. McCartin, off to the side, tells an officer that he does not like addressing groups. "Chuck is into this shit. He's going to be a patrol sergeant one of these days. He likes taking charge. That's why we bump heads sometimes. I'll be a homicide dick until the day I retire."

A man shyly approaches McCartin and says he wants to talk to him privately, away from the other residents. McCartin follows him to the parking lot.

"There's a black guy, a big dude, who lived here with this woman for a while," he says. "He was here Saturday, the day before Easter. I saw him smoking in the patio. He's strange. A very different kind of guy. Anyway, I thought you should know this."

When he mentions the man's apartment number, excitement flashes in McCartin's eyes: the man lived in the same unit as the woman who claimed she was raped and then recanted when officers hauled her and the suspect to the police station.

When Knolls finishes answering residents' questions, he and McCartin head for the stairs to the woman's apartment. The detectives are relieved when she answers the door. They introduce themselves to the woman, who is in her mid-forties, and follow her through the living room, which is lined with African masks, and into the kitchen.

After some casual chat about Unson—the woman occasionally ran into her in the laundry room—McCartin asks, "Wasn't there an incident involving a man who lived here?"

"No . . . not really," she says, pursing her lips and shaking her head. "He's a friend."

During the Luda Petushenko investigation the detectives often interrupted each other and shattered the flow of interviews. Now, however, they question witnesses seamlessly. Knolls senses that McCartin has established a rapport with the woman, so he leans back in his chair and observes.

"How big is this guy?" McCartin asks.

"About six-two, two-twenty."

"How'd you meet?"

"I used to be involved in the film industry," she says, grabbing a spoon off the table and tapping it on a palm. "I did some extra work. I met him two and a half years ago. He was an extra, too."

"Did he live here?"

"No. He moved to Seattle, but moved back and stayed here just for a few days last year. And he stayed with me again this month in early April . . . for about seven days."

McCartin asks if he visited her during the Easter weekend.

"Yes, but he left on Saturday at four P.M. I dropped him off at the bus station. He was going to New York."

"Is he your boyfriend?" McCartin asks.

"We were on the outs."

"What happened when the police came?"

"He was very possessive. I wanted him out," says the woman. "I had to go to school"—she attends community college—"and take care of business." She raises a hand and flutters her fingers. "But all he wanted to do was talk, talk, talk."

"Were you scared of him?"

"Not really. I wanted him out of my space."

"The patrol officer says he forced himself on you."

She shakes her head. "It wasn't really a rape. Sometimes a woman doesn't feel like it."

"Was it against your will?"

"Yes and no," she says, shrugging.

"When did the police come?"

"A few weeks ago. What used to really bug me was I'd want to go to the lab at school and he wanted to make love. This was cutting into my time. I resented it." She bites her lip, and stares at her shoes. "During one of his visits I called the police."

McCartin senses she is trying to protect her former boyfriend. "When my wife doesn't want to have sex, she doesn't call the police."

"That's *your* wife," the woman says sharply.

McCartin does not want to alienate the woman so he drops the subject. He asks her a few questions that will help him track down the man, locate his criminal record, and confirm that he actually boarded the bus on Saturday:

"Where's he from?"

"Chicago."

"Has he ever been arrested?"

"Yes, when he was nineteen. He said he was doing salesman work and saw an open door. . . ."

"Has he been back here since Easter?"

"No. I don't want someone in my space that much."

"Did he have money for the bus, or did you pay?"

"He had money."

"How much did the ticket cost?"

"I think $147."

McCartin studies her for a moment and asks, "You think he's involved in this incident?"

"No," she says angrily. "What kind of creature would do this?" The man called her recently, she says, and "I even jokingly asked, 'Did you do it?' These days you don't know. He monopolized my time, but he's not vicious. He's not a coldblooded person."

"Did he know her?"

"No."

"You ever see anyone who doesn't belong here?"

"Just the guy who found her. He kept shouting, '¡Es muerte! ¡Es muerte!' I said, '¿Quien?' He said, 'El doctor.' "

McCartin asks her where her friend stays in Los Angeles when not with her.

"In a hotel near downtown in a transient area." He recently left New York, she tells McCartin, and may return to Los Angeles next week.

McCartin hands the woman his business card and tells her to contact him when she talks to the man again.

The detectives linger in the courtyard after the interview. McCartin says, "I get the feeling that woman's not telling us the *whole* truth. I didn't like the way she backed off on the rape."

"We've got to make sure he really *did* leave on a bus on Saturday," Knolls adds.

"We've got to talk to Greyhound and check their records," McCartin agrees, nodding.

"Hell, she says he lived in a hotel near Skid Row," Knolls says. "That's pretty strange right there."

They walk around the building to the jazz club parking lot where the bloodhound picked up the suspect's trail. The dog's handler suspected that the killer fled to the back of the apartment building, climbed the fence to the parking lot, and then hopped over another fence to the sidewalk. The detectives have stopped by the jazz club several times, but never spotted the attendant. Tonight he is working. They ask him if he has ever seen anyone acting suspiciously in the parking lot.

"I saw one thing that was very strange," he says. "There's this big guy who looks like he just got out of prison. He's four times the size of me. I've talked to him a few times. He's an Armenian. I know his mother and sister live in the building." He points to the cyclone fence bordering the apartment building. "One night he jumped over that fence and ran across this lot. I asked him what was going on. He said it was a shortcut."

McCartin asks softly, attempting to conceal his excitement, "When was this?"

The attendant runs his fingers through his hair and clicks his tongue against the roof of his mouth. "Let me see. Must have been about four months ago. And I haven't seen him since."

Discouraged the detectives question the man for a few more minutes and discover that the club closed early on Easter Sunday, so no attendant was on duty at the time of the murder. But as they walk to their car they realize that the attendant's story was helpful.

"This means that at least he's familiar with that route," McCartin says. "If he's taken the route once, he could take it again."

"And then there were two."

"I agree," McCartin says. "It's either the Armenian or this lady's boyfriend."

Knolls opens the car door. "I'll be curious to see if he ever got on that bus."

Part VI

22

At 12:30 A.M. on the first Saturday in May, Lieutenant Hartwell calls Detective Ron Ito, who groggily reaches for the phone near his bed.

"Good morning," Hartwell says. "We got a callout. The wife of that actor, Robert Blake, was killed in Studio City. The captain wants us to go out there and take the case."

"Is it a whodunnit?"

"I don't know," Hartwell says. "But before you roll out there I want to make sure your plate's clean. Any court cases coming up? Anything I should know about?"

"No. I'm clear."

"Okay," Hartwell says. "I'll see you out there."

About an hour later, they meet in the squad room. Ito, who is Japanese-American, is about five-nine, compactly built, and dressed in a muted green suit, white button-down shirt, red print tie, and gleaming black oxfords. His hair is cut military style, sheared on the sides and longer on top.

Hartwell is dressed in a manner few detectives could afford—custom-made blue suit of the finest Italian wool, made-to-order creamy white Egyptian cotton shirt, and shimmering silk tie. He spends all his vacations in Thailand and buys his clothes from a Bangkok tailor at only a fraction of what they would cost in the United States. He is fascinated by Thai culture, cuisine, and history, enjoys scuba diving on remote islands far from the tourist sites, and plans to retire to Thailand in a few years. Hartwell is fifty-nine, the oldest man in the unit. Divorced, he lives in an apartment a few blocks from the beach and looks perpetually sunburnt.

"The North Hollywood detectives have talked to Blake," Hartwell says. "Now he's in the interview room with his attorney."

"What's he need an attorney for?" Ito asks. "Is he a suspect?"

Hartwell shrugs. "You know how these things are. He's not a criminal lawyer. It's his entertainment attorney."

Ito is immediately suspicious. *Why does Blake need an attorney? His wife has just been murdered. Why isn't he still with the North Hollywood detectives trying to help them find out who killed her?*

Chuck Knolls joins Ito and Hartwell in the squad room, greeting North Hollywood detective Martin Pinner and his supervisor, Mike Coffey, who were the first to be called out to the crime scene and have just interviewed Blake. Last August, Pinner and Coffey investigated the Luda Petushenko murder before Knolls and McCartin took over. While Knolls explains how he and McCartin solved that case, two other Homicide Special detectives arrive, and they all head for a conference table at the side of the squad room.

Coffey tells them they interviewed Blake for about an hour while investigators questioned some residents near the murder scene. He then provides a precis of the case: the union between Blake and his wife, Bonny Lee Bakley, Coffey says, was not one of Hollywood's great love stories. She was a star stalker who made a living selling dirty pictures of herself, advertising in sex magazines, and corresponding with lonely suckers whom she conned out of cash. Blake knocked her up, she had the baby—a daughter, Rose—about eleven months ago, and they fought for custody of her. Eventually, a few months ago, they married.

On Friday night, Blake and Bakley had driven to Vitello's, an Italian restaurant in Studio City. But instead of parking at the restaurant, Blake had parked a block and a half away, on a dim street, beside a Dumpster.

Hearing this, Ito raises an eyebrow.

After dinner, when they returned to the car, Blake told Bakley that he had left his .38 snub-nose revolver—which he has a permit to carry—in the restaurant, on the seat in their booth. He jogged back to retrieve the gun. When he returned he found Bakley slumped in the car and noticed blood coming out of her nose and mouth.

A North Hollywood detective steps in to announce, "Blake's getting antsy."

"Tell him the case is being transferred downtown," Ito says, "and the downtown detectives are being briefed."

Ito asks Coffey, "Is the scene secured?"

Coffey nods. One casing was found in the street, he says, and another on the passenger seat.

"It's a nine-millimeter, but that's not totally confirmed," Pinner says. "There was a shot to the body and the right side of her head."

The North Hollywood detective interrupts again. "Blake's ready to go. He's in the hallway."

Blake wears jeans, a tight black T-shirt, and black cowboy boots. His hair is shaggy and an unnatural shade of jet black, which gives his pale skin, stretched taut from a facelift, a ghostly pallor. He looks exhausted and a bit sheepish as he stares at the floor.

"I don't want to be sixty-seven years old, but I am," he mutters, standing in the hallway beside his lawyer. "I'm sixty-seven fucking years old." He sounds disgusted. "I'm tired and just want to lie down."

Ito subtly scrutinizes Blake's hands, clothes, and shoes, looking for specks of blood, but he finds nothing. He knows that the North Hollywood detectives have tested Blake's hands for gunshot residue, but the results are not yet available. Ito asks the lawyer whether he can question Blake. Not tonight, the lawyer answers, but maybe tomorrow morning.

Ito then asks to search Blake's house. "He can take a nap while we check out the house." The attorney refuses, but gives detectives permission to examine the guest house in back where Bonny Lee Bakley lived. Hartwell dispatches two detectives.

Ito is frustrated, but he cannot detain Blake unless he arrests him. "Go home and get some sleep," he says. "We'll talk tomorrow."

Ito watches the lawyer and Blake saunter toward the door and thinks, *This is not how a man acts whose wife has just been murdered. He did not seem distraught. He did not ask how his wife was killed. He did not show any curiosity about the case. He seemed more concerned about getting to bed than finding his wife's killer.*

The detectives return to the conference table, where Coffey resumes his briefing. "She's from Tennessee and travels back and forth," he says. "I asked him when they got married and he gave the phony crying with no tears. He loves to talk about how dirty she is."

"Anybody interviewed from the restaurant?" Ito asks.

Coffey nods. "Three of them. All employees."

"Did you run him for guns?" Ito asks.

"He's got three or four," Pinner says.

"The officers at the hospital want to know what to do with her clothes," Coffey says.

"If they're still on her, we can't take them," Ito says. "The coroner will handle it."

A patrol officer walks into the room carrying a large envelope with Blake's gun and hands it to Pinner.

Ito, who has investigated hundreds of murders, calmly delegates tasks and coordinates various aspects of the investigation. "I need someone to write a chain of custody on the gun. And let's see if the gun's loaded or if a round's been fired. Someone get gloves and check it out." He turns toward Hartwell and says, "Can you ask the coroner to hold all press? Refer all calls to the LAPD." Then he asks Coffey, "A casing was found inside the car?"

"Yeah," Coffey replies.

"Everything circumstantial is going against him," Ito says. "A few things are interesting. That story about coming back to the restaurant. . . . He has to have someone see him so he can say: 'I didn't shoot her.' "

Pinner tells him that the restaurant's co-owner, who greeted customers by the front door, said Blake returned only once—after he spotted his wife's bloody body in the car. He was in a panic and shouted for a doctor. A nurse who was dining in the restaurant followed him back to the car. The co-owner never saw Blake return for the gun.

"This is a dark street," Coffey says. "No light at nine-thirty. And he says she's paranoid. But he leaves her there. He's full of shit."

Ito smiles ruefully, shaking his head. "We'll never get another statement from him."

Knolls laughs. "That's for sure."

"She's on full-scale probation from Little Rock from one of her scams," Pinner says.

"He's blaming it on the mob she was running with," Coffey says.

"He never cried?" Ito asks.

"No," Coffey says. "He pretended to. . . . And he never asked what happened to her." Coffey drums his fingers on the conference table. "Good luck on this one. He's a character."

After the briefing, Ito and Steve Eguchi head to the crime scene. Ito is between partners, but has been assisted recently by Eguchi, a member of Metro, the LAPD's elite tactical patrol unit, which is dispatched to problem spots throughout the city. Eguchi and another Metro officer have temporarily been assigned to Homicide Special to assist detectives working a few difficult investigations.

Ito and Eguchi, both Japanese-American, have similar family backgrounds. Although Ito, at forty-seven, is only three years older than Eguchi, he has become his mentor. Eguchi joined the department in his mid-thirties and has no detective experience. Ito has helped him plot his future and is teaching him the rudiments of homicide investigation. Eguchi recently passed the detective exam and is waiting for assignment to a division. Meanwhile he will assist on the case. Ito does not really need a partner, but because the case is so high profile, Homicide Special supervisors decided to free up several detectives to work with him.

As Eguchi drives them through the dark, desolate city streets, Ito yawns. "I was watching *M*A*S*H* last night. I got about an hour of sleep when the phone rang."

At about four A.M., they arrive at the murder scene. Reporters, photographers, and television cameramen have started gathering behind the yellow tape. Several patrol cars, overhead light bars pulsing, block off the street. Paramedics have already transported Bakley's body to a local hospital, where she was pronounced dead on arrival.

Blake's black Dodge Stealth is parked in front of an enormous Dumpster filled with chunks of stucco and strips of lumber. The Dumpster is beside a house, encircled by a chain-link fence, which has been almost completely demolished and will, no doubt, be rebuilt on a grander scale. The street is lined with ranch-style houses with carefully pruned shrubbery and well-kept lawns. The night is cool and the full moon and scattering of stars are veiled in a thin film of fog.

Ito and Eguchi study the area around the car, which is littered with a bloody towel and ribbons of bloody gauze, left behind by the paramedics. Ito grips his flashlight like a patrol officer—knuckles up—raises it above his shoulder, and illuminates the inside of the car. Both front windows are open.

"I see a glove," he tells Eguchi, who peers inside. "I think it's O.J.'s glove."

Eguchi chuckles and Ito continues studying the car's interior. There is a single shell casing on the passenger seat, near a small pool of blood, surrounded by a few reddish streaks on the gray upholstery.

Coffey, Pinner, and Homicide Special detective Mike Whalen join

Ito and Eguchi. Whalen has just returned from Blake's house, where he and his partner searched the guest house and then obtained Blake's clothing, which will be tested for gunshot residue. The entertainment attorney said Blake would not talk to detectives and that a criminal lawyer would soon take over.

Coffey points out the streaks of vomit that dapple the exterior of the car from the driver's door to the taillight, and sections of the inside, near the driver's seat.

"Patrol says he was throwing up," Coffey says.

Whalen says to Ito, "We should go back later this morning and ask Blake some questions that weren't covered in the interview."

"He'll lawyer up," Ito says.

"I don't think so," Whalen says. "He's playing games. Let's listen to the tape and prepare."

Ito, Whalen, and Eguchi slip into the squad car. Eguchi starts the engine and flips on the heat, while Ito slides in the cassette of Blake's interview with the North Hollywood detectives. The three detectives sprawl out on the seats and listen intently.

Blake sounds like the detective he played in *Baretta,* cursing and infusing his speech with an East Coast tough-guy inflection, although he moved from New Jersey to California when he was five. While his attorney monitors the interview, Blake begins by providing some background on Bakley. Coffey then asks him about the murder.

"Who would want to do anything like this?"

Blake sighs.

"You know a lot more about her than we do," Coffey says with a hint of impatience.

Blake tells a confusing story about a man from New Jersey named John—Blake does not know his last name—who he says tried to kill Bakley two years ago. "He tried to crash both of them. He said they were going to commit suicide or something." But Blake cannot provide any details.

"Can you fill us in on what happened tonight?" asks Coffey. "What were your activities tonight?"

Blake is silent for about ten seconds and finally says, "We went to the restaurant. We parked. . . . And things were going really good. We were talking about bringing Holly—her daughter—out here. And when I sit down, the gun, which I don't always carry, but with her I carry the fuckin' gun . . . usually I just leave it in a car or leave it at home . . . I took it out and put it on the seat, under my sweatshirt."

Blake says he keeps the gun in a small holster and had owned it since he starred in *Baretta* in the mid-1970s.

"So you had the gun on the seat under your sweatshirt. Then what?" Coffey asks.

"I picked up my sweatshirt to leave. Then we got to the car and I realized I'd left the gun there. And I was afraid I was going to lose my license or that somebody would find it and it would be a bad scene."

Ito yawns, and turns to Whalen and Eguchi. "The gun's an alibi."

"If he's so worried about her, why'd he leave her alone?" Whalen says.

"He parked a block and a half away," Ito says. "He could've driven right up to the restaurant and got the gun."

On the tape, Coffey asks Blake, "Did you leave and think the gun was missing? Or were you just sitting in the parking lot and said, 'My gun is missing.' "

"No, we were on the street and I said, 'I left my gun in the restaurant. I got to go back.' . . . So I went back into the restaurant and the gun was on the floor. Under the booth."

Blake digresses, telling Coffey that Bakley was fearful and in hiding because she had made numerous enemies as a result of her business scams. "She puts ads in all kinds of sex papers all over the U.S., Australia, and Canada. . . ." Blake says. "What she does, and she's been doing it for twenty, thirty years . . . guys write to her from these ads and then she calls them on the phone. . . . They send her money to come and see them and she never shows up. They send her plane tickets and credit cards. It's a whole mail fraud scheme behind something that seems legit. . . . She says, 'Wire the money to my bank,' or 'My credit card is used up.' She's got a million different ways of doing it."

Whalen snorts derisively and says, "He's trying to talk about everything except what happened."

Blake, referring to Bakley's enemies, tells his lawyer, "I want to write out a will tomorrow, because if those motherfuckers are looking for me, I want Rosie protected."

Coffey ignores this. "Robert, what happened? You left the restaurant, discovered you didn't have your gun, went back. . . . Did you say anything to the people in the restaurant when you went back and got it?" He is trying to lock Blake into his chronology so he can eventually use the co-owner's statement against him.

"I just said, 'I left something in the booth,' and went in and got it. And I left. . . . Then I went back to the car." He stifles a sob. "And it looked like Bonny was sleepin'."

"So in that time you went into the restaurant, somebody came by and did this to her," Coffey says—flatly, without a hint of sympathy.

Blake pauses. "Are you askin' me? That's how it must have happened. 'Cause she was perfect when I left."

"Then what did you do?"

"I went to a couple of houses and banged on doors that had lights on them. I was screaming, 'Help.' And their dogs were barking." He stifles another sob. "And there wasn't a motherfucker that would come to the door. And I finally went to one guy's door"—his voice cracks—"and he recognized me. . . . And I said, 'Call 911.' And then I said, 'Something happened to my wife and I saw blood on her mouth.' "

Blake pauses. "The first thing that came to me. I had no fuckin' idea why. When I was a kid, when I was about nineteen years old"—his voice quavers with emotion—"I saw a young guy that didn't pay his gambling debts. And I saw some people beat him with a hammer. And when they left I went up and looked at him." He cries. "And for some reason or another, that's what came to me."

"Meaning that's what she looked like to you?" Coffey asks.

"It just came to me." He sobs. "I don't know if I consciously thought someone hit her or robbed her. I just didn't know. That thing came to me from when I was a kid and I just started running around yelling. I just lost it."

A few minutes later Blake says, "I know this sounds weird, but I got to pee again. I hope I don't dehydrate. I'm not drinking any water."

Coffey leaves for the crime scene and Pinner and another detective eventually resume the interview. Blake tells them about a suspicious-looking man driving a black pickup truck who had been cruising by his house recently. On one occasion the man parked in front. Another time, Blake says, "he walked past my house. He was wearing an old plaid shirt, a windbreaker, Levi's and he had on dark glasses and a baseball cap, like I wasn't supposed to recognize him." Blake and his bodyguard, Earle Caldwell, nicknamed him "Buzzcut."

After Blake tells a long, disjointed story about the times he spotted Buzzcut lingering near his house, Pinner cuts him off and says, "Okay, so tonight when you're out to dinner . . . you keep your eyes out for these guys?"

"I've been looking over my shoulder ever since I met Bonny and . . ."

Pinner asks about Blake's curious decision to park a block and a half away from the restaurant.

Blake tells him there is no valet parking at Vitello's and on weekends the lot is full.

Pinner asks Blake to recount, again, the events of the night.

Midway through his story, Blake says, "I just thought of something." He tells Pinner that he was worried recently about two men sitting inside a van that was parked in front of his house one night.

Whalen raps his knuckles on a window and says to Ito, "See how he's always changing the subject. He doesn't want to talk about what happened here."

On the tape, Blake says he brandished a pistol and scared the men off.

Pinner steers Blake back to the events at the restaurant. After Blake again recounts what happened after he retrieved his gun, Pinner asks, "Let's go back to the van, the two guys in the van."

"I hate to ask you, but can we wrap it up? I'm beat," Blake says in a weary tone.

The other detective in the room says, "What's holding it up now is the downtown detectives. The big shots. They're here and they're being advised of what happened."

"Oh God," Blake groans.

"They'll be coming to briefly talk to you. They just want to figure out what happened. They'll be here in a few seconds. It's because of your status."

"I can't make it, man," he says softly. "I can't make it. I'm sixty-seven years old."

Blake's lawyer, who was silent during most of the interview, says, "Tell them we've got to go."

"Tell 'em," Blake says, "I'm sixty-seven years old."

Ito, Whalen, and Eguchi climb out of the car and stretch. The first hint of sunrise streaks the horizon with a pale orange band. The sky is clear now, without a hint of mist, and chirping birds perch on tree limbs, fences, and roofs.

Ito walks over to the Dumpster and tells Eguchi, "Let's take this to the dump, empty it all out on something, and go over it all."

They walk over to Blake's car, crouch by the curb, and study the passenger seat, which is smeared with blood.

"There was no contact wound, so it's hard to figure the scenario," Whalen tells Ito and Eguchi. "If the entry wound was on the right side of her head, how does the casing get in the front seat of the car? Since casings kick out to the right you'd expect it to be here," he says, pointing to the curb. "But maybe the doctor was wrong. Maybe it was an exit wound."

Knolls points to the passenger-seat headrest. "This is a weird one. Why isn't there any blood here?"

"Another strange thing," Ito says, "is none of the neighbors heard any shots."

"Maybe she was shot somewhere else," Knolls speculates. "Maybe she was tossed into the car and someone drove her here."

The detectives scour the crime scene again in the buttery morning light, walking past lawns slick with dew. A soft breeze carries the scent of roses, planted behind a white picket fence across the street.

Hartwell calls the LAPD's press relations department from his cell phone and updates them. He clicks the phone off, shakes his head wearily, and says to Ito, "They say it's going to be an avalanche. The press is going crazy. They're all asking: 'Is this an O.J.-type crime?' "

When a woman is murdered, detectives usually focus on the husband or the boyfriend first because crime statistics reveal that in the vast majority of cases he is the killer. If the detectives clear him, they will then move on to other suspects. Now is the time, in this early stage of the Bakley investigation, to obtain as much information about Blake as possible. So when the detectives finish examining the area, Ito heads back to the office to write the lengthy search warrant for Blake's house.

During the past few months, Ito had been increasingly frustrated by the abundance of officer-involved-shooting callouts. He occasionally muttered to other detectives, "I hope my next case is a homicide."

Now he turns to Eguchi and says, "Yeah, I wanted a homicide. But not *this* homicide."

Ito is one of the few detectives who was a member of the unit during the O. J. Simpson case, although he was not subjected to criticism because his role was peripheral. Still, he knows the problems and pitfalls surrounding a murder investigation of a celebrity's wife. Robert Blake might be considered a B actor at this point, but Ito knows the case will generate extensive press coverage anyway. As he drives back toward downtown, he thinks of the adage "Be careful what you wish for."

Ito's great-grandfather immigrated to California in the 1880s, but his grandfather returned to Japan fifty years later. He wanted his son to have a more traditional Japanese education. The family was fortunate that World War II ended when it did, because in the summer of 1945, Ito's father was in kamikaze school, training for a suicide mission.

Ito's family moved back to Los Angeles when he was seven. His father owned a Japanese restaurant in West Los Angeles and his grandmother—who had stayed in California and spent the war years in an internment camp—opened a café in Little Toyko. Ito grew up washing dishes and busing tables. His family lived a few miles west of downtown, in a fourplex; they occupied one apartment and his aunts, uncles, and cousins lived in the other units.

Ito enrolled in a community college police-science class because he thought the class would be an easy A and he wanted to raise his grade-point average. But he found the subject matter so interesting that he eventually quit school and joined the LAPD. After six years working patrol and a vice unit, he was assigned to the Hollywood Division as a detective trainee in robbery. He had always been interested in homicide, so Russ Kuster, the detective in charge of Hollywood Homicide who trained Rick Jackson and Jerry Stephens, occasionally called him to murder scenes. Ito never turned down a chance to assist and learn, and Kuster eventually hired him.

Kuster appreciated Ito's work ethic, how he sifted through cold cases during lulls in the action, attempting to solve them. One of the first old cases he checked out involved an immigrant from Mexico who had doused his wife with lighter fluid and tossed a match on her. She gave a dying statement to police, identifying her husband. The suspect, however, fled after the murder and detectives had never been able to find him. Ito studied the thirteen-year-old file, called a few acquaintances and relatives of the suspect, and discovered that he was hiding out in a small village in the state of Michoacán. An LAPD fugitive squad located him. Since both he and his victim were citizens of Mexico, he was tried there, and convicted of murder. Kuster was impressed that Ito had cleared the case with just a few phone calls.

After four years at Hollywood Homicide, Ito joined the RHD, eventually transferring to the division's bank robbery squad. In the wake of O. J. Simpson's arrest, Homicide Special needed a coordinator to handle the deluge of data, so for a year Ito collated the almost five hundred tips from all over the world and organized them in order of urgency. Much of his time was spent separating the legitimate tips from the crank calls. One man called from Greenland with a tip on where to find the murder weapon. Psychics called, and dog psychologists told Ito they could interpret barks and identify the killer. When the Simpson trial was over, Ito stayed at Homicide Special.

Ito, whose mother lives in a Little Toyko retirement village a few blocks from Parker Center, is active in the Japanese community, serving as president of the San Gabriel Valley Japanese Community Center and teaching judo classes there. After years of enduring bad Japanese jokes, Ito enjoys working with Eguchi. They have much in common, but their paths to the LAPD have been quite different.

Eguchi studied auto mechanics at a trade school and was eventually hired at the Parker Center garage, where he became friends with a few detectives whose cars he serviced. When he joined them for racquetball at the police academy, a few told him that since he was in such good shape he should join the LAPD. But Eguchi believed that, at five foot seven, he was too small and, at thirty-three, too old. They convinced him that his size and age would not be a problem, so he applied and was immediately accepted.

Eguchi's mother was not happy. "Japanese," she told him, "are not police officers." But as he quickly rose through the ranks—from patrol to training officer to Metro—she finally accepted his decision. And Eguchi, whose 200-pound bench press set the LAPD record for officers in his 131-pound weight division, soon realized that his size was not a problem on the streets.

Now that he has decided to become a detective he feels his assignment to Homicide Special was serendipitous. And although the Bakley murder is a daunting case, Eguchi is grateful for the opportunity to learn alongside some of the best homicide investigators in the city.

More Homicide Special detectives arrive at the crime scene and start knocking on doors and interviewing neighbors. Eguchi waits for the Dumpster to be moved so he can sift through the rubble. Knolls drives to St. Joseph's Hospital in Burbank to examine Bakley's body before Sunday's autopsy.

In the hospital morgue, an orderly opens a stainless-steel cold-storage vault, rolls out a gurney, and unzips a white body bag. Before examining Bakley's body, Knolls tucks his tie inside his shirt so it will not pick up bloodstains: the reflex of a veteran homicide detective. Bakley is still wearing the cervical collar and blue plastic breathing tube that the paramedics inserted before they transported her to the hospital. Knolls leans over and studies the perfectly round circle on her right shoulder—an obvious entry wound. Her hair is stringy and matted and her face and ears so bloody that Knolls cannot locate the head wound. He shines his flashlight on the right side of her face and finally locates what appears to be an entry wound, in front of her earlobe. To be sure, a technician posts Bakley's head X ray on an illuminated viewing box. Knolls studies the X ray, frowns and shakes his head. The X ray reveals that the bullet entered on the *left* side of Bakley's head—a small white circle—and then exited from the right side—a wider, jagged pattern. Knolls can identify the exit wound on the X ray because bullets, especially hollow-points, mushroom after the initial impact.

Knolls is troubled because this contradicts the findings of the coroner's criminalist. He crouches and studies the wounds from several angles. Finally, he sees the problem: the technician posted the X ray backward. When he flips it around, the X ray clearly shows the entry wound on the right side of her face.

As Knolls drives away from the hospital, he flips on his cell phone, calls his wife, and asks her to give his son a message: "Robert Blake is ruining my weekend. I'm not going to be able to make the UCLA volleyball game."

Knolls returns to the North Hollywood station and spots Eguchi in the squad room.

"We found the gun," Eguchi says.

Knolls flashes him a skeptical look.

"I'm serious."

"If you're bullshitting me, I'll beat your ass."

Eguchi turns around and bends over. He grins at Knolls and says, "It was at the landfill and recycling center. I was with the criminalist and the photographer. There were two big piles. There was nothing in the first pile. The criminalist goes through the second pile. There was a bunch of lumber and dirt. He says, 'Hey, hey, hey,' and motions me over. And there it was. The hammer was cocked, the safety was off, and there was one in the chamber."

The pistol is a Walther P-38 semiautomatic, a German World War II relic. It was slick with oil, so fingerprints are unlikely.

Knolls claps Eguchi on the shoulder. "Good thing we went through that Dumpster."

More detectives have been summoned to the crime scene, they canvass the neighborhood in the harsh glare of a hot May morning and attempt to find witnesses or, at least, locate someone who heard a gunshot. Because there are so many neighbors and this is such a high-profile case, investigators from both Homicide I and Homicide II are called out.

Detective Robert Bub is preparing to interview the only resident who talked to Blake that night. Blake banged on his door and asked him to call 911. North Hollywood officers have already talked to the man, but Bub wants to interview him more thoroughly.

The man lives down the street from where Blake's Dodge Stealth was parked, in a modest single-story stucco house with an air conditioner jutting from the front window. Bub walks down a cement path bracketed by rosebushes and knocks on the front door. The man, who is in his mid-thirties and wears jeans, a T-shirt, and a baseball cap, appears dazed as he leads Bub to the breakfast room table. He tells Bub he is a film director.

"First thing I'm going to do is to have you run through the story for me real quick, as to what you heard," Bub says.

"I was at my back computer, in my bathrobe and I heard *ding, dong, ding, dong, ding, dong,* like crazy. Knocking and ringing . . . I open the door and the first thing I heard is"—he imitates Blake's panicked cries—" 'You got to help me! You got to help me! She's bloody and she's beaten! Oh my God.' "

The man, reenacting the encounter, says incredulously, " 'Robert Blake? Robert?' "

"He's like, 'Yeah, yeah, yeah. It's me.' "

"I said, 'Please come in, Robert. What's going on?' "

The man again imitates Blake's breathless manner: " 'She's bloody! She's bloody! My wife is bloody! They beat her up! She's been beaten!' "

"And I'm like, 'Where is she? What do you mean?' "

"He goes, 'She's in the car.' "

"The first thing I thought of: I looked at his hands to see if it was him who beat her up. You know, a domestic kind of situation. He looked like his eyes were totally dilated. He was in shock. He looked a little inebriated to me, to be quite honest. So he goes: 'I got to call the police. I got to call 911.' "

The man says he ran to the bedroom and called 911; the dispatcher told him to grab a towel and apply pressure to the wound. He rushed outside to the car, carrying the towel. Blake headed back to the restaurant.

"I found that odd," the man says. "Like, why isn't he going with me to help her?"

The man describes how he tried to stanch the bleeding. "All I see is blood coming out her nose. Like a lot. It wasn't completely runny and didn't look completely fresh. It was mucusy already. . . . It looks like a bullet wound, because I've seen bullet wounds. I'm a director and they do a lot of research and stuff. . . . She was totally catatonic. I looked into her eyes. They were all over the place. No focus. No anything."

When Blake returned, the man says he tried to console him. After the paramedics arrived, Blake began crying.

"What I found odd," the man says in a confidential tone, "was there were no *tears*. I'm a director so I'm looking at him as an actor and his emotions and da, da, da. It's really weird to see someone go"—the man acts out heart-wrenching sobs—"and nothing is coming out. I don't know if it's shock that shuts it off. I have no clue."

As the man hugged Blake to comfort him, an LAPD sergeant approached them and asked who was related to the woman. Blake told him, "That's my wife. I knew this was going to happen. I knew it. She was afraid. And I'm carrying my piece." Blake then handed his revolver to the sergeant. When Blake said he was thirsty, the man returned to his house and brought back a glass of water.

Before concluding the interview, Bub says, "Let's go back to the beginning."

The man again describes how after he called 911 Blake dashed back to the restaurant.

"And you said you thought that was kind of odd," Bub says.

"Completely," the man says. "If it was my girlfriend or my wife, I wouldn't let her alone for a *minute*."

When the man describes the bullet wound to the side of her head, Bub asks, "Can you get any sense of direction?"

"This is what would go in my head, as a director, if I did the scene: she was totally trusting of this person. You know what I'm saying? He comes around. He says something to her. And boom. Because it looks like she just . . ." He pauses and demonstrates how the body was slumped in the car seat. "Her hands were down."

Most of the detectives meet for lunch at the Aroma Café, less than two blocks from the crime scene and across the street from Vitello's, where Blake and Bakley dined. While Vitello's is a traditional, family-style Italian restaurant, with a plain redbrick façade and a menu of standard pasta dishes, this strip of Tujunga Avenue is lined with a number of trendy businesses, including a power yoga studio, an aromatherapy spa, a wine and cheese store, and several boutiques.

The Aroma Café is a quaint, ivy-covered restaurant–coffee shop–bookstore. About half a dozen detectives, along with Captain Tatreau and Lieutenants Hartwell and Farrell, gather in a cozy room with screenwriting books lining the shelves, a tiled fireplace, and a brass chandelier overhead. Emblazoned over an archway is the message "May the Coming Hour O'erflow with Joy." The detectives, all wearing pressed white shirts, ties, and dark suits, with their 9-millimeter Berettas and .45-caliber Smith & Wesson semiautomatics hanging from their belts or peeking out of their shoulder holsters, appear decidedly out of place on this warm Saturday afternoon. They draw countless stares from the hip young customers wearing shorts, sandals, and tank tops, and sipping cappuccinos.

Most of the detectives order bacon and eggs or omelets, since this is their first meal of the day. "If this murder was on the south end," Tatreau jokes, "we'd probably be eating lunch on the trunk of our car."

The detectives are perfectly aware that this case will attract tremendous media interest and that their actions will be scrutinized by a national audience. Still, they are accustomed to working high-profile cases and jousting with reporters, and they seem matter-of-fact about the murder. As the detectives eat, they trade insults and swap their favorite lines from *Baretta*:

" 'If you can't do the time, don't do the crime,' " one offers.

" 'You pull the trigger and somebody dies,' " another adds.

" 'And you can take *that* to da bank,' " a third announces in a mock-serious tone.

The detectives then attempt to recall the name of Detective Tony Baretta's pet cockatoo. Finally one blurts out, "Fred," and the others smack their foreheads and nod.

Tatreau tells the detectives that he is a fan of the movie *Electra Glide in Blue*. Tatreau's favorite line from the movie is when Blake's character, a Vietnam veteran motorcycle cop who cruises the Arizona desert, pulls over a driver who complains about how he has been treated since he returned from Vietnam.

" 'I'm going to do for you something that it took six months for people to do for me,' " Tatreau says, acting out Blake's part, and pausing for dramatic effect. " 'Nothin'!' "

Tatreau picks up the tab and everyone drives off to Blake's house, located less than a mile from the crime scene, in a more upscale section of Studio City. The area is an amalgam of architectural styles—Spanish, ranch, colonial, Cape Cod, English Tudor—and the flora are a typical Southern California hodgepodge, with sycamores, live oaks, palm trees, and magnolias shading the street. But even in this eclectic neighborhood, Blake's house, down the street from where the television series *The Brady Bunch* was filmed, is an eccentric anomaly. Constructed of rough-hewn redwood planks, with a horseshoe hanging over the door, a lantern and deer antlers nailed to the walls, and two large signs in front—MATA HARI RANCH and BUZZARDS GULCH—the place looks like a rustic lodge, better suited to the Wyoming backcountry than the Southern California suburbs.

The detectives arrive to find Blake stretched out in a lawn chair on the patio, unfiltered cigarette in one hand, matches in the other, wearing maroon sweatpants, a blue T-shirt, white sneakers, and a baseball cap. He looks stunned and his eyes are glassy. He is flanked by Harland Braun, his criminal lawyer, whom he just hired, and a private investigator, and he now refuses to speak with detectives. Tatreau talks to the lawyer about the terms of the search warrant, and then Blake and his entourage drive off.

A few minutes later, Tatreau tells Hartwell and Farrell that he just called Chief Bernard Parks and updated him. "I told him Blake was here and he's leaving, but there wouldn't be another white Bronco chase."

About a dozen Homicide Special detectives and supervisors assemble on the front porch, some dozing in lawn chairs while they wait for Ito to finish preparing his search warrant and obtain a judge's approval. The area is blocked off to keep the reporters at bay, and the street, which has no sidewalks, is now a peaceful, bucolic setting, with broad lawns edged with rosebushes, Mexican sage, and jasmine. A soft Valley breeze rattles the bloodred climbing roses against a metal fence. Across the street, thick wisteria in full bloom drapes a house in pale purple blossoms.

When Ito returns with the warrant in the late afternoon, the detectives, accompanied by two deputy district attorneys, fan out and search the house. The living room features a wagon-wheel light fixture and is cluttered with dirty clothes, baby toys, a leather saddle in one corner and a stroller in the other. Other rooms suggest a man trapped between adolescence and old age, with shelves and cabinets filled with toy soldiers, vintage Lone Ranger comic books, BB guns, cowboy memorabilia, and Indian relics. Most of the pictures on the walls trace Blake's career, from his first parts as a child actor to his role as a killer in *In Cold Blood*. While most of the house is messy, the nursery is immaculate. Peter Rabbit curtains shade the windows; a crib and a new rocker with green upholstery stand on one side of the room and stuffed animals are arranged neatly on top of the dresser.

Behind the house is a sprawling two-story guest cottage. On the ground floor is a carpeted, well-equipped gym, with barbells and workout machines, and a mirrored aerobics room. Bakley briefly lived in the loft, which features a fireplace, a wood-beamed ceiling, a skylight, and a kitchen.

The detectives spend hours, from afternoon to night, carefully examining every closet, drawer, and cabinet on the property. When they finish, they are disappointed: they do not find anything that definitively links Blake with the Walther. They have, however, made a few interesting discoveries. On the wall of a bathroom and on the gym mirror, Blake has scrawled: "I'm not going down." One detective turned up $12,000 in a bedroom dresser. Another found in a cabinet a hundred-bullet box of 9-millimeter ammunition with three rounds missing. Ito is excited by the discovery: Walther P-38s use 9-millimeter ammunition, Bakley was shot twice, and the Walther found in the Dumpster had a third round in the chamber.

The detectives cart off boxes of Blake's financial records, briefs documenting his custody dispute with Bakley, other paperwork, several pistols, and the ammunition. When Ito finishes itemizing everything, the detectives decide to meet at Astro's, an all-night coffee shop north of downtown. Over cheeseburgers and fries, they discuss the case.

"Steve and I are probably going to fly back to Tennessee and Arkansas to interview people close to Bonny," Ito says.

"Oh, you two will fit in *real* well there," Whalen says sarcastically. "Just tell 'em, 'Sure we look different. We're Italian.' "

Bub tells Ito about his interview this morning with the neighbor who called 911 for Blake. "The guy contacted me later and said that

Larry King personally called him," Bub says. "King wants to fly him to New York. After that, *Good Morning America* called the guy."

"O.J. all over again," a detective says.

"Not quite O.J.," Bub says. "Maybe an off-Broadway O.J."

A detective asks Eguchi about the gun he found in the Dumpster. "Looks like an antique German gun," Eguchi says. "No markings."

"Wouldn't it be great if the gun was a Beretta?" Ito says.

Although the Walther was unregistered, a detective says, "If there's some way to connect Blake to it, he's through."

"We'll have to go to the ATF and hope they have a record of it," Ito says.

At about eleven P.M., the detectives finish eating. Ito sends two detectives off to interview the nurse who accompanied Blake from Vitello's back to the car. Ito and Eguchi would do the interview themselves, but they plan to arrive at the office early Sunday morning, write the chronology, set up the murder book, and find out whether LAPD technicians can lift any fingerprints off the gun.

The squad room is thrumming with activity on Monday morning. All the phone lines are tied up with calls from reporters, tipsters, and criminalists, so a civilian crime analyst is recruited as a temporary receptionist. The detectives bustle around, organize their notes from the weekend, and call various LAPD units to set up evidence testing. A commander marches through the room, asking for a briefing from Hartwell.

A detective tells Ito with disgust that Blake's attorney, Harland Braun, is already "dirtying the victim," telling the press all about her shady past.

"He's really spinning," another detective says. "I heard him say on the radio that it was a professional hit because of her scams."

Tatreau wants an update on the case, so he calls a meeting in his office. Ito, Eguchi, and Hartwell, along with four other Homicide II detectives drafted to help with the Bakley investigation—Chuck Knolls, Brian McCartin, Mike Whelan, and Whelan's partner, Jim Gollaz—assemble around the conference table. The mood in the room is uncharacteristically tense and subdued, with little of the usual humor and razzing. The supervisors and detectives knew this murder would attract some attention, but because the victim was an aging grifter and Blake is best known for a television show canceled more than twenty years ago, they did not the anticipate the firestorm of publicity. Now the specter of the O. J. Simpson debacle hovers over this investigation.

Ito opens the meeting by telling the detectives that Sunday's autopsy revealed that either shot could have been the fatal one. "The one in the shoulder severed the carotid artery, lodged in the aorta, and caused severe internal bleeding." The trajectory of the shots was almost level, with a slightly upward tilt. "This means the shooter was crouching," Ito says. "He was using the Dumpster for cover. Since she allowed the shooter to get so close, she probably knew him."

The coroner removed a slug from the aorta, "with stria visible, so it's good for comparison," Ito says. He is still waiting for ballistics to confirm that the Walther was the murder weapon. "There was no stippling, so the head shot wasn't a contact wound. But since the casing was in the car, she was probably shot at pretty close range. No defense wounds on her hands."

Ito then delivers the bad news: LAPD technicians could not lift a single print from the gun. "Not even a smudge," he says. "And we keep trying to run the gun different ways. Nothing. We figure it's unregistered."

The ammunition box found at Blake's house, Ito says, was "a gangster load," meaning that it contained a variety of rounds, about half of them hollow-point. Only if all ninety-seven rounds in the box had been the same—and they matched the three in the Walther—could the detectives have linked the gun to Blake's house.

In the Sunday morning newspapers, Ito discovered that LAPD press officers told reporters that Blake was a witness, not a suspect. "I wish they would have been a bit more vague and not made him look as clean as a Safeway chicken."

"Initially we just said he was *interviewed* as a witness," Hartwell says. "That's all."

"Can we verify that Blake returned to the restaurant to pick up the gun?" Tatreau asks.

Ito shakes his head.

"Let's document who did what and when," Tatreau says. "I don't want to see you all end up on the stand saying, 'We all did a lot of stuff, but I don't know exactly what.' "

Tatreau then questions Ito's decision to return to the office and write the search warrant rather than remain at the scene and supervise the investigation. Someone else, Tatreau says, probably should have written the warrant.

Ito is clearly irritated that his judgment has been questioned. "I knew the case best, I was working with the DA, and it needed to be done." Ito then delegates various tasks, asking detectives to trace the Walther through the U.S. Bureau of Alcohol, Tobacco, and Firearms, to find out whether any of the men Bakley corresponded with had threatened her recently, and to have the vomit, blood splatter patterns, and possible gunshot residue inside the car tested.

Ito and Eguchi walk across the street to the LAPD parking lot. Ito is still miffed that Tatreau second-guessed him about the search warrant.

"I don't need that," Ito mutters. "I've got enough pressure as it is."

"Well, you wanted a murder real bad, and you finally got one," Eguchi says.

"Yeah." Ito shakes his head. "But I wanted a regular one. I don't want to be the LAPD's sacrificial lamb."

Eguchi drives to the Firearms Analysis Unit, housed in a weathered single-story structure about five miles north of downtown. He clutches the Walther, in a large Manila envelope. Ito explains to a supervisor that the gun was found in the Dumpster. He then adds that two shell casings were picked up at the scene and two 9-millimeter pistols were recovered from Blake's house, where they also found a box of ammunition. The ninety-seven semiautomatic rounds are all "reloads," Ito says—used casings reloaded with bullets, gunpowder, and primers. Ito wants firearms technicians to analyze the casings and determine whether they can be linked to the Walther or to Blake's two 9-millimeter pistols. (When a semiautomatic is fired, distinctive "ejector marks" are imprinted on the casings.) But first he wants to know whether the Walther fired the bullet that was extracted from Bakley's body during the autopsy.

"This is a hurry-up thing," Ito tells the supervisor.

"We don't do anything hurry-up anymore," the supervisor says, sounding bored.

"This is a high-priority case," Ito says, exasperated.

"*Everything* we have now is high priority," the supervisor says.

"I guarantee you the chief will tell you to drop everything to work on this one." Ito shows him the gun. "Does a Walther eject like a Beretta?"

The supervisor shakes his head: a Walther is the rare semiautomatic pistol that ejects casings to the left.

Ito now knows how one of the casings ended up inside the car. The shooter was crouching beside the car, slightly behind Bakley, when he shot her in the head. The casing flew right into the open window.

"This is a war gun," Ito says. "It probably came back with one of General Patton's guys."

The supervisor explains that before he can test the gun, Ito has to return to Parker Center and book it at the Property Division. Then he can check it back out and return to the firearms unit.

Eguchi drives back downtown while Ito mutters about the LAPD's bewildering, bureaucratic evidence procedures: "What a waste of time. The sheriff's department would do it right now, while we waited."

Ito and Eguchi wait at the Property Division, a musty office in the bowels of Parker Center. When a clerk is finally free, she boxes up the evidence, enters it into the computer system, and provides Ito with a receipt and the box. Through heavy freeway traffic he and Eguchi drive back to the Firearms Analysis Unit.

After they finally finish briefing another technician and filling out paperwork, Ito asks, "You going to do this tonight?"

"No," the technician says flatly.

"The chief will be calling your supervisor," Ito says.

The man shrugs. "I can't do anything until I'm told to."

On the way back to Parker Center, Ito calls Hartwell on his cell phone and says, "Please call the supervisor in firearms so we can get this thing started."

He checks his watch and says to Eguchi, "It's four-fifty-three now and our day has been wasted. If they'd done it this morning we'd know now if it was the murder weapon. See how much time we waste on this BS?"

The next morning, Tatreau, knowing he has offended Ito, stops by the squad room. "I have the lineup in the Blake case for you," he says, tossing the record album soundtrack of *Electra Glide in Blue* on Ito's desk. On the cover, a group of motorcycle cops from the movie stand against a wall, with Blake, about a foot shorter than the others, in the middle. Ito shows the album to Eguchi and displays it on his desk.

All the detectives on the Bakley case now meet in Tatreau's office, including Robert Bub, who has just been assigned the job of clue coordinator. He will sift through all the tips and phone calls, grade them in order of importance, and then a civilian employee will enter them on the computer. One of the first calls was from Blake's third cousin, who had not talked to Blake since childhood. She had no information to impart; she merely wanted Blake to call her.

"I got a call at home from Firearms last night at eleven," Ito says, opening the meeting. Everyone looks up immediately. "They made the coroner's bullet to the Walther." He pauses, as the detectives nod appreciatively. "So we have the murder weapon."

"Any news on the ejector marks?" Hartwell asks.

"We're still waiting," Ito says. "What do we have on tracing the gun?"

"A manufacturer does not have to report sales on guns made before 1968," Whalen says.

"Let's see if there's a way to trace guns brought over here from Germany after the war," Ito says.

Whalen reports the findings of an LAPD blood splatter expert: "The crime lab determined she was shot right there, at that location"— not shot, dumped in the car, and then driven to the street near Vitello's. "She was most likely shot in the shoulder first. And when she was leaning over the console, she was shot the second time. There were a few specks of blood on the driver's seat. They would have smeared if someone sat in the seat after she was killed. The blood splatters have what's called a directional tail, so we can determine where the shot came from."

Hartwell, looking embarrassed, says, "I know this is an administrative situation, but we do need your overtime slips."

"Are you kidding?" Ito says, laughing. "We want the money. That's our first priority."

Before the meeting breaks up, Ito says, "I've been around a lot of these big cases, and we've always had problems with security. When you go home for the day, put your shit away. I walked around last night and saw notes, search warrants, and other things lying around."

As they walk back to the squad room, Bub says to Ito, "You know what bothers me? The press is already calling this the *Blake* murder. It's like the victim doesn't count. Her past might have been pretty questionable, but she's still the victim. It's not the Blake murder. It's the Bakley murder."

Bonny Lee Bakley ended up in what writer Nathanael West called "the dream dump" of Hollywood because she wanted to be a star. When her plan did not work out, she decided to marry one and ruthlessly pursued her goal.

Finally, in her mid-forties, she snagged Robert Blake. Although he was sixty-seven and had not worked in years, she decided he would do. She moved from Little Rock to Los Angeles, but in the dim light of her husband's fading fame, Bakley never received the attention she desperately sought. West portrayed this kind of frustrated dreamer in his bleak Hollywood novel *The Day of the Locust*. He described their "fever eyes and unruly hands" and explained that they did not move west to loll under the palms. "They had come to California to die."

When, as her friends had predicted, Bakley met her fate, she was interred at Forest Lawn in the Hollywood Hills—where many stars were buried, including Clark Gable, Liberace, Errol Flynn, and Bette Davis. While the news helicopters hovered above and the television reporters and cameramen jostled for position, Bakley finally achieved the fame she had frenetically pursued her entire life.

She was born in Morristown, New Jersey, and her father, a tree surgeon, was a nasty drunk. When she was seven, she later told friends, and her mother was at a hospital in labor, "my father tried to get fresh with me." Later that year, her parents split up and she moved in with her grandmother, who lived in a trailer in northwest New Jersey and was so thrifty she hoarded water. She rarely allowed Bakley to bathe; at school, other students teased her unmercifully about her greasy, stringy hair and threadbare clothing. She told a friend years later, in a conversation she tape-recorded, "I was the kid that everybody hated in school 'cause I was like poor and couldn't dress good and, you know, everybody always made fun of me. . . . So then you grow up saying, 'Oh, I'll fix them. I'll show them. I'll be a movie star.' "

When she was sixteen, Bonny dropped out of high school and enrolled at the Barbizon School of Modeling. But she soon discovered that her features were too sharp and her appeal too coarse for legitimate modeling jobs. By this time her mother had remarried and moved from New Jersey, and her father had died in jail. Bakley began modeling for nudist publications and what used to be called girlie magazines. When she was twenty-one, she sent a graphic, gynecological shot of herself to *Hustler* and was featured in the "Beaver Hunt" section.

Now that she had a collection of nude pictures at her disposal, her life's work was launched. She began advertising in swinger publications and men's magazines, fleecing marks with a con she employed in various forms during the next two decades. She sent nude pictures of herself to the mostly older men who answered the ads, and then sought to separate them from their money. To some, she was a struggling student who needed cash for tuition. To others, she had just broken up with her fiancé and needed rent money. After a few letters, she promised to visit the correspondent, but claimed she needed cash to repair her car. Then she would send another letter, explaining that she had been on the road, halfway there, when her car stalled, and now she needed more money—or a credit card number— for repairs, or perhaps a bus or airline ticket. She would string out the con as long as the cash kept coming. When the man finally realized he'd been bilked, there was little he could do, since Bakley operated out of post office boxes and mail drops across the country.

One of her friends described her to detectives as a "mail-order whore. Once in a while she had to put out."

When Bakley was twenty-one, she married her first cousin Paul Gawron, a New Jersey pipe grinder, and they soon had two children. He eventually quit because her scams were more lucrative than his job. When they divorced, he assumed most of the child-rearing responsibility and continued to help Bakley with her burgeoning business.

Bakley's first celebrity infatuation was with Frankie Valli—he, too, was a New Jersey native, and his song "Rag Doll" describes a girl forced to wear hand-me-down clothes: "They always laughed at her. . . . Called her Rag Doll, little Rag Doll." Bakley had the dreamy goal of earning enough money to buy a house near Valli's. "Wouldn't it be something if we were neighbors," she fantasized to friends. Living near Valli would give her the social standing she craved, would prove to the high school kids who had taunted her that she had made it, had accomplished something in life.

She soon became more obsessive in her pursuit of reflected celebrity. Bakley had read a biography of Jerry Lee Lewis and she identified with his troubled background and how, through talent, grit, and drive, he ascended to country music fame. She soon began tracking him like a stalker, following his shows across the country, befriending his sister, and bribing backstage guards so she could talk to him. Bakley even bought a house in Memphis, moving her ex-husband and two children with her, so she could be close to Lewis.

Friends said Bakley and Lewis occasionally dated. When she gave birth to a baby girl in the summer of 1993, she claimed he was the father and named the baby Jeri Lee Lewis. But he has insisted that he was out of the country when the baby was conceived. Bakley finally realized that her pursuit of Lewis had reached a dead end, but she did not mourn the loss for long. She quickly shifted her sights to other stars.

Despite her obsession with Lewis, her mail-order business had thrived. She had conned a number of elderly men into marrying her, swindling a few of them out of their savings and their life insurance. For Bakley, the occupational hazard of arrest was not a deterrent. She was busted for forgery, fraud, and once for drug possession, but was only briefly jailed, fined, and placed on probation. Still, the cash-stuffed envelopes kept rolling in, and Bakley invested the money wisely, purchasing two houses in Memphis and several undeveloped lots. She earned enough to fund frequent trips to Hollywood, where she unsuccessfully pursued a singing and acting career under the name of Leebonny. But she could not sing and she could not act. This was when she finally concluded, according to a conversation with a friend that she had taped, that to "be a movie star . . . was too hard . . . so I figured well, why not *fall* for movie stars . . . instead of becoming one."

Bakley was clever enough to know that her best chance at insinuating herself into the life of a celebrity was to search for a vulnerable one. After Robert Downey, Jr., was imprisoned on drug charges, she wrote to him, but he, like a few other actors, was savvy enough to elude her. Although Christian Brando was more infamous than famous—he had just finished his prison sentence for murdering his half-sister's boyfriend—his father, Marlon, was a big enough celebrity for both of them. So she tried the same approach with him, this time including a few porno tapes. They began corresponding, and when he moved to rural Washington state she visited him a few times.

Smart enough to hedge her bets, Bakley also began to troll for stars in Hollywood. She bought a house at the northern edge of the Valley and frequently flew to Los Angeles. In 1998, on an August evening, she attended a birthday party for the veteran character actor Chuck McCann at Chadney's, a now-defunct jazz club across the street from Universal Studios. She accompanied Will Jordan, a New York comic and impersonator almost twice her age whom she had met back in New Jersey when she was in her early twenties. Jordan needed Bakley because he did not drive; Bakley needed Jordan as an entrée to Hollywood parties.

When she spotted Blake across the room she did not know who

he was. But when she noticed how people fawned over him, she assumed he was famous and decided he might be worth pursuing. She caught his eye and smiled. He wandered over to her table and they chatted. Eventually Blake asked her, "Can I drive you back to your hotel?"

"No problem," she responded.

When they arrived at the parking lot of the North Hollywood Holiday Inn, where she was staying, they had a fast fling in the backseat of Blake's SUV. She later told a relative she had decided to seduce him after saying to herself, *Don't let this one go. This one you're going to marry.*

When she returned to Little Rock she still did not know who Blake was, just that he was an actor, which was titillating enough. She immediately rented every movie of his that she could find. Although Bakley was on probation for possessing stolen credit cards and false identification and prohibited from leaving the state, she managed to slip out to Los Angeles again for a few more trysts. She always paid for her own flights and hotel rooms. Sometimes Blake would deign to see her; sometimes he snubbed her.

When she became pregnant in September 1999, which had been her goal all along, she immediately informed a tabloid that she was carrying Robert Blake's child. Then she called Blake, who was apoplectic. "You double-crossed me; you double-dealt me and that's who you are," Blake shouted, according to a conversation that Bakley recorded. "You have to live with yourself and I don't know how you do it. You swore to me on your life that no matter what, I didn't have to worry, and that was a rotten, stinking, filthy lie, and you deliberately got pregnant. For the rest of your life, you'll have to live with that, and for the rest of my life I'll never forget it."

Blake immediately changed his phone number and she could no longer reach him, except by letter, so she decided to tell Christian Brando the child was his. She liked Brando better anyway, she told a friend. He was younger, better looking, nicer, and—most important—more malleable.

"Who would you go for more if you were me—Blake or Christian?" she asked one friend, according to a tape recording of the conversation. She added that she was unsure if she wanted to be married to Blake "the rest of my life . . . because he's going to get even older and worse looking, and I'm already in love with Christian. So I should just leave it like that."

She discussed the situation with Gawron, her ex-husband, who told her to forget Brando: "Christian has killed someone. Go with Robert Blake. He's the better deal."

But she continued to equivocate. On June 2, 2000, she gave birth in Little Rock to a baby girl whom she named Christian Shannon Brando. But she soon changed her mind again and sent Blake photos of the baby. He eventually agreed to a DNA test to establish paternity.

In August, Bakley flew to Los Angeles, violating her probation in Little Rock again. Blake picked her and the baby up at the airport, and where he had once been contentious he was now charming— affectionate with the baby and solicitous toward her. Back at his house, he showed Bakley the nursery, which he had just finished decorating, and introduced her to a nanny he had just hired. Blake handed the baby to the nanny and drove Bakley to a restaurant for lunch. Before they could eat, two men who identified themselves as police officers arrived and arrested Bakley for probation violation. As they hustled her out the door, Blake assured her that he would care for the baby until her legal problems were resolved.

On the way to the station, one of the cops told Bakley he was about to retire and did not want to waste his last few days writing arrest reports and dealing with red tape. If she would return to Little Rock and immediately contact her probation officer, he would not throw her in jail. She readily agreed, and he drove her to the airport.

When Bakley returned home and called her probation officer, she realized that Blake had pulled off a sting. The two men who had "arrested" her were not police officers; they were private investigators hired by Blake, and they had informed her probation officer that she had left the state. Bakley was placed under house arrest.

She eventually hired a family law attorney, filed a police report accusing Blake of kidnapping, and demanded child support. Then, in a decision that was a mystery to her friends, and even to Bakley herself, he decided to propose.

Bakley's friends eventually concluded that Blake believed it would be easier for him to gain custody of the baby if the two were married. A prenuptial agreement was drawn up, and Blake bought an opal wedding ring at a flea market. In November, they were married in his backyard. While Bakley was disappointed by the chintzy ceremony, she was thrilled that the justice of the peace that Blake had found in the Yellow Pages had recently married Drew Barrymore. She immediately insured that a tabloid carried an item on the nuptials.

Bakley spent her wedding night back at her hotel alone, and flew back to Little Rock the next morning—without the baby.

On Tuesday afternoon, four days after the murder, Bakley's sister, Margerry, arrives at the squad room door, accompanied by a tabloid reporter who has paid for her exclusive story. Margerry, four years younger than her sister, is heavyset and pasty-faced and wears black stretch pants, a coral-colored T-shirt, and brown leather sandals. Ito and Eguchi are busy examining the evidence, so Whelan and Gollaz escort her to an interview room—without the tabloid reporter. Margerry recounts the night Bonny met Blake, and her occasional visits back to Los Angeles.

"Every time they had sex, he'd call her afterwards, worried about her being pregnant. He'd say, 'You've got to be pregnant. I'm Italian. We have very strong sperm.' "

Sometimes they would have sex in the car. But even when they had sex at Blake's house, Margerry says, he would not allow Bakley to spend the night or even sleep in his bed. "She had to talk about it," Margerry says. "She was *so* elated. Some of the conversations were for six or seven hours. I'd fall asleep or hang up."

Margerry then tells the detectives about Christian Brando. "She had a better relationship with him than with Blake. He was nice," she says earnestly, "for a murderer."

"Nicer than most murderers?" Whelan asks dryly.

Margerry looks flustered. "I don't know how to put it."

"Let's talk about the baby," Whelan says.

Bakley timed her visits to Los Angeles when she was ovulating and, to enhance her chances, she took the fertility drug Clomid, Margerry says.

"Why'd she want to get pregnant?" Gollaz asks.

"She wanted to marry him and she knew she couldn't get him unless she got pregnant. She read an article on how to take a tampon, put cellophane on it, insert it afterwards, and stand on your head so the sperm won't come out." Margerry holds her palms together as if praying.

"This is what she did?" Whelan looks incredulous.

"Yes," she says, her face flushed now in the warm interview room.

"Did she try this for a while or did it work the first time?" Gollaz asks.

Margerry smiles. "I think it worked the first time."

She primly folds her hand on the table like a schoolgirl and says Bonny missed her period the next month. But she waited another few months, until she was sure she would not miscarry, to inform Blake.

"She told him over the phone. He says, 'Can you get the morning-after pill? Is it available in the U.S.? Can you go to Mexico? . . . He's going on and on about abortion and the pill."

When he realized that Bakley was not enthusiastic about terminating the pregnancy, Blake told her he had a terminal illness and would probably not live to see the child grow up. When she still would not agree to an abortion, he asked her to visit his daughter's gynecologist for an amniocentesis. Bakley refused, because she knew that there was a small chance of losing the baby as a result of the procedure.

"She finally got pregnant by a movie star and she wasn't going to do it," Margerry says.

Blake called and told her he wanted her to take the test so he could check the fetus's DNA. When she still refused, he told her the baby was probably not his and hung up on her.

Margerry shrugs and says blithely, "So she proceeded with Christian Brando and told him the baby was his, because she didn't want to lose another star."

She sips her Pepsi and tells the detectives a confusing story about how Bakley eventually pressed Blake about the baby, their convoluted negotiations, and his threats.

"She was saying all the time, 'He's going to kill me, he's going to kill me,' " Margerry says. Bonny once told her that Blake said, "I'm going to blow my brains out, but don't worry. You're coming with me 'cause I got a bullet with your name on it."

In April, five months after the wedding, Bakley changed the baby's name to Rose Lenore Sophia Blake. A few weeks later Blake invited Bakley and Margerry to join him and Earle Caldwell, his bodyguard, on a vacation to Arizona. This was supposed to be the honeymoon Blake and Bakley had never had. Margerry drove partway, but then she decided to return home.

"Why'd he want you to come?" Gollaz asks.

"Because he knew I knew everything . . . to kill me and her at the same time. I wasn't going to do that. This is her game."

Blake asked Bakley, Margerry says, " 'to sign some papers, so if anything happens to us on this trip, the baby will go to my daughter.' She wouldn't. She said, 'I'm not signing my death warrant.' "

When she moved in with Blake after the vacation—just a few weeks before she was murdered—she was still frightened.

"She was very afraid for her life and she wanted me to record what she was saying . . . ," Margerry says.

On Friday morning, the day Bakley was killed, she called Margerry. "We were talking and she hears a loud bang and says, 'Oh my God. The burglar alarm is going off. Oh my God. I think he's coming to kill me now. If I scream—hang up and call the police.' One bang and she was freaked. . . . I said, 'Maybe the idiot blew his own brains out.' She said, 'No. He said he was taking me with him.' "

At the end of the interview, Margerry waves a scrap of paper with the phone number of a tabloid reporter scrawled on it. "She left me this number and told me to call when it happens. She said he's always done good stories on her in the past and treated her fairly. She said, 'Call him and make sure he has a nice picture of me.' "

Margerry cries and dabs her eyes with her knuckles. "I think it's revenge. . . ." She pauses and says softly, "Just revenge."

On Wednesday morning, the detectives meet again in Tatreau's office. Ito and Eguchi, both of whom worked until almost midnight Monday and Tuesday, look exhausted, their eyes red-rimmed. Ito has a cough that is worsening. He plans to leave in midafternoon and visit a doctor.

Ito tells the group that firearms technicians, studying the extractor marks, have determined that the ninety-seven bullets in Blake's ammunition box cannot be traced to the Walther. Also, the three bullets from the Walther, Ito says, are "factory ammunition," not reloads, and do not match the other rounds in the box.

Ito coughs. "So we can't trace the Walther to Blake. Firearms was hoping the three rounds would match the ninety-seven in the box. They're the same brand—Remington-Peters—but they're *not* reloads."

When Tatreau asks whether there was gunshot residue on Blake's hands, Ito reports that the crime lab's GSR equipment is on the fritz. The coroner will conduct the test.

"I heard Braun tell reporters that the GSR test on Blake was negative," a detective says.

"How could he say the test is negative?" Eguchi asks, outraged. "The test hasn't even been done yet."

Ito flashes him a sympathetic smile; Eguchi is unfamiliar with defense lawyers' tactics. During the early stages of an investigation, the defense can make all sorts of claims, without fear of being challenged, because neither the cops nor the deputy district attorneys assigned to the case will comment.

Tatreau asks why no neighbors heard the two shots.

"The house across from the car was vacant and under construction," McCartin says. "Across the street, the lady was in New York. Another neighbor said her kid was watching *Elmo* real loud. And at the corner houses, when we went to the doors, there was no answer."

"Maybe the shooter had a sweater or clothing wrapped around the gun," Bub says. "And maybe that's how the casing ended up in the car."

Bub, the clue coordinator, says he has already chronicled thirty-three tips. "Here's my latest. A lady called this morning with some real helpful information about Blake. And this is how she found it out: she can read souls by seeing them on television."

Ito laughs and then coughs. "I need a travel team," he says.

"Is Tahiti on the itinerary?" Whalen asks.

"New Jersey, Arkansas, and Tennessee," Ito says.

Knolls and McCartin pick up the assignment, which will complicate their efforts on the Lourdes Unson murder.

The Blake case has forced them to temporarily suspend their investigation, but during the past few days they have managed to squeeze in a few phone calls. They have narrowed their suspect list to two men: the Armenian whose mother lived next door to the victim—he recently skipped parole—and the six-foot-two-inch black man whose girlfriend accused him of rape and then recanted. She had told detectives that the man boarded a Greyhound bus for New York on Saturday, the day before the murder.

McCartin calls a Greyhound official, who searches the company's records. The officials discover that the man's name was not listed on any passenger register for the entire weekend. McCartin also discovers that during the past few years a woman filed a restraining order against him in Seattle, he was arrested for robbery in Barstow, and he served almost a year in the Los Angeles county jail for grand theft. Last year, when he applied for a California driver's license, he provided his girlfriend's Los Feliz address.

"Let's ease him in here," McCartin says. "Then we'll swab him for DNA."

Knolls calls the girlfriend and asks whether she knows where the man is staying. She says he called a few days ago and told her he is "on the road," on his way back to Los Angeles from New York.

"This guy's looking better and better," McCartin says.

"Yeah," Knolls says. "But it's just our luck. We got two suspects and both are in the wind. I wish we had more time to search for them."

"This Blake case," McCartin says, "is burning everyone out."

Bub, who calls himself the "clue clown," now has a prop. A detective gave him a bicycle horn, so whenever he gets a call and adds another clue to his growing list, he hangs up the phone and toots the horn. By Thursday morning Bub has fifty-three clues, including one from a psychic who told him that Blake killed Bakley "because she didn't return his love."

This is the first morning the detectives do not meet in Tatreau's office: he is too busy negotiating with Braun. In Blake's guest house, Bakley had left numerous boxes of letters from her male correspondents; Braun plans to turn them over to the LAPD. He has told reporters that many of these men had a motive to kill Bakley and are potential suspects because she ripped them off. The detectives believe he is simply trying to bury them in paperwork, dissipate their time and energy, and deflect press attention from Blake. Still, if a plausible threat appears in the letters, they are prepared to question the writer.

Tatreau has asked Braun to meet the detectives at Piper Technical Center—where the crime lab is based—at the edge of downtown because the LAPD can keep the press out and supervise the area. Braun wants the exchange at the Parker Center parking lot, Tatreau believes, because it is a more public spot and the media can chronicle the proceedings.

"Our interest is getting the truth," Hartwell complains to Ito. "His interest is getting publicity."

Tatreau, hoping to resolve the impasse quickly, reluctantly agrees on Parker Center. By noon the street is teeming with dozens of photographers, cameramen, and television, radio, and newspaper reporters. At two minutes after the hour, Braun, driving a silver Mercedes and trailed by his private investigator in a yellow Mercedes station wagon, pulls into the parking lot. As an LAPD Property Division employee wheels out a large dolly for the three steamer trunks, four suitcases, and two boxes, television reporters shout to their cameramen, "Get the boxes! Get the boxes!"

After the exchange, Braun holds a press conference in front of

Parker Center. "My duty as a criminal defense attorney is to turn over to the police department evidence that might be relevant to the investigation. I've had lots of dealings with the LAPD over the years. In the past, the LAPD has been obstinate. On this investigation they've reevaluated the situation and showed a flexibility they haven't shown in the past."

The reporters' mostly softball questions include "Is Mr. Blake getting support from the Hollywood community?" and "How is the baby?"

Later in the day, Knolls returns from an interview with a doctor at UCLA Medical Center who, on the night of May 4, was walking to his car with a date when he spotted Blake. Knolls pulls out his notes and updates Ito.

The doctor, who did not know at the time that the man was Robert Blake, saw him banging on a door and shouting, "She's bleeding! Help! Call 911!" Because the doctor found Blake's behavior peculiar, he was reluctant to approach.

When paramedics arrived, the doctor watched Blake sit on the curb, next to a woman. Blake repeatedly asked: "What's wrong with her?"

"Two things struck me as odd about his behavior. First, he was sitting off at some distance—fifteen feet away from the car. Things are going on with her and he is seemingly distraught, but he didn't seem to show much interest into what was happening to her. . . . I just thought 'What's wrong with her?' is such an unusual line."

The doctor said that in emergency rooms, "it's usually very hard to keep the families away. . . . So that's what I was struck by. That he did not get involved and showed no interest. . . . I just think that throughout all of this . . . there was something that was not right, that seemed strange. From the first time he called for help . . . and from a professional view, I hear people call for help. I know what that's like. And it just didn't seem . . . genuine."

Ito tells Knolls that the interview could prove to be important during a trial. The doctor is the second witness to question Blake's behavior that night. And because he is accustomed to seeing grief-stricken spouses, his opinion would impress a jury.

A few hours later, in the early evening, Earle Caldwell, whom friends described as Blake's bodyguard and handyman, stops by the squad room. Ito believes Caldwell may be a key to the case.

Fortuitously, a friend of Bakley's has just called the station with a tip about Caldwell: Bakley had confided, the friend said, that after her trip with Blake to Arizona, they visited Sequoia National Park and she suspected that Caldwell was supposed to kill her, but he was so nervous he became sick and could not pull the trigger.

Ito had attempted to interview Caldwell yesterday, but he refused, saying he wanted a lawyer with him. Today he is accompanied by one—paid for by Blake. Caldwell, unshaven and balding, is about six feet tall, slender and fit, yet he does not have the physical presence of a bodyguard.

Caldwell tells Ito that he worked at a car stereo and alarm shop in Studio City and met Blake when he brought his car in. He eventually began working at Blake's house as a handyman and was hired full-time last year. When Caldwell describes Blake's relationship with Bakley, Ito's tone turns confrontational and incredulous. He believes Caldwell's comments are scripted, slanted to protect Blake and condemn Bakley. Several times Caldwell is prompted by his attorney, or he says, "I'm supposed to tell you this," before he recounts an anecdote.

When Bakley lived in the guest house, Caldwell says, she and Blake "were lovey-dovey."

"Don't you think that's odd when they were sleeping in separate residences?" Ito says sarcastically, but Caldwell does not respond.

When Bakley visited, Caldwell says, he served as her bodyguard. He noticed that she was constantly looking over her shoulder, as if she feared someone was following her. Bakley was afraid of an old boyfriend from New Jersey. Caldwell says, "His attitude was: 'If I can't have you, no one can.'"

Caldwell then recounts a story similar to the one Blake had told to North Hollywood detectives about a man they called Buzzcut, who appeared to be staking out the house. When Caldwell says the man was in his late twenties, Ito points out that Buzzcut does not fit the profile of the men writing to Bakley, who were much older.

Ito asks about the trip to Sequoia National Park and Caldwell, after prompting by his attorney, said Blake and Bakley held hands, kissed, and seemed to be having a fine time. He did become sick, he says, probably because of the altitude, and he spent a few hours in a nearby emergency room. Because of the tip, Ito is skeptical; besides, the spot is not much higher than 6,000 feet. But he lets Caldwell continue. Bakley disliked him, Caldwell says, and wanted Blake to fire him and hire her brother as a bodyguard. A few days before her murder, to ease the tension, Blake asked Caldwell to take some time off, so he spent a few days in the San Francisco area.

At the end of the interview, Ito asks Caldwell who he thought would want to kill Bakley. Caldwell says he believes Blake was actually the target of the hit and Bakley was killed by accident. Bakley had the motive, Caldwell says, because she would benefit financially.

But Bakley signed a prenuptial agreement before the marriage, so Ito knows she would not inherit his estate. Barely disguising his irritation, Ito asks Caldwell if he will take a polygraph exam. Caldwell refuses, saying he does not trust the results.

At about nine P.M., Ito returns to the squad room, coughing and scowling. Knolls pulls up a chair next to him. "Well, Ron, where do we stand?"

"Blake did it, man," Ito says. He tells Knolls he had been perplexed because he did not know why a sixty-seven-year-old man would want custody of a baby. But, through interviews with acquaintances of Blake, he recently learned that the actor's daughter, who is in her mid-thirties, is childless. During the past year, ever since Blake's private investigators hustled Bakley to the airport, she has been caring for the baby at her Hidden Hills home.

"So how're we going to prove he did it?" Knolls asks.

"I want to find someone who Blake told that he did it," Ito says.

"We're not going to find that," Knolls says.

"It's still early on," Ito says. "Someone may surface."

Although Ito's cough is worsening and he is losing his voice, he spends the weekend listening to Blake's original interview again, studying witness statements, and sifting through hundreds of Bakley's letters that Braun had dropped off at Parker Center.

The papers document Bakley's operation, the various post office boxes and addresses she used, and include copies of the handwritten letters she sent out, the lascivious photographs she enclosed—some of herself more than twenty years ago; some of other young women— and the responses she received from men across the country. One of her typical come-on ads, which she ran in various trashy swinger publications, begins:

"Men wanted. Any age from anywhere to write to a young, single pretty girl. I promise to answer all. I am 22, 36-24-35, 127 lbs. I can travel if you can't, in order to meet. I am sad and lonely due to a recent break up with someone I was engaged to. I need your letters to cheer me up. Looks are unimportant as well as age, and I do love older men mostly. Hurry and write!" Most of the men who replied seem lonely and desperate, their letters pathetic attempts at seduction. Some seem forlorn, merely seeking companionship. Others are crude or psychotic. A few try the clever approach, like the man from North Hollywood who plays off a quote from the movie *The Elephant Man:* "Hi pervert," he wrote. "I love you. I'm not an animal. Okay, sometimes I am. . . ."

After a man responded, Bakley typically sent him a form letter—

but handwritten—designed to play on his sympathy and establish that she was a young woman in a temporary fix, not a hardened hustler. She explained that she had recently broken up with her boyfriend, moved out of his house, and now survived day-to-day. To let him know her living situation was tenuous and potentially dire, she wrote on motel stationery.

Then, to pique his interest and ensure the hook was firmly implanted, she slipped in a few graphic sentences that sounded like a cheesy parody of a 1950s pornographic novel: "Just tell me your desire and what you enjoy. I'm sure you will be pleased with my hot nest and hot mouth. French is my favorite giving and receiving but I enjoy all positions and I can cum over and over again."

Bakley then explained she could not afford to stay in her motel much longer and promised to visit the man—if he sent her fifty dollars for gas and traveling expenses. She also promised to send him her "collection of photos my last love took of me nude and doing sexy things to let you know what you're missing."

If a man wrote back, sent money, and asked her to move in with him, she dashed off another letter and stalled, asking for more cash, usually sixty dollars. She concluded with a line such as "Hope we will have some spicy sex soon!" and signed the letter, "Frenchingly."

If a man did not include cash, she pressured him for the money and also asked for books of stamps and prepaid phone cards. If he continued to write but did not send money, Bakley harshly rebuked him, writing that unless he "helped her out," she could not afford to visit him and become his "love pet."

Bakley is not the most sympathetic victim. But most detectives in Homicide Special learned their craft working gang murders in busy homicide units. They learned to investigate all cases professionally, not judge the players in the drama, and simply do their jobs.

Ito and Eguchi find the letters amusing, but also revealing. On the back of each envelope Bakley received, she wrote the amount of cash enclosed, usually less than $40. While Braun tells reporters that the men she stiffed are potential suspects, Ito believes that someone who was ripped off for a small amount of cash, or stamps and phone cards, is not going to be angry enough to kill her. Still, he tells Eguchi, they will study the letters, and if anything appears that can be construed as a threat, they will question the writer. Ito is also examining all the radio calls in the area on the night Bakley was killed and recent crime reports to learn whether there are any other potential suspects to investigate.

"We've got to do that to be fair," he tells Eguchi. "But let's be realistic. Look at Blake's actions: He leaves her alone in the car. The windows are down. He takes the keys. Plus he tells the bodyguard earlier that week to split. Yet he's supposed to be concerned about her safety."

By Monday, May 14, ten days after the murder, the investigation's initial frenzy has subsided. For the first time since the murder, there is no news about Blake in the Southern California newspapers. Tatreau does not hold a meeting in his office, the squad room has returned to normal, and detectives begin joking about the case.

Otis Marlow calls out to Ito, "I'm taking my wife to Vitello's tonight. I'm going to tell her to wear her best clothes and put on all her jewels. Then I'm going to park by that big Dumpster, throw all my credit cards on the dash, and leave her there."

"If that doesn't work and you want to be single again," Bub says, "hire Caldwell as her bodyguard."

A detective then tells the group about a case he is investigating and calls the suspect an asshole.

Marlow raises an index finger and says primly, "I don't approve of calling a murder suspect an asshole. You should refer to him as someone who simply hasn't found his niche in life."

Hartwell turns to Knolls and says, "If I wasn't on the job, I wouldn't be interested in this case at all. Our poor doctor in Los Feliz is a lot more tragic, and her case is a lot more interesting."

"I agree," Knolls says, grabbing his briefcase. "I just wish we had time to work on it." He is headed for an apartment complex in the Valley, to interview two men who dined at Vitello's the night of the murder. Detectives briefly talked to them that night, but Ito wants Knolls to question the two more extensively. Knolls talks to one of them in the dining room while the other waits in the back of the apartment.

The man, who works for a furniture store and is middle-aged with thinning gray hair, says he and his friend sat at a table near Blake's booth and they spotted him walking past them a few times on his way to the rest room.

"I don't know him, but he seemed neurotic," says the man. "Pulling his hair, running his hands through his hair. He looked preoccupied. . . . He acted nervous. Another ten or fifteen minutes and he's back again. He did this three or four times. Enough so we commented on it. . . . It was kind of odd behavior. He seemed . . . kind of keyed up. At his table he was still pulling his hair."

The man says he heard on the news that Blake claimed he had returned to the restaurant to pick up his gun. But, he says, "I didn't see him."

Shortly after Blake rushed back into the restaurant asking for a doctor, the man and his friend paid their bill and left. Then they spotted the fire truck and the paramedics on the street. "We did find it odd that he parked behind the Dumpster—safety-wise. Particularly since there was so much parking on the street and he didn't arrive much after us. We both commented that this was a very odd place to park."

Knolls then interviews the other man, who reiterates how nervous Blake seemed. Shortly after Blake passed their table on his way to the bathroom for the second time, this man also went to the bathroom, where he noticed that someone had vomited in the trash can.

"I've been going there twelve years and I'd never seen that before," the man says. "I thought it was odd and wondered, because Blake was so wound up, if it was him."

The man noticed bits of spinach and pasta in the vomit, which he found significant when he later learned that Blake was such a regular customer the restaurant named a dish for him—"Fusilli e minestra alla Robert Blake"—corkscrew pasta with garlic, olive oil, spinach, and fresh tomatoes. Blake ordered the dish that night.

The man found Blake's behavior so odd that the next night, when he was eating in the restaurant again and he spotted the police interviewing people, he approached them rather than wait for them to come to him.

Later in the afternoon, Ito and Eguchi interview Bakley's brother Joey in his room at the Best Western motel off a bustling stretch of Colorado Boulevard in east Pasadena. He lives in Mexico, he says, and recently arrived in Los Angeles for the funeral. Joey, who is thirty-seven, wears a T-shirt with an NYPD insignia and answers the door barefoot. He is about five foot eight, chubby, and unshaven. He tells Ito and Eguchi that he used to pave roads for a living but now, after an injury, lives on state disability.

"She was a good person," he announces immediately. "I loved her."

"Was she having a problem with anyone?" Ito asks.

"Only *him*," he says, with disdain.

"How long was the problem going on?" Ito asks.

"Since day one. He's a snake, in my opinion."

After Joey describes the first time he met Blake, Ito asks, "With the mail-order business, was there anyone who was trying to get even with her?"

"No one even knew she was out here," he says.

Ito asks whether her ex-husband Paul Gawron, who is caring for their young daughter, would have a motive to kill her.

"He's pussywhipped." Joey sounds disgusted.

"No one ever stalked her? . . . Anyone who ever tried to hurt her or threaten her?"

"No."

"She ever tell anyone outside the family that she's coming out here to live?"

"No."

While Joey tells the detectives about the day he met Blake, Ito checks his pager, which is buzzing. He calls the number and reaches Mike Coffey, the supervisor for North Hollywood Homicide. "We've got a guy here who says he was solicited by Blake to kill his wife," Coffey says.

As Eguchi speeds to the North Hollywood station, Ito, keyed up about the upcoming interview, considers a series of questions for the man. If this interview goes the way he hopes, Robert Blake's tumultuous and tortured life may end in a prison cell.

Robert Blake and Bonny Lee Bakley were both born poor in New Jersey, children of abusive, alcoholic fathers, and both landed in California, on the fringes of Hollywood, but by distinctly different routes. Hollywood was Bakley's dream destination, and when she finally arrived she immediately began trolling for stars. Blake was transported to the city like a commodity, his father hoping to parlay his toddler's waiflike looks and precocious poise into a meal ticket for the family.

Blake was born Michael Gubitosi during the height of the Depression, in a tenement near Newark. When he was a toddler, his father dressed him and his older brother and sister in overalls, dubbed them the Three Little Hillbillies, and demanded that they sing and dance at political rallies and other events, where people threw money onstage.

When Blake was five, and already a show-business veteran, his family piled into a 1928 jalopy and headed for California, where his father knew child actors would not have to grub for dimes on park stages but could secure lucrative contracts from movie studios.

Blake's father shepherded his children to countless Hollywood casting offices where he showed off the Three Little Hillbillies act. The jaded agents were not impressed, but Blake earned a spot as an extra in the "Our Gang" short films and mugged alongside Spanky, Alfalfa, and Buckwheat. One morning on the set, when one of the other child actors repeatedly muffed his lines, Blake marched up to the director and told him, "I can do that." He was hired for the role of Little Mickey and for the next five years his $100 a week from "Our Gang" and other small movie roles helped support the family. Instead of being pampered, however, Blake was reviled and abused by his father.

Blake loved acting, "desperately and completely," he once said. "It was the only place where I could come alive, but the consequences were terrible because my father . . . [was] horribly jealous of me. . . . He couldn't help it, because I was supporting the family. And I was also giving him what little reflected glory he got. But he despised me for it."

His brutal childhood tormented him for the rest of his life. He was beaten and sexually abused by his father, he told interviewers decades later, sometimes locked in a closet all day and forced to eat on the floor like a dog. His mother was a cold, remote woman who paid little attention to him. His first hug was from Donna Reed, when he was eight years old, on the set of the 1942 movie *Mokey*.

When Blake outgrew "Our Gang," he had little trouble finding work. He played Little Beaver in the "Red Ryder" Western movies, and the street urchin in *The Treasure of the Sierra Madre* with Humphrey Bogart. By the end of the 1940s, he had appeared in more than seventy-five films.

Because Blake was small, he was able to play children's roles well into adolescence. But by the time he was in his late teens, the parts dried up. With his short bandy legs, barrel chest, swarthy looks, and brooding manner, Blake now looked like a hood—and he soon began acting like one. He was thrown out of high school, and when he was discharged from the army in the mid-1950s—after he was stationed in Alaska—he shot heroin and sold drugs. He was estranged from his father, who later committed suicide, and his mother, whom he never talked to again.

Acting, the only respite from his parents' abuse, had saved him once. Now, as his life bottomed out, acting was once again his salvation. He signed up for classes, began therapy, and realized again that the only time he felt good about himself was when he was onstage or in front of a camera.

During the late 1950s he landed numerous spots in television Westerns, and by the early 1960s, he was picking up parts in movies such as *Town Without Pity* and *The Greatest Story Ever Told*. He married Sondra Kerr, an actress, in 1964, had two children, and appeared to have finally established some stability.

The film that defined him as an actor was 1967's *In Cold Blood*. Blake was magnificent as the diminutive, aspirin-popping murderer Perry Smith, in a performance that captured both the killer's vulnerability and his menace. The movie was critically acclaimed and received four Oscar nominations, but did not relaunch Blake's career as he had hoped. Six years later he starred in *Electra Glide in Blue*, a critical success but a commercial failure.

In 1975, against the advice of his agent and lawyer, he pursued the easy fame and fast money of television as the macho, quirky street cop in *Baretta*. The show garnered excellent ratings and he won an Emmy. Blake, who had been ambivalent about sacrificing his film career for television, was now a huge star. But he was miserable. On the set he was a terror, threatening to punch out directors, demanding that scripts be repeatedly rewritten, berating executives. During his frequent appearances on *The Tonight Show* Blake railed against the corruption of Hollywood and went on about how the money-grubbing network "suits" destroyed artistic integrity. Blake's denunciations of Hollywood were sincere, and he eschewed the typical trappings of a television star. He cruised to the studio lot in an eleven-year-old car, dressed in faded jeans and T-shirts, and lived with his family in a modest North Hollywood neighborhood in the house he had purchased years earlier for $30,000 with a GI loan.

Blake walked away from *Baretta* after three and a half seasons, unaware that his career had reached its apogee. The late 1970s were the beginning of a long, frustrating decline, both personally and professionally. Blake's marriage ended in divorce and he worked only sporadically. In 1985, he starred as a skid row priest in *Hell Town,* but the series did not last long. Blake descended into a haze of booze and drugs and was so depressed he was unable to muster the energy to seek roles. The many missed opportunities, the squandered promise, the way his own arrogance had undermined him tormented Blake. Over the years he had rejected a number of roles that could have changed the course of his desultory career. When John Schlesinger attempted to contact him in the late 1960s to discuss the role of Ratso Rizzo in *Midnight Cowboy,* Blake never even returned his call.

He feared that he would soon join the many other "Our Gang" child actors whose lives had ended tragically. Alfalfa was shot to death at thirty-one. Stymie's life was plagued by drugs and crime. Brisbane committed suicide. Chubby died at twenty-two after losing 164 pounds on a crash diet. Scotty was beaten to death at thirty-eight. Froggy was killed at fourteen in a motor-scooter accident. Wheezer died at nineteen in a military plane crash. Even Pete the Pup suffered an untimely demise—he was poisoned.

"The fear that I could end up that way haunted me for years," Blake said in a 1977 *Playboy* interview. "I was positively maniacal about being identified as a kid actor."

In the early 1990s, Blake fired his therapist of thirty years, hired a new one, and joined Alcoholics Anonymous. After emerging from his self-imposed exile, he was ready to work again.

He starred in the 1993 television movie *Judgment Day,* portraying John List, a New Jersey accountant who killed his mother, wife, and three children, disappeared, and started a new life, then was caught seventeen years later. Blake understood the motivation of murderers, he told a reporter at the time: "I could very easily have killed myself at some point, which is no different from murdering someone else. There's no difference between me and a lot of people on Death Row, except that they crossed the line."

While promoting the movie, Blake released to entertainment writers a rambling twenty-six-page autobiography that chronicled his abysmal childhood and his arduous journey to self-discovery and spiritual renewal. He finally seemed at peace. Although he only picked up a few minor roles during the next decade, he lived comfortably in what he called the third act of his life. He had invested wisely in Southern California real estate, owned several homes and rental properties, and in the late 1990s had an annual income of more than $800,000. He was no longer famous, just famous for once being famous, and while that did not give him much cachet in Hollywood, a place where aging actors are treated shabbily, it was a sufficient lure for Bonny Bakley.

Mike Coffey, the detective supervisor at North Hollywood Homicide, waits in an interview room with a man named Gary McLarty, who called the station with the revelation that Blake asked him to kill Bakley. McLarty is a retired stuntman who first met Blake when he worked on the *Baretta* set more than thirty years ago. At sixty-one, stocky and weather-beaten, he still looks fit enough to perform stunt work.

Coffey walks out into the hallway, greets the detectives, and quickly briefs them. Then Ito and Eguchi join McLarty in the interview room and introduce themselves.

"We're from RHD—downtown," Ito tells McLarty. "We stole this case from Mike Coffey. The reason we did is we have a little more time to work on one case. More manpower."

"Well, I'm a little late in revealing this, but I got so many personal problems," McLarty says sheepishly. He tells the detectives about a messy divorce and difficulties with some property he owns. "It finally got to the point where . . . I didn't want to lead you guys on a wrong trail, and this could tighten things up for you. I thought I better come in and reveal this thing."

"I'm glad you did," Ito says in a reassuring tone.

"That woman didn't deserve what she got," McLarty says.

"No one does," Ito says.

"With Robert, he knew I'd killed a guy a while back . . . so he figured because of that and I got off and everything and he, you know—" McLarty sputters. He speaks in staccato bursts and sometimes breaks off in midsentence when he loses his train of thought. He briefly tells the detectives about the incident. The victim was an ex-convict who had raped a family friend; McLarty says he shot him in self-defense.

Until recently, the last time he saw Blake was more than twenty years ago when they worked together on a movie called *Coast to Coast.* Then, about six weeks ago, a mutual acquaintance, an old stuntman everyone called Snuffy, asked McLarty to meet Blake for lunch at Du-Par's restaurant in Studio City.

"Did he say why?" Ito asks.

"I figured it was a stunt job, a movie job," McLarty says.

"What happened when you met?"

"We just bullshitted, a little small talk. Then he started talking about this gal he wanted something done with. I thought—" He stops abruptly. "Hmmm . . ."

"Did he specify who this girl was?"

"He said it was this girl he met at a party and fucked one night and got pregnant. It turned out it was his kid. She was bilking him out of a lot of money. To be able to keep the kid there, he was giving her a couple thousand a month. That's why he wanted to get her bumped off, I guess."

Detectives always pray for that one golden phone call that will provide the critical break in a case. Ito and Eguchi, who attempt to remain poker-faced and conceal their excitement, realize they have just received that call.

"He took me," McLarty says, "and showed me the backyard and layout like I might come in there and do it. He takes me to this back house and opens the sliding glass door. . . . She was living in the house behind his house. . . ."

McLarty remarks on how Blake cleverly set up the meeting through Snuffy: "That motherfucker's smart. He didn't leave a paper trail with he and I in case I did this thing. That's how smart he is."

During the next few days, McLarty says he worried about the meeting. "How the fuck can someone think . . . that I'd kill an innocent person? I don't even know what she had done wrong, just bilking some guys out of a little bit of money. She wasn't doing anything to cause havoc on anyone. . . ."

Ito steers him back to the meeting at Du-Par's. "What exactly did he say at the restaurant?"

"We just met and had some small talk about movies. I thought he wanted me to do a stunt coordinating job or double or something. But it turned out he wanted me to kill his wife. . . ." McLarty sounds incredulous.

"How'd he say he wanted you to do that?" Ito asks.

"I really can't tell you word for word. I just know that in the conversation that's what it finally boiled down to."

"At the restaurant did he mention something about killing his wife?"

"No. I think he wanted to get me to the house and show me what a bad person she was. . . . Oh man," he says breathlessly. "Like reality was overwhelming to say the least."

McLarty tells them that after bringing him to the back house, Blake took him inside and showed him stacks of the letters Bakley sent to lonely men across the country.

Ito again asks him to recall exactly how Blake proposed he kill Bakley.

"He showed me where she slept and insinuated someone could sneak in here at night, slide open the door, and sneak up there and pop her."

"Did he say 'pop her'?"

"Something to that effect."

McLarty says they then left the house, and strolled a few blocks around the neighborhood while Blake explained that he was planning to drive to Bullhead City, Arizona. He could stop at a restaurant, he told McLarty, and someone could kill Bakley in the parking lot. "Just like what happened. When I heard that on the news I thought––" He pauses and whistles, looking amazed. "Talk about hitting close to home. I said it sounded awfully suspicious to me."

The detectives are intrigued. Bakley's friend told detectives that Blake wanted Earle Caldwell to kill her on an out-of-town trip. And Blake, Bakley, and Caldwell spent a few days near Bullhead City, along the Colorado River.

"He said Bullhead City?" Ito asks.

"He talked about [getting] her there and going for a walk one night. Apparently there's some kind of a walk-run along the river where there's a restaurant or casino and he could lure her down there to somebody and they could do it. . . . He talked about on a highway, stopping to pee or going down a hill to take a dump."

"What are you supposed to be doing all this time?" Ito asks.

"From what he was insinuating, somebody could follow him so when he did that, when he was down there taking care of business, somebody could slide in there and pop her that way." He pauses and takes a deep breath. "Like I said, it's pretty overwhelming, boys."

The afternoon of the meeting, McLarty tells detectives, Blake then drove him back to the restaurant where his car was parked and said, "You want to call me?"

"You call *me*," McLarty told Blake. Then he asked, "And what are you really talking about anyway, *moneywise*."

"How does ten thousand sound?" Blake replied.

About a week later, Blake called McLarty, who told him, "I don't want to have anything to do with this thing at all."

"Why?" Blake asked.

"Well, number one, I don't want to do anything like that. And the other one is your notoriety."

Blake abruptly ended the conversation.

Then, when McLarty heard on the news that Bakley had been killed, he knew he should have contacted police earlier. "But I let it go and I let it go and I let it go. Finally I said, 'I can't let it go any further.' "

"Did he ever come out with the exact words of him wanting you to kill his wife?" Ito asks.

"More like . . . 'You walk over and pop her.' "

"That's what he said?"

"Yes."

According to McLarty, Blake showed him a gun in the house that day and then suggested he obtain a silencer. But McLarty cannot describe the gun in much detail. "I don't know anything about guns except you pull the trigger and it goes bang."

McLarty says he was talking to a friend this morning who persuaded him to contact the police. "He was saying I should get in there and say something. To hide something like this would be ludicrous."

After the interview, as the detectives head back downtown, Eguchi and Ito exchange a high five. "We have to do a lot of work to check out his story, to confirm what he's saying. But there's no doubt that this is a big break."

The next day, the detectives question Snuffy, a retired stuntman in his late sixties. He confirms that he set up the meeting, but says he thought Blake just wanted to talk to McLarty about a book deal. Although Ito is disappointed, at least Snuffy has confirmed he contacted McLarty, which will give the stuntman some credibility with a jury.

Later in the day, when the detectives return to the squad room, they learn that a handyman from the high desert has contacted San Bernardino County sheriff's deputies with information about the Bakley murder. The deputies called Homicide Special while Ito and Eguchi were interviewing Snuffy, so Hartwell sent Rich Haro, whose retirement continues to be delayed, and Adrian Soler to question the informant.

In the early evening, as Ito and Eguchi type up witness statements, Haro and Soler call from the desert to describe their interview with the handyman. A few days after the murder, a stuntman named Ronald

Hambleton confided in the handyman that Blake asked him to kill Bakley. Hambleton told the handyman, who once worked for him, that he had met Blake at Du-Par's about a month before the murder. Later, Blake drove Hambleton back to his house and offered him $100,000 to kill Bakley, the handyman said.

Haro and Soler then interviewed Hambleton, who acknowledged that Snuffy had contacted him and set up a meeting with Blake at Du-Par's about a month ago. But he said the meeting was about a movie project and he denied that Blake had ever mentioned the murder.

In the morning, the detectives and Hartwell meet with Haro and Soler in the captain's office to hear more about the interviews. "Both the informant and Hambleton say the same thing about the meeting at Du-Par's and how it was arranged," Soler says. "The only discrepancy is regarding the solicitation by Blake."

"You have a good feeling about this informant?" Ito asks.

"Yes," Soler says. "Especially after hearing what McLarty said."

Ito shakes Soler's and Haro's hands and says, "That's good shit."

"The timeline's perfect," Hartwell says.

"The case is good and it keeps getting better," Ito says. He plans to reinterview Snuffy, he says, and maybe he will get more information from him the second time around.

"Unless we get pressure, we'll keep working on the case instead of going to the DA with the minimum," Ito says.

"Like O.J.," Bub says.

Ito shakes his head. "With O.J., it wasn't premature. It was just the way we popped him that was a problem. This case is the complete opposite of O.J. We had so much lab results with O.J. and this one we have very little, just a lot of witness statements. I'm still hoping the lab will help us."

Back in the squad room, the detectives are giddy after the sudden headway in the case. Whalen picks up a ringing phone and calls out to Ito, "They want to speak to the Emperor Detective."

Ito grunts some mock-Japanese phrases and takes the call. When he hangs up, he tells Whalen, "We'll target the trial for December seventh and me and Steve will come into the courtroom as [World War II Japanese] Zero pilots."

Eguchi laughs but his mood quickly turns somber when Ito tells him, "You think this case has got a lot of attention? You ain't seen nothin' yet. Wait until we arrest or indict this guy. All hell will break loose and everyone will go after us. They'll try to make us look like the scum of the earth."

A detective calls out to Bub, "I've got a psychic on the line who senses something and wants to talk to a detective."

Bub, who has been inundated by false leads and erroneous tips, says, "If he's such a good psychic why didn't he ask for *me*?"

Bub grabs the phone, listens for a minute, rolls his eyes, and says in a bored monotone, "So you talked to Bonny *after* she was killed, and now you're connecting psychically with the suspect. . . ."

In the late morning, Ito searches the RHD supply cabinet and discovers there are no notepads left. Eguchi drives to Office Depot while Ito grumbles, "This is ridiculous. I'm on a case like this and I have to take time out to shop for pads. And I have to pay for them myself!" Afterward they head to a Chinese restaurant on a bleak stretch of Western Avenue in South-Central. Ho Sai Kai is a cop favorite because the food is fast, tasty, and cheap and the owners do not mind when detectives slip off their coats, displaying an array of weaponry in their shoulder and belt holsters. In this neighborhood, business owners always welcome cops.

A few other Homicide Special detectives join them and as they slurp their wonton soup, they discuss the case and complain about the way Braun has manipulated the press by leaking Bakley's letters and tapes to reporters, who have been enthusiastically limning her squalid past and dehumanizing her to the extent that some potential jurors probably believe her murder was justifiable homicide.

One detective saw Braun on CNN ripping the LAPD, claiming that detectives did not search the Dumpster in which the gun was found until forty-eight hours after the murder.

"That's total bullshit," says Eguchi, who searched the Dumpster himself hours after he arrived at the crime scene.

"Get used to it," Ito says. "It's just beginning."

He cracks open his fortune cookie and nods in appreciation. Considering the recent break in the case, Ito says, the fortune is entirely appropriate. He holds it up and reads: "A surprise announcement will free you."

After four hectic days on the East Coast and in the South interviewing Bakley's friends and family, Knolls and McCartin, the designated travel team, return to squad room, spread out their interview notes in the captain's empty office, and brief Ito, Eguchi, and Hartwell.

McCartin says a close friend of Bakley's who lives in Mississippi related an interesting conversation: Bakley had told her that if she was killed, "Call the L.A. police department and tell them that Blake did it and don't let him get away with it." Bakley explained to the friend that she believed Blake and Caldwell had conspired to murder her during the vacation a few weeks before her death. After they visited Arizona and drove to the Sequoia National Park in central California, Bakley and Blake were in the woods having sex—for the first time on the trip—when she heard a noise. Bakley then saw Caldwell holding a gun and vomiting in the bushes. Blake walked over to Caldwell, Bakley told the friend, and attempted to comfort him, saying "It's okay, don't worry about it. I'll have someone else do it."

Knolls and McCartin talked to another friend of Bakley's in New Jersey, who said that she had told him the same story.

Most of Bakley's immediate family and close friends have sold their stories to the tabloids, McCartin says, but he still believes they are credible. None of them could identify any angry victims of her scams who were likely suspects.

The friend from New Jersey said he told Bakley, "I don't know what's going on, but you need to get the hell away from him. Something is going to happen. You're going to get hurt."

"I want to get my baby," Bakley responded. "If anything happens, be sure to tell the police." Then Bakley asked him, "Do you think I'll feel any pain? I hate pain."

He told her, "I'm sure it will be over quick. But don't put yourself in this harm."

"I always wanted to be famous," she told him. "If it happens, I guess I will be. I'll get my dream."

About a week after Haro and Soler first talked to the stuntman Ronald Hambleton, they decide to pay him another visit. He denies that Blake solicited him to kill Bakley, but the detectives are certain he is lying. They believe the informant, the handyman who once worked for him. So they will employ another approach with Hambleton: they obtain a search warrant. Sometimes this can be an effective interrogation tool. If detectives unearth evidence related to the case, that might convince a person to talk, or if they stumble upon evidence of other crimes—illegal drugs, for example—the threat of jail can also be used to pressure a reluctant witness.

In the late afternoon, Ito and Eguchi head out for Hambleton's place at the edge of the Mojave Desert, several hours from downtown. As they drive through the city streets on the way to the freeway, they pass stands of jacaranda trees in full bloom, the vivid lavender blossoms heralding the end of spring. Eguchi drives east on the freeway, inching along in rush hour. As traffic thins and the housing tracts give way to verdant foothills, he cuts north, climbs four thousand feet over the crest of the San Bernardino Mountains, and cruises down into the dusty, dun-colored flatlands of Southern California's high desert.

Ito stares out at the limitless horizon and says, "We need this guy to 'fess up."

McLarty's comments were crucial, he tells Eguchi, but if Hambleton levels with them, "Blake is bought and paid for." Tonight's interview could wrap up the case.

They finally reach a sheriff's substation, where Hartwell and a few other detectives are gathered in a meeting room. After they plot out how they will approach Hambleton and conduct the search, Ito asks a sheriff's deputy for a dinner recommendation. When he suggests a Chinese place, all the detectives stare at him skeptically. The deputy assures them the food is excellent, so they walk down a stretch of desert road and stop in front of the small restaurant, its windows coated with dust. They venture inside, where the owner, excited at seeing another Asian in the desert, asks Ito whether he is Chinese. When Ito responds that he is Japanese, the owner shuffles forlornly back to the kitchen. Ten minutes later, he returns with heaping plates of kung pao beef, beef with snow peas, and almond chicken. The detectives take a few bites and then turn toward Hartwell for an expert assessment. In culinary matters they always defer to him.

"Not bad at all," Hartwell says. "Actually, it's surprisingly good."

Hartwell has an improbable background for a gourmet. He grew up in a small blue-collar town in the Northwest and after high school worked a union job in a Washington paper mill for six years. Searching for sunshine, he eventually moved to Los Angeles and joined the LAPD. He married young and raised a son. His wife did most of the cooking, but occasionally, after dining out, Hartwell experimented in the kitchen and attempted to re-create the dishes he enjoyed.

He was first exposed to French cuisine when his mother joined the Cookbook of the Month Club and received Julia Child's *Mastering the Art of French Cooking*. His mother, who was more interested in meat and potato recipes, tossed the book aside. But Hartwell was entranced by the exotic ingredients and complex sauces. He began experimenting, occasionally inviting his cop friends over for small dinner parties. He soon started collecting cookbooks, occasionally taking days off to search specialty stores for truffles, foie gras, French beans, and young spring lamb. His avocation soon became a passion. He installed in his kitchen a commercial range, a Sub-Zero refrigerator, and side-by-side sinks, bought a set of heavy hammered-copper pans, and built a wine cellar in his basement.

When his marriage dissolved and he found his evenings suddenly free, Hartwell began taking classes at restaurants and cooking schools throughout the city. At one class, he met Patrick Jamon, the renowned chef of Les Anges in Santa Monica. Les Anges was one of the finest French restaurants in Southern California, popular with actors and directors. Hartwell had dined at the restaurant several times and marveled at the intensity of Jamon's sauces and his signature dishes, such as poached oysters with sea urchin sauce and turbot stuffed with scallops and lobster mousse. Hartwell, the only man in the class, often chatted with Jamon. His knowledgeable questions impressed the chef, who invited Hartwell to visit the kitchen, have a glass of wine, and watch him work.

One Friday night, Hartwell stopped by and Jamon told him, "As long as you're just standing around, why don't you slice some leeks." When Hartwell saw how much faster and finer the others in the kitchen sliced vegetables, he realized that for all his enthusiasm, he was still a rank amateur. Over the next few months, he stopped by the restaurant several nights a week after work and volunteered. When Jamon was satisfied that Hartwell had learned the basics, he allowed him to prepare hors d'oeuvres and then a few fish dishes. After Jamon's sous-chef was hired as head chef at another French restaurant, Hartwell was promoted.

A new owner took over the restaurant, but he liked Hartwell's cooking and asked him to stay on. Hartwell began cooking the fish, another chef prepared meat dishes, and Jamon supervised. For weeks at a time, when Jamon was on vacation, Hartwell assumed the role of head chef—ordering the meat, fish, and poultry, and rising early to shop for vegetables at the produce market. For the next four years he worked during the day as a detective lieutenant in charge of the missing persons section and other downtown units, then spent his evenings at the restaurant.

The days were long, but he loved the creativity and freedom he was afforded in the kitchen, a bracing contrast to the bureaucratic tedium of the LAPD. In 1989, Les Anges closed, but Hartwell continued to work with Jamon occasionally at private clubs and at banquets. Today, he no longer cooks professionally, but is still a fervent epicure. He owns almost a hundred cookbooks, stores cases of first growth Bordeaux and vintage California Cabernets and Zinfandels at wine warehouses, and dines at the city's most celebrated restaurants.

The other cops used to view Hartwell as an eccentric, but now value his expertise. Before special occasions, they often ask him for restaurant suggestions or wine recommendations. And a few detectives who will admit that they like to cook come to him for tutorals on sauce preparation or sautéing techniques.

Ito and the other Homicide Special detectives enjoy working for Hartwell because he respects their knowledge and skills, allows them to work their cases with minimal interference, handles most of the administrative tasks, and runs interference with the brass. And Hartwell's interests are so eclectic that he can explain why he paid top dollar for a 1961 Bordeaux, but still discuss the Dodgers' pitching woes and USC football.

When the detectives finish their Chinese food, they caravan to Hambleton's house. The dusk is warm, a bone-dry breeze kicks up clouds of dust, and a few low stars prick through the sky, milky white against the enameled blue of the desert horizon. The detectives pull off the highway onto a long, serpentine dirt road, bumping over ruts and rocks, bugs smashing against their windshields. Finally, they reach Hambleton's isolated four-acre compound. Hours ago they were in Los Angeles; now they feel as if they are at the ends of the earth, standing in a barren moonscape with a few jagged Joshua trees looming on the perimeter like lonely sentinels. It is perfectly quiet in the gloaming as the light suddenly fades, cobalt to black, sky to ground. Soon there is an infinite expanse of stars overhead, more stars than are ever visible in the neon glare of Los Angeles.

Hambleton's property, encircled by a chain-link fence, is cluttered with more than a dozen cars, trucks, and motorcycles in various states of disrepair and a vast carpet of engine parts. When the detectives show him the search warrant, he reluctantly lets them through the gate.

Because Haro and Soler have already questioned Hambleton and established a rapport, they, along with Ito, will interview him in RHD's traveling command post, a mobile home outfitted with a table and chairs that another detective has driven to the desert. Eguchi and a few other detectives will search the cluttered ranch-style house—a bachelor's residence with a dartboard in the living room and a coffee table covered with *National Enquirers*. Tacked on a wall, beside a window shaded by threadbare drapes, is a newspaper article about how police cannot protect witnesses.

Hambleton, in his mid-sixties, is a desert rat, a wrinkled, grizzled character with a bushy mustache and a fringe of gray hair. He frustrates Haro and Soler by sticking to the story that Blake discussed only a movie project with him. Eventually he acknowledges that a few days after Bakley was killed, he told the handyman that Blake had offered him $100,000 to kill her, but he insists he made up the story only because he wanted to "seed" his friend—to determine if he was a snitch.

"I knew that if it came back to me, then this gentleman was, in fact, nothing more than a snitch. And I don't like snitches around me. . . . After the incident I figured, well, we'll find out if he's a yackety yacker. . . . That's why we're talking now."

Ito eventually joins in the questioning. "Don't you think it's kind of odd that you meet with Blake and a few weeks later she's dead?"

"Yes it is," Hambleton says earnestly.

"Isn't it true," Ito asks, "that . . . he gets ahold of you for one reason: it's to kill his wife. And you turned him down. Isn't that the main reason you met with him? And it wasn't for no bull script."

"It was specifically for a script," he insists.

Soler asks whether he is willing to take a polygraph exam.

Hambleton says he is not familiar with polygraphs and does not trust them. After a few more minutes of jousting, he finally acknowledges that he is afraid to cooperate with the detectives because he associates with members of the Hell's Angels and the Mongols motorcycle gangs. They hate snitches: "I know for goddamn sure if I go and testify in a huge case of this nature, I know the collar I'll be wearing and I know my life's not going to be worth a shit."

"How do you know we'll ever need you to testify?" Ito asks. "You don't know that for sure."

"If you guys give me an affidavit that I don't have to testify, I'll be happy to tell you what I know."

"We can't do that," says Ito.

"Then I don't know nothin'," he says sullenly.

Soler asks, "What would it take to get you to tell us the truth? Would it take a relocation out of state?"

Hambleton considers the question for a few seconds. "You guys can prove the case without me being involved. I have no doubts in your capabilities. You guys are sharp as a tack. It isn't worth it to me to put myself in that position."

Ito says, "You didn't answer my partner's question. What would it take?"

"I don't know," Hambleton says wearily.

"You're not being totally truthful with us," Ito says.

Hambleton laughs. "I think I've copped to that. I think *that's* pretty well established." His mood quickly changes and he says, his voice straining in frustration, "For crying out loud, I'm trying to be righteous. But I'm over a barrel."

Finally, when Ito is certain Hambleton will not deviate from his story, he asks, "If you were on your deathbed, would you tell us the truth?"

"I imagine on my deathbed I would," he says, chuckling.

When the interview is over Ito discovers that the detectives searching the house did not have much luck, either. Eguchi drives back to the city in a glum mood as Ito dozes off in the front seat.

After the Memorial Day weekend, Ito compiles a list of about a dozen stuntmen who worked with Blake in the past. During the next few weeks, he plans to slog through the list, interview each stuntman, and hope Blake solicited one of them. Ito also plans to question Snuffy again—since he was Blake's go-between with both McLarty and Hambleton—and hopes he is more forthcoming.

For three and a half weeks, the investigation has hummed along briskly, the detectives following up on critical clues and tracking down significant leads. Now the next phase of the case begins, the tedious process of reinterviewing people, attempting to persuade reluctant witnesses to talk, pressing the crime lab for results, chasing marginal tips and peripheral players. As Ito compiles a to-do list, a detective informs him that the film *Pearl Harbor* just opened and says, "That's one movie that should cheer you up."

"I'll be yelling in the theater, 'Go get 'em, Uncle. Way to go. You got another one.' " Ito laughs and says, "I'll watch *Pearl Harbor* every night. I just won't see *Midway*."

"You'll get shot in the theater and it'll be just another OIS we'll have to respond to," another detective says.

The deputy district attorney assigned to the Blake case is Greg Dohi, who is half Japanese, which inspires more kidding by the detectives. Rick Jackson, who investigated the murders of Yuriko and Michelle Taga, calls out across the room to Ito: "In my case the victims are Japanese but the detectives and the DA are white. How come in your case the victim is white but the detectives and the DA are Japanese? We should switch."

Later in the morning Dohi stops by to confer with Ito and Eguchi. Ito stands up when he sees Dohi, gives him a mock bow, and grunts, "Dohi-san."

"We need to get Lance Ito [the Japanese-American judge assigned to the O. J. Simpson trial] on this case," jokes Ito. (He is not related to the judge.) "Then we'll really know we've taken over the L.A. justice system."

Crisscrossing the country interviewing Bakley's friends and family, Knolls and McCartin have neglected the Lourdes Unson murder. But on a late afternoon in early June, a Hollywood detective calls them. Their Armenian suspect, a parole violator, has just been picked up and is being held at the Hollywood station.

As they cruise toward Hollywood, Knolls realizes that this might be one of his last interviews as a Homicide Special detective. In a few weeks he will transfer to a Valley division where he will work as a patrol sergeant. Knolls is tired of all the late-night and early-morning officer-involved-shooting callouts and the mountains of paperwork that must be filed. He joined Homicide Special because he wanted to work only complex homicides, and he has been increasingly frustrated by the distractions. But he is also leaving because he has missed the street, missed teaching rookies the nuances of patrol work, missed the satisfaction he felt when he grabbed a young cop by the gun belt and pulled him off a belligerent suspect before he took a swing and endangered his career.

McCartin and most of the other detectives believe that Homicide Special, despite its drawbacks, is the apex of investigative work and they think Knolls is making a mistake. One day, Knolls figures, he will probably return to detective work, but for now he is ready for a patrol car. He tells McCartin that he is looking forward to returning to the Valley, where he was raised. But the Valley now bears no resemblance to the bucolic place he recalls from his boyhood, when he would hop on his bicycle and ride east from his home in Panorama City and pedal past orange groves, the blossoms redolent on warm afternoons, and through dairies where the dust and smell of cow manure hung in the air.

A century ago, the San Fernando Valley was a vast, dusty wasteland encircled by low-lying mountain ranges. Not yet part of Los Angeles, the sparsely populated landscape lacked the one element farmers needed to harvest crops and investors needed to subdivide the land: water.

The story of how the San Fernando Valley evolved into the country's prototypical suburban development is, like so many other chapters of Los Angeles history, a story of how a group of powerful men despoiled the environment, defied nature, and duped the public in order to make a great fortune on Southern California real estate.

At the turn of the century, 100,000 people lived in Los Angeles. During the next four years the population doubled and the area suffered an extended drought—two intertwined events that prompted ambitious civic leaders to seek additional water sources.

In 1904, William Mulholland, the superintendent of the Los Angeles Department of Water and Power, and Fred Eaton, who preceded

Mulholland as superintendent and was also a former mayor, devised an improbable plan. After a trip to the eastern slope of the Sierra Nevada Mountains, they decided that an aqueduct could siphon off water to Los Angeles from the Owens River, 233 miles to the northeast, and solve the city's problems.

This new supply greatly exceeded Los Angeles's needs, so instead of selling the excess water, Mulholland believed, Los Angeles should annex great swaths of land, such as the San Fernando Valley, and provide the new territory with the surplus. An aqueduct, Mulholland told a city commission, "will give Los Angeles standing as the metropolis of the Pacific Coast."

In order to buy Owens Valley land and water rights cheaply from local ranchers and to prevent land speculation based on inside information, the aqueduct plan was kept secret.

But not long after Mulholland and Eaton had returned from their fact-finding mission in the Owens Valley, where they concluded that the aqueduct plan was feasible, a syndicate of investors, which included some of Southern California's wealthiest and most influential men, quietly optioned 16,000 acres of San Fernando Valley real estate at the rock-bottom price of $35 an acre. The syndicate members included the *Los Angeles Times*'s owner, Harrison Gray Otis; his son-in-law, *Times* general manager Harry Chandler; Edwin T. Earl, publisher of the *Los Angeles Express;* Henry E. Huntington, founder of the Pacific Electric Railway; and Edward H. Harriman, chairman of the Union Pacific Railroad.

Eaton and Mulholland had surreptitiously secured land and water rights along forty miles of the Owens River. Later, Eaton and a group of Los Angeles officials, posing as cattle ranchers, claimed their option on the property.

In the summer of 1905, one day after the city's Board of Water commissioners privately approved the aqueduct plan, the prominent syndicate members purchased the San Fernando Valley acreage. It defies credulity to suggest that these powerful men were not aware of the privileged information. Many believed they had been tipped off: one of the syndicate members, a streetcar magnate named Moses Sherman, also sat on the water board.

During the next few years, Otis and Chandler regularly ran articles in the *Los Angeles Times* about the city's great water crisis and the critical need for the aqueduct. In one editorial the paper railed that anyone who voted against the funding of the aqueduct would be "placing himself in the attitude of an enemy of the city." When the bond issue was approved in 1907, few were aware of the great fortune Otis and Chandler were about to make and their role in the real estate scam.

In 1909, four years before the aqueduct was completed, Otis, Chandler, Sherman, and two other partners, using their profits from the previous land grab, bought a massive Valley tract of almost 50,000 acres, again for a bargain price: $53 an acre.

When the aqueduct opened, more than 40,000 people gathered along a hillside in the San Fernando Valley for a fireworks show and the firing of military guns. As mountain snowmelt cascaded down the spillway, Mulholland turned toward the mayor and said, "There it is. Take it."

The San Fernando Valley was the beneficiary of so much water that until development ranged from mountain range to mountain range, agriculture thrived between the subdivisions. But the Owens Valley, drained of its vast water supply, was ravaged. Eventually most farmers and ranchers abandoned the land, and several towns in the area shut down. The once immense, turquoise Owens Lake was sucked so dry the wind kicked up huge alkaline dust storms, spewing noxious clouds and creating a health risk for residents.

Los Angeles, however, prospered. Aqueduct water fueled the massive growth and watered the lush lawns—and later the backyard swimming pools—of countless subdivisions. By 1925, the city's population had grown to 1.2 million. Soon, Los Angeles was—after Cairo—the largest desert city in the world.

The Armenian suspect is waiting for Knolls and McCartin in a Hollywood Division interview room lined with graffiti-scarred perforated panels. He is in his late twenties, big and burly, with close-cropped black hair, and he wears a V-neck velour shirt, khaki pants, and black loafers. His left arm is cuffed to his chair. After a few preliminary questions, the detectives conclude he is not very bright. He has difficulty responding to even the most basic query and stares at them with a bovine expression, mouth open, eyes opaque.

"Where do you work?" McCartin asks.

He stares at McCartin, concentrating on the question. "I don't."

"How do you get money?"

"My cousin gives me money," he says. "I can't read too good. I have a slow memory."

"Where does your mother live?" Knolls asks.

"What does that have to do with anything?" he asks. He knows that Knolls and McCartin are homicide detectives, so he asks whether the interview is connected to the murder at his mother's apartment building.

"How'd you hear about that?" Knolls asks.

A neighbor told his mother, he says.

"When was the last time you were there?" Knolls asks.

The suspect spends several minutes trying to figure out where he lived the past few months and when he last stopped by his mother's apartment, but the story is so convoluted that McCartin finally asks in frustration, "Are you under the care of a doctor?"

"I use to be," the man says. "I use to take stress medication."

Eventually he figures out that he visited his mother around Christmas.

Because he was so vague about the dates, Knolls tells him, "You're giving us a lot of reasons for you to do bad things."

He nervously massages his collarbone. "I'm not stupid enough to harm somebody."

Knolls asks whether he knew the woman who was killed.

"She lived in the building," he says, avoiding Knolls's gaze.

"What part of the building?" McCartin asks.

"Next door," he says, still looking away.

"You know her?"

"Not really."

When they ask him a few more questions about where he lived recently and the cousin he briefly stayed with, he tugs at his hair and cries, "My head is blowing up. I'm getting frustrated. Why you want to know about my family?"

After the detectives calm him down, he explains that after Christmas he spent a few months in Mexico.

The man has difficulty remembering when he returned, so Knolls asks him, "Do you know when Easter is?"

"Is it in June?" he asks.

"We're in June *now*," Knolls says impatiently.

"I don't know," the man says, closing his eyes and grimacing. "My head's messed up. I'm stressed out." He eventually figures out that he left Mexico in April.

Unson was murdered in mid-April and McCartin wants to pin

down an exact date for the the man's return to Los Angeles. But he says he cannot remember. McCartin then asks whether it is possible that he visited his mother at her apartment *after* his trip to Mexico.

The man stares at McCartin suspiciously. "What for?"

"Because you're a good son," Knolls says sarcastically.

McCartin loses his temper and snaps, "It's a simple question."

The man finally says that because he was on the run from his parole officers, he avoided his mother's apartment when he returned from Mexico: he knew they would look for him there.

When McCartin presses him about exact dates, the man clenches his teeth and groans, "I don't know. Something's fucked up in my head. I got fucked-up head problems."

When he calms down, Knolls shows him a picture of Unson and asks if he ever talked to her.

The man shakes his head.

"How often did you see her?" McCartin asks.

"A few times."

"Did you ever visit her in her apartment?"

"No."

"You ever been to her apartment?"

He drops his chin to his fist and says, "No."

McCartin leans across the table and says sharply, "Did you do it?"

He crosses his arms and says, "No."

"Did *you* kill her?"

"No!" he says, emphatically.

"You ever hear of DNA?"

He nods.

"If you ever visited her, tell us now, so if we found some of your DNA in there—"

The man interjects that he never once visited the apartment.

"You sure we're not going to find your DNA?" McCartin asks. "If there's a reason for it, I want to know now. This little case you have here is *nothing*. You'll be facing a murder and end up on Death Row."

The man shakes his head and waves a palm.

"You willing to take a poly?" McCartin asks.

He nods without hesitation. "Bring it."

After the interview, both detectives have throbbing headaches. They walk out into the squad room and collapse into chairs.

"This guy's a friggin' numbnuts," McCartin says with disgust.

"He's definitely a wack job," Knolls says. "My concern is because he's such a dumb fuck, he could have been manipulated into going along. Maybe he's involved but he didn't do it himself."

"At least we know where he is now," McCartin says. "He'll be locked up for a while."

The detectives believe it is significant that the man readily agreed to take the polygraph. And he insisted he never visited Unson's apartment, even when they continued to press him. A guilty man might have said that he was once inside the apartment for some innocuous reason. Even a suspect this dim is familiar with fingerprints and DNA. But until they receive the lab results from the murder scene and track down the other suspect, they will not know for sure whether he is the killer.

A few days later, a television reporter in Louisiana calls Homicide Special and tells a detective he recently talked to a friend of Bakley's who has inside information on the murder. McCartin and Bub—who has replaced Knolls on the travel team because he is preparing to transfer—fly to Louisiana to question the woman. Once they hear what she has to say, they immediately call Ito.

One Friday night in early May, the woman told detectives, Bakley called from her cell phone. She said she had just dined with Blake and was sitting in his car, alone, down the street from the restaurant. After they chatted for a few minutes, Bakley whispered, sounding frightened, "There's somebody coming."

The friend told Bakley to flee.

"It's okay," Bakley responded with obvious relief. "It's Blake."

Then the friend heard two pops and the line went dead. She was so shocked she dropped the phone and fell down, injuring her eye so badly she had to go to the emergency room. The next day she learned that Bakley had been murdered.

McCartin and Bub tell Ito they will try to confirm her story by checking hospital records for the time and date she was treated.

"If her story checks out," Ito tells Eguchi, "we could book Blake tomorrow."

26

Exactly a month after the Bakley murder, Ito and Eguchi greet a new partner, Detective Brian Tyndall. Tyndall is fifty-three and, with his shaved head, looks like an Irish Telly Savalas. Almost three years ago he was working in RHD's bank robbery section when he was assigned to an LAPD task force investigating the Rampart scandal. Ito, who just learned that the task force is breaking up, asked Tatreau if Tyndall could be assigned to the Blake case. Ito knows Eguchi, who recently passed the detective exam, eventually will be shipped out to another division.

During the 1980s, when Ito worked Hollywood Homicide, he investigated a case with Tyndall, who was a homicide detective at the old Venice station. Ito was impressed with Tyndall's intelligence and professionalism and they stayed in touch over the years. Ito figures that Tyndall's experience on the Rampart task force, which was such a high-profile, politically sensitive assignment, will be extremely helpful on the Blake investigation.

Ito spends the morning in an interview room briefing Tyndall. He relates the story told by Bakley's friend from Louisiana—which he says, ruefully, has only one thing wrong with it. When McCartin and Bub examined hospital records they found that the friend—who said she visited the emergency room after the conversation—was treated about three hours *before* Bakley was killed.

A few days later, on an overcast June morning, Ito, Tyndall, and Eguchi, along with Hartwell and Tatreau, walk a few blocks to the Criminal Court Building, take the elevator to the eighteenth floor, and meet with several lawyers from the district attorney's office in their conference room. Ito details the investigation, from the night Blake and Bakley met, to her pregnancy and their custody battle, to her murder, to the interviews with the retired stuntmen. He concludes with the friend from Louisiana. McCartin and Bub, Ito says, think she's highly unreliable.

"I don't think so," Tatreau says, laughing. "I think she's a witness who can definitely be rehabilitated."

After a few of the deputy DAs and their supervisors pepper him with questions, Ito says, "You know what's interesting? During his interview with the North Hollywood detectives, Blake never asks what happened to her—did she get shot, stabbed, beat with a baseball bat, or whatever."

Ito adds that a few days after Blake met with McLarty, he called him back at home, but McLarty again refused to do the job.

"You know why he wouldn't do it?" Tatreau says, as the DAs nod thoughtfully. "Because he knew Ito was on call."

A prosecutor chuckles and then suggests that the detectives question Snuffy again.

Ito nods. "We want to work on some other stuntmen first and then we'll go back to him.

"Why do you think Blake did it?" another prosecutor asks.

"He wanted the kid and his daughter's in her thirties with no kids," Ito says.

A prosecutor recommends that the detectives interview Blake's nanny, who witnessed how he lured Bakley out to California, grabbed the baby, set up the phony arrest, and sent Bakley back to Arkansas.

"That's motive, too," a prosecutor says.

Ito explains that he believes Blake shot Bakley, coated the gun with oil to eliminate fingerprints, and then tossed it in the Dumpster. He is still trying to trace the provenance of the gun.

The prosecutor asks Ito whether he thinks a hitman hired by Blake could have shot Bakley and dumped the gun.

"That's kind of Hollywood," Ito says.

"This *is* Hollywood," the prosecutor retorts. Everyone laughs.

Ito shakes his head and says, "A third party wouldn't dump it."

"Why not?" the prosecutor asks.

"I've been working murders eighteen years and I've never seen a contract killer dump a gun at the scene."

Another prosecutor says that the McLarty solicitation is a break, but the key to the case is persuading Hambleton to talk.

Ito mentions that Hambleton is facing a misdemeanor weapons charge in San Bernardino County for brandishing a rifle at sheriff's deputies at the edge of his property.

"A misdemeanor's not much leverage," a prosecutor says.

Ito tells them that Blake had an income of more than $800,000 in 1999.

"So he can fund a pretty good defense team," a prosecutor says. He looks around at the scuffed linoleum floor and generic county furniture and deadpans, "But they won't have as nice a conference room as this one."

When the meeting concludes, they walk back to Parker Center and Hartwell tells Ito, "What remains from the meeting is how much still needs to be done."

Ito adds a number of items to his to-do list, including interviewing the nanny, checking to see whether Blake usually parks in the lot at Vitello's, interviewing other stuntmen, reinterviewing Snuffy and Hambleton, obtaining Hambleton's phone records, checking on whether any of Blake's acquaintances recognize the murder weapon, and attempting to determine why no neighbors heard the shots.

Ito is discouraged. Although he has built the framework, there is still much work to do before the investigation is complete. An avid golfer, he has not been able to play since Bakley's murder. Every weekend he has either worked or been too tired to drive to the golf course. Usually in June, the days are long enough so he can play eighteen holes before dark. Now, he complains to Eguchi, he does not know when he will swing his clubs again.

Ito, Eguchi, and Tyndall spend the next few weeks attempting to track down a dozen stuntmen who once worked with Blake. Most of them know one another and the detectives soon gain insight, they believe, into why Blake contacted McLarty and Hambleton.

Hambleton, who was known to have a nasty temper, once had a beef with another stuntman who attempted to break the men's land speed record. His car's parachute, which was supposed to serve as a brake, did not open and the stuntman's car sped off in the desert for about five miles before it finally came to a stop. Later, he discovered the strings to his parachute had been severed with battery acid, accord-

ing to a stuntman Ito recently interviewed. He added that nothing was
ever proved, but at the monthly stuntman meetings, Hambleton, fear-
ing a reprisal, began packing a gun. During the past few years, Hambleton, suffering from serious health problems and needing a liver
transplant, has not worked.

McLarty had worked on more than a hundred television shows and
movies, including *Last Action Hero, Beverly Hills Cop,* and *Convoy.*
In 1982, he was involved in one of the worst stunt disasters in Hollywood history, on the set of *Twilight Zone—the Movie.* McLarty was
one of the pilots of a helicopter that crashed in a riverbed near two
child actors and Vic Morrow, all three of whom were killed. Although
that accident did not derail his career, more recently he had been out
of work, embroiled in a bitter divorce, and short of money.

The detectives also discovered that a few months before the murder Snuffy had called a stuntman's organization and told the secretary
he wanted to ask Bobby Bass, a former *Baretta* stuntman, to call
Blake at home. But the secretary would not give out his phone number. Snuffy finally obtained the number elsewhere, but Bass, who was
suffering from Parkinson's disease, was not interested in meeting
Blake.

After the detectives interview many of the former *Baretta* stuntmen,
they discern a pattern. Blake was interested in Hambleton and Bass,
they believe, because they are both critically ill, need money, and have
little to lose. McLarty, too, is financially strapped. And he once killed
a man.

Now that Ito has a better feel for the stuntmen and their relationship
with Blake, he calls Snuffy and attempts to reinterview him. But now
Snuffy will not talk. He tells Ito to call his attorney.

A few days later, the detectives brief Deputy District Attorney Greg
Dohi, who has been spending more and more time in the squad room,
conferring with the detectives. They meet in one of the small windowless interview rooms, which is sweltering. During frigid winter mornings, the air conditioner in the squad room often blasted cold air.
Now, on a hot June afternoon, heat emanates from the vents. Ito tugs
on his collar and says, "Let's cut to the chase. Blake either fired a gun
or was in an area where a gun was fired."

"So we have GSR particles?" Dohi asks.

Ito nods and tells him gunshot residue was found on Blake's clothing. And Ito recently received a positive result from the GSR test on
Blake's hands—but, he explains, the criminalist hedged a bit, writing

in his report that "if Mr. Blake is in the environment of firearms, i.e. handles firearms on a regular basis, then these results could be the result of contact."

Frowning and crossing his arms, Ito tells Dohi that the detective in charge of Blake's clothes left them boxed up in the trunk of his car all night, instead of booking them into evidence that evening.

They are all aware of how a defense attorney can spin this information into a massive web of police conspiracy. "Uh-oh," Dohi says. "Any guns in the trunk?"

"I don't think so," Ito says.

"We're going to need a statement from him about what he keeps in the trunk, and have the area checked for GSR."

"We'll swab the area," Ito says.

Dohi shakes his head and says weakly, "It is what it is."

But as Ito tells Dohi more about his interviews with the stuntmen, his mood brightens. Even with the clothing in the detective's trunk, Dohi says, the GSR results are good news.

The next afternoon, the detectives, armed with a search warrant, stop by Earle Caldwell's apartment. Ito is not hopeful that he will find anything important, but Dohi urges him to make the attempt anyway.

Caldwell lives the life of the Hollywood fringe player. His studio is perched over a garage, overlooking an alley, in a modest Burbank neighborhood of nondescript apartment buildings. The detectives find $2,000 in cash inside, as well as two pistols and two shotguns. Caldwell tells them that he recently cashed his last paycheck and that he inherited the weapons from his father, who was a gunsmith. But then, from the bottom of a cup holder in Caldwell's car, beneath a few gas and food receipts, Eguchi pulls out a folded-up piece of yellow legal paper, torn in half, with a handwritten list: "2 shovels, small sledge, 25-auto, get blank gun ready, old rugs, duct tape—black, Draino [sic], pool acid, lye, shovels." Eguchi also finds a World War II-era Mauser in a desiccated leather case in the car's center console. Caldwell claims this, too, was part of his father's collection.

The detectives are ecstatic. The list, they believe, implies that Caldwell intended to dispose of a body. And if he owns one vintage German pistol, maybe he was in possession of a Walther P-38, too.

In the morning, Caldwell's attorney calls Ito and explains that there is an innocent explanation for the list. Most of the items, which Caldwell never ended up purchasing, were for repairs at Blake's house; the lye was for the swimming pool.

After Ito hangs up, Tyndall says, "It looks to me like a 'kill Bonny' list."

"I think we hit the jackpot," Eguchi agrees.

The detectives are always amused by the frequently inaccurate television news reports and Hartwell shares the latest: "I saw one guy on TV who said that the LAPD is replacing the entire Blake team."

Another detective calls out across the room, "I saw another one last night who said, 'Some crimes never get solved and this will be one of them.'"

The next week Tyndall flies to the Bay Area, where Caldwell's wife lives. (They are apparently separated.) He confirms that Caldwell and his wife spent the evening of Bakley's murder with another couple. Tyndall also attempts to learn whether any of Caldwell's friends, acquaintances, or former coworkers ever saw him or his father with a Walther P-38. Tyndall brings a photograph, but no one can identify the gun, which remains a mystery. Neither ATF documents nor any state databases list the weapon. The detectives' last hope is that ATF employees, who are now hand-searching archives of German war relics brought to the United States, will unearth some record of the Walther.

The detectives are still attempting to determine why no neighbors heard the gunshot. They confer with a firearms expert at an LAPD gun range, who suggests several possibilities. Because the tip of the slug is somewhat flat and crimped at the edges, someone might have removed it with a "bullet-puller," he says, dumped half the gunpowder out, and pounded the tip back on. The noise from the shot, he says, would have been muffled significantly. A simple, handmade silencer, he tells the detectives, can also significantly cut the decibel level. Demonstrating, he cuts the top off a plastic water bottle and tapes it to the muzzle of a pistol. He aims toward a target surrounded by countless brass shell casings that glitter in the sunshine. When he fires, the sound is merely a dull thud.

The detectives decide to visit the Indiana factory where the Remington-Peters bullets were manufactured and see if they can learn more about the ammunition.

The detectives spend the Fourth of July in the squad room, sifting again through the stacks of letters sent to Bakley to ensure they have not missed a threat. During a break, Ito convinces Eguchi to help him this weekend at the annual Obon festival at a temple in Little Tokyo.

The festival resembles All Souls' Day: Buddhists honor the dead, and the temple sponsors Japanese cultural exhibits.

On Friday afternoon, the day before the festival, Ito, Eguchi, and Tyndall drive to the Hollywood Hills to interview Cody Blackwell, the woman who posed as Blake's nanny when Bakley was duped into handing over the baby. Blackwell has already sold her story to a tabloid, so the detectives have a general sense of her role in the drama. Witnesses who were paid by tabloids proved controversial in the O. J. Simpson case; prosecutors, believing their credibility had been compromised, never called them at trial. Ito hopes that when the Blake case is filed the prosecutors will have a more open-minded view.

Blackwell lives in a small pink cottage, a rustic aerie grafted onto the side of a steep canyon overgrown with brush. The detectives have to climb more than a hundred rickety wooden steps to reach her door. The morning is warm and unusually humid. July is typically hot and dry in Los Angeles—desert weather—but yesterday a muggy monsoon from northern Mexico, a wind-fed summer storm, blew into Southern California, generating lightning and thundershowers. Now, standing on Blackwell's porch, with the clusters of eucalyptus, squat palm trees, and bamboo dripping with moisture, Ito feels as if he is in a Hawaiian rain forest, not ten minutes from Hollywood Boulevard.

When the detectives introduce themselves, Blackwell says, "I've been waiting for you guys to show up," and invites them inside. The cement floor is splashed with swirls of yellow, purple, and blue paint, and plants hang from the ceiling. Beside her bed, yoga books and Indian statues are stacked on purple milk crates, and Native American drums, feathers, and pictures of wolves line the walls. Blackwell, who is sixty, has bright red hair and wears khaki shorts and a T-shirt. She sits on the side of her bed, her two enormous dogs—an Alaskan malamute and a wolf hybrid—growling at her feet. The detectives pull up chairs beside her.

"I'm glad you're Japanese," she says to Ito. "I have a new Japanese friend and I don't know how to pronounce her name."

After Ito helps her out, she recounts her role in the drama with the baby. She had once worked as Blake's personal assistant, she says, but had not talked to him for a while. In September he called, told her about his two-month-old baby, Rose, and said that the mother would be arriving in a week. He asked Blackwell if she would move into his house and temporarily play the role of nanny.

"I moved some stuff in . . . and he says, 'No. I want you to move your *homey* stuff in. Make it look like you've been living here.' "

Blackwell shopped with Blake and he spent $900 on items for the baby, including a car seat, stroller, diapers, bibs, and toys. He then began vilifying Bakley. "She's the scum of the earth," he told Blackwell. "She's involved with drug dealers, racketeering, bikers, and all these seedy people that rip people off. She's horrible. She's awful and I can't stand her."

The way Bakley had duped Blake enraged him, she says. "He doesn't kiss anyone's ass. He's a total control freak. For him to have someone manipulate him must have sent him over the edge. Just up a tree. He said, 'I'll do whatever's necessary to get this baby.' "

Blake introduced her to a man he called Moose, who was wearing camouflage fatigues and combat boots. When she describes him, the detectives realize Moose is Caldwell.

Blake told Blackwell, " 'I want her to feel really secure with you watching the baby. We're going to tell her you're a nurse and your name is Nancy.' Then I started wondering. I said, 'Robert, this is really weird.' "

When he drove to the airport to pick up Bakley, Blackwell remained at the house and chatted with Moose, who told her, "I'm just here to make sure things don't get out of hand. . . . If things get wild and crazy I'm here to subdue her."

When Blake returned, Moose dropped to the ground and crawled to the tool shed and hid inside. Blackwell demonstrates by jumping off her bed and inching along the floor on her hands and knees. "I'm thinking, 'Oh my God! Oh my God!' Then I saw her and my mouth fell open. She didn't look exactly like I expected. Her hair was fried, like cotton candy. She was chubby, old. I was surprised. She didn't look like a woman he'd have a baby with. But she seemed nice."

Blake pulled Blackwell aside and said, "We're going to lunch. Moose is hiding. You take care of the baby." He then told Bakley, "It's okay. She's a nurse."

Fifteen minutes later, Blake called her and said, "I want you to take the baby up to your house. Leave now!" Blackwell hugs one of her dogs and says, "That's when I started getting really scared. I didn't know what to do. I haven't been a mother in thirty or forty years."

An hour later, Blake called Blackwell at home and told her to meet him at a liquor store parking lot near his house. When she arrived, she handed the baby to Blake and he paid her $300. Blake rocked his daughter and whispered to her, "Well, kid, from here on out it's just you and me. Just the two of us." Blackwell tells the detectives, "I'm going, 'Oh my God! I've been involved in a kidnapping.' I'm freaking out." Blake then said to Blackwell, "Okay, you're coming with me." He instructed her to lie down in the back of the SUV and hold the baby while he drove. He stopped at a McDonald's in Calabasas, where he gave Blackwell $10 for a meal.

"I know he'd just bought his daughter a big house [nearby]. It doesn't take a rocket scientist to know why we were there. He was taking the baby to his daughter's."

An hour later Blake returned, without the baby, and said that Bakley "is out of the state. I don't have to worry about her." As he drove Blackwell back to Studio City so she could pick up her car, he ranted about what he would do if Bakley's friends returned for the baby. "Just let those motherfuckers come to my house," he told Blackwell. "I'm ready for them. Let 'em come over the fence. I'll shoot 'em like dogs and let the birds pick their bones."

"I thought I was in a B movie," Blackwell says. Back at home, she panicked.

"Oh my God," she says. "Now I'm an accomplice to a kidnapping." She cries, dabs her eyes with a tissue, and asks the detectives, "Am I going to be in trouble? Am I going to be arrested?"

Ito shakes his head and says softly, "No."

Ito shows her a photograph of Caldwell and she shouts, "That's Moose!"

Later, as the detectives stand up to leave, Ito asks her, "Why didn't his daughter have kids?"

"He mentioned his daughter and her boyfriend were trying to have a baby but weren't having any luck. And he was implying if anything happened, that's where Rosie would go."

As the detectives head back down the canyon, through the mist, Ito says, "She's the first person to confirm the angle about the daughter."

Tyndall taps the murder book and says, "Blake's shit just got a whole bunch weaker."

27

Three months after Lourdes Unson's murder, McCartin is still waiting for fingerprint and lab results. Knolls is working as a patrol sergeant in Van Nuys, so, for now, McCartin is tracking the case alone.

One hair was found on Unson's body and one on the mattress. If technicians can find a root, DNA can be obtained from the hair. But even when there is no root, sometimes the race of the suspect can be determined, which would help McCartin enormously. No body fluids were recovered after the sexual assault, but skin tissue was found under Unson's nails, which is also being tested for DNA.

McCartin has been so busy on the Blake case he has had little time to devote to the Unson murder. He felt particularly guilty when he met one of her brothers, a monsignor in the Philippines, who recently visited Los Angeles to settle her estate. The man stopped by the squad room and told McCartin how many Irish priests he had enjoyed working with in Manila. Then he shook McCartin's hand, stared into his eyes intently, and murmured, "I have faith in you."

Two other cases from the past year have lost momentum. Dave Lambkin and Tim Marcia have been so busy investigating the murder of an elderly Valley couple, they have had little time for the Stephanie Gorman case. And Paul Coulter and Jerry Stephens, after months of intensively tracking the Susan Berman homicide, are discouraged because the more they learn about Nyle, the more certain they are that he is not the killer. After questioning many more people, they have a better understanding of Nyle. What motive he might have remains obscure and he simply does not seem to be the type who would kill a woman. His friends and acquaintances contended it was unlikely he would own or even have access to a gun. Although the handwriting analyst reported that it was "highly probable" that Nyle wrote the note to the Beverly Hills Police Department alerting them to the corpse, that finding was far from a conclusive identification. Coulter and Stephens still hope to interview Robert Durst, but a few weeks ago they were pulled off the Berman case to investigate the murder of a teenage girl whose body was dumped in Elysian Park.

Ito and his team have been working the Bakley homicide since early May, and they feel they have put together a comprehensive enough case to book Blake for murder. Greg Dohi recently presented the evidence to his superiors at the DA's office; now, he sets up a meeting with the detectives on a Monday afternoon in mid-July.

Ito, Eguchi, Tyndall, Lieutenant Hartwell, McCartin, Bub, and Whelan meet with Dohi in the captain's empty office. Dohi, who slips off his suit coat, is wearing suspenders with a blue and white diamond pattern, a blue button-down shirt, and a red tie. While some deputy district attorneys imperiously order cops about, Dohi always couches his requests in a respectful, soft-spoken manner that the detectives appreciate.

Dohi hands out a document he has put together: "The Case Against Robert Blake." After they spend several minutes riffling through the pages, Dohi says, "I think we have a number of bases for prosecution."

He points to the document, which lists the main points: "Scientific/Physical Evidence"; "Motive/State of Mind"; "Hitmen"; "Statements"; "Witnesses at the Scene."

"Tell me if you think I'm wrong," Dohi says, "but I feel we're getting close."

"I think you're right," Ito says.

Dohi begins by asking Ito about the scientific evidence. "What more can we get on the gun?"

"We're not done yet," Ito says. The World War II–era German pistol found in Caldwell's car, he explains, suggests that the bodyguard may have provided Blake with the Walther P-38. They still plan to interview more friends and acquaintances of Caldwell and his late father.

"If we get a friend who says they saw him with several war relics, we've got a circumstantial case," Tyndall says.

Dohi nods.

Ito is still waiting to learn whether the DNA in the vomit found on Blake's car was his.

"How could he shoot her twice and no one hear?" Dohi says.

"If you fire in a car I don't know what it sounds like," Ito says.

"No stippling?" Dohi asks.

Ito shakes his head. "But if you take half the powder out there'd be less sound and less stippling." He adds that he will soon visit the plant that manufactured the bullets.

"What do you think about the oil on the gun?" Dohi asks.

"He could have told her the car needed oil," Tyndall says. "Then he opens the hood, pulls the gun out, and boom, boom."

"He'd oil the gun *after* he shot it," Ito says.

"Anyone see grease on his hands?" Dohi says.

"He had plenty of time to wipe them," Ito says.

They then discuss a number of tapes Blake made—apparently for himself, as a cathartic exercise—in which he describes how his father abused him, declares he hates his mother, and says both parents robbed him of his childhood.

"After dating a psychologist for eight years," Dohi says, "my interpretation is he wanted to save this little girl from the exploitation and abuse that he endured. And we've got a victim who leeched onto a guy with a hair-trigger temper."

"If those North Hollywood detectives had your psychological insight," Whalen jokes, "Blake would have copped right then and saved us all this hassle."

"The baby's real but the marriage is a farce," Ito says.

"I think this will be the strongest part of our case—how much he hates her," Dohi says. "Was it obvious to him that she was shot?"

Ito laughs. "Well, there was a bullet hole in her head."

"But all he said that night to witnesses was that there was something wrong with her," Dohi says.

"In my experience," Ito says, "suspects avoid saying exactly what happened to avoid particulars."

"You feel comfortable there's no more potential hitmen out there?" Dohi asks.

Ito nods.

"You going to talk to Blake's daughter?" Dohi asks.

"Isn't that risky?" Ito asks. "What'll we gain?"

"She'll probably tell you to pound sand, but you never know until you try," Dohi says.

Ito asks Dohi about the witnesses who have been paid by the tabloids.

"I don't see it as a major problem in this case."

Dohi then directs them to the heading "To Be Done," which includes questioning Bakley's probation officer in Arkansas, her oldest daughter, and several of her ex-husbands; setting up a second interview with Caldwell and one of Blake's friends; rechecking Bakley's correspondence for any more possible threats; and a number of other time-consuming tasks.

After the meeting, Ito is a bit deflated. He has no doubt the case is a strong one, and he is encouraged by Dohi's certainty that a murder charge will eventually be filed. But he has spent two and a half months investigating this homicide—up to twelve hours a day, sometimes seven days a week—laboring under immense pressure and intense scrutiny. Now, realizing that he may have to spend more months reinterviewing witnesses, reexamining countless documents, retracing Blake's steps during his vacation with Bakley, reviewing every step of the investigation, he is suddenly exhausted and disheartened and knows he will feel no relief until he drives out to Blake's house and slaps the handcuffs on him.

One evening two weeks later, while Ito, Eguchi, and Tyndall are slogging through Dohi's To Be Done list, McCartin returns to the office and spots a note on his desk with a message to call the LAPD's latent print section. Although McCartin is weary at the end of a long day, he feels a rush of excitement because he figures a fingerprint technician has just identified a suspect in the Lourdes Unson murder. There are only two potential suspects, McCartin believes: the Armenian whose mother was a neighbor of the victim, and the tall black man who lived with a woman in the building. He has a distinctive name—Jammie Hendrix. But McCartin has not been able to do much work on the case lately, and every time he spots the murder book, which has been gathering dust on the edge of his desk, he feels a pang of conscience.

He immediately calls latent prints and hears the news he was hoping for: "We got a match on your case."

"Jammie Hendrix?" McCartin says.

"How'd you know?" the technician asks.

McCartin is exultant. "He's one of the guys we're looking at."

Hendrix left two fingerprints in the apartment: one inside the front door, and one on a bathroom wall. The print on the front door was lifted the first day. But the one on the bathroom wall is a testament to McCartin's and Knolls's thoroughness. Because they did not believe the fingerprint technician at the crime scene was sufficiently meticulous, they made arrangements for a new group of technicians to dust the apartment. That second team lifted the print on the bathroom wall.

The day after McCartin learns the good news, he calls Hendrix's former girlfriend and casually asks whether she knows where he is living. McCartin explains that he has talked to everyone else loosely connected to the case and just wants to bring Hendrix to the station for a routine interview. Hendrix is living in Austin, Texas, she says, and working for a telephone company.

A security officer at the company informs McCartin that Hendrix was hired June 4 and was involved in a sexual harassment incident the next month. He received one hour of counseling, never showed up for work again, and was officially fired July 24. Unfortunately, the only address he gave his employer was a post office box.

From an Austin Police Department detective, McCartin learns that Hendrix recently pawned five pieces of women's jewelry and a man's ring. A detective e-mails McCartin pictures, which he shows to several of Unson's coworkers. They recognize three of the pieces as Unson's.

On a Monday afternoon, a week after McCartin learns of the fingerprint match, he presents the case to a deputy district attorney, who files murder charges against Hendrix and issues an arrest warrant.

The next day McCartin and his new partner, Tom Mathew, fly to Texas and search for Hendrix. They cannot find him, but they do interview two women in Austin who recently filed assault reports against him. The women tell similar stories. When they first met the thirty-one-year-old Hendrix, they were drawn to his looks, charm, and affectionate manner, but when they were not in the mood for sex, he turned violent. Hendrix smacked one woman so hard, she said, he knocked her off the bed and then stomped on her. The other woman told police Hendrix picked her up by the neck and choked her until she passed out—which, since Unson was strangled, will be powerful testimony in court.

After examining Greyhound bus records, the detectives discover that Hendrix left Austin on July 30 and arrived in Los Angeles in August. McCartin searches a computerized database service that includes extensive public records and turns up an address for Hendrix in Los Angeles. He then checks utility records and discovers that the woman who rents the apartment works for a nonprofit organization that aids homeless people. The detectives, now familiar with Hendrix's approach, suspect that he has insinuated himself into this woman's life.

McCartin and Mathew decide to find the woman in the hopes she can lead them to Hendrix. Mathew, who was born in India and lived there until he was thirteen, is McCartin's best friend in the department. They have an easy camaraderie, but the other detectives—and some suspects—often haze him because Mathew is one of the few Indian cops in Southern California. In the squad room, the detectives call him Hadji after the elephant-riding character on the cartoon show *Jonny Quest,* and on the street suspects sometimes call him Snake Charmer, Gandhi, or 7-Eleven King. McCartin is one of the few detectives who uses his actual first name.

On a warm afternoon in mid-August, the detectives head to South San Julian Street, the central artery of downtown's skid row. In many areas of Los Angeles the sidewalks are almost always empty, but here they are clotted with the homeless, who sleep in cardboard boxes, sit on plastic milk crates, read Bibles beneath tarpaulins, push shopping carts, and lug black plastic garbage bags filled with clothes. Enterprising winos trudge down the street selling cigarettes and dollar T-shirts. A few transvestites, juggling pocket mirrors, apply makeup. The gutters overflow with trash, and pigeons peck at the rubble. Boom boxes blare along both sides of the street and the smell of ripe garbage, cheap wine, and marijuana drifts along the sidewalk. A few daring denizens fire up crack pipes with plastic lighters. In the distance, the skyscrapers of Bunker Hill tower above skid row, shimmering in the August heat.

The detectives stop by the homeless center where the woman they are looking for works. She is out for a few hours, so they leave a message for her with a clerk. They then show him a picture of Hendrix, whom he immediately recognizes. Hendrix is staying at a nearby hotel, he says.

The detectives walk through the dingy lobby, which smells of Lysol, past a few toothless residents staring vacantly at a small television. The manager confirms that Hendrix checked in for a few nights, but says he recently moved to another nearby hotel.

"We're just one step behind this fucker," Mathew mutters.

They stop by a few more dilapidated flophouses and end up at the Los Angeles Mission. When they find no record of Hendrix there, Mathew says, "Let's just walk the streets. Maybe we'll run into him."

There is a pocket park across from the mission and they decide to check it out. The park, enclosed by an eight-foot metal fence, teems with people dozing on the grass, sprawling on benches, or playing cards, chess, or dominoes on the cement tables beneath the jacarandas and spindly palms.

McCartin and Mathew, in their dark suits, white shirts, and ties, immediately draw suspicious stares and hostile glances as they cut through the park. When they reach the center, McCartin whispers, "Tom, I think it's him," and motions toward a black man with a small gold hoop earring standing beside a group of domino players and watching the game.

"I can't see his face too good," Mathew says. "He's looking down."

When the man briefly looks up, Mathew says, "That's him, man. Let's go."

As McCartin and Mathew casually stroll toward Hendrix, people in the park look up in alarm and scurry out onto the street. When the detectives reach the table, the players freeze. The detectives know they can cuff Hendrix, lock him up, and book him for murder. But they would much rather persuade him to ride with them to the station voluntarily and interview him first. Although his fingerprints were found in Unson's apartment, he might be savvy enough to devise an innocuous explanation. If, however, Hendrix denies ever visiting Unson, the case will be infinitely stronger.

They hope to immediately lower the tension level and convince Hendrix that he has nothing to fear. Just in case, Mathew has a hand in his pocket, on his Mace canister.

"Hey Jammie, where the fuck you been?" asks Mathew, who picked up a ghetto inflection during the years he spent as a gang cop in South-Central. "We been lookin' everywhere for you."

Hendrix shrugs. Unlike many of those in the park, he is clean-shaven and well groomed. Tall and muscular, he wears black and red Air Jordan basketball shoes with no laces, baggy beige shorts, and a T-shirt with a large DARE insignia, which the detectives find amusing, because DARE is an antidrug program created by the LAPD—Drug Abuse Resistance Education.

McCartin guides Hendrix away from the domino players, mentions the Unson murder, and asks Hendrix to ride with them back to the station for a routine interview.

Hendrix looks down at the detectives through his sunglasses, which are perched at the end of his nose, and asks sullenly, "What for?"

"You're the last witness we need to contact," McCartin says. He then adds reassuringly, "You'll be back before the next domino game."

"Why can't we do it here?" Hendrix asks.

"It's too noisy, too many people," McCartin says. "Come to our office. It's more comfortable."

Mathew puts his hand on Hendrix's shoulder and says, "Hey man, we're not trying to fuck with you. Ain't no big thing. If you saw some shit, you can tell us. If not, fuck it, you're gone."

"You're free to go whenever you want," McCartin adds. "We just got to get this done. It won't take more than a half hour."

Finally, Hendrix nods and follows them back to their car.

In the interview room, he keeps his sunglasses on and stares at the detectives, fists clenched. McCartin attempts to put him at ease so he can lure him into a trap.

"You're here as a witness," McCartin says. "You're free to go. You're not under arrest, obviously. We brought you over to talk to you, like we said. Hopefully no longer than a half hour and we'll bring you back. You aware of that?"

"I understan'," Hendrix says.

Then McCartin, with the bonhomie of a real estate agent showing off a property to a prospective buyer, says cheerily, "I know you have some questions, which is fine. As soon as we're done, you can shoot away and ask as many questions as you want and we'll see if we can answer them for you."

McCartin then spends a few minutes questioning Hendrix about his relationship with the woman he lived with in the Los Feliz apartment building. Hendrix stares at him, arms crossed, with an arrogant expression, and says he cannot recall when he moved out and headed east on the Greyhound.

"Did you ever hear about this murder?" McCartin asks. "She's a little Filipino woman. Her name is Lourdes Unson. Were you there when it occurred?"

Hendrix considers the questions for a few seconds. "I don't know when it occurred," he says defensively. He explains that his ex-girlfriend told him about the murder over the phone, while he was living in Texas.

"Did you know the woman?" McCartin asks.

"I didn't know her," he says flatly.

"Did you ever wave to her or say hi to her or any of that? Or were you friendly with her in any way?"

"No," Hendrix says. "I wouldn't say I was friendly with her. I'd seen her here and there, going to and fro."

McCartin bides his time with more background queries and then, finally, asks, "Did you ever go in her apartment?"

Hendrix pauses for a moment. "Umm . . ." McCartin and Mathew stare at him poker-faced, trying not to reveal how anxious they are about his response. He stares at his hands and says, "One time. I was going downstairs to the laundry and she was going upstairs and she had some bags. I carried them to her apartment for her."

While Hendrix is still looking down, McCartin and Mathew exchange a quick glance and roll their eyes in frustration. Hendrix, they figure, knows the system, knows he left prints in the apartment, and is protecting himself.

"Where did you go in the apartment?" McCartin asks.

Hendrix leans back and folds his hands on his lap. "The kitchen area."

"Did you ever go in there and socialize with her and hang out with her?" McCartin asks.

"Naw," Hendrix says dismissively. "I set the bags in there. She offered me a couple of dollars for taking her bags and I said I didn't want the couple of dollars. And that was pretty much it."

McCartin backs off and asks a few general questions about Unson so Hendrix will not know that the detectives are keying on what rooms he entered.

"Where did you put the groceries when you got into the house?" McCartin asks.

"I put them on the counter, by the kitchen."

McCartin pauses for a few seconds and decides to ask the critical question, the question that could determine the outcome of the Lourdes Unson murder investigation and the fate of Jammie Hendrix. "Did you go in any other part of the house after that?" he asks matter-of-factly. "Did you see what the rest of the house looked like, by chance?"

Hendrix studies McCartin for a moment. "No," he says softly.

"Did you go anywhere else in the apartment?"

"I went into the living room," Hendrix says. "I went over by the kitchen area. And between the kitchen area there's a counter there. I put the bag up on the counter. . . . And that's it."

McCartin now poses a few quick questions so Hendrix will not have a chance to construct an alibi. "Did you go in the bedroom for any reason?"

"No."

"Did you go in the bathroom for any reason?"

"No."

McCartin has the key denial, but he continues peppering Hendrix with questions to prevent him from hedging. "Go through any of the drawers or closets for any reason?"

"No."

"Move stuff or lift stuff?"

"No."

"Did you open the door or did she open the door?"

Hendrix considers the question for a moment and says, "I can't remember. . . ."

"Okay, you were never in any other rooms of the house?"

"No," Hendrix says weakly.

"No?" McCartin asks again.

"It's like what I said. And that's it. . . ."

"After that time you helped her with the packages, you ever been in her apartment again?"

"No."

While the detectives ask him about his stay at the ex-girlfriend's Los Feliz apartment, why he left, and when he moved to Texas, Hendrix studies their cards on the table. He asks who is McCartin and who is Mathew.

"I'm Tom—that's a good Indian name," Mathew says sarcastically. Hendrix smiles wanly.

McCartin asks Hendrix if he wants something to drink, but he shakes his head.

"Let me get a drink," McCartin says. He and Mathew head for their desks, but not for a drink. They grab DNA swabs and return to the interview room.

"One more thing," McCartin says, dropping the swabs on the table. "You ever hear of DNA?"

Hendrix slips off his sunglasses, drops his palms on the table, and says, "Yes."

"We got all sorts of DNA tests going on," McCartin says. "What we want to do is take a swab of your throat and the inside of your mouth so we can rule out that you were ever in the house or had anything to do with her in any way. That make sense?"

Hendrix abruptly sits up and grabs the side of the table. "That makes sense," he says uneasily. "I understand what you're saying."

McCartin is still amiable, because he wants Hendrix's cooperation. He knows he can obtain a court order for the DNA, but it would be easier if Hendrix provided the sample voluntarily. McCartin explains the complexities of DNA, then asks, "Am I getting clear to you?"

"I'm listening . . ." Hendrix responds warily. "I guess one of my questions is . . . am I under arrest?" His voice is tinged with fear.

After McCartin takes a deep breath and slowly exhales, his manner changes. He casts a cold, disdainful glance at Hendrix. "You *are* under arrest."

Hendrix stares at McCartin, a look of pure hatred. His body tenses.

Mathew believes Hendrix is going to attack McCartin. The detectives' guns are in the squad room, so Mathew stands up, prepared to restrain him.

After McCartin reads Hendrix his constitutional rights, he says, "Do you want to discuss it further, what happened out there that day?"

"Do you want to tell *your* side of the story?" Mathew adds.

"My side of the story?" Hendrix asks uneasily.

"DNA does not lie," McCartin says. "We have a lot of information. Do you want to keep going with it or end it right here?"

"What do you mean go on with it?"

"You're acting *stupid*," McCartin snaps. "It's a simple answer. I read you your rights. Now the question is: do you want to continue talking with us about this case? Tell us your side of what occurred with this poor woman?"

"I know one thing for certain," Hendrix says with resignation. "I won't be leaving today."

McCartin tells him about the evidence they have amassed—the fingerprints lifted at the apartment and Unson's jewelry pawned in Austin.

"I've murdered no one," he says without conviction.

"You want to take a lie detector test?" McCartin asks.

Hendrix refuses. "I'll tell you this. I do know an important thing. And the important thing is I'm under arrest."

McCartin stares at him contemptuously. "Yes, you are."

"Then counsel's in order," Hendrix says.

"So you want a lawyer now. That's what you're telling us?"

"Yes."

Now that McCartin knows the interview is over, he feels immense satisfaction. He thinks to himself: *This guy's a predator who preys on the vulnerable. He raped and killed one woman and attacked a few others. I'm glad I got this piece of shit off the street and nipped his act in the bud.* McCartin believes he has saved other lives. Also, he has grown fond of Unson's brothers and sisters and is pleased he will be able to tell them that he has caught their sister's killer and avenged her murder. Tracking down Jammie Hendrix, putting together the case against him, and locking him up is why McCartin became a homicide detective.

He jumps to his feet and commands, "Turn around and face the wall! Now you're in *our* custody. You'll do what you're told."

"*Whose* custody am I going to be under?" Hendrix asks.

"You're in the custody of the Los Angeles Police Department. You're going to jail for murder."

Epilogue

Several of the suspects I wrote about have either been tried or are awaiting trial. Other cases are still lingering in the limbo of the un-solved files. As of this writing, close to two-and-a-half years after I completed my research at Homicide Special:

Alexander Gabay was sentenced in March 2002 to twenty-five years to life in prison for killing Luda Petushenko. His girlfriend, Oxana, testified against him and was not prosecuted.

The preliminary hearing for Kazumi Taga was held in the fall of 2001. A judge determined there was enough evidence to hold him for trial in the murder of his wife, Yuriko, and daughter, Michelle. Friends of Yuriko's testified at the hearing that she became violently ill on two occasions after eating food prepared by Taga. Detectives suspected he attempted to poison her, and he faced two additional counts of attempted murder.

Taga pleaded not guilty at his arraignment. But two years later, to avoid the possibility of receiving the death penalty after a trial, Taga pleaded guilty to killing his wife and daughter and was sentenced to life in prison without the possibility of parole.

The murder of Stephanie Gorman remains unsolved. Detectives, however, have renewed hope. Currently, LAPD detectives looking for palm print matches have to manually compare them with those found at crime scenes. But a new FBI system will soon be available and detectives looking for a match will be able to enter anonymous palm prints into an automated identification system filled with databases containing the palm prints of millions of felons.

Dave Lambkin and Tim Marcia hope that the unidentified palm prints from the Gorman house will lead them to the killer.

The murder of Susan Berman also remains unsolved. But detectives are interested in a bizarre development involving Berman's longtime friend Robert Durst.

In September 2001, a teenage boy discovered the headless torso of a Texas man floating in Galveston Bay. Nearby, divers found the man's arms and legs stuffed in garbage bags, which also contained papers that led police to a Galveston apartment building. They followed a trail of blood between the seventy-one-year-old murder victim's apartment and a spartan studio that the landlord said was rented by a middle-aged mute woman named Dorothy.

Investigators believe that Durst—disguised as a woman and wearing a blond wig, pantsuit, and low heels—rented the apartment and stayed there occasionally. The new tenant told the landlord that she would have to communicate with him by writing notes because her voice box had been operated on numerous times.

A week after the body parts were found, Durst was arrested, charged with the murder, and released after posting bail. At his next court hearing, he did not appear and was finally apprehended seven weeks later in Pennsylvania, where he was arrested for stealing a sandwich from a grocery store.

Detectives eventually obtained a court order for Durst's handwriting sample and compared it to the note that alerted police to Berman's body. LAPD handwriting analysts have concluded that Durst's sample is closer to the writing on the note than Nyle's sample. They are now certain Nyle was not involved in Berman's murder.

While Paul Coulter and Jerry Stephens were not happy that they might have been misdirected because of the original handwriting analysis, they know that the person who wrote the note was disguising his writing, which makes the analyst's job quite difficult.

In November 2003, a Texas jury found Durst not guilty of murder, even though he admitted he dismembered his neighbor's corpse, stuffed the man's limbs in garbage bags, and tossed them into the ocean. Both the defense and the prosecution decided not to ask jurors to consider lesser charges, such as manslaughter.

Homicide Special Detectives are currently trying to determine Durst's whereabouts on the night Berman was murdered.

Jammie Hendrix, who pleaded not guilty at his arraignment, was bound over for trial after his September 2002 preliminary hearing. He has not yet been tried.

In April 2002, Robert Blake was arrested and charged with the murder of Bonny Bakley, in addition to solicitation of murder and conspiracy. His bodyguard, Earle Caldwell, was also arrested and charged with conspiracy. Caldwell was released on $1 million bail, but Blake was denied bail and remained in jail.

I followed only the first few months of the Bakley case. Detectives eventually interviewed more than 150 witnesses and traveled to more than twenty states. I am not going to attempt to summarize the mammoth investigation, which I did not observe.

The case against Blake was significantly advanced when detectives persuaded a second stuntman, Ronald Hambleton, to talk. Hambleton previously denied that Blake had asked him to kill Bakley, but when he was faced with a subpoena to appear before a grand jury he acknowledged that Blake solicited him to kill his wife. Hambleton told detectives a story similar to Gary McLarty's, the other stuntman who said Blake asked him to kill Bakley.

About two months before the murder, Blake suggested to Hambleton a number of different ways to kill his wife, he told detectives. On one occasion, Hambleton said, Blake drove him to the parking lot next to Vitello's restaurant and discussed several potential spots nearby where Bakley could be killed. Blake told Hambleton that as Bakley sat in a car on the street, he could walk up next to her and kill her.

Several times, Blake asked how much Hambleton would charge for the hit. Hambleton, however, did not name a price because he never intended to kill her.

A critical piece of evidence, the detectives believe, is the prepaid phone card that Hambleton suggested Blake purchase. Hambleton was under the impression the card could not be traced. But the detectives tracked down the phone card and a record of all the calls made on it. They discovered that Blake had called Hambleton's home more than fifty times and had called the other stuntman, Gary McLarty, several times.

Detectives also interviewed a private investigator and former LAPD detective who said that Blake told him in October 1999 that if Bakley would not have an abortion, he intended to "whack" her.

A judge ruled at the preliminary hearing that Blake had the motive and the opportunity to murder his wife and ruled that he and Caldwell must stand trial. Blake, who pleaded not guilty at his arraignment, was released on $1.5 million bail.

Eight months later, the judge ruled there was insufficient evidence proving that Blake conspired with his handyman to murder Bakley and threw out the entire case against Caldwell.

The murder trial was delayed, partly because two of Blake's lead criminal defense attorneys had differences with him and quit the case.

As of this writing, Blake is still awaiting trial.

Homicide Special recently created a cold case unit and appointed Dave Lambkin to head the section. His partner, Tim Marcia, and Rick Jackson were also transferred to the seven-detective team. Most of the other detectives I wrote about are still in the squad room, except for Jerry Stephens and Rich Haro, who have retired, and Chuck Knolls, who works as a patrol sergeant in the Wilshire Division.

Source Notes

CHAPTER 2

35 "*a* vor v zakonye": Robert I. Friedman, *Red Mafiya: How the Russian Mob Has Invaded America* (Little, Brown and Company, Boston, 2000), p. 9.

CHAPTER 3

45 *Polygraphs cannot determine guilt*: David Fisher, *Hard Evidence: How Detectives Inside the FBI's Sci-Crime Lab Have Helped Solve America's Toughest Cases* (Dell, New York, 1996), p. 367.

CHAPTER 5

68 *San Pedro and its neighbor*: Joan Didion, *After Henry* (Simon & Schuster, New York, 1992), pp. 225–26.

73 *When Kuster was still a bachelor*: Christopher Darden with Jess Walter, *In Contempt* (Regan Books, New York, 1996), p. 140.

CHAPTER 6

101 Two resources were helpful in compiling the history of Fish Harbor: Susan Moffat, "A Paradise Lost, Never Forgotten," *Los Angeles Times*, Jan. 5, 1994; and Leonard Pitt and Dale Pitt, *Los Angeles A to Z* (University of California Press, Berkeley, 1997), pp. 497–98.

CHAPTER 8

122 *As a result, crime*: Kevin Starr, *The Dream Endures: California Enters the 1940s* (Oxford University Press, New York, 1997), p. 168.

123 *By the late 1940s* and *"Los Angeles has become the dumping ground"*: Bernard Potter, *Los Angeles—Yesterday and Today* (Wetzel Publishing Co., Los Angeles, 1950) p. 28; Kevin Starr, *Embattled Dreams: California in War and Peace, 1940-1950* (Oxford University Press, New York, 2002), p. 232.

124 *They dressed in double-breasted suits*: Aggie Underwood, *Newspaper Woman* (Harper & Brothers, New York, 1949), p. 108; Starr, *Embattled Dreams*, p. 218.

124 *There was an acute housing*: Starr, *Embattled Dreams*, p. 218.

125 *The LAPD's road to*: A few passages on the modern history of the Los Angeles Police Department were taken from the author's book *The Killing Season: A Summer Inside an LAPD Homicide Division* (Simon & Schuster, New York, 1997).

126 *launched an immense investigation*: Myrna Oliver, "Robert Houghton: Former LAPD Official," (Obituary), *Los Angeles Times*, Jan. 7, 1998.

126 *Houghton envisioned a specialized unit*: Author interview with Robert Perry, the first captain of Robbery-Homicide Division.

127 *Yet Homicide Special detectives decided*: Vincent Bugliosi with Curt Gentry, *Helter Skelter* (W.W. Norton & Company, New York, 1974), p. 41.

127 *A Homicide Special detective also made another critical error*: Bugliosi and Gentry, *Helter Skelter*, pp. 33-34.

128 *Los Angeles had the lowest*: According to a Police Foundation study based on 1986 statistics.

128 *Rodney King, a drunk, African-American motorist*: Lou Cannon, *Official Negligence* (Westview, New York, 1999), p. 39.

129 *"It was about as hardball"*: Hank Goldberg, *The Prosecution Responds: An O. J. Simpson Trial Prosecutor Reveals What Really Happened* (Birch Lane Press, New York, 1996), p. 193.

130 *During the decade*: Matt Lait, "Analyzing a Turnaround," *Los Angeles Times*, Feb. 5, 1999.

CHAPTER 10

157 *in Hollywood, Lambkin*: Bob James, "Room in His Heart for Crime Victims," *Los Angeles Times*, April 5, 1988.

CHAPTER 14

201 *"I am never secure"*: Susan Berman, *Easy Street* (Dial Press, New York, 1981), p. 210.

201 Several sources were helpful when I was researching Susan Berman's life, including her autobiography, *Easy Street,* and two magazine stories by Lisa

DePaulo: "The Gangster's Daughter," *New York Magazine,* March 12, 2001, and "The Devil in Bobby Durst," *Talk Magazine,* February 2002.

206 *Deputy District Attorney Christopher Darden described*: Darden and Walter, *In Contempt,* p. 91.

CHAPTER 17

232 *"There are scars within me"*: Berman, *Easy Street,* p. 210.

236 *On Sunday, January 31, 1982*: Kevin Flynn and Charles V. Bagli, "Reopened Mystery," *New York Times,* March 6, 2001.

CHAPTER 23 and 24

318 Three magazine articles were helpful when I was researching the lives of Bonny Bakley and Robert Blake: David Grann, "To Die For," *The New Republic,* Aug. 13, 2001; Mary Murphy and Dennis McDougal, "To Live and Die in L.A.," *TV Guide,* March 16, 2002; and Deanne Stillman, "A Murder in Hollywood," *Rolling Stone,* May 23, 2002.

337 *Blake loved acting*: John Engstrom, "Actor Emerges Reborn from Abyss of Childhood Horrors," *Seattle Post-Intelligencer,* Jan. 13, 1993.

337 *Sometimes locked in a closet*: Mark Goodman and Craig Tomashoff, "Endangered Species: A Man of Private Torment and Public Fury, Robert Blake Returns to TV as a Killer," *People,* March 1, 1993.

339 *He feared that he would soon*: "The Curse of the Little Rascals," *Los Angeles Times,* May 16, 2001, excerpted from the *Las Vegas Review Journal.*

339 *"I could very easily have killed myself"*: Goodman and Tomashoff, "Endangered Species."

CHAPTER 25

354 *An aqueduct, Mulholland*: Norris Hundley, Jr., *The Great Thirst: Californians and Water, 1770s–1990s* (University of California Press, Berkeley, 1992), p. 158.

354 *one day after the city's Board of Water*: Kevin Roderick, *America's Suburb* (Los Angeles Times Books, Los Angeles, 2001), p. 57.

355 *In 1909, four years before*: Mark Reisner, *Cadillac Desert* (Penguin Books, New York, 1987), p. 105.

355 *By 1925, the city's population*: Reisner, *Cadillac Desert,* p. 105.

Author's Note

I spent a year in Homicide Special's squad room, from the summer of 2000 to the summer of 2001, and was with the detectives through every stage of their investigations. Although the unit's supervisors granted me complete and unfettered access, I was subject to no restrictions or edicts.

After I finished writing the book, I discovered that I had become a part of the story. During Robert Blake's preliminary hearing for the murder of his wife, Bonny Bakley, my presence during the first few months of the investigation was raised by the defense as a controversial issue. Police officials were criticized, and the judgment of the detectives was questioned.

I am chagrined that my access was used to attack the investigation and will probably be employed as a defense strategy during the trial. The detectives were criticized for letting me follow them, but my presence was not their decision. Police officials approved my project. Although they obviously hoped I would portray the department in a positive manner, I criticize the LAPD when I see fit and depict flaws as I encounter them. I believe that allowing a journalist to scrutinize police investigations is clearly in the public interest, sheds light on a traditionally secretive institution, and is a safeguard against police misconduct.

My research approach is not unique. Other writers have employed similar methods, including David Simon, who wrote the critically acclaimed book, *Homicide: A Year on the Killing Streets*. During the research for my first book, *The Killing Season*, which was set in South-

Central Los Angeles, I also shadowed homicide detectives. And as a crime reporter for the *Los Angeles Times*, I followed investigators to numerous crime scenes, autopsies, witness interviews, death notifications and other stages of their cases.

During my year with Homicide Special, the detectives picked up more than a dozen cases, but I could not recount every one. I focused on the cases I felt were the most interesting, varied, and limned both investigative successes as well as failures. Most of the events of this book I observed; those I did not I re-created through transcripts and interviews with the detectives. Some of the lengthier interviews have been condensed. All of the names in the book are real except for Vincent Rossi and Michael Goldsmith.

I want to thank the detectives for their support and for making me feel at home during my year in the squad room. Their graciousness and generosity went above and beyond the call of duty. Lieutenants Clay Farrell and Don Hartwell always patiently answered all of my questions and helped me understand the nuances of homicide investigation. They are true gentlemen. Captain Jim Tatreau never attempted to influence what I wrote or how I portrayed the unit. "Yes, these guys will make mistakes and screw up sometimes," he told me. "I don't care if people see that. But I'd also like them to see that most of our detectives are hard-working people who generally try to do the right thing."

I'd also like to thank my agent, Barney Karpfinger, who is more than just a business representative. He is a good friend. Over the years, he has helped me so often, in so many ways. He did it again this time around.

My editors, Jennifer Barth and George Hodgman, had excellent insights and suggestions, which made *Homicide Special* a much better book. I really appreciate their energy, enthusiasm, and refusal to accept any chapter that did not meet their standards. Ruth Kaplan was also extremely helpful.

I thank an old friend, Michael Shapiro, for reading the manuscript and offering encouragement when it was needed most.

My sister Leni Corwin was a wonderful confidant, friend, and ally during the final stages of the book. Her assistance was invaluable.

I am especially grateful for the help of my wife, Diane. I simply could not have written this book without her support.

ABOUT THE AUTHOR

A former award-winning reporter at the *Los Angeles Times*, MILES CORWIN is the author of *The Killing Season*, a national best-seller. His second book, *And Still We Rise*, was a *Los Angeles Times* Best Book of the Year and the winner of the PEN West award for nonfiction. He lives outside Los Angeles.